Merry Christmas
Joan

from Aunt Josie
1952

THE
HOLLOW
REED

THE
HOLLOW REED

By

MARY J. J. WRINN

HARPER & BROTHERS PUBLISHERS
New York and London

And I pluck'd a hollow reed,

And I made a rural pen,
   And I stain'd the water clear,
And I wrote my happy songs
   Every child may joy to hear.

—WILLIAM BLAKE

CONTENTS

PREFACE

THESE pages are addressed to youth. While they speak directly to high-school and college students, they include all the young in heart, for the spirit of youth has nothing to do with schools or birthdays unless it be that, like Gilbert and Sullivan's apprentice pirate Frederic, it celebrates on the twenty-ninth of February; and counting that way—well, you know how it was with the apprentice pirate, slave of duty. In any event it was at the request of young persons for definite training in the craft of poetry that this book was conceived.

They wanted to experience poetry, they said, with the maker "from the bottom up" in terms that they could understand. What they read was too indefinite or too far beyond them, they felt, to guide their own experiments very far, and they wanted to experiment, some with breathless eagerness, others with tremulous misgivings as to their own powers. "I don't think I shall ever be able to write a poem!" is a repeated understatement of an all-consuming wish.

Why should we not approach poetry from a single essential element? Why should we not consider its medium one step at a time? Stage by stage, from the sentence to the essay and the argument, prose composition is developed in our schools with the changing interests of the growing writer as motive power. For sixteen years young persons are invited, cajoled, encouraged to prose utterance, but in the highest form of all expression they are left more or less to their own devices. There are those who feel that this is the wisest course; that a teacher may play only a silent albeit sympathetic part in the development of poetic expression.

And yet, if you ask the youthful natural-born sonneteer how he came to write his sonnet, he will tell you, simply enough, that he sat down with Keats or Wordsworth, with David Morton or Edna St. Vincent Millay, and one or the other taught him the pattern, which he applied to his own material. He did just what the amateur dress-maker does with her first dress—cuts it to pattern; what the boy boat builder does with his first sailing vessel—fashions it after a model. He has done what Keats did when he studied Spenser; what Shakespeare did with Marlowe's mighty line; what Tennyson did when he went to Vergil; what Coleridge did at the feet of William Lisle Bowles. After all, there are principles underlying every art. It is not wholly the way of madness to teach them. And they may be presented simply, without the befuddled mysticism and technical verbiage that so often cloud the subject of poetry as an art. Furthermore, the apprenticeship need not be devoid of delight. It may indeed be the most thrilling venture of youth, revealing depths undreamed of.

This book aims merely to suit the subject to the mind and heart of modern youth and to prevent waste in his efforts. It extends an invitation to those who have never written a line of poetry but would like to test the sweet yoke of the Muse; to those who enjoy writing but have never attempted verse; to those who have written some poetry and wish further to develop their technique; to those who, enjoying other forms of literature, feel that they "could never like poetry"—meaning perhaps that they have not found the way to its secrets; and to those who may enrich the pleasure of reading by a consideration of the maker's viewpoint. In short, it invites the curious, the incredulous, the shy. It is planned to meet the need of the teacher who has been deterred from delightful experiment for lack of suitable material in convenient form. For the effective teaching of composition—prose or verse— objective material is needed, but in this age of high pressure there is not always time to search for it.

If these pages are to fulfil their promise, the beginner must participate actively and progressively. This is a work-book even as the crossword puzzle or the page of music or the drawing leaf is a work sheet. It offers to show the sweetness of solitude. Time and quiet are requisites. The pleasure of the experience is a light-blown freedom.

The first chapters are concerned solely with the spirit of poetry. The poet is a poet first, a technician afterward. We enjoy the experience of bringing together out of time and space strange things: wind and a wolf, fire hydrants and mushrooms, aërial wires and cobwebs. We probe the nature of things, their actions and qualities, physical and spiritual. We test the logic of the imagination and apply the test to our images. While we search our familiar highways and hedges with a new eye, gathering the crumbs of experience in a notebook lest they be lost, we carry on laboratory experiments with rhythm and meter, rhyme and assonance. There are copious exercises to help the inner ear recapture a lost delight in a music that over-sophistication has banished from the child heart. They are the five-finger exercises for daily practice.

After careful preparation we fuse one day the imaginative element with the simplest metrical pattern in a couplet bound by rhyme. We have created our first metrical poem. From this point on development is a matter of further practice, the poets themselves offering "so sweete a prospect into the way as will entice any man to enter it." The poems included have delighted young persons of varying tastes and interests and at various stages of maturity. High-school poetry is presented with the discussion out of which it grew for two purposes—to encourage other beginners and give them a standard for judging their own efforts, and to answer the question: Is the method workable? Contributions of some young authors have been carried right through the book to show their progress.

In each chapter assignments encourage practice to make straight the way for the genuine poem that some day will sing itself free of the pounding blood. The masterpiece does not spring full-armored from the head of genius. Before immortal David came forth from a shapeless mass of marble waste, a sensitive little boy had served an apprenticeship in the gardens of Lorenzo de Medici, studying anatomy, modeling in clay, and gaining a Titan's power over the chisel and the mallet. If genius feels the need of such discipline, how much more, O we of lesser talents!

After the first nine, the chapters need not be read in exact sequence. Some units, however, have particular functions. Without peer for training in compact and suggestive expression is the little miracle of design, the Japanese hokku with its American derivative, the cinquain. For developing skill in the handling of words there is nothing to equal the French forms. When the beginner reaches "The Rondel," he may find it helpful to alternate a fixed form with a poem in less restricted pattern. If he does not attempt the most difficult of the forms, he will at least wish to be acquainted with them. Those who mind babies or have younger relatives and acquaintances may find "Verse for Children" of practical use and at the same time enjoy a sense of superiority through appealing to outgrown tastes and interests which they are able to look upon with tolerant wisdom. In an age which has literally brought fire from heaven to light its piers of progress it is wholesome to consider "What hath God wrought!" through man and his engines, his test tubes and his gases, his slide and his lens. "A Thought to Vigor" seeks to turn the eyes of the young poet toward the strength and majesty of a world as yet unsung.

Humor is given no separate place in these pages, but flashes from seasoned poet and amateur throughout. There is nothing like laughter for letting in light. What if the effect be verse as distinct from the "flower of a high seriousness"? We do not scorn the bright music of neatly turned verse.

Because no one may say how or when or where the creator begins, four approaches have been planned: through matter, through manner, through a mood, through a theme. By experiment the novice will find *his* way. For the advanced worker, devices to heighten effects—which he has doubtless employed with or without the name, traditional patterns not previously considered, and the latest extension of rhyme are presented in the closing chapters. When the apprenticeship is over there will be independent adventuring.

The mastery of a technique grows in significance as the young poet becomes self-critical. Gradually, as he strengthens the standards for his own just judgments, he frees himself of outside criticism. "Indeed," says T. S. Eliot, "the larger part of the labour of an author in composing his work is critical labour; the labour of sifting, combining, constructing, expunging, correcting, testing: this frightful toil is as much critical as creative." When the young poet has appeased his own dissatisfaction with his work, he is ready to ask with Longinus: "How would Homer, had he been here, or how would Demosthenes, have listened to what I have written, or how would they have been affected by it?" Today, however, youth will choose his peers from poets nearer his own time. They are here to answer him.

A book designed to invite writing has no concern with schools of poetry, the history of poetry, age-old disputes over "borns" and "mades," or quibblings over teaching and learning. The devil can cite scripture for his purpose. The fruits are presented with the method. That has grown out of my own experience in a public high school numbering more than fifty-five hundred pupils.

Quite accidentally the experiment began in a second-year class with a lesson on Japanese hokku designed to invite original poems in the hokku pattern, one simple enough, I felt, to be attempted in a few periods of the all-too-brief time allowed for contemporary poetry. It evoked surprisingly interesting fragments, some of which are reprinted in Chapter X. The experiment made the pupils hokku conscious. One told the other about the little form, and between classes, in the lunchroom, in the study hall, during the official period, everyone was counting syllables with an excitement to rival that of the sixteenth century tournaments. Not all were poems, to be sure!

But from that slight beginning a poets' club emerged. At the request of its members it became in reality an after-school class. High above the city in the Tower, we sat around a table reading poetry, giving ourselves assignments, and exchanging criticism. I worked with them and for any lapses had my knuckles soundly rapped. That joyous half year made the club members want to go farther.

A term later we had the first in-school class of its kind in the City. It was open to students of third-year English and to others as an elective. All the club members still in school enrolled. The others had no burning urge for poetic expression, but had applied for membership because they liked to write, because they were curious, or because a former teacher, sensing the unsuspected spark, had advised them to. Not the least influence in the success of the experiment has been the genius of my colleagues for discovering gifted pupils. It is due largely to their confidence and coöperation that the Poetry Class is an institution at George Washington. Through the interest of Edwin Van B. Knickerbocker and Edwin A. Kane, chairmen of the English department, and of Arthur A. Boylan, principal, selected work of class and club has been preserved in a graceful little volume, *The Poets' Pack*. Some of the poems have won prizes; some have even found their way into professional periodicals.

The value of creative experience, however, lies not so much in the product as in the attitude which the experience engenders in the young poet. He carries that within him which touches life with magic; the poetry of earth responds to him because he brings it a lover's heart. Furthermore, his creative effort has given him an insight into all recorded poetry that no amount of outside "appreciation" can give. To be able to commune with true poets is to enjoy an experience transcending life.

Give youth an interest in the making of verses and he has a pastime to absorb his leisure. Life has its limitations; the imagination has none. He does not need the excitement of the moment; his is an abiding excitement. Song has a way of revealing the eternal things. For his delight he needs no instrument, no easel, no platform, no mass of clay. He should have time to make music out of his deepening sympathy and his growing insight, time to hear his music and that of his young companions even as once Daphnis and Menalcas heard "on the long ranges of the hills." No less worthy is the changeless theme of life in his staccato world, but until he has tried his pipe, he may not be aware of his own gifts or of the joy in a lyric. If these pages have succeeded in their purpose they have given him, for the blowing of his songs, a hollow reed with "nine stops, fitted with white wax, and smoothed evenly, above as below."

Mary J. J. Wrinn

New York

ACKNOWLEDGMENTS

GRATEFUL appreciation is due to the following for their kind permission to include in *The Hollow Reed* the poems and other material which have made the book possible:

Brandt and Brandt for "She Is Overheard Singing" and "Daphne" from *A Few Figs from Thistles*, published by Harper and Brothers, copyright 1922 by Edna St. Vincent Millay.

Bruce Humphries, Inc. for hokkus from *Japanese Hokkus* by Yone Noguchi, copyright 1920 by The Four Seas Company.

The Columbia Review for "Ballade of the Wasted Moon" by Edward Stasheff, published in *The Morningside.*

Curtis Brown, Ltd. for "Sea Sonnet" from *Collected Poems* by V. Sackville West.

Dodd, Mead and Company, Inc. for "The Great Lover" by Rupert Brooke; "A Ballade of Suicide" by G. K. Chesterton; "Villanelle of His Lady's Treasures" by Ernest Dowson; "A Vagabond Song" by Bliss Carman.

Doubleday, Doran & Company, Inc. for "Villanelle" with Stevenson's Assistance from *Weights and Measures* by Franklin P. Adams, copyright 1917 by Doubleday, Doran & Co., Inc.; "Easter" from *Trees and Other Poems* by Joyce Kilmer, copyright 1914 by Doubleday, Doran & Co., Inc.

Farrar and Rinehart, Inc. for "Truth" and "Love Came Back at Fall of Dew" from *The Selected Poems of Lizette Woodworth Reese*, copyright 1926 and reprinted by permission of the publishers.

Harcourt, Brace and Company, Inc. for "Austin Dobson Recites a Ballade by Way of Retort" from —— *And Other Poets* by Louis Untermeyer.

Harper and Brothers for "For a Pessimist" from *Color* by Countee Cullen; selections from *Poetical Works* of Algernon Charles Swinburne; "Words," "Is This the Lark?" "Water," "Sandal String," and "Touch" from *Sunrise Trumpets*, and "Steel" from *The Cyclops Eye* by Joseph Auslander; excerpts from *Some Modern Poets* by Edward Davison.

Henry Holt and Company for "Fog" from *Chicago Poems* and "Prayers of Steel" from *Cornhuskers* by Carl Sandburg; "Four Little Foxes" from *Slow Smoke*, "Clipped Wings" and "Coyote Brood" from *Wings Against the Moon* by Lew Sarett; "Mending Wall,"

"A Hillside Thaw," "Birches," "The Tuft of Flowers," "Fire-flies in the Garden," "House Fear" (from "The Hill Wife"), "The Road Not Taken," "Nothing Gold Can Stay," and "An Old Man's Winter Night" from *Collected Poems* by Robert Frost; "Alas, Alack" and "Miss T." from *Peacock Pie*, and "The Listeners" from *Selected Poems* by Walter de la Mare; "Words Before Twilight" from *Bright Harbor* by Daniel Whitehead Hicky.

Houghton Mifflin Company for "Awake, Awake" from *The Poems of Frank Dempster Sherman*; "The Monk in the Kitchen" from *Rose of the Wind* by Anna Hempstead Branch; "Calvary" from *The Door of Dreams* by Jessie B. Rittenhouse; "Love Planted a Rose" by Katherine Lee Bates; by permission of and by arrangement with Houghton Mifflin Company.

Alfred A. Knopf for "On Seeing Weather-Beaten Trees," "The Immortal Residue," "Song," "Dirge," and thirteen cinquains from *Verse* by Adelaide Crapsey; "Sonnet II" from *Angels and Earthly Creatures* by Elinor Wylie; "A Dance for Rain" by Witter Bynner; by permission of and special arrangement with Alfred A. Knopf, authorized publishers.

Little, Brown and Company for "Pedigree" and "Indian Summer" from *The Poems of Emily Dickinson*, Centenary Edition, edited by Martha Dickinson Bianchi and Alfred Leete Hampson.

Longmans, Green and Company for "Scythe Song" by Andrew Lang.

The Macmillan Company for "Philomela" from *Lyric and Elegiac Poems* by Matthew Arnold; "St. Valentine's Day" from *Poetical Works* by Wilfrid Scawen Blunt; "My Garden" and "Vespers" from *Collected Poems* by T. E. Brown; "The Paisley Shawl" from *Collected Poems* and "John's Wife" from *Hazards* by Wilfrid Wilson Gibson; "On Sturminster Foot-bridge" and "'Regret Not Me,'" from *Collected Poems* by Thomas Hardy; "Alons au Bois le Mai Cueillir," "The Villanelle," "What Is to Come," "Ballade of Ladies' Names," "Ballade of Youth and Age" from *Poems* by William Ernest Henley; "On Growing Old" from *Collected Poems* by John Masefield; "A Birthday" from *Poetical Works* by Christina Rossetti; "The Lake Isle of Innisfree" from *Early Poems and Stories* by William Butler Yeats; lines from *Tristram* by Edwin Arlington Robinson; excerpt from *The Early Life of Thomas Hardy* by Florence Emily Hardy; "Appraisal" from *The Dark of the Moon* by Sara Teasdale; author as well as publisher for "Crystal Moment" from *The Yoke of Thunder* by Robert P. Tristram Coffin, and for "Hound at Night" from *Eve Walks in Her Garden* by Louise Ayres Garnett.

The British Museum, London, and The Macmillan Company for a page from the manuscript of *The Dynasts* by Thomas Hardy.

Robert McBride and Company, with the special permission of the author, for "The Conqueror Passes" from *From the Hidden Way* by James Branch Cabell.

Minton, Balch and Company, Publishers, New York, for "Little" from *Everything and Anything* by Dorothy Aldis.

Thomas Bird Mosher for "Tears" from *A Wayside Lute* by Lizette Woodworth Reese.

Oxford University Press and Mr. Alban Dobson for "The Ballade of Prose and Rhyme," "The Dance of Death," "In Town," "The Kiss," "I Intended an Ode," "'Urceus Exit'" from "Rose Leaves," "The Wanderer," "In After Days," "Rondeau" by Austin Dobson.

Poetry (Chicago) and the authors for "Antelope with Cattle" by Robert McBlair; "Autumn Crickets" by Glenn Ward Dresbach; "Meteor" by B. A. Botkin; "Mother with Young Kittens" by Richard Hart; "The Dark Song" by Shirley Brownrigg; "A Cow" by Julia Van der Veer; "Ancestral" by Jessica Nelson North; "In March" by Harriet Monroe; "The Wind Is My Neighbor" by Margery Mansfield.

The Poetry Bookshop, London, for "Wind" and "Summer" by C. Lovat Fraser.

Charles Scribner's Sons for "Ready for the Ride" by H. C. Bunner; "Song of the Chattahooche" from *Poems* by Sidney Lanier; "Breath of the Briar" from *Poems* by George Meredith; "To a Snowflake" by Francis Thompson; "The House on the Hill" and "Aaron Stark" from *Children of the Night* by Edwin Arlington Robinson.

Vanity Fair for epitaphs reprinted by permission of *Vanity Fair*.

The Viking Press for "April's Amazing Meaning" from *Boy in the Wind* by George Dillon, copyright 1927; "High Tide" from *Growing Pains* by Jean Starr Untermeyer, copyright 1918; the author as well as the publishers for "John Bird" from *The Espalier* by Sylvia Townsend Warner.

Yale University Press for "Rondel for September" from *Blue Smoke* by Karle Wilson Baker.

Bureau of Publications, Teachers College, Columbia University, and Dr. Allan Abbott for a leaf from *Exercises in Judging Poetry* prepared by Allan Abbott and M. R. Trabue.

Ada Alden for "As a Star from the Dust" and "Unhearing."

Gelett Burgess for "The Chant Royal of Pure Romance" first published in *The Lark*.

Robert P. Tristram Coffin and *The Saturday Review of Literature* for "The Spider."

Isabel Fiske Conant for "Sakura," "Dear Friend," "Kwannon, the Compassionate," and "Homeless"; and for "Icarus" by Evelyn Ahrend from *Iron Moths* edited by Isabel Fiske Conant.

Mary Cummings Eudy for "Oxen"; "Three Lonely Women," published in *Palms*; and "Crystals and Flame," published in *Decimal*.

John Gould Fletcher for "The Skaters."

John L. Foley, literary executor for the late Thomas S. Jones, Jr., for "Sometimes" from *The Rose Jar*; "To a Greek Statue" from *The Voice in the Silence*; "Quatrains" from *Sonnets and Quatrains*; "Clonard" and "A Roman Road" from *Sonnets of the Cross*; "Michelangelo," "Copernicus," and "Tycho Brache" from *The Unicorn and Other Sonnets*; "Socrates" and "Solomon" from *Akhnaton and Other Sonnets* by Thomas S. Jones, Jr.; publisher, Thomas Bird Mosher.

Hamlin Garland for "Magic" and "A River Gorge."

Agnes Kendrick Gray for "Ducks and Heron."

Jessie Lemont for "Snake," published in *The Nation*.

Francis A. Litz for "Gone," "God's Likeness," "Deep Unto Deep," "Vestiges," "God," "Shelley," "Opportunity," and "The Voyager" from *The Poetry of Father Tabb*, edited by Francis A. Litz and published by Dodd, Mead and Company, Inc.

Justin Huntley McCarthy for "If I Were King" and "Rondel."

Thomas McCrae for "In Flanders Fields" from *In Flanders Fields* by John McCrae, published by G. P. Putnam's Sons.

Edwin Markham for "The Man with the Hoe," copyrighted by Edwin Markham and used with his permission.

Don Marquis and Doubleday, Doran and Company, Inc. for "Sapphics" from *The Awakening and Other Poems* and for "The Rondeau" from *Dreams and Dust* by Don Marquis.

Florence Ripley Mastin and *The Saturday Review of Literature* for "Old Hound."

F. L. Montgomery for "All Souls Night."

David Morton for "Visitor," "Guest," "Legend," "Moths," "Scars," and "And Now These Jonquils" from *Harvest*; "Expedition" from *Earth's Processional*; excerpts from *The Sonnet Today and Yesterday*, published by G. P. Putnam's Sons; and for "Glimpses" by Russell M. Spear, published in *Amherst Undergraduate Verse*, edited by David Morton.

Helene Mullins for "To John Hall Wheelock."

Curtis Hidden Page for the inscription of his book, *Japanese Poetry*, and for translations from it.

Marie Tello Phillips for "Late Chrysanthemums" from *The Honey-suckle and the Rose*.

Lizette Woodworth Reese for "Ellen Hanging Clothes."

Jessie B. Rittenhouse, literary executor for the late Clinton Scollard, for "Where Are the Ships of Tyre?" by Clinton Scollard.

Edwin Meade Robinson for "Ballade à Double Refrain."

Siegfried Sassoon for "Aftermath," from *Picture-Show*.

Charles Wharton Stork for "Standards."

Leonora Speyer for "New Excavations" (from "Pompeii") in *Fiddler's Farewell*, published by Alfred A. Knopf and for "Ballad of Old Doc Higgins," published in *The Nation*.

Virginia Lyne Tunstall for "Porcelaine de Saxe."

John Martin's Book and The New York *Sun* for poems by Mary J. J. Wrinn.

J. J. for three couplets, "Lucy," and "Malay Shopping Carol."

Julia Van der Veer for "Calf in the Goldenrod."

In a very special way, the author is indebted to the following:

Basil Hall Chamberlain and the late Frederick V. Dickins, whose works on the Japanese language and literature have made accessible many transliterations of Japanese poems, as well as authentic information on the history and practice of the ancient singers of Japan.

The high-school poets whose work appears in these pages.

THE
HOLLOW
REED

CHAPTER I

THE ESSENCE OF POETRY

To THINK the poet's way is to invest the moments of life with the great breath of the imagination. To the poet the primrose by the river's brink is much more than a yellow primrose. Its significance may arouse in him thoughts that "lie too deep for tears." The imaginative energy in the poet is communicated through his utterance to the imagination of his listener, and through the imagination touches his heart. Imaginative energy in either the poet or the reader and feeling, or what is called emotional effect, are inseparable.

The poet seeks to turn his imaginative experience into a thing of beauty. His poem is a work of art. All art implies a mastery of technique; in other words, discipline, else it is not art. Therefore, to consider poetry we must consider artistic expression, but for the moment let us be content to put our finger on the heart of poetry. Let us pin our faith to the imaginative element alone as a workable beginning for our own creative efforts.

Without it, we may have prose. We may have prose which deals only with fact, as scientific works do. Without it, we may have artistic expression which follows the laws of rhyme and meter; that is, we may have verse, excellent verse. But unless the imaginative quality is woven in the fabric of thought and expression, we have not poetry.

Applying the imaginative test to each of the following passages, you will not find it difficult to say which is poetry and which is verse.

> The thistle is a pasture weed
> Which, all too soon, has gone to seed.
>
> The thistle is a powder puff
> With Nature's softest silk for fluff.

Before we proceed further, let us get rid of one idea, which, if it persists, will prove ruinous to all attempt at poetic expression. *Rhyme does not make poetry.* It is not even necessary to it. Our first efforts toward poetic expression will ignore rhyme completely—will utterly banish rhyme, until we have learned to think the poet's way; to look at life with the poet's eye and feel life with the poet's heart.

Shakespeare's great plays, the high water mark of English poetry, are in blank verse; the lines do not rhyme. The Bible, a large part of

which is poetry, is unrhymed. Much other beautiful poetry is unrhymed. Rhyme has its uses for musical and structural effect. It is a
shaper, an embellisher, not a necessary element. There are many
qualities that contribute to the beauty of poetry, but the imaginative
element seems to be the great force which gives them life.

Let us then examine some of the effects of an exercise of the
imagination.

Along the river bank nearby are tall flowers, the blossoms of which
burn along the stem in a raceme. Close examination will show a
strange two-lipped construction of the corolla: the upper lip erect and
two-lobed; the lower spreading and three-cleft. Some early poet-at-heart
was struck by the brilliance of this bloom. It reminded him of the
flaming robes of a cardinal. Once you have heard the name, cardinal
flower, you cannot see the wild growth without being struck by the
appropriateness of the name to the image which immediately leaps
to the mind. The effect is a pleasurable one.

Close by are clusters of another plant with a violet-purple blossom.
Its tubular corolla also is two-lipped: the upper erect and flaring, the
lower spreading and three-lobed. Its throat is half choked with yellow
fuzz. The whole effect is that of a grinning face. Some poet-botanist
with a sense of humor named it *monkey flower*!

Everyone recognizes the quaint little preachers of the woods, our
jack-in-the-pulpits. Who ever calls them by their other name, Indian
turnips! No one who loves the poetry of things. Through the same
imaginative insight we have our Dutchman's breeches, butter-and-eggs,
devil's paint brush—names familiar and dear to every school boy.

The Japanese seem to live poetry. One of the truest poets among
them renounced the world at twenty-three to become a monk. Now
the Buddhist Paradise is a country far to the West. He assumed as his
name *Sai go jō*, meaning *westward-wanderer*. A wanderer . . . a poet
. . . a monk . . . westward-wanderer. And the name of the greatest
master of the hokku form, which we will study later, is no less charged
with the spirit of imagination, the essence of poetry. Bashō is his name.
It means *banana leaves*. Banana leaves are very flexible; they respond
to the whims of wind and temperature. The poet felt the similarity
between his own ephemeral life and these leaves; hence his name,
Bashō.

This feeling for resemblances is the essence of poetry. It seems to
be the first fruit of imaginative activity. We may train ourselves to
be on the lookout for striking resemblances in otherwise very unlike
things. In the presence of one experience another will leap into the
mind. Delight in the discovery is the natural effect.

Let us imagine that it is a cloudy night. The moon is out, but it is
blurred by mist and white clouds that move slowly across it. A matter-

of-fact person looks toward the sky and says, "The moon looks hazy." If he is a farmer, he may add, "Rain is not far off." An imaginative person sees it and his mind leaps to a ship at sea, a galleon. "The moon is a ghostly galleon." For him the moon is no longer a moon, but a ghostly galleon. The clouds are not clouds and nothing more, but a rough sea in which the galleon is sailing. "The moon is a ghostly galleon tossed upon cloudy seas." If you were an artist and wanted to illustrate that picture you would have no difficulty. The image is sharp and clean-cut. Every word is precise. Though the galleon is blurred, there is no blur in the impression. Not all images are visible to the eye, however. There are sound, touch, taste, and smell images. Poetry is a succession of these.

When an image takes the form, "The moon is a ghostly galleon," that is, when one thing is transmuted to another through the intensity of the poet's imagination, we speak of it as a metaphor.

If the poet had said, "The moon is like a ghostly galleon," he would have created a simile instead. A simile is a slightly weaker metaphor. In the galleon-simile imagined above, the creator does not forget the moon as a moon. He expresses the identity of both the moon and the galleon. He shows how his mind put the two together by using the linking word, "like." They are like each other. Alfred Noyes, who created the metaphor in "The Highwayman," is carried away with the intensity of his feeling; to him the moon *is* a ghostly galleon.

A very important use of the simile is to clarify what is obscure, what is difficult to describe. Further, it supplies deficiencies in a limited English vocabulary. "It is the excellent merit of similes and metaphors," George Meredith once wrote, "to spring us to vault over gaps and thickets and slippery places."

"She is as changeable as the wind" is a much more precise characterization than "She is very changeable." *How* changeable is "very"? Perhaps you have never been to the desert. "What do yucca palms look like?" you ask. "Like twisted old mediums on intimate terms with the supernatural spirits that haunt the yellow sands." Here is suggested the eeriness of the palms that a scientific explanation of spines and branches would not give. That is what poetry does: it gives impressions.

Our daily speech yields many traces of poetry created by the man in the street, though he would be surprised to hear it. Long use and familiarity has destroyed the pleased shock of surprise which his images originally gave, but they are instances of imaginative activity nevertheless. A feeling for the significance of things is not a gift of the high brow's possessing. It is often latent where we least expect to find it.

The most striking similarities seem to exist in the nature of things; in their qualities; in their actions. These similarities are revealed through names or nouns, through qualifying words such as adjectives and past participles, and through verbs. Here are some illuminating glimpses through commonplace things, the nature of which is familiar to us:

> He was like a fish out of water; she was like a hen on a hot griddle *or* like a chicken with its head off.
> The effect was like water rolling off a duck's back. Isn't she a cat! He's nothing but a stripling. That boy is a regular circus!

Below, things unlike are brought together with respect to a quality which is a marked characteristic of both things:

> This is not worth a continental; my head is as heavy as lead; she is as light as a feather; stupid as an ox; stubborn as a mule; *or,* she is a feather head; he's mulish; her cheeks are like apples; she was as white as a ghost.

Through the verb we catch the similarity of actions.

> The train flashed by like lightning; he kicked like a steer; she sang like a lark.

When people speak this way, they are using figurative language; that is, they are making objective what is subjective. Out of the physical world they are creating images or figures to clarify ideas of the immaterial world. Their words and the pictures which their words call to the mind suggest something more than the fact-meaning of the words. When meaning is true to fact and fact alone, the language is literal.

Experiences out of which some images have emerged are no longer a part of our every day lives, but the imagery is still a vivid part of our daily speech. "Castles in Spain"; "when my ship comes in"; "she stole a march on me," are examples. Slang too is figurative. You can see how pictorial these examples are: "step on it"; "don't high-hat me"; "blockhead."

Not all comparisons are figurative. "He worked like a slave," for instance, is vivid; it is not a simile, however, because both slave and man are alike in most respects; they belong to the same class: man.

"The flounder spun around like an eel" is not a simile. The flounder and the eel are alike in all fundamental qualities. They are both fish. There is a comparison but not an imaginative comparison. It is the imaginative comparison that creates an image. *The flounder caught on the hook spun around like a pinwheel.* Here is a simile. Things unlike in all other particulars—family, kingdom, functions, use— have one striking point of similarity: spinning. To clear up the point: Some striking quality in an object, as the color of the cardinal flower, suggests a thing of widely different character, a dignitary of the Church, because a quality of the first is striking in the second: a Cardinal wears flame-colored robes. The name of the flower is a condensed form of the expression, "This red flower is like a Cardinal," or "This flower is a Cardinal." The wider apart the two things are, that is, the greater the difference in all but one prominent characteristic, the more striking is the image.

While strangeness is an element of enjoyment, the strangeness must not be so strange as to seem strained or to cause disbelief, and so halt the pleasure of surprise which it is intended to convey.

> Hail, sister springs,
> Parents of silver-footed rills!
> Ever bubbling things,
> Thawing crystal, snowy hills!
> Still spending, never spent; I mean
> Thy fair eyes, sweet Magdalene.
>
> —RICHARD CRASHAW

The grotesqueness of eyes *the parents of rills* or *bubbling things that thaw hills* defeats any serious purpose. Rills and hills are too big to link with eyes. Our credulity will not stretch to meet the exaggeration.

On the other hand, a mean thing to explain a thing of beauty or dignity fails of serious effect.

> Like a lobster boiled, the morn
> From black to red began to burn.
>
> —SAMUEL BUTLER

When the author compared lovely dawn to the lowly boiled lobster, instead of making the fine thing clearer to the understanding and satisfying to the heart through the imagination—which is what images should do—he made dawn seem absurd and so caused a laugh at the absurdity. Boiled lobsters suggest feeling so at variance with those aroused at the coming of dawn that our sense of the ludicrous rather than our sympathies is challenged. This is exactly the effect which Samuel Butler intended; but serious verse demands the dignity of congruity.

Let us now enjoy some striking similes created by our recognized poets for their serious poetry. Let us turn them over in our hands, feeling their heartbeats, delighting in their vitality. Thomas Hardy's *Collected Poems*—there are more than a thousand—abounds in sharp similes. In "The Music Box" he speaks of

> Swart bats, whose wings, be-webbed and tanned
> Whirred like the wheels of ancient clocks.

Hear how light falls:

> . . . the frail light shed by a slim young moon
> Fell like a friendly tune.

Hardy played the violin. Only a lover of music would interpret light through song as he does. A poet's imagery is colored by his interests, his observation, and experience.

Now imagine an old man sitting propped up in a chair before the fireplace. See what the simile does to your sympathies.

> The open fireplace spread
> Like a vast weary yawn above his head.

And how appropriate to age is the suggestion of weariness in the yawn.

But here is spring in an apple-orchard:

> Then like popcorn in a shaker
> The trees began to burst in bloom.
> —Dorothy Aldis

No less alive with vivid similes is any poet's prose. Here is a passage from Hardy's comment on the annual dinner of the Royal Academy, dated 1887.

> In speaking the Duke of Cambridge could not decide whether he had ended his speech or not, and so tagged on a bit more, and a bit more, till the *sentences* were *like acrobats* hanging down from a trapeze.
> —Florence Emily Hardy: *The Early Life of Thomas Hardy*

In the "Rime of the Ancient Mariner" are many striking similes:

> And every soul, it pass'd me by
> Like the whizz of my cross-bow!

> And thou art long, and lank, and brown,
> As is the ribb'd sea-sand.

> No voice; but oh! the silence sank
> Like music on my heart.

In "Adonais" Shelley leads us to the grave of Keats beneath the slope of a hill,

> Where, like an infant's smile, over the dead,
> A light of laughing flowers along the grass is spread.

In one of his sonnets William Wordsworth gives us the feeling of a beauteous evening.

> The holy time is quiet as a Nun
> Breathless with adoration . . .

Two others in opposite mood will suffice, I hope, to send you on a tour of discovery for others.

And all went merry as a marriage bell.
—GEORGE GORDON, LORD BYRON

Sue's man's mind is like good jell—
All one color and clear.
—EDNA ST. VINCENT MILLAY

Sir Philip Sidney once said: "The poet doth not only show the way but giveth so sweet a prospect with the way as will entice any man to enter it." No more enchanting prospect was ever given than by our "sweetest Shakespeare, fancy's child." Let him lead us for a little while by way of his surprising metaphors.

Cinna points to what he believes is the east, saying

> . . . and yon grey lines
> That fret the clouds are messengers of day.

When Oberon commands Puck to procure the little western flower, love-in-idleness, Puck shows his readiness through a metaphor:

> I'll put a girdle round about the earth
> In forty minutes.

Says Florizel to Perdita in *Winter's Tale*

> . . . When you do dance, I wish you
> A wave o' the sea, that you might ever do
> Nothing but that.

In *Macbeth* the great tribute to sleep paid by a man who realizes that his conscience will never sleep again, is through a series of metaphors.

> Sleep that knits up the ravell'd sleave of care
> The death of each day's life, sore labour's bath,
> Balm of hurt minds, great nature's second course,
> Chief nourisher in life's feast.

He has made sleep a knitter of a raveled skein, a death, a bath, balm, a course, a nourisher.

Keats calls autumn

> Close bosom-friend of the maturing sun

and he shows her

> . . . sitting careless on a granary floor
> Thy hair soft-lifted by the winnowing wind
> Or on a half-reap'd furrow sound asleep.

Edna St. Vincent Millay sees the sunrise:

> . . . the sun rose dripping, a bucketful of gold.

As in the simile, the resemblance may be suggested through quality or action. In either case, then, one of the two things compared is not definitely expressed. The metaphor is implied. But the act of the poet's imagination is revealed through the qualifying words or through the action. The most subtle metaphors are thus implied.

Says Macbeth, after a series of murders

> . . . I am in blood
> Stepp'd in so far that, should I wade no more,
> Returning were as tedious as go o'er:

It is clear that he had in mind the act of wading across a river or stream. When you reach the middle where it is deepest, it is just as easy to go one way as it is the other.

Feel the wind in this line:

> And maple tassels somersaulting by.
> —DOROTHY ALDIS

What magic in that action "somersaulting!"

Metaphors that are implied by the adjective modifier are perhaps more elusive. In "Snow" Madison Cawein has the line

> The waters are *stern* with frost.

The land which Jacques Cartier looked upon when as a missionary he came to America, Thomas S. Jones calls "a land of morning." A great deal is implied in that phrase, "of morning" (a *morning* land), with a suggestion of all that fresh morning promises! Lew Sarett describes a little cabin as wearing

> Such a *panic-stricken air.*

The details of his poem justify the little cabin's panic. With pointed magic Joseph Auslander pictures roots "on edge with April" and

> The sky is even water-tone behind *suave* poplar trees.

That "suave" catches the very personality of poplars.

Sometimes the metaphor takes this construction:

> the rickety staircase of the moon.
> —JOSEPH AUSLANDER

Could anything describe a waning moon more perfectly than that "rickety staircase"?

> Clung to the *whistling mane of every wind*
> Drew the *bolt of Nature's secrecies* . . .
> —FRANCIS THOMPSON

That "whistling mane" transforms the wind into a plunging stallion; and the bolt makes those intangible secrecies a closed door.

When the qualities or the actions are human qualities or human actions given to inanimate things, the metaphor may be called personification. Some of the metaphors above—you will be able to select them—may be called personification, as are these following:

> Blow, winds, and crack your cheeks!
>
> —SHAKESPEARE

Obviously here the wind is a human being. The comparison is implied in "crack your cheeks."

> But, look, the morn, in russet mantle clad,
> Walks o'er the dew of yon high eastern hill.
>
> —SHAKESPEARE

The morn here is a person walking on the hill. And again

> Night's candles are burnt out and jocund Day
> Stands tiptoe on the misty mountain top.
>
> —SHAKESPEARE

> The broad bold moon edged up where the sea was wide,
> Mild, mellow-faced.
>
> —THOMAS HARDY

> The lamps of the Bay
> . . . make a long display
> Under which in the waves *they bore their gimlets of light.*
>
> —THOMAS HARDY

In the lines that follow, it is the verb alone that reveals the human personality:

> How sweet the moonlight sleeps upon this bank!
>
> —SHAKESPEARE

> When the sweet wind doth gently kiss the trees.
>
> —SHAKESPEARE

You will delight in many others as you read. Then you must begin to create some of your own. A ready notebook is indispensable for this adventure. You will not want to lose the moments which your imaginative mind has found significant. Your notebook will hold your riches until you are ready for withdrawals. If you care to see how a keen and sympathetic observer of human nature kept a notebook, you ought to dip into *The Early Life Of Thomas Hardy* by Florence Emily Hardy, published by the Macmillan Company, New York. Many pages of Hardy's notes, as he jotted them down day by day, show how a great mind gathered material, speculated on life, and set forth his theories of art for later reference. The virtue of writing down our impressions as we experience them is that we capture some of the moment's fire which dies down with time.

The letters of many poets are now available, to give an insight into how they thought and worked out their poems. They even give us glimpses of how they happened to write this poem or that. None are more pulsing with life than those of John Keats.

By observing keenly all the little things along our daily way and by exercising our imagination daily we are acquiring the poet's way of looking at life. The habit gives to life a vividness and intensity that is wholly absent from the days of those who never see with the poet's eye. For there is beauty in all things, indeed beauty varying and varied in each moment, if we but seek it.

"The poetry of earth is never dead." And it is the poet's pleasure to interpret what he finds, to translate, to suggest so that others may enjoy. In the images which he creates the poet reflects his observations and his habits of life and work. His images give pleasure as they are sharp and fresh. He should make his own, by exercising his own imagination, not by echoing the work of poets dead and gone. With our new age teeming with new activity we should be able to create many vivid original pictures. Imagine what Shelley or Keats or Chaucer or Shakespeare would do with our material. Even such poets as they made a beginning. Even they grew with practice.

Because poetry gives impressions, the words which we choose to convey our imaginings should be words that create impressions: suggestive or associative words, words that appeal to the senses—sight, sound, touch, taste, smell. Abstract, vague or general words, such as *goodness, philosophy, misrepresentation, virtue, institution, length, congruity,* do not create definite impressions. When our poets use them, they make them objective at once by an image expressed in concrete words. They never use them to explain a concrete thing. "How poor are they that have not patience!" says Shakespeare through the mouth of Iago. But in the next line he makes that abstract patience a thing that you can see and touch and feel:

What wound did ever heal but by degrees?

In *Twelfth Night*

> . . . She never told her love
> But let concealment, like a worm i' the bud,
> Feed on her damask cheek: she pin'd in thought;
> And, with a green and yellow melancholy,
> She sat, like patience on a monument,
> Smiling at grief.

Here the abstract "concealment" is pictured, "a worm i' the bud"; "melancholy" by the "green" and "yellow" suggests the color of a face that results from a disordered liver; and "patience" smiles at grief. The illustrator would have no difficulty in painting these abstract ideas. Keats shows

> . . . Joy whose hand is ever at his lips
> Bidding adieu.

Gray in his famous "Elegy" has "Grandeur hear with a disdaining smile." And see what Edwin Arlington Robinson does to image rumor!

> Let rumor's noise, like thunder heard far off,
> Rumble itself to silence and as nigh
> To nothing as might be . . .

As abstract a thing as philosophy takes *shape* in George Meredith's handling:

> Cold as a mountain in its star-pitched tent,
> Stood high Philosophy, less friend than foe.

Yes, today as in the days of Elizabeth,

> The lunatic, the lover, and the poet,
> Are of imagination all compact . . .

And we might go even further and suggest that the poet is a little of the lunatic and largely the lover. And is not Shakespeare with us in the suggestion?

> The poet's eye, in a fine frenzy rolling
> Doth glance from heaven to earth, from earth to heaven,
> And as *imagination bodies* forth
> The *forms* of things unknown, the poet's pen
> Turns them to *shapes,* and gives *to airy nothing*
> *A local habitation and a name.*

A CHALLENGE TO YOUR IMAGINATION

The first suggestions are offered to start your notebook.

1. Take your notebook and pen. Make a list of things that have pleased you today. Do you see in one thing on that list possibilities of imaginative development so that a reader will be touched with a feeling of pleasurable surprise at what you have discovered? Is there something on your list so familiar to us all that we will be pleased at recognizing it? Here are some familiar things that might do that: a fruit stand, a news stand, a newsboy, a shop window with the latest costumes from Paris, advertisements in a street car.
Add to this list from day to day.

2. Jot down a situation which suggests life in its simplicity; complexity; its most alluring aspects; in its almost completeness; in its homely familiarity.

Note what moves you to wonder. Note what thrills you with beauty.

Do you see anything that inspires you with indignation at injustice; at stupidity of man; at circumstances?

Are you saddened by something?

What do you find that fills you with admiration for heroism; sacrifice; honest struggle; independence; loyalty?

Do you see circumstances which move you by their irony?

3. Can you discover the poetry of imagination in names along your highways: in names of towns, creeks, canyons, rivers, trademarks? Here is one: *Minnehaha,* which means *laughing water.* The Indians call whiskey firewater. Can't you feel it burn? Then there are Sleepy Hollow, the Gypsy Trail, Lonesome Water, Lost River, Nineveh, Bagdad.

A poet's imagination touches the feelings of those who read his work. What actual words can you think of which preserve the effect of imagination, that is, make you feel their meaning rather than understand it? *Rustling* is one; *lonely* is another.

4. Make a list of from five to ten things that excite your eye, or are interesting to your sight. It is not necessary that the eye approve of them. Make a list so vivid that a stranger will see the picture.

Here are some things that students found exciting: Sparks from a subway train, a dilapidated house, type in a print shop, a flint arrow head, hard packed snow flying beneath the runner of a sled, a wheat field, laughing child, brown and white collie, little red-haired girl in an orchid dress, and some bitter-sweet—its fantastically curling branches and brilliant color. ("Color" in the last picture was criticized as too vague. The student changed it to *orange berries.* His line became: "Some bitter-sweet—its fantastically curling branches and brilliant orange berries.")

5. Make a list of things that excite your ear. In other words, what do you find interesting to hear? Try to suggest through the exact word the sound that excited you.

Beginners who tried this exercise found many interesting sounds. You will add to the few that follow: squawk of a parrot, dripping water, clinking of ice against the glass, crackle of woodfire, grinding of automobile gears, rain on a tin roof, the rat-tat-tat of riveting, static on the radio, gentle lapping of waves against a canoe, airplane flying overhead, shades thumping against the window at night. ("Airplane flying" was criticized because "flying" suggests motion rather than sound. The author revised it to "Drone of airplanes overhead; hum of airplanes overhead; or roar of airplanes overhead.") ("Thumping" was criticized as indefinite. Sounds suggested in "flapping," "beating," "rattling," "snapping," "tapping" were more exact for shades.)

"Banging of a boat faintly seen in the darkness, against a dock side" was a contribution criticized as follows: (1) "Banging" did not suggest the sound a boat would make against the dock. The author agreed that "hollow thudding" expressed his idea more exactly. (2) Seeing the boat had nothing whatsoever to do with the sound effect. In fact if the impression is to come through the ear the suggestion of "faintly seen" weakens the effect. Revised this contribution is:

Hollow thudding of a boat in the darkness, against a dock side.

6. List things that excite your sense of touch. To put the question another way: What do you remember especially for its feel? Try to bring out the feel of the thing by appropriate words.

Here are some notes which beginners made: peach fuzz, a thistle leaf, smooth pebbles, water running over the wrist, lamb's fleece, sandpaper, the sting of iodine on a wound, wet snow down the back, bare feet on a thick carpet, bare feet on a polished floor, tickling of a daddy-long-legs down your arm, a dog's wet cold nose in your palm, the curve of a crystal globe.

7. Make a list of things that excite your sense of smell. Try to suggest the smell by your words.

Some smells that beginners found stimulating follow: freshly cut grass after rain, a pine forest, newly ploughed earth, coffee cooking on an outdoor fire, burning brakes, green logs burning, fresh paint, musty old books, leaves burning, a freshly laundered towel, lumber and tropical fruits and river water blowing off the dock, Dad's cigar, spilled gasoline.

8. List some things that please or displease your palate. Try to suggest the taste through your choice of words.

Students found interest in the following tastes: lime juice, cold potatoes, crisp bacon and freshly made coffee, a fresh mint leaf, sassafras root, cold spring water, ice-cold soda pop after a hard game of tennis, honey, a mouthful of sea water, the inner bark of the cherry birch, candied ginger.

9. Note how taste is suggested in the following passage from "The Eve of St. Agnes" by John Keats. He appeals to all the senses; but in one stanza to your sense of taste largely through his selection. If you count the foods you will not find a great many but you will find a strong suggestion of oriental richness.

XXIX

Then by the bed-side, where the faded moon
Made a dim, silver twilight, soft he set
A table, and, half anguish'd, threw thereon
A cloth of woven crimson, gold, and jet:—
O for some drowsy Morphean amulet!
The boisterous, midnight, festive clarion,
The kettle-drum, and far-heard clarionet,
Affray his ears, though but in dying tone:—
The hall-door shuts again, and all the noise is gone.

XXX

And still she slept an azure-lidded sleep,
In blanched linen, smooth and lavender'd,
While he forth from the closet brought a heap
Of candied apple, quince, and plum, and gourd;
With jellies soother than the creamy curd,
And lucent syrops, tinct with cinnamon;
Manna and dates, in argosy transferr'd
From Fez; and spiced dainties, every one,
From silken Samarcand to cedar'd Lebanon.

10. Read Rupert Brooke's "The Great Lover" printed below. Note how many things have grown dear to each of his senses.

I have been so great a lover: filled my days
So proudly with the splendour of Love's praise
The pain, the calm, and the astonishment,
Desire illimitable, and still content,
And all dear names men use, to cheat despair,
For the perplexed and viewless streams that bear
Our hearts at random down the dark of life.
Now, ere the unthinking silence on that strife
Steals down, I would cheat drowsy Death so far,
My night shall be remembered for a star
That outshone all the suns of all men's days.
Shall I not crown them with immortal praise
Whom I have loved, who have given me, dared with me
High secrets, and in darkness knelt to see
The inenarrable godhead of delight?
Love is a flame;—we have beaconed the world's night.
A city:—and we have built it, these and I.
An emperor:—we have taught the world to die.
So, for their sakes I loved, ere I go hence,
And the high cause of Love's magnificence,
And to keep loyalties young, I'll write those names
Golden for ever, eagles, crying flames,
And set them as a banner, that men may know,
To dare the generations, burn, and blow
Out on the wind of Time, shining and streaming . . .
These I have loved:
      White plates and cups, clean-gleaming,
Ringed with blue lines; and feathery, faery dust;
Wet roofs, beneath the lamp-light; the strong crust
Of friendly bread; and many-tasting food;
Rainbows; and the blue bitter smoke of wood;
And radiant raindrops couching in cool flowers;
And flowers themselves, that sway through sunny hours,

Dreaming of moths that drink them under the moon;
Then, the cool kindliness of sheets, that soon
Smooth away trouble; and the rough male kiss
Of blankets; grainy wood; live hair that is
Shining and free; blue-massing clouds; the keen
Unpassioned beauty of a great machine;
The benison of hot water; furs to touch;
The good smell of old clothes; and other such—
The comfortable smell of friendly fingers,
Hair's fragrance, and the musty reek that lingers
About dead leaves and last year's ferns. . . .

                      Dear names,
And thousand other throng to me! Royal flames;
Sweet water's dimpling laugh from tap or spring;
Holes in the ground; and voices that do sing;
Voices in laughter, too; and body's pain,
Soon turned to peace; and the deep-panting train;
Firm sands; the little dulling edge of foam
That browns and dwindles as the wave goes home;
And washen stones, gay for an hour; the cold
Graveness of iron; moist black earthen mould;
Sleep; and high places; footprints in the dew;
And oaks; and brown horse-chestnuts, glossy-new;
And new-peeled sticks; and shining pools on grass;—
All these have been my loves. And these shall pass,
Whatever passes not, in the great hour,
Nor all my passion, all my prayers, have power
To hold them with me through the gate of Death.
They'll play deserter, turn with the traitor breath,
Break the high bond we made, and sell Love's trust
And sacramented covenant to the dust.
—Oh, never a doubt but, somewhere, I shall wake,
And give what's left of love again, and make
New friends, now strangers. . . .

                      But the best I've known,
Stays here, and changes, breaks, grows old, is blown
About the winds of the world, and fades from brains
Of living men, and dies.

                Nothing remains.

O dear my loves, O faithless, once again
This one last gift I give: that after men
Shall know, and later lovers, far-removed,
Praise you, "All these were lovely"; say, "He loved."

11. Now read "L'Allegro" and "Il Penseroso." You may find them among
Milton's poetry, in Palgrave's *Golden Treasury*, or in *The Oxford Book
of English Verse* to be found in every library. These two poems suggest

the pleasures enjoyed by a man in a happy frame of mind and pleasures enjoyed by the same man in a contemplative or pensive mood. Draw a vertical line down the center of your paper. Head one side "L'Allegro," the other "Il Penseroso." Under the proper heading list the things which the eye enjoys in each poem. Then list what you might enjoy if you were blind but could hear. By running over your two columns you will see how a change of mood changes the aspect of one's pleasures. A poet needs to bear this in mind.

12. Write down what the following things suggest to your imagination. Use this form:

> A hooked fish spinning on a line—pinwheel
> Tall red flower—cardinal

Mack truck in the dark   Gate post with snow on top   Bare tree in winter   Birch tree bent by the wind   A gnarled apple tree   Light rain   Stiff brownstone houses in a row   Full moon   Crescent moon   Ocean waves   White caps on the water   A caterpillar crawling on your arm   Silence after a great tumult   Petals blown by the wind   Smell of mignonette   Flight of swallows   Sounds of wild geese   A frigidaire motor   Brakes in need of oil   Branches scraping the window pane

Beginners found likenesses as follows:

Wood fire—swaying red robed priests

—RUTH KLEIN

New York skyline seen from the ship *Siboney*—a broken fence in an old back yard

—ELINA PRINCE

Trees in winter—scarecrows

—IRMA TERR

Large wheatfields with a strong wind blowing—surging sea

—ALEX TALMADGE

Moon—smiling skull

—MARJORIE DE GRAFF

Bridge at night—steel lace work

—ARTHUR GOEBEL

Petals blown by the wind—flakes of snow

—VICTOR WOLFRAM

Petals blown by the wind—butterflies

—ELEANOR CHAPMAN

13. See what you can do in the way of creating similes by making the things listed below more real through other things suggested by your imagination. Let your comparison be illuminating and fresh. Head your work: Similes Through Names.

Gnarled apple tree   The moon   Wind in the trees   Aërial
wires   Her hands   Brick houses   Highbridge in fog
A lighted house in a fog   A gate post with snow on it   Steam
roller   Stubble field   A field of corn stacks   A determined person   A scolding woman   An avenue of trees
Peace after a quarrel   Confidence in a friend   Stiff date palms
        An egotistical man, boy, woman or girl (select one)
Crooked streets

Here are some similes which beginners created this way, by seeing a
likeness in things a world apart in time, in space, and in nature.

The moon is like a clumsy oyster in a sea of stars.

—MURIEL WELCHER

Wind in the trees is like dryad's breath.

—DORIS LECKY

Aërial wires are like cobwebs spun across the sky.

—ARA TIMOURIAN

Her hands were like twin lotus flowers.

—WILLIAM ROEHRICK

Rain, falling off the roof, is like silver slipping through a miser's hand
in little joyful bursts.

—SYDNEY ABRAM

14. Complete each of the following with a vivid simile:

He walked like _____.   He whistled like _____.
She danced like _____.   Her anger broke like _____.
Evening came like _____.   Her faith is as tepid as _____.

15. Supply the blanks with action appropriate to the image:

Sunlight _____ the garden path like rain.
His jaw _____ like a rat trap.
Her word _____ with the softness of snow.

Here are students' creations in which the action is illuminated by a simile.
There is no rule against humor.

He sang like a crow who thinks he's a nightingale.

—JEAN DECKER

Sang like a wounded lion.

—WILLIAM ROEHRICK

He walked like an animated stick.

—MURIEL WELCHER

16. A quality may be intensified by a vivid image. What is the softest thing
you know in the world? Thomas S. Jones, Jr., thinks "the corn silk in the
south wind's breath." What is the stillest thing? "The mouth of one just
dead," says Adelaide Crapsey. What is the gayest thing? Daffodils?

Illuminate the quality by filling the blanks with appropriate and surprising words: gay as _____; sullen as _____; durable as _____; communicative as _____; fragrant as _____; loyal as _____; adaptable as _____; clear as _____; simple as _____; sweet as _____; sour as _____; melodious as _____; rough as _____

Here are some beginners' similes suggested by a quality:

> He was as unresponsive as a turtle sleeping on a stretch of sand.
> —JOHN MCGUIRE

> She was as gay as a summer breeze.
> She was as light-hearted as a thrush.
> She was as frank as a mirror.
> She was as unresponsive as a photograph.
> —WILLIAM ROEHRICK

17. Experiment five times with the lines below by filling the blanks each time with appropriate words.

> The _____ might have been a _____. It was so _____.
> Example: The birch might have been a ghost. It was so white.

18. Here are some clichés (trite expressions, hackneyed expressions) which we want to rule out of our writing, prose or verse. The life has been used out of them, they have been repeated so often. Observe closely, find new things that have the qualities emphasized, and put new life into each expression through a fresh image: white as a sheet, ghost; face as red as a beet, rose, boiled lobster; flat as a pancake; happy as a lark; hands as cold as ice; as still as a mouse; at break of day; ran like lightning.

19. Why is the following image incongruous?

> The garden walk is like the long veil of a bride walking among the flower-beds.

20. Take the things listed in question 13 above and intensify the comparison by omitting the word of comparison, thus changing each simile to a metaphor. Head your exercise: Image in Noun.

Here are some metaphors created by students who did this exercise:

> The moon is a leaf crumpled against the breast of the midnight.
> The moon is the icy laughter of the gods.
> Moonlight is dust on the shelves of darkness.
> Moonlight is echoed laughter from the walls of morning.
> —MURIEL F. HOCHDORF

> The fire hydrants are black thick-stemmed toadstools.
> The steam shovel is a giant hermit crab, slowly moving his unwieldy claw in search of food.
> —WILLIAM ROEHRICK

Her word was a shiny pebble disturbing the cool waters of tranquillity.
—RUTH H. HAUSMAN

The gate-post is a stiff sentry, guarding my castle.
White jasmine blossoms are thin, white ghosts, swaying in the moonlight.
—DORIS V. LECKY

21. Here is a paired list of unlike things. Each pair has a striking common characteristic. Without naming the second thing, for instance "dog," show that the first is like it—"wind" like "dog"—through what the first thing does. *The wind whines outside.* In other words, let the first thing *do* what is a strongly characteristic action of the second.

wind—dog; Ford—asthmatic man; wind—wolf; wind—dancer; star—fire; moon on a cloudy night—drunkard; sumac trees—bonfires; harpstrings —loom; trees—lyre; kettle—singer; baseball—knife; autumn—artists; waves—slave master; autumn—gipsy; night air—dagger

This is how some student beginners did this exercise. They are showing by what the wind *does* that it is a dog.

It *yelps* and *whines, begging* leaves from the trees.
—WILLIAM ROEHRICK

It *barked* down the chimney.
—JEAN DECKER

The wind *snapped* at gentlemen's coat tails and *nipped* little boys' ears.
—MURIEL WELCHER

Below, they show by what the old Ford does that it is an asthmatic old man; but they do not *say* that he is an asthmatic old man.

The old Ford *climbed* the hill *with labored breath.*
—JEAN DECKER

The Ford *coughs* and *wheezes* down the street.
—JOHN McGUIRE

The old Ford *stood still, wheezing* out its sad story; then *coughed* on.
—DORIS V. LECKY

This is the most vivid kind of metaphor. Sometimes it is called an implied metaphor. Here are others created by students who did this exercise.

A little wind lay fast asleep upon the shoulder of the dunes.
The wind slunk away, whining softly, with his tail between his legs.
The wind ran its fingers through the curling hair of the grass.
Music splintered through the moonlight.
—MURIEL F. HOCHDORF

The black clouds perspire beneath the wind's cutting whip.
Docks reach into the river to grasp and hold the giant ships.
The moon reeled and stumbled across the sky; then fell in a stupor behind a cloud.
—WILLIAM ROEHRICK

Gargoyles of cloud spurt water from the roof of the sky.

—ROSALIE MAHER

22. Make your own verb images now. The action metaphor, sometimes called implied metaphor, has immense possibilities for development. It is the most vital of metaphors. Remember: The VERB's the thing!

23. Why are the following not metaphors and not similes?

The garden walk is a path through paradise.
She was as gay as the merry widow.
The skyline is like a silhouette that a baby giant has snipped with scissors.
He was light-hearted as a tramp after a good meal.
An air drill is like a sputtering machine gun as it jacks its way through the rock.

24. From the following material make metaphors by bringing out a *feeling* in each case; that is, think of the effect.

Clothes on a line in a high wind.
   Example: The clothes flapped gaily in the wind. Woolen arms and legs danced crazily. The "gaily" and "crazily" suggest feeling.
Autumn leaves on a windy day   Chrysanthemums from a child's viewpoint (A child's interests should influence the choice of image).
      Hares running in the meadow   A young colt   Rain against the pane   Wind in the rigging of a ship   A kettle of water on the stove

25. Turn the following expressions into vivid metaphors.

Her hair is yellow. (What is the yellowest thing you know?)
She had the tiniest hands I ever saw on a girl her size.
Her mouth was beautifully formed and suggested a sweet disposition.
She was very intelligent looking.
She showed poise as she walked.
Her hands were large and coarse looking.

26. Put into figurative language; that is, lift these literal expressions into the realm of the imagination by metaphor or simile.

The moon looks full and clear. Not a cloud is anywhere near it.
It makes me sad to think of you.
The automobile went very fast that night.
The top of the skyscraper was not visible through the fog that was settling down.
We could see the road in the moonlight stretching through the meadow.
I watched him until I could see him no more.
The fog obscured the hills.
Arc lights are reflected in the park lake.
You could hear the motor as it turned steadily.

You hardly realized that you had taken-off in the plane. There was
no sensation as you left the earth.
We went through the dark at a high rate of speed.
The waves came up the beach with a deafening noise.
The view was wonderful.
I watched the sunset with you beside me.
She laughed happily.
Time seemed never ending as I waited.

27. Write five figurative sentences which you then turn into literal language.
Give the literal sentences to one of your associates to translate into figurative
language. Compare notes. Does the imagery reveal differences of interest,
aptitude, taste?

28. From the sense exercises you did—questions 4 to 8—select the things
that appeal to you most and weave them into a paragraph beginning,
"These are the things I know and love," or a variation of it. Perhaps you
can now illuminate a quality or an action by a sincere simile or metaphor.

CHAPTER II

THE EXTENDED IMAGE

WHEN Alfred Noyes shows us that "the moon is a ghostly galleon," he does not stop. He follows the course of the galleon. A wind is driving the clouds, scattering them, piling them up around and across the moon. But the moon is no longer a moon to the poet; it is a galleon. Galleons sail the seas. This one is rising and falling on a rough sea.

> The moon is a ghostly galleon
> Tossed upon cloudy seas.

The sky has become sea. Furthermore, imagination has put this sea in a place appropriate to a moon ship. It is a sea of clouds—a cloudy sea.

If the poet had wanted to tell more about this galleon on the seas, he would have had to select details appropriate to this ghost ship on its rough course. He could not have added, "It has a happy face," because galleons have not faces. Human beings have. If he had wanted to indicate that after awhile the moon stopped shining, he could not have added, "By midnight it ceased shining." He would have had to suggest something like this: "Before it reached port it foundered and went down." A ship must be a ship to the last detail of the experience. Every image must be carried out appropriately in its own terms. Any lack of sincerity or illogical imagining will quickly show in developing an image; that is, when we enlarge the picture by adding details, or by filling in a background.

Coleridge once said: "Poetry . . . had a logic of its own, as severe as that of science; and more difficult, because more subtle, more complex, and dependent on more and more fugitive causes."

Here is a famous passage from Shakespeare's *As You Like It* in which he compares the life of a man to the acts of a play. He never once loses sight of the image which he is elaborating down to "the last scene of all that ends this strange eventful history."

> All the world's a stage,
> And all the men and women merely players:
> They have their exits and their entrances;
> And one man in his time plays many parts,
> His acts being seven ages. At first the infant,
> Mewling and pewking in the nurse's arms.

Then the whining schoolboy, with his satchel
And shining morning face, creeping like a snail
Unwillingly to school. And then the lover,
Sighing like a furnace, with a woeful ballad
Made to his mistress' eyebrow. Then a soldier,
Full of strange oaths, and bearded like a pard,
Jealous in honour, sudden and quick in quarrel,
Seeking the bubble reputation
Even in the cannon's mouth. And then the justice,
In fair round belly with good capon lin'd,
With eyes severe, and beard of formal cut,
Full of wise saws and modern instances;
And so he plays his part. The sixth age shifts
Into the lean and slipper'd pantaloon,
With spectacles on nose and pouch on side,
His youthful hose, well sav'd, a world too wide
For his shrunk shank; and his big manly voice,
Turning again toward childish treble, pipes
And whistles in his sound. Last scene of all,
That ends this strange eventful history,
Is second childishness, and mere oblivion,
Sans teeth, sans eyes, sans taste, sans everything.

While this passage is part of a play, a monologue of one of the characters, such an extended image is sometimes the material of a complete lyric: William Watson's "Song," for instance, in which April is
like a young girl ready to laugh or to cry upon the slightest provo-
cation, or Robert Frost's poem below, in which a hillside thaw lets
go "ten million silver lizards."

A Hillside Thaw

To think to know the country and not know
The hillside on the day the sun lets go
Ten million silver lizards out of snow!
As often as I've seen it done before
I can't pretend to tell the way it's done.
It looks as if some magic of the sun
Lifted the rug that bred them on the floor
And the light breaking on them made them run.
But if I thought to stop the wet stampede,
And caught one silver lizard by the tail,
And put my foot on one without avail,
And threw myself wet-elbowed and wet-kneed
In front of twenty others' wriggling speed,—
In the confusion of them all aglitter,
And birds that joined in the excited fun

By doubling and redoubling song and twitter,
I have no doubt I'd end by holding none.

It takes the moon for this. The sun's a wizard
By all I tell; but so's the moon a witch.
From the high west she makes a gentle cast
And suddenly, without a jerk or twitch,
She has her spell on every single lizard.
I fancied when I looked at six o'clock
The swarm still ran and scuttled just as fast.
The moon was waiting for her chill effect.
I looked at nine: the swarm was turned to rock
In every lifelike posture of the swarm,
Transfixed on mountain slopes almost erect.
Across each other and side by side they lay.
The spell that so could hold them as they were
Was wrought through trees without a breath of storm
To make a leaf, if there had been one, stir.
It was the moon's: she held them until day,
One lizard at the end of every ray.
The thought of my attempting such a stay!

The developed metaphors which we have cited are in metrical
verse. Beautiful effects are often created by adapting the cadences of
natural speech to a single basic image. The pauses made by the
breath mark the movements, line upon line. The poem is built on a
metaphor or a simile. It is all metaphor or all simile. Read this one:

High-Tide

I edged back against the night.
The sea growled assault on the wave-bitten shore,
And the breakers,
Like young and impatient hounds,
Sprang, with rough joy, on the shrinking sand,
Sprang—but were drawn back slowly,
With a long, relentless pull,
Whimpering, into the dark.

Then I saw who held them captive;
And I saw how they were bound
With a broad and quivering leash of light
Held by the moon,
As, calm and unsmiling,
She walked the deep fields of the sky.

—JEAN STARR UNTERMEYER

Note how logical to the scientific theory underlying the image is every detail. The moon controls the tides. Here the imagination unrolls the picture with a logic as severe as that of science. This logic is the truth of imagery.

Here are some others, shorter, but quite as vivid:

The Skaters

Black swallows swooping or gliding
In a flurry of entangled loops and curves;
The skaters skim over the frozen river.

And the grinding click of their skates as they impinge upon the surface,
Is like the brushing together of thin wing-tips of silver.

—JOHN GOULD FLETCHER

Three Lonely Women

One alone
As a thorn tree in winter
Where even cattle find no rest;
That has only known
The press of a bird's breast
When seeking death.

Another . . . lonely
As an underground stream
Quiet . . . unseen
Freshening roots of trees.

And one lonely
As an eagle
That lifts away from these.

—MARY CUMMINGS EUDY

Hound At Night

I did not know how brittle
Was the silence
Till quick, shrewd barks of a hound
Pelted over the hills
Breaking the stillness with fragments
Like slivers of bright looking glass.

—LOUISE AYRES GARNETT

No single image is perhaps more familiar today than this:

Fog

The fog comes
on little cat feet.

It sits looking
over harbor and city
on silent haunches
and then moves on.

—CARL SANDBURG

Below are some extended images created by beginners in the art of expression beautiful. They may encourage you to invent others.

Sleep

He shall not get me
The many-armed octopus—
He shall not twine his waving arms
About me.
I struggle:
He is fascinating;
He is cruel:
And I—am
Weak.
One scintillating tendril catches me
Slowly.
I sink
Into cool waters
Wrapped
Deep in his embrace.
I sleep. . . .

—HARRIET DOKTOR

Icebergs

Winter,
Greedy Midas,
Has touched the laughing waves
And transformed them into frozen
Silver.

—ESTELLE ROOKS

Fog

It embraces the river
Like a jealous lover
Who would shut out
The rest of the world.

—SYLVIA ADELMAN

March Wind

The wind blusters
around the corner—
with round, red cheeks
and a mighty stomach—
and knocks me flat
with a hearty bump;
then, coat-tails flying
and hat awry,
he lumbers on—
clumping
into ash-cans and fences,
leaving behind him
a shattering clatter
of ear-splitting sound.

Does he hurry so
to catch the express
for Eternity?

—NAOMI ROGIN

Buzzard

The wind swooped down with flapping wings
Upon a host of dying trees.
When they were dead he pecked their flesh
And gorged himself with it;
Then left their skeletons behind
Against the blue wall of the sky . . . .
And now he lies asleep
Beneath the autumn sun.

—WILLIAM ROEHRICK

Full Bloom

Last week
The moon was only a bud,
Delicate and ethereal,
But now it is a great yellow blossom,
Nestled in the black branches of a tree.
—RUTH KLEIN

In this poem the young poet uses three similes to extend her image:

April

April comes tearfully,
Like a child that has just dropped
Its lollypop,
Like a maiden
Mourning for her lover,
Like me
When you have hurt my heart.
—ESTELLE ROOKS

Sculptor

I shall carve a vision
More delicate than frost design,
Symmetrically pure
As the crescent of the moon.
I shall carve a vision
Elusive as a plume of spray
Tossed
Through the light of summer sun
By wind-spun wave.
The fantasy and wonder
Of spring's imagined music
Will mingle
With the melancholy softness
Of an autumn sky. . . .

I shall carve Beauty's image
And perish with creation.
—GILBERT O'CONNOR

Plea

The Autumn breeze
Strips the last vestiges of beauty
From the remaining flowers:
Here a petal,
There a leaf.
So, too,

Experience strips from my heart
Here a faith,
There an ideal.
Shamefaced skeletons are left.
They ask only
That the charitable snows cover their nakedness.

—SYLVIA LAPIDUS

The Singer

The kettle on the fire
Practices her music lesson,
Bubbling over in her effort
To reach the highest notes.
Why should she be so overjoyed?
For, in spite of all these lessons,
She still keeps singing through her nose!

—ALICE LEVY

A CHALLENGE TO THE LOGIC OF
YOUR IMAGINATION

1. Take any one of the images that you created as an exercise in the previous chapter and develop it. Do not use rhyme. Let your medium of expression be perfectly free. As you write, indicate the rhythm of speech by breaking your lines to suggest the sweep of the voice from breath to breath. In this exercise your imagination must catch the inflections of the speaking voice. Test your result by reading aloud to see whether the cadence suits your material.

2. Try a wholly new image which is suggested by material in your notebook.

3. Build images on any of the following: Caprice of the wind   Patience of winter trees   Wind   Garden walk   Daffodils in the breeze   Hyacinth blooms in a flower shop   Late chrysanthemums   Traffic signals   Subway platform   Variability of weather   Cat-tails in the wind   Docks   Mystery of trees in leaf   Inconstancy   Crooked streets   Lane   Galoshes   Tea things   Kettle boiling   A river   Swamp

4. Build an image to suggest one of the following: Power   Strength   Durability   Strangeness of someone you thought you knew   Eternal value   Hardness   Transitoriness of things

CHAPTER III

RHYTHM AND METER

In the days when hand labor rolled barrels of cotton down the dock for shipping the worker sang at his task. The movements of his body made the tune to which his words were set.

> Oh, roll the cotton, roll it down,
> Oh roll the cotton down;
> Oh roll the cotton, roll it down,
> Oh roll the cotton down.

Sailors drawing in their anchors, put words to the movement of their bodies as they tug at the rope: heave—ho—heave—ho! The accented note of the song marks the finish of the pull, while the next accent marks the limit of the next pull.

When you and a companion go walking along a country road, one sets the pace; the other falls into step. There is harmony of movement while both keep step. But if one loses a step a bumping of sides results to remark the disturbance. If you have ever ridden horseback you know how you let your body swing into the horse's motion before you can post. You know too how the movement varies with different animals; one will have a long trot; the other, a short trot. If you travel on the railroad it is not long before you catch the measured song of the wheels on the rails: clackity-clack, clackity-clack. Beside the sea you hear the surge of the waves rolling in, breaking, receding; rolling in, breaking, receding. One accent tells you when they are in, another when they break, another when they are all out,—even when you are not looking.

You may have seen your grandmother darning stockings as she rocked back and forth, back and forth. Her whole body responded to the rise and fall, rise and fall of her rocker. This clackity-clack; this rolling in, breaking, receding; this rise and fall—in short all this measured movement is rhythm.

Every motion mentioned above has its own peculiar song. The universe moves to many rhythms; the heart of man beats in rhythm; you can feel it at your wrist.

Rhythm marks our daily speech, though this rhythm is not always the regular clackity-clack of the cars, or the break, break, break of the waves. As feeling heightens, however, speech tends to grow more and

more regular. The six-year-old child, whose father has promised to
take him to the circus, claps his hands while he dances up and down
chanting in glee:

> I'm go' ing to' the cir' cus
> I'm go' ing to' the cir' cus
> I'm go' ing to' the cir' cus.

His delight is expressed in rhythmical utterance which flows in a
definite pattern. He marks the pattern by the clapping of his hands
and the up and down movements of his dance. Here is the spontaneous
overflow of feeling which Wordsworth called poetry.

Passionate utterance of any kind has marked rhythm whether a
torrent of angry words; or the spontaneous prayer from the depths
of the soul; or the intense declaration of the lover. The nature of the
feeling seems to shape the flow of the pattern.

Because poetry is usually the result of intense feeling, its music
flows in definite patterns. Indeed, the chief difference between the
music of prose and the music of verse is that prose rhythms flow in
no definite pattern; whereas verse rhythm flows in a pattern which
the ear soon detects just as the horseback rider detects the gait of the
animal beneath him. Having detected the pattern, the ear listens for
its recurrence. It feels and expects it. There is pleasure in having the
expectation fulfilled. If there is a disturbance—as the loss of step in
the walk on the country road, the trained ear is offended. Even an
untrained ear may detect a difference between the music of

> dum' ta ta, dum' ta ta, dum' ta ta, dum'

and

> ta dum', ta dum', ta dum', ta dum'.

Note the different rhythms in these passages from various poems.

> Summer is coming
> Summer is coming
> I know it, I know it, I know it.

> 'Tis the star-spangled banner! O long may it wave
> O'er the land of the free and the home of the brave!

> The curfew tolls the knell of parting day,
> The lowing herd winds slowly o'er the lea.

> There is something in the autumn
> That is native to my blood.

You might still keep the music of these lines by dispensing with the words and substituting *la la*, accenting the beats that are now accented. In the first instance the music would sound

la' la la   la' la
la' la la   la' la
la la' la,   la la' la,   la la' la!

This movement of the poem, which we feel as we listen, makes the lilt of one poem differ from that of another. Let us call it the outer pattern. To recognize it we need not analyze what comprises its music any more than we need to analyze the music of "The Star-Spangled Banner" to distinguish it from "Oh, Holy Night." When the pattern is repeated in large units the recurrence gives pleasure through recognition as the recurrence of the musical theme of the Ninth Symphony brings delight to ears that recognize it.

We feel this outer music without thinking about the why of it. We hum as the automobile moves along, or whistle as we walk, catching the rhythm of the motion without giving heed to how we are interpreting the song. But the poet who creates this outer music knows that it is put together by light and sharp accents, that is, by the recurrence of accent or beat arranged in groups, which form a kind of inner music. As accented sounds and unaccented sounds are strung together the music unrolls in the outer pattern. Various kinds of verse music are made by arranging these accented sounds and unaccented sounds in various combinations. Any combination of accented and unaccented sounds is called meter. From the point of view of the composer, the kind of meter makes the rhythm.

There are four common kinds of meter. We may as well learn the name of each kind for convenience in talking about it to other verse makers. When you answer the telephone with *hello'*, you have answered with an iamb; that is, a word of two syllables, with the accent falling on the second syllable. Listen to the accent: *hello'* soft *loud*. Tap it with your pencil. Represented graphically it is

./   ta dee'

Some other iambic words or words which are iambs are: *delight, delay, content, machine, believe, caprice, convey.*

When you call out *Mother!* or *Father!* you have used a trochee. The first syllable *Moth* is accented; the second *er* unaccented.

/.   dee' ta

Some other trochaic words, or words which are trochees, are: *steering, axle, gaily, rocker, grasses, velvet, gritty, moonlight, Sunday, gentile.*

The iamb and the trochee, you see, are made of two syllables.

The other two combinations are made of three syllables. The first is soft, soft, *loud*. Tap it with your pencil.

../ ta ta dee′ *effervesce′*

Such a combination is called an anapest. Some anapestic words or words which are anapests are: *undeserved, represent, supersede, incomplete.*

The last of the fundamental group is *loud,* soft, soft. Tap it.

/.. dee′ ta ta *hick′ ory*

This is called a dactyl. Other dactylic words, or words which are dactyls are: *gaiety, happiness, merrily, telegram, violet, history, brotherhood, Saturday, beautiful, calico, indigo, Caucasus.*

Each one of these groups: one accent with one unaccented syllable or one accent with two unaccented syllables, is a metrical unit, called a foot. You might say *unit* or *measure*, but if you wish to use the verse maker's term, "foot" is the word. Here you have them briefly:

./ iamb
/. trochee
../ anapest
/.. dactyl

As one of these metrical units predominates more than the others in poetry, we call the verse pattern iambic or trochaic, anapestic or dactylic.

When you sing

My coun′ try 'tis′ of thee′
Sweet land′ of lib′ erty′—
Of thee′ I sing′

you are using iambic verse. Perhaps we use iambs more frequently than we use any other kind of meter both in our daily speech and in English versification. Our language seems to lend itself to the music of iambs. Some other examples, more or less familiar, follow:

If all the world were apple pie
And all the sea were ink

The lion and the unicorn
Were fighting for the crown

The Queen of Hearts
She made some tarts

A Book of Verses underneath the Bough

In Flanders fields the poppies blow
Between the crosses, row on row.

I think that I shall never see
A poem lovely as a tree.

Here are some lines in trochees:

Twinkle, twinkle, little star
How I wonder what you are.

Sing a song o' sixpence

Ring-a-round-a-rosy.

Twenty froggies went to school
Down beside a rushy pool.

Mary had a little lamb.

Gin a body meet a body
Coming through the rye.

All are architects of fate
Working in these walls of time
Some with massive deeds and great,
Some with ornaments of rhyme.

Bards of passion and of mirth,
Ye have left your souls on earth.

Com and trip it as ye go
On the light fantastick toe.

Teach me half the gladness
That thy brain must know;

Dig the grave and let me lie.

In most of the lines above, the last foot is not a perfect trochee.

Twink' le, twink' le, lit' tle star'

"Star" is the accent of a trochee; the unaccented syllable is omitted. Such an omission is quite usual in trochaic verse. It makes possible a strong ending to the line. An accented syllable at the end of a line is a strong or masculine ending. By singing softly to yourself the syllable left out, just as you count softly the value of a rest when you are learning to play a musical instrument, you will see that the rhythm is undisturbed by the omission. Because the line lacks a syllable to make it complete it is a *catalectic* line. Whether or not you remember that word is of no importance; it simply means *incomplete*. A student once said it sounded like a fit—it seemed associated with old Silas Marner.

Teach' me   half' the   glad' ness

is made up of perfect trochees.

The last foot is a trochee and so ends with an unaccented syllable, "ness" of "gladness." Such an ending is a weak or feminine ending. These feminine endings, properly handled, may lend sweetness and delicacy to verse—too many make it over sweet. Notice further that *Ring-a-round-a-rosy* is composed of three perfect trochees. It neither lacks a syllable nor has an extra one; such a line is called an *acatalectic* or complete line.

When you stand and remove your hat as the band strikes up "The Star-Spangled Banner" you sing in anapests:

Oh say'   can you see'   by the dawn's'   early light'.

Other lines in anapestic meter are:

Be it e'   ver so hum'   ble, there's no'   place like home'.

Twas the night'   before Christ'   mas and all'   through the house'
Not a crea'   ture was stir'   ring not e'   ven a mouse'

I am mon'   arch of all'   I survey'

With a heigh'   and a ho'   and a heigh'   nonino'

The Assyr'   ian came down'   like a wolf'   on the fold'

In every case above, the last foot ends in a true anapest, and so is a masculine or strong ending, because an anapest is accented on the last syllable. Because the lines are complete, they are acatalectic. Suppose the line

Not a creature was stirring not even a mouse

were

Not a crea' ture was stir' ring not e' ven a mous' *ie*.

There would be one syllable more than is needed to make the perfect line. Such a line which has an excess of syllable or syllables is called a *hypercatalectic* line. In iambic lines there is frequently such an extra syllable at the end of a line.

Farewell'   thou art'   too dear'   for my'   pos sess'   ing

It is not at all necessary that you burden yourself with these technical words. But understand about the complete line, the incomplete line, and the excess of syllables for intelligent criticism of your own work.

It is always the number of verse accents that determine the number of feet on a line.

As a child, you played a game while you pretended to wind a clock, saying,

Hickory, dickory, dock.

You were winding in dactylic lines. You can fill in the music of the last foot by softly saying *ery* as you did with the trochees that omitted a syllable. Other dactylic lines are:

Rock′-a-bye, ba′by thy cra′ dle is   green′

Lad′ y bird, lad′ y bird, fly′ away   home′

Oh′ how I   love′ to go up′ in a   swing′.

This′ is the   for′ est pri   me′ val. The   mur′ muring   pines′ and the hem′ locks . . .

Cannon to right of them,
Cannon to left of them.

Merrily, merrily shall I live now,
Under the blossom that hangs on the bough.

Over the river and through the wood.

So much for lines of iambs, trochees, anapests, and dactyls. When verse makers become proficient in handling meter they seek to put variety into their rhythms by introducing a strange foot into the line here and there. For example, just above in the last dactylic line

Over the river and through the wood

you have *through′ the* which is a trochee, in place of a dactyl. "Wood" is the accent of a dactyl, incomplete by two unaccented syllables.
In

Much′ have   I trav′   eled in′   the realms′   of gold′

Keats begins an iambic line with a trochee: *Much′ have.* The next foot, *I trav′,* is an iamb, and all the other feet in the line are iambs. But he needed a trochee first to emphasize "Much."

The predominant pattern of "The Rime of the Ancient Mariner" is iambic. The regular beat runs like this:

He holds him with his skinny hand,
'There was a ship,' quoth he.
'Hold off! unhand me, gray-beard loon!'
Eftsoons his hand dropt he.

But Coleridge frequently substitutes another foot for an iamb. "The Rime" begins

It is an ancient Mariner,
And he stop'   peth one' of three'.
By thy long'   gray beard' and glit' tering eye'.

In the second two lines above he has substituted an anapest for the first regular iamb. Below, he puts an anapest for one of the middle iambs:

For all averr'd *I had kill'd* the bird.

And again:

The Sun now rose upon the right:
Out' of   the sea came he.

"Out of" is a trochee substituted for the initial iamb.

Glimmer'd the white moon shine.

"Glimmer'd" is another instance of the same kind of substitution. Go through "The Ancient Mariner" and you will find other examples. With all his substitutions, Coleridge never loses sight of his fundamental patterns. He substitutes to enrich his music; then immediately recovers the iambic foot.

To summarize: We have noted how one syllable may be dropped in a trochee ending and two in a dactylic ending. We have seen how an anapest may be substituted for an iamb, an iamb for an anapest, a trochee for an iamb. In fact almost any foot may be substituted for another foot in working out a pattern.

Besides the four fundamental feet that are most generally used in English verse, there are two often introduced to give variety. They are usually substitute feet, although occasionally you will find a whole line of them. The first is the spondee, two accents. // It is doubtful whether in English there is such thing as a true spondee but such words as *heartbreak, houseboat, craft-made,* are pretty near it. A combination of two words of one syllable makes a spondee as nearly as we can get one in English verse. Any versifier, however, may interpret the spondee as a trochee or an iamb, according to the character of the outer musical pattern. Here are some lines which have substitute spondees,

I have lived long enough, having seen *one thing*, that love hath an end.
—Algernon Charles Swinburne

A sonnet is a moment's monument
Memorial from the soul's eternity
To one *dead death*less hour.
—DANTE GABRIEL ROSSETTI

Another substitute foot is the amphibrach—soft, *hard,* soft ./.
Words to illustrate the amphibrach are: *contentment, delightful, outrageous, together, Italian, mechanic, deserving.* Here are examples of
amphibrachs:

The old oaken bucket, the iron bound bucket,
. / . . / . . / . . / .

Summer is coming, summer is coming,
I know it, I know it, I know it.
. / . . / . . / .

O Captain, my captain, our fearful trip is done.
. / . . / .

Briefly, the added feet are:

Spondee   //
Amphibrach   ./.

There are many other combinations which give many varieties of
feet, but as an introduction to the handling of meter the six here
described are a sufficient working basis.

As the poet works out his pattern, he may plan on a line any number of feet from one to eight, hardly more than eight. He may combine
these lines in any way he chooses: a long line alternated with a short
one; three longs and a short, four lines the same length, and so on.
He may gather these lines into sheaves of from two to nine or more
lines to suit the flow of his thought. He may repeat the design of one
sheaf in another. He may keep on repeating this design to suit the
flowing of his thought. Each sheaf then forms a stanza. The line is
one of the builders of structure.

According to the number of metrical accents on a line we speak
of lines as one-foot, two-foot, three-foot, four-foot, five-foot, six-foot,
seven-foot, or eight-foot lines. The number of musical units depends
upon the number of accents. If there are three accents, there are three
feet to the line.

Here is a poem with only one foot on each line:

A Poet Sets His Price
For this?
A kiss!
—J. J.

The name for one foot is *mono* (from the Greek word meaning "one") *meter* (meaning "measure"). So the line length and the character of the music in the above short poem are designated *iambic monometer*. In other words, iambic meter; one accent on the line.

A two-foot line is a di (two) meter, *dimeter*:

> Sun comes, moon comes,
> Time slips away.
>
> —ALFRED, LORD TENNYSON

Three-foot lines are designated *trimeter;* four, *tetrameter;* five, *pentameter;* six, *hexameter;* seven, *heptameter;* eight, *octameter.* If you forget the Greek word use the number. Examples of each are given below:

> Thou point'st at me
> In mockery;
> If I come nigh   *2-foot or dimeter*
> Shade-like thou'lt fly
>
> —WILLIAM CARTWRIGHT

Lines of one or two feet are seldom found except in light or humorous verse. Lines of two feet lend themselves admirably to poems of an airy nature.

> In this secluded shrine
> O miracle of grace,
> No mortal eye but mine   *3-foot or trimeter*
> Hath looked upon thy face.
>
> —JOHN B. TABB

> Thy voice is on the rolling air;
> I hear thee where the waters run;
> Thou standest in the rising sun,   *4-foot or tetrameter*
> And in the setting thou art fair.
>
> —ALFRED, LORD TENNYSON

> Drink to me only with thine eyes   *4-foot or tetrameter*
> And I will pledge with mine;   *3-foot or trimeter*
> Or leave a kiss but in the cup
> And I'll not look for wine.
>
> —BEN JONSON

In Ben Jonson's lines we have lines of four feet and three feet alternately combined. The ballads furnish many examples of this line combination.

The five-foot line moves with dignity. It is suited to gravest thought.

> Thou still unravish'd bride of quietness,
> Thou foster-child of silence and slow time,   *5-foot or*
> Sylvan historian, who canst thus express   *pentameter*
> A flowery tale more sweetly than our rhyme:
>
> —JOHN KEATS

This is the forest primeval; but where are the hearts that
    beneath it
Leaped like the roe, when he hears in the woodland the
    voice of the hunstman?   *6-foot or*
Where is the thatch-roofed village, the home of Acadian   *hexameter*
    farmers,—

           —HENRY WADSWORTH LONGFELLOW

Beyond the path of the outmost sun through utter dark-
    ness hurled—
Farther than ever comet flared or vagrant star-dust swirled—   *7-foot or*
Live such as fought and sailed and ruled and loved and   *heptameter*
    made our world.

           —RUDYARD KIPLING

Comrades, leave me here a little, while as yet 'tis early morn:
Leave me here, and when you want me, sound upon the   *8-foot or*
    bugle horn.   *octameter*

           —ALFRED, LORD TENNYSON

Lines of seven and eight feet seem ungainly; hence they are not so
popular among poets as the shorter lengths. They tend to break into
lines of four feet and three feet; or four and four. Swinburne was fond
of long lines; so is Kipling.

It is fun to have some one beat out metrical lines with a pencil while
you name them; that is, you tell how many feet there are in the line
and what kind of feet they are. The line beater will have to understand
meter, of course, to be of help. He must act as umpire. For example:
Umpire beats with a pencil /./././. You answer, "Four beats: tetrameter; accent, unaccented: trochee." Ask some one to tap the patterns
below and see whether you are able to recognize them; or sing them
from the printed pattern below. Then name the kind of metrical unit
and how many of the kind in the pattern.

././././   ../../
./././   ../../../../
./././././   /././.
/./.   /../../../..
/././/.   /../../../..
/././   ../../../../
../../   /../../..

When you are accustomed to the sound of the accents, try to recognize the line length and the meter of lines of verse.

If winter comes can spring be far behind?

I think that I shall never see
A poem lovely as a tree.

Take her up tenderly.

Merrily, merrily shall I live now.

The hare limped trembling through the frozen grass.

I am sick o' wastin' leather on these gritty pavin'-stones
An' the blasted Henglish drizzle wakes the fever in my bones.

I am monarch of all I survey.

Love took up the glass of Time, and turn'd it in his glowing hands;
Every moment, lightly shaken, ran itself in golden sands.

Tiger, tiger, burning bright
In the forests of the night.

My fugitive years are all wasting away.

And no one shall work for money, and no one shall work for fame,

Ring out, ye crystal spheres!
Once bless our human ears.

Phoebus, arise!

Who hammered you, wrought you
From argentine vapour?

When you can recognize various meters, experiment further by fitting some words to short patterns. For example, here is a pattern:

$$/./././$$

These lines fit the pattern:

Come here, my dear, and play with me.

I wish that you might never go.

The rain is falling gently down.

Supply words for the following patterns:

·/·/·/·/

/·/·/·/·   *Use as the last word a word of two syllables, the second unaccented,*

/·/·/·/·   *such as* heather, weather.

··/··/··/

/··/··/··/

/··/··/··/··   *Here you will need to end with a word of three syllables or the equivalent, such as* happiness.

The thing that the young versifier must bear in mind is that the accented syllable of the word must fall upon the accent of the pattern. Take the last example: The rain'-is fall'-ing gent'-ly down'. The words "falling" and "gently" are accented on the first syllable. They fall quite naturally into the pattern:

$$. \quad / \quad . \quad / \quad . \quad . \quad / \quad . \quad /$$
$$\text{The rain} \quad \text{is fall} \quad \text{ing gent} \quad \text{ly down.}$$

The accent of the word falls on the accent of the pattern. But we must not force an accent on an unaccented syllable.

The rain gently is falling down. In our daily speech we do not accent the word this way: *gent ly'*. But if this line were fitted to the pattern, it would have to sing:

The rain' gently' is fall' ing down.

This is called wrenching the accent. We must not do it. Furthermore, words that we do not normally emphasize, should not fall on the beat of the pattern: prepositions—*to, for, in,* and the like; conjunctions; articles; and other unimportant words.

$$/ \quad / \quad / \quad /$$
$$\text{Mary} \quad \text{Ware just} \quad \text{came to} \quad \text{town.}$$

is as we should say it in ordinary speech. The accents coincide with the accents of the pattern. But

$$/ \quad / \quad / \quad /$$
$$\text{Mary} \quad \text{Ware came} \quad \text{to the} \quad \text{town.}$$

is not as we should say it. In phrasing, we slur our prepositions and accent the nouns. If we wrench accents this way in writing our verse, the reader (who will phrase the words normally, with the accent as in habitual speech) will find little music in the line. And if such a line appears in a stanza with metrically perfect lines, it disturbs the rhythm, and the line is therefore unmusical.

This wrenching of accents occurs in the early ballads made by unlettered folk and imitated to preserve the homely ballad effect. The music in them is so strong that you are compelled to mispronounce if you feel the meter. Here is an example from "The Bludy Serk," a 15th century poem.

This hinder yeir I hard be told   *hinder yeir = last year*
    Thair was a worthy King;
Dukis, Erlis, and Barronis bold,
    He had at his bidding.

In humorous verse too accents are deliberately wrenched to evoke laughter. But the young versifier who is acquiring the mechanics of verse must not wrench accents.

By supplying or deleting syllables and rearranging the words so that the normal speech accent will fall upon the metrical accent, he may turn any rhythm into any other rhythm. Here are three examples:

I think that I shall never see
A poem lovely as a tree.   *Iambic*

Never shall a poem be
Lovely as a growing tree.   *Trochaic*

I am sure that my eyes shall not see anywhere
In a poem the loveliness found in a tree.   *Anapestic*

Surely no poem that I ever looked upon
Sheds half the loveliness trees scatter everywhere.   *Dactylic*

If winter comes can spring be far behind?

Winter comes with springtime close behind him.

Winter is coming with springtime close following.

If the winter has come how can spring stay behind!

Come and see the moonlight dancing.

Will you come where you'll see how the moonlight can dance?

Come, won't you, out where the moonlight is toe dancing.

Come out to see the moonlight dance.

While you are studying rhythm, read poetry aloud. Try to bring out the music of the line: the inner pattern; as well as the music of the whole: the outer pattern, in your reading. There are really three rhythms which go into the making of metrical verse: the rhythm of the stanza; the rhythm of the line pattern; the rhythm of speech, which is the rhythm of the underlying thought with its tints and shades of meaning.

FIVE-FINGER EXERCISES

1. Answer each question below in exactly the same pattern as the question. Let every accent in your answer match the accent of the question. Do not try to rhyme. Say or sing question and answer aloud.

    a. Where has all the snow been taken? /./././.
       Some answers by pupils are listed below:
       How can anybody answer? /././././.
       Ask the unemployed; they'll tell you.

    b. Will you come out and play with me?
       I will if you can wait awhile.

    c. Whose books are these?
       I think they're mine.

    d. Did you see where I laid Minnie's key?
    e. If it rains shall we go?
    f. Will you take tea with me today?
    g. Where are the poems due today? /../ ./ ./
       (Be sure to have your accents fall beneath the accents of the question)
    h. Have you time to talk a moment?
    i. Why did you leave so soon, Jeanette?
    j. When did you hear that you passed in geometry?
    k. Why have you written illegibly?
    l. Who's there?
    m. Who said, "Yes, sir?"
    n. Where is Robert?
    o. Have you a pin?
    p. If you please, will you lend me your pen?
    q. What's that?

2. Match every line below, beat for beat, with a suitable line. If possible say the given line aloud or sing it; then say or sing your matching line before you write it.

    Examples—   I wish I were a butterfly
    Pupils' answers: *I'd flit about the fields all day.*
                I'd sip the nectar from the flowers.
                With gauzy wings of midnight blue.
                With not a thing to do but play.

Group I

The wind is laughing on the hill	The thistle is a powder puff
The wind went whining down the lane	I wish I were a butterfly
The Ford went wheezing up the hill	Romance came by in shabby coat
Where there are patterns on the grass	

Group II

Moonlight dances on the lake	Come and see the moonlight dancing
Shadows come with noiseless footfall	Patience is a lovely thing
Laugh and sing	Once a song went wrapped in silver
Wind-swept heights are often cold	(There is no word to rhyme with "silver")
Life is so much joy and sorrow	Laugh and sing, for life is lovely
Even songbirds love the silence	
Evening walks the world with beauty	

Group III

When you dream
If you wish
Let's away to the woods at the end of the town
With a skip, with a song
Where the lilies grow thickest and shadows are long
Through the grind and the rumble and clank

Group IV

Summer is coming and how do I know it is?
Autumn is lighting its fires for a holiday
Where are you going, you fat little puppy dog?
Life is a jolly companion
Spring is a bride dressed in lace that her mother wore
Why must I { weep / sing at the sound of the rain? / laugh
Whither, oh whither, the young generation?
Down where the birches are
In through the sunlight and shadow we paddle
Out in the garden the flowers in a carnival
Milk for a kitten as creamy and white
Merrily, merrily shall I live airily

3. Using an oblique line to represent an accented syllable and a dot to represent an unaccented syllable write out the pattern of each of the lines in Question 2 above. Tell the number of feet on the line, the kind of foot. Indicate whether the line is a full line. If incomplete, note the number of syllables missing. State whether the ending is masculine or feminine.

Example: I wish the kitten were my brother ./././././.
4 iambs plus an extra unaccented syllable   feminine.

4. Retell each passage below in metrical pattern, made four ways: in iambs, trochees, anapests, dactyls. As an exercise, hold yourself to a strict pattern—no substituting, no wrenching of accent. Rearrange and substitute words and phrases only when necessary to the meter. Preserve the meaning as closely as you can.

a. The Cat only grinned when it saw Alice. It looked good-natured, she thought: still it had *very* long claws and a great many teeth, so she felt it ought to be treated with respect.
—LEWIS CARROLL: *Alice's Adventures in Wonderland*

b. After a time she heard a little pattering of feet in the distance, and she hastily dried her eyes to see what was coming. It was the White Rabbit returning, splendidly dressed, with a pair of white kid gloves in one hand and a large fan in the other: he came trotting along in a great hurry, muttering to himself as he came, "Oh! the Duchess, the Duchess! Oh! won't she be savage if I've kept her waiting!"
— LEWIS CARROLL: *Alice's Adventures in Wonderland*

c. He was very fond of animals and kept many kinds of pets. Besides the gold-fish in the pond at the bottom of his garden, he had rabbits in the pantry, white mice in his piano, a squirrel in the linen closet and a hedgehog in the cellar. He had a cow with a calf too, and an old lame horse—twenty-five years of age—and chickens, and pigeons, and two lambs, and many other animals.
— HUGH LOFTING: *The Story of Doctor Dolittle*

This passage is about Burns.

d. He seemed a living proof of what Rousseau had said—that truth and poetry were found among simple men. The troubadour in homespun became the lion of the season.
— AUSLANDER and HILL: *The Winged Horse*

e. And through the beauty of his poetry Shelley planted in the hearts of men a bright restlessness that still fires Youth, urging it to some higher and purer endeavor.
— AUSLANDER and HILL: *The Winged Horse*

5. Put these passages into the various meters. Do not strive for rhyme. Aim only to catch the music of the pattern you are attempting.

> Willows whiten, aspens quiver,
> Little breezes dusk and shiver.

> Be not the first by whom the new is tried
> Nor yet the last to lay the old aside.

> In Flanders Fields the poppies blow
> Between the crosses row on row.

> Twinkle, twinkle, little star,
> How I wonder what you are.

> I wandered lonely as a cloud
> That floats on high o'er vales and hills.

As an exercise, hold yourself to a strict pattern—no substituting, no syllables omitted at the ends of lines in the patterns you make. When you are master of this much rhythm you may substitute, and you may drop syllables or add them to the end of a line.

6. Write an original line in the four kinds of meter. Label each and state whether the line is complete, lacks one syllable or two, or whether there is a syllable or two in excess.

7. What is the matter with the following lines when sung to the pattern indicated at the right?

> You can't have any of my peanuts, ./././.
> When your peanuts are gone. ././.

8. How do the lines below those marked "To Be Matched" fail to match the pattern that is indicated at the right?

To Be Matched:

> *The Ford went wheezing up the hill* ././././
> To the surprise of driver Bill.
> The horse went galloping up the hill.
> The sight of it gave me a thrill.

To Be Matched:

> *Oh, why do I weep at the sound of the rain* ./../../..//
> As it gently patters upon the pane.
> As it pitters and patters on the window pane.
> It's such a cooling, refreshing refrain.
> Whenever it beats upon my window pane.

CHAPTER IV

RHYME AND ITS USES

IF WE judge from the form of poetry written in English since the rise of the morning-star of English song, the ear delights in rhyme.

Exactly what is rhyme? *Beau* rhymes with *toe* but *sew* does not rhyme with *dew*. The spelling in the first pair, *beau—toe,* is different; the spelling of the second pair is the same except for the initial consonant. But rhyme has nothing to do with spelling, or with what we see. It has to do with what we hear.

Rhyme is the identity in sound of an accented vowel in a word together with all the sounds following, while the immediately preceding consonantal sounds differ. For example: *bite, kite, fight, height,* de*light* are rhymes, as are *playing, saying, weighing, spraying, sleighing.* The accented syllable *ā* (spelled *eigh* or *ay*) and all sounds following: *ing,* are identically the same to the ear. (The looks do not matter.) The immediately preceding consonant sounds: *pl, s, w, spr, sl,* differ. You may apply the same test to: super*stitious,* de*licious,* pro*pitious, vicious,* am*bitious,* of*ficious,* Alo*ysius* and find them true rhymes.

By the application of the same test, *tell* and fore*tell* are not true rhymes: the accented vowel *ĕ* with the succeeding consonants *ll* fulfill the requirements; but the immediately preceding consonants, *t* and *t,* do not differ. Such pairing is called identical rhyme or no rhyme at all.

If the identity after the differing initial consonant is of single syllables, the rhyme is said to be single or masculine, as *bite, kite;* de*light, spite;* if two syllables are identical, with the accent on the next to the last, the rhyme is double or feminine, as *double, stubble; vicious,* de*licious;* if three syllables are identical, with the third from the end accented, the rhyme is double feminine or triple, as *tenderly, slenderly.*

Of course words as well as syllables may be combined to form double or triple rhymes, as

> fender, send her, spender, mender, lender.
> sing to me, ring to me, bring to me, fling to me.

Examples of masculine or single rhyme follow:

> To market, to market, to buy a fat pig,
> Home again, home again, jiggety-jig.

> Old King Cole was a merry old soul
> And a merry old soul was he;
> He called for his pipe, and he called for his bowl,
> And he called for his fiddlers three.

Soul and *bowl*, *he* and *three* are masculine rhymes.
Here are some double or feminine rhymes:

> I tisket, I *tasket*
> A green and yellow *basket*
>
> Hey, diddle *diddle*
> The cat and the *fiddle*
>
> A diller, a *dollar*
> A ten o'clock *scholar*

Masculine and feminine rhymes are often combined in a group of lines as in

> Little Miss Muffet
> Sat on a tuffet
> Eating of curds and whey;
> There came a great spider
> That sat down beside her
> And frightened Miss Muffet away.

Whey and a*way* are masculine rhymes. *Muffet* and *tuffet*, *spider* and *side her*, are feminine. Note how two words form the second of the pair in *spider* and *beside her*.
Keats combines masculine with feminine rhymes in the following:

> In a drear-nighted December
> Too happy, happy brook,
> Thy bubblings ne'er remember
> Apollo's summer look.
> But with a sweet forgetting
> They stay their crystal fretting
> Never, never petting
> About the frozen time.

De*cember*, re*member*; for*getting*, *fretting*, *petting* are feminine rhymes. *Brook*, *look* are masculine. Double feminine or triple rhymes are not so common as the other two.

> Take her up *tenderly*
> Lift her with care;
> Fashion'd so *slenderly*
> Young, and so fair!
>
> —THOMAS HOOD

"Tenderly," "slenderly" are triple rhymes. Humor sometimes has its way with triple rhymes:

> Little Miss Muffet discovered a tuffet,
>   (Which never occurred to the *rest of us*)
> And, as 'twas a June day, and just about noonday,
>   She wanted to eat—like the *best of us*.
> Her diet was whey, and I hasten to say
>   It is wholesome and people grow *fat on it*.
> The spot being lonely, the lady not only
>   Discovered the tuffet, but *sat on it*.
>   —GUY WETMORE CARRYL

Here "rest of us" and "best of us," "fat on it" and "sat on it" are triple rhymes.

To wrench the accent and otherwise strain pronunciation are two of the humorist's devices for inviting a smile.

The most important function of rhyme is to shape the structure of verse. A buttress gives character and strength to the walls of a cathedral; so does rhyme to the poem. In the blue-print of a poem the rhyme plan or rhyme scheme may be represented by the letters of the alphabet, each new letter representing a change of word ending; rhymed groups are represented by the same letter. Here is a poem with its rhyme scheme:

My Garden

A garden is a lovesome thing, God wot!	a
Rose plot,	a
Fringed pool, ...	b
Ferned grot—	a
The veriest school	b
Of peace; and yet the fool	b
Contends that God is not—	a
Not God! in gardens! when the eve is cool?	b
Nay, but I have a sign;	c
'Tis very sure God walks in mine.	c

—THOMAS EDWARD BROWN

In this ten-line poem the one rhyme pattern, *a a b a b b a b c c*, is sufficient to express the thought. But in a longer poem it would be necessary to repeat developed units of thought to develop the poem. Each unit of developed thought would be expressed in a group of lines called a stanza, which is to the poem what the paragraph is to a prose work. Stanzas are built on a rhyme pattern. Usually the rhyme pattern of the first stanza is repeated unchanged in succeeding stanzas.

Sometimes there is a slight variation. The ear derives a great deal of pleasure from the repetition.

Here is a very simple poem in which the rhyme pattern of the first two lines is repeated.

Gone

1. The sunshine seeks thee, and the *day*,	a
2. Without thee, lonely, wears a*way*:	a
3. And where the twilight shadows *pass*,	b
4. And miss thy footprints on the *grass*,	b
5. They weep; whereat the breezes *sigh*,	c
6. And, following to find thee, *die*.	c

—JOHN B. TABB

In shaping the structure of the stanzas and so determining the architecture of the poem, rhyme emphasizes words which tip the line. Unimportant words, which are never emphasized in our daily speech, such as conjunctions, prepositions, and articles, should therefore be avoided as line endings.

Another simple rhyme scheme is this from the ballad "Sir Patrick Spens":

1. The King sits in Dunfermline town	a
2. Drinking the blude-red wine:	b
3. O whaur will I get a skeely skipper	c
4. To sail this gude ship of mine?	b

Notice that 1 and 3 are unrhymed; 2 and 4 are rhymed. This pattern is followed in the successive stanzas.

Rhyme performs another function in the four lines above: it unifies the group by binding it together as the binder holds the sheaves. "Wine" in the poem above fills the ear with expectancy which is realized in "mine." If 1 and 3 rhymed and 2 and 4 were left hanging without rhyme, there would be a feeling of falling apart that would spoil the pleasure of realization which we experience through "mine," which ties up the group. The last line of a stanza should tie up the stanza, not let it fall apart. Any falling apart should be left for lines above the last unless there is a definite reason for leaving the reader nowhere. It might be appropriate to the thought to arouse expectation only to deny fulfillment.

Many variations of rhyme pattern result from the arrangement of rhymes. Here is one; exquisite in workmanship of an intricate design.

Season of mists and mellow fruitfulness,   a
Close bosom-friend of the maturing sun;   b
Conspiring with him how to load and bless   a
With fruit the vines that round the thatch-eaves run;   b
To bend with apples the moss'd cottage-trees,   c
And fill all fruit with ripeness to the core;   d
To swell the gourd, and plump the hazel shells   e
With a sweet kernel; to set budding more,   d
And still more, later flowers for the bees,   c
Until they think warm days will never cease;   c *(inexact)*
For Summer has o'erbrimm'd their clammy cells.   e
                              —JOHN KEATS, *To Autumn*

This rhyme pattern is twice repeated with a slight variation. Notice how every expectation aroused is realized—the group is well woven and exquisitely bound. Thus it is that rhyme is a shaper and unifier of verse. When you begin to use rhyme it will be your pleasure to see how far your ingenuity can combine rhymes into fresh stanza patterns.

Beyond its building function, rhyme delights the ear by enhancing the melody of the music. Poetry was intended to be read aloud. A listener who does not understand a word may derive pleasure from its music. Some poems, such as Poe's "The Bells" were meant to give sheer musical delight. Rhyme is one of the melodic devices which contribute to this pleasure.

Because of the musical effect of rhyme, the poet has a care to what rhymes he combines in the same stanza. He aims for variety of sound in distributing his rhymes; for instance, in the second stanza in the poem, "To Autumn":

Who hath not seen thee oft amid thy store?   a
Sometimes whoever seeks abroad may find   b
Thee sitting careless on a granary floor,   a
Thy hair soft-lifted by the winnowing wind;   b
Or on a half-reap'd furrow sound asleep,   c
Drowsed with the fume of poppies, while thy hook   d
Spares the next swath and all its twinèd flowers: e
And sometimes like a gleaner thou dost keep   c
Steady thy laden head across a brook;   d
Or by a cyder-press, with patient look,   d
Thou watchest the last oozings, hours by hours.   e

We have st*ore* followed by f*ind* which gives a markedly different sound. *Ore* followed by *own* would not be so pleasant, because the vowel sounds would be so nearly like. His next variation is as*leep*, which is followed by h*ook*, then h*ours* varying both vowel and consonant.

The similarity of sounds in rhymes with a marked variation of sounds in the changing rhymes brings delight to the ear.

It is well to remember that the ear does not ordinarily carry the sound of rhyme over more than three intervening unrhymed lines. In six lines of poetry, for instance, to have only lines 1 and 6 rhyme would not be very effective because the anticipation aroused by 1 or 2 would be forgotten before 6 was reached.

Not more than four consecutive lines of serious verse may rhyme and preserve a serious effect. Four seems to be the limit as

> A bow-shot from her bower-eaves
> He rode between the barley-sheaves,
> The sun came dazzling thro' the leaves,
> And flamed upon the brazen greaves
>   Of bold Sir Lancelot
> A red-cross knight forever kneeled
> To a lady in his shield
> That sparkled on the yellow field,
>   Beside remote Shalott.
>   —ALFRED, LORD TENNYSON: *The Lady of Shalott*

In this work of shaping, unifying, and accenting the melody, rhyme must give the effect of naturalness. There should never be any straining any more than there should be straining in images. If rhyme calls attention to itself, it is like the glittering jewels with which vulgar persons overload themselves. While rhyme is highly artificial, it must *seem* spontaneous. It must be as inevitable as the keystone of the arch.

There are times, however, when the best of poets are hard put for a rhyme word. A good rule for the versifier to remember is this: If there must be any slight straining, let the forced word appear *above* the spontaneous or inevitable one. In the pleasurable effect of the inevitable rhyme, the clumsy effect of the first will probably be forgotten, for

> . . . those that write in rhyme still make
> The one verse for the other's sake;
> For one for sense, and one for rhyme,
> I think's sufficient at one time.
>   —SAMUEL BUTLER

While restrictions of rhyme sometimes thus force matings not wholly satisfactory, on the other hand they often provoke expression of rare beauty. Necessity *is* the mother of invention. The revisions of our finest poets teach us a great deal about the exquisite children born of this mother. Turn to Keats's poem, "On First Looking Into Chapman's Homer." He is telling of the experience of coming upon a translation of Homer, by an Elizabethan writer, James Chapman. In his second quatrain Keats wrote:

Oft of one wide expanse had I been told
That low-browed Homer ruled as his demesne
Yet did I never know what men could mean
Till I heard Chapman speak out loud and bold.

In accordance with his scheme, 1 and 4, 2 and 3 were to rhyme. He noticed that he had *mesne* (pronounced *meen*) rhyming with *mean*, identical or no rhymes. If you go through the alphabet you will find few *ean* words that would suit. Necessity, boring to rich unsounded depths, yielded

Yet did I never breathe its pure serene,

so that *mesne* and *rene* are perfectly matched. The revised line is exquisite for its significance, its poetry, and its music. The true artist finds freedom in the restraints of art.

Thus far we have been speaking of rhyme that tips the ends of the lines. For musical effects, poets sometimes introduce rhyme in the line:

Little Jack Horner sat in a corner

He put in his thumb, and pulled out a plum

As Tommy Snooks and Bessy Brooks
Were walking out one Sunday

Jack Sprat could eat no fat.

"Horner" and "corner," "thumb" and "plum," "Snooks" and "Brooks," "Sprat" and "fat" rhyme. Such pairing in the line is called internal rhyme. Every other line of Shelley's "The Cloud" contains internal rhyme. Here are some of them:

I bring fresh *showers* for the thirsting *flowers*

I wield the *flail* of the lashing *hail*

When I widen the *rent* in my wind-built *tent*

Coleridge used internal rhyme freely in his "The Rime of the Ancient Mariner."

The guests are met, the feast is set

The ship was cheered, the harbour cleared.

The wedding-guest here beat his breast

The ship drove fast, loud roared the blast.

In the third line of every stanza of Sidney Lanier's "Song of the Chattahoochee" internal rhyme is part of the pattern. The stanzas are indicated by number:

1. I hurry a*main* to reach the *plain*
2. The rushes *cried* Abide, *abide*.
3. The hickory *told* me mani*fold*
   Fairy tales of shade . . .[1]
4. The white quartz *shone*, and the smooth brook-*stone*
5. And oh, not the valleys of Hall[1]
   Avail: I am *fain* for to water the *plain*

You will find many instances of internal rhyme as you read the great
poets. Like the fine lady with rings on her fingers and bells on her
toes internal rhyme makes music wherever it goes.

As in images and word combinations that have become worn out
by over use, (*white as snow, pale as a ghost,* and the like) so in
rhyming, pleasure is lessened by the too familiar. He is a slovenly
artist who must always match *bliss* with *kiss*; whose lady wears *blue*
if she be *true*; who for you *only* is always *lonely*; whose heart is
burning while he is *yearning*. Through long association do not these
rhymes sound cheap and sentimental, reminiscent of the world's worst
popular ballads with a tremolo voice sustaining the chorus? Resource-
fulness in rhyme, no less than originality in the handling of any other
poetic device, brings delight to the reader.

It is indeed true that some words, such as *anguish, mountain, winter,* have few mates; hence the same pairing will be made again and
again if these words are used. Some have no mates at all, as *April,
August, chimney, coif, crimson, forest, film, microcosm, month, nothing, open, orange, rhomb, poet, scarce, scarf, silver, statue, squirrel,
temple, widow, window, zebra.* A young poet should therefore have a
care for his choice of words that require mates for the shaping of a
pattern. Furthermore, to rhyme accurately, students must pronounce
accurately. The versifier who says "ro'mance" "exquis'ite," "crule"
for "cruel," and the like, is following "wandering fires lost in the
quagmire" on his rhyme quest. An unabridged dictionary, not a
rhyming dictionary, is the most valuable possession for the rhyme
craftsman.

Determination to avoid trite rhymes frequently forces poets to pair
words which are not true mates. Thomas Hardy believed that "inexact
rhymes and rhythms now and then are far more pleasing than correct
ones." And many of our living poets feel that a suggestion of rhyme or
an echo of rhyme is far more pleasing to the sophisticated ear than
rhyme combinations which have been worn threadbare. Mother Goose
gives us inexact rhymes:

[1] The line is quoted so that the sense of the passage will be clear.

> Goosey, Goosey, gander,
> Where shall I wander?

"Wander" does not exactly match "gander."

> See-Saw-Jack in the hedge
> Which is the way to London Bridge?

See how the vowel sound in "bridge" slants off a bit from that in "hedge." This kind of pairing is called consonance, off-rhyme, near rhyme, slant rhyme, sour rhyme—your choice!

The lyrists of Shakespeare's time also were fond of using off-rhymes. Sometimes they broke the laws of correct rhyming because they wished to create novel effects. In three stanzas from a single poem see how Richard Crashaw uses off-rhymes:

> Till that ripe *birth*
> Of studied Fate stand *forth*
> And teach her fair steps to our *earth*
>
> A Face, made *up*
> Out of no other *shop*
> Than what Nature's white hand sets *ope*
>
> Smiles that can *warm*
> The blood, yet teach a *charm,*
> That chastity shall take no harm.
> —RICHARD CRASHAW: *Wishes to His Supposed Mistress*

> Foolish prater, what dost *thou*
> So early at my window *do?*
> —ABRAHAM COWLEY

Certain pairs, while not true mates, are accepted as mates because authentic poets have coupled them again and again since before the days of Elizabeth, such as *come—home; heaven—even; river—ever; love—prove* or *love—move.* That is, the habit of poets has built up some conventions in the use of off-rhymes. Thomas Campion, sweet singer of Elizabeth's time, rhymes "love" and "move":

> There, wrapt in cloud of sorrow, pity move,
> And tell the ravisher of my soul I perish for her love.

And again in "Vobiscum est Iope":

> To hear the stories of thy finish'd love
> From that smooth tongue whose music hell can move.

> Now yellow waxen lights
>> Shall wait on honey love,
> While youthful revels, masques, and courtly sights
>> Sleep's leaden spells remove.

This convention is still observed in modern poetry. Find some examples. Edna St. Vincent Millay comes a bit closer to vowel identity when she rhymes "love" with "of" in the line:

> She tells her love what he's thinking of.

In the "Hound of Heaven" Francis Thompson, almost a contemporary of ours, couples "home" with "come"; "ever" with "shiver"; "over" with "lover."

> I have stored for thee at *home*
> Rise, clasp my hand, and *come*!

> Wherein tear-drippings stagnate, spilt down *ever*
> From the dank thoughts that *shiver*.

> With thy skiey blossom heap me *over*
> From this tremendous *lover*.

The same convention appears in

> Willows whiten, aspens *quiver*
> Little breezes dusk and *shiver*
> Through the wave that runs for*ever*
> By the island in the *river*.
>> —ALFRED, LORD TENNYSON

and

> I knew the Spring was come. I knew it *even*
> Better than all by this, that through my chase
> In bush and stone and hill and sea and *heaven*
> I seem'd to see and follow still your face.
>> —WILFRED SCAWEN BLUNT

Another convention is that of rhyming end *y* pronounced *ēē* as in eternity, with *i* as in *eye*. For instance

> Once more I pray unto your courtes*y*:
> Be heavy for me again or else I *die*!
>> —GEOFFREY CHAUCER

> What immortal hand or *eye*
> Dare frame thy fearful symmetr*y*.
>> —WILLIAM BLAKE

And in some weaker glories *spy*
Some shadows of eternity
—HENRY VAUGHAN

There is, phonetically, a close relation between the sounds *ī* and *ē*. Long *ī* seems to be made up of a combination of *ah* and *ē*.

Changes in pronunciation have made some formerly correct rhymes sound inaccurate. The obsolete pronunciation of "wind" to rhyme with "find" is still preserved in verse. Says Shelley in the "Ode to the West Wind"

Be through my lips to unawaken'd earth
The trumpet of a prophecy! O *wind*,
If Winter comes, can Spring be far *behind*?

You will find "wind" so used in many poems. The tendency today, however, is to adhere to current pronunciation. Five centuries hence our pronunciation may sound as strange to readers of 2400 as Pope's Eighteenth Century English, *join* rhymed with *wine* and *tea* with *obey*.

We may not read "been" used as an end rhyme by any English versifier without giving it the English pronunciation:

And many goodly states and kingdoms seen;
Round many western islands have I been.
—JOHN KEATS

More closely related to true rhyme is assonance. In true rhyme we have identity of accented vowel sound with consonantal sounds succeeding; in assonance or vowel rhyme we still have identity of the accented vowel sound but dissimilarity in both the subsequent consonantal sounds and the immediately preceding consonantal sound: *man, pass, gap, bat, catch, dash, fan, has, jam, alack, snag, mad, shall.*

See a pin and pick it *up*
All day long you'll have good *luck.*

Assonance is frequent in nursery rhymes:

Little Tommy *Tucker,*
Sang for his *supper*
What shall he have?
White bread and *butter.*

Rock-a-bye baby on the tree *top*
When the wind blows the cradle will *rock.*

> One for my master, one for my *dame*
> And one for the little boy who lives in the *lane*

This substitute for rhyme was used in Provençal and old French poetry, and in early Latin poetry of the church. It is still used in Spanish poetry. George Eliot makes use of the device in Juan's song of her "Spanish Gypsy":

> Maiden crowned with glossy *blackness*
> Lithe as panther forest *roaming*
> Long-armed naiad when she *dances*
> On a stream of ether *floating*.

"Roaming" and "floating," "blackness" and "dances" are assonances. In the lines

> The splendor falls on castle walls
> And *snowy* summits old in *story*

there is assonance within the second line: "snowy—story," as there is internal rhyme in the preceding line: "falls—walls."

Assonances are often effectively combined with true rhyme to tip lines.

> I wield the flail of the lashing hail
> And whiten the green plains under;
> And then again I dissolve in rain,
> And laugh as I pass in thunder.
> —PERCY BYSSHE SHELLEY: *The Cloud*

Here "hail" and "rain" are assonances; "under" and "thunder" are feminine rhymes; "flail" and "hail" (1), "gain" and "rain" (3) internal rhyme. ("Gain" of *again* is here pronounced to rhyme with "rain.")

Emily Dickinson is fond of off-rhyme and assonance as well. In a stanza of "Chartless" she pairs "God" and "spot"—assonance; "Heaven" and "given"—off-rhyme—a convention. The most striking effects are made when, familiar with your pattern, you surprise your reader by an echo or a suggestion of what he expects. Keats is a master of this art.

To illustrate this point: Just as the architects of the Middle Ages built cathedrals in Gothic style, so Edmund Spenser shaped a stanza into a form which bears his name. The design of the Spenserian stanza is like this: nine lines, the first eight with five iambic feet, the last with six iambic feet. The lines rhyme *a b a b b c b c c*. This is the pattern of *The Faerie Queene*. Now Keats, who went through the scenes of the romance "as a young horse would through a spring meadow ramping," used this pattern in the "The Eve of St. Agnes" with many subtle suggestions of his master's rhyme scheme rather than the actual scheme

1. A casement high and triple-arch'd there *was*, a
2. All garlanded with carven *imag'ries* b
3. Of fruits, and flowers, and bunches of knot-*grass*, *off-rhyme* a
4. And diamonded with panes of quaint *device*, *off* b
5. Innumerable of stains and splendid *dyes*, *off* b
6. As are the tiger-moth's deep-damask'd wings; c
7. And in the midst, 'mong thousand herald*ries*, *off* b
8. And twilight saints, and dim emblazonings, c
9. A shielded scutcheon blush'd with blood of queens and kings. c

To derive full enjoyment from modern verse you will want to be able to recognize these subtle substitutes for rhyme. The young versifier, however, should hold himself strictly to perfect rhymes until he has mastered the art of mating words with skill and some degree of freshness.

> True ease in writing comes from art, not chance,
> As those move easiest who have learned to dance.

This is the warning of a great artist. There is no art without discipline and no beginner can produce subtle effects through assonances and off-rhymes until he has learned to manage the rhymes which he seeks to suggest or echo. The consonant chart on page 60 may be of assistance to you in making your rhymes.

> . . . Rhyme the rudder is of verses
> With which like ships they steer their courses

said Samuel Butler.

Let us delight in handling this rudder with a firm, wise grasp—our eye on the course ahead.

A CHALLENGE TO YOUR EAR

1. Match these words with all the words you can think of:

   a. fun, shake, raft, light, dawn, can, confer, resign
   b. merry, spender, Harry, fictitious. (Use two words if you wish.)
   c. eternity, airily, sinuous, tenderly, milliner, filigree (Use more than one word if you wish to.)

2. From the following list mate and label the proper words as rhyme, identical rhyme, assonance: hap   moan   discreet   bowl
shows   feet   compete   cheat   mishap

Consonant Chart

To the maker of verses *consonant* means *consonant sound*. The letter is the symbol of sound.

```
b........bl........br........bw
c (k) .....cl.........cr.......                    s.........scr........scl
c (s)
d .................dr........dw
f ........fl ........fr........
g........gl........gr........gw
h
j (g)
l ...........................sl
m...........................sm
n...........................sn
p........pl........pr........pw        sp........spr........spl
qu ..........................squ
r (wr)
s ........sl
t.................tr........tw         st ........str
v ...........................sv
w...........................sw
x
y
z ........zl
sh.................shr
th.................thr
th
ch
zh
wh
```

Double consonants are treated as single in rhyming; that is, *ray*, *fray*, *gray*, *tray* are perfect rhymes, because *r* and *fr* are regarded as different initial sounds.

3. Write out the rhyme pattern of the following:

> Fair pledges of a fruitful tree
> Why do ye fall so fast?
> Your date is not so past
> But you may stay yet here awhile
> To blush and gently smile,
> And go at last.
>
> —ROBERT HERRICK

This pattern is repeated twice in the poem; the shaping words in the second are

> be, delight, night, forth, worth, quite

and in the last

> we, have, brave, pride, glide, grave.

List any imperfect rhymes.

4. Using the pattern you have made, write new rhymes to suit the plan. Words only, not lines. This is merely an exercise. Have a difference in the vowel sounds of your rhyme sets; that is, if you use *en* words for your *a* rhyme, do not use *el* words in the *b* rhymes.

5. Take any popular song of today. Analyze its rhyme pattern. Is it fresh? Do the rhymes give pleasure of surprise? Or are they hackneyed?

6. Invent a rhyme pattern for a stanza of six lines. Supply words for the pattern. See how many patterns you can invent. Try to find models from authentic poets.

7. From the chapter, "Patterns to Try," at the back of this book discover the metrical pattern and the rhyme scheme that Chaucer used in stanzas of *The Monk's Tale*. Look at the later Spenserian stanza (page 59). How do the stanzas differ? When you have had some practice in versification you may want to try them.

8. Note how Shakespeare varies the rhyme-sets combined in these stanzas. List the vowel sounds used in the successive rhyme-sets.

> Under the greenwood tree
> Who loves to lie with me,
> And turn his merry note
> Unto the sweet bird's throat—
> Come hither, come hither, come hither!
> Here shall he see
> No enemy
> But winter and rough weather.

Who doth ambition shun
And loves to live i' the sun,
Seeking the food he eats
And pleased with what he gets—
Come hither, come hither, come hither!
Here shall he see
No enemy
But winter and rough weather.

9. In what particular, so far as the music of rhyme is concerned, is stanza I below superior to stanza II?

Else I with roses every day
  Will whip you hence,
And bind you, when you long to play,
  For your offence;
  I'll shut my eyes to keep you in;
  I'll make you fast it for your sin;
  I'll count your power not worth a pin;
  —Alas! what hereby shall I win,
    If he gainsay me?

What if I beat the wanton boy
  With many a rod?
He will repay me with annoy,
  Because a god.
  Then sit thou safely on my knee,
  And let thy bower my bosom be;
  Lurk in mine eyes, I like of thee,
  O Cupid! so thou pity me,
    Spare not, but play thee!
      —Thomas Lodge

10. From the following, list the internal rhymes, the masculine and feminine rhymes. Are there any off-rhymes?

Pack, clouds, away, and welcome day,	a
With night we banish sorrow;	b
Sweet air blow soft; mount, larks, aloft	c
To give my Love good-morrow!	b
Wings from the wind to please her mind	d
Notes from the lark I'll borrow;	b
Bird, prune thy wing; nightingale, sing,	e
To give my Love good-morrow:	b
To give my Love good-morrow	b
Notes from them both I'll borrow.	b

—Thomas Heywood

CHAPTER V

THE COUPLET

THE simplest kind of sheaf to make, with rhyme as a binder, is the couplet.

There can be no shorter poem. But even so brief a form may be packed with beauty. In the couplet is fused the imaginative breath of poetry with its simplest artistic expression. In your own writing of the couplet you will bring together the essence of poetry and the form: what you have learned of the image and what you have learned of rhythm, meter, and rhyme.

The rhyme scheme of a rhymed couplet may be represented *a a.* The lines may be any metrical pattern and of any length, to suit the thought.

Catch the beauty of these poems in couplet form. The first two are translations from the Japanese.

Waiting

The trees stand hushed, on tip-toe for the sight
Of moon-rise, that shall glorify the night.

—CURTIS HIDDEN PAGE

Shadows

The moon is risen, and without a sound
They write their welcome-songs along the ground.

—CURTIS HIDDEN PAGE

On Seeing Weather-Beaten Trees

Is it as plainly in our living shown
By slant and twist, which way the wind hath blown?

—ADELAIDE CRAPSEY

Truth

The old faiths light their candles all about.
But burly Truth comes by and blows them out.
> —Lizette Woodworth Reese

Standards

White is the skimming gull on the somber green of the fir-trees,
Black is the soaring gull on a snowy glimmer of cloud.
> —Charles Wharton Stork

Notice how the title "Standards" lifts the picture up to the realm of the imagination, making the poet's observation something more significant than a white gull on green; and a black gull on snow white cloud.

Frequently the title is the bridge between the ethereal world of fancy and the place of reality, especially in very short poems.

Here are perhaps the shortest poems in the language—rhymed couplets:

Philosophical Poem

I?
Why?

The Antiquity of Fashions

Eve's
Leaves.
> —J. J.

A Lover to His Doubting Lady

Who?
You!
> —J. J.

Below are some couplets created by students. Applying the imagination test, which is the first test of poetry, you may judge how well the young versifiers have succeeded in their first metrical poems.

Winter

A wan and wavering sunbeam peeps
Into the room where Nature sleeps.
> —Naomi Rogin

Moon Rise

She dips her finger tips of light
Into the finger bowl of night.
> —Nan MacKenzie

Night in a Ravine

The wind is a ventriloquist who throws his mournful tones
From peak to peak, across the stream above the shrubs and stones.
—WILLIAM ROEHRICK

Poet's Prospect

My lover will buy me a wedding ring, soon;
It's studded with stars, and it's cut out of moon.
—GEORGIA H. COOPER

Spring Cleaning

Spring is a housewife who walks through the land
Carrying sunlight and warmth in her hand.
—WILLIAM ROEHRICK

Retort to Time

Fly madly, oh time, fly fast and fly free;
I'm racing *with* you; you can't worry me!
—SHYRLEE KOHN

Avarice

Bees are robbers, fleet and daring,
Not the smallest flower sparing.
—HILDEGARD KOHNER

Gold

Like the will o' the wisp was her hair
As it twinkled and danced in the air.
—FLORENCE LUFT

Family Shame

Does April weep because of March, the naughty child,
Who plays so many tricks and is so wild?
—FANNIE WILLIAMS

Coup d'Etat

The moon is a princess in garments of gray,
Dethroned by the sun with the coming of day.
—MARJORIE DeGRAFF

Wonder

Did you get your hair from strings of harps?
And pick your lips from berry tarts?

—Lois Dawson

Miss Dawson tried assonance instead of rhyme as a binder.

In "Sea Fantasy" the young versifier wrote a couplet sequence of four poems.

Sea Fantasy

I

SEA SHELL

Swan-white, with velvet flush, like wondering waking sky,—
A sea-nymph brushed it with her toe in passing by.

II

SEA MOON

The moon weaves a ladder of stars to the sea
For the sea-prince, waiting impatiently.

III

JELLY FISH

The old sea-chef is angry today;
He upset his preserves and they're floating away.

IV

SEA WEED

The sea king popped his head up and blinked upon the land;
Wind-elf pulled his whiskers out and strewed them on the sand.

—Louise Fischer

The couplet may be an outlet for humor also. There is no reason that we should not laugh through our poetry.

Preference	*Ann*
Your love is candy, very sweet— Ah for the taste of blood red meat! —Georgia H. Cooper	As frank as a mirror was Ann; She never could hold any man. —William Roehrick

Cure for Ennui

When I am bored with all this world of men
Nothing can cheer me like the Five and Ten.
                              —EVELYNE LOVE COOPER

NOW YOU EXPERIMENT!

1. Think of these titles figuratively or literally, and write a couplet on what one or two of them suggest. Use them as they are or in modified form. If they make no appeal to you write on something remotely suggested by any idea in any of them.

Leaf Magic   Shadow   Cloud   Boat on the River
The Old Home   Wind Magic   Dancing Moonlight
Young Light   Leaf Movement   Spring Fancy (Autumn, Summer, Winter)   Old Lace   Spring Breath   Birth
Song   Shadow Patterns   Absence   Possession   Fragility   Daybreak   Bird Song   Rain   City Rain
Mud Puddles   Sunset   Cloud Effect   Gaiety   Lampposts   Spring Cleaning   Bonds (Home Relationship, Tastes, Suffering, Understanding, or the like)   Gifts   Without You

2. Do the following suggest anything to you?

A fountain in the park   Cherry tree over a wall   A wisp of beauty   A broken wall   Play space in the city   Beauty parlor   Deserted barn   Retort to time   Rodeo
Breath of arbutus (any fragrance)   Amusement park   Tiptoeing wind

3. Use the following any way you choose:

A drooping....   A long dusty road....   Out of night....
From blue distance....   Bird song....   Ragged shadows....
Where the sky and earth met....   Cascade of stars....
Agile as a Persian cat....   My life is free as April winds.....

When you finish a poem—any poem, even your most advanced work—pencil the pattern of each line at the right (./././). Correct metrical disturbances that your pattern shows up.

FIVE-FINGER EXERCISES

Every day this week

1. Match a line from each of the four groups in "Rhythm and Meter," pages 43 and 44, exercise 2. This time bind with rhyme.

2. Turn a passage into the four standard metrical patterns.

3. Add a thought to your notebook.
    In the florist's at the corner I saw a vase full of bare branches from winter trees. They had been dipped into calcimine which gave the

appearance of snow. City people were buying them for Christmas. I think I have material for a poem which I am burning to write. What did *you* find today for a poem?

THE LONGER FORM IN COUPLETS

Now you may want to try a longer poem. You may use the couplet as a stanza and repeat it in a poem of four, six, a dozen—any number of lines. Or you may build a stanza of four or more lines—two or more couplets—and repeat that stanza pattern. The nature of your flow of thought will determine the choice. As you indent the first word of a paragraph in prose, in poetry you enlarge the space between stanzas. Long poems in couplet form are frequently written with no stanza divisions. Read the following poems by authentic poets and by young versifiers; then you try one. Use the suggestions, "Now You Experiment," page 67, or write on a subject of your own choice.

In planning your sentences see that they give pleasure through variety. Let them fill successive couplets differently. If in the first couplet they come out this way

$$\underline{\hspace{4cm}}^|$$
$$\underline{\hspace{4cm}}^|$$

Vertical line indicates end of sentence.

in the next, one may run over the first line to the end of the second like this:

$$\underline{\hspace{2cm}}^|\underline{\hspace{1.5cm}}$$
$$\underline{\hspace{4cm}}^|$$

or like this

$$\underline{\hspace{2cm}}^|\underline{\hspace{1.5cm}}$$
$$\underline{\hspace{0.5cm}}^|\underline{\hspace{3cm}}^|$$

or the couplet may be all one sentence

$$\underline{\hspace{4cm}}$$
$$\underline{\hspace{4cm}}^|$$

Each stanza grows out of the preceding stanza, as in prose, paragraph grows from paragraph. Each added stanza drives ahead in the further development of the poem to its completion in unity and compactness, suggesting rather than repeating.

When you finish your work, go over it carefully. Remove matter that does not contribute to the effect which you want your poem to create; vague words; disturbances in rhythm. Remember that your poem must suggest. The imaginative is the essence of poetry, whatever its form.

Here are some longer poems written in couplets.

To Dianeme

Sweet, be not proud of those two eyes
Which starlike sparkle in their skies;
Nor be you proud, that you can see
All hearts your captives; yours yet free:
Be you not proud of that rich hair
Which wantons with the lovesick air;
Whenas that ruby which you wear,
Sunk from the tip of your soft ear,
Will last to be a precious stone
When all your world of beauty's gone.

—ROBERT HERRICK

The Passionate Shepherd to His Love

Come live with me and be my Love,
And we will all the pleasures prove
That hills and valleys, dale and field,
And all the craggy mountains yield.

There will we sit upon the rocks
And see the shepherds feed their flocks,
By shallow rivers, to whose falls
Melodious birds sing madrigals

There will I make thee beds of roses
And a thousand fragrant posies,
A cap of flowers, and a kirtle
Embroider'd all with leaves of myrtle.

A gown made of the finest wool,
Which from our pretty lambs we pull,
Fair linèd slippers for the cold,
With buckles of the purest gold.

A belt of straw and ivy buds
With coral clasps and amber studs:
And if these pleasures may thee move,
Come live with me and be my Love.

Thy silver dishes for thy meat
As precious as the gods do eat,
Shall on an ivory table be
Prepared each day for thee and me.

The shepherd swains shall dance and sing
For thy delight each May-morning:
If these delights thy mind may move,
Then live with me and be my Love.

—CHRISTOPHER MARLOWE

Glen-Almain, the Narrow Glen

In this still place, remote from men,
Sleeps Ossian, in the Narrow Glen;
In this still place, where murmurs on
But one meek streamlet, only one:
He sang of battles, and the breath
Of stormy war, and violent death;
And should, methinks, when all was past,
Have rightfully been laid at last
Where rocks were rudely heap'd, and rent
As by a spirit turbulent;
Where sights were rough, and sounds were wild,
And everything unreconciled;
In some complaining, dim retreat,
For fear and melancholy meet;
But this is calm; there cannot be
A more entire tranquillity.

Does then the Bard sleep here indeed?
Or is it but a groundless creed?
What matters it?—I blame them not
Whose fancy in this lonely spot
Was moved; and in such way express'd
Their notion of its perfect rest.
A convent, even a hermit's cell
Would break the silence of this Dell:
It is not quiet, is not ease;
But something deeper far than these:
The separation that is here
Is of the grave; and of austere
Yet happy feelings of the dead:
And, therefore, was it rightly said
That Ossian, last of all his race!
Lies buried in this lonely place.

—WILLIAM WORDSWORTH

Words Before Twilight

Look long upon this daylight. Soon, too soon,
It will be utterly ravished by the moon.

Look long upon these sunlit leaves that blow
Like bells rung by the wind. Watch daylight go

As incense rises from a scarlet rose;
Drink deep the last faint flicker, and bend close

To read blue grief in every pansy's face
As darkness gathers. Watch a slow snail trace

His glittering pathway to a hidden stone
Whose purple shelter he will seek alone.

Look long upon this daylight. Not again
Shall it return. A thousand thousand men

Can never bring it back though they may call
Until stars shatter and the mountains fall

And once again are dust. Look long upon
This day, for soon, too soon it will be gone

As swiftly as a sparrow, as a breath—
As surely as no heartbeat follows death.
                          —DANIEL WHITEHEAD HICKY

Calvary

I walked alone to my calvary,
And no man carried the cross for me.
Carried the cross? Nay, no man knew
The fearful load that I bent unto,
But each as we met upon the way
Spoke me fair of the journey I walked that day.

I came alone to my calvary,
And high was the hill and bleak to see,
But lo, as I scaled its flinty side,
A thousand went up to be crucified!
A thousand kept the way with me,
But never a cross my eyes could see.
                          —JESSIE B. RITTENHOUSE

In "Calvary" Jessie Rittenhouse has built a pattern of six lines on the couplet and repeated this pattern as the second stanza. Such a division is suited to the content of the poem, you can readily see. The manner must suit the spirit of a poem as the glove fits the hand that wears it.

In the next poem the effect of the couplet is entirely different. "My Last Duchess" is a dramatic monologue. The Duke of Ferrara is talking to an envoy who has come to discuss prospects of the Duke's second marriage. Notice how the Duke gives character pictures of himself and of his "last duchess," and how the action of the Duke and the envoy before the painting is suggested—all through the words of the Duke. Browning is *the* master of the dramatic monologue. His masterpiece, "The Ring and the Book," comprises nine dramatic monologues giving the evidence of nine witnesses at the trial in Rome of Count Guido, who has murdered his beautiful young wife, Pompilia.

My Last Duchess

FERRARA

That's my last Duchess painted on the wall,
Looking as if she were alive. I call
That piece a wonder, now: Frà Pandolf's hands
Worked busily a day, and there she stands.
Will 't please you sit and look at her? I said
"Frà Pandolf" by design, for never read
Strangers like you that pictured countenance,
The depth and passion of its earnest glance,
But to myself they turned (since none puts by
The curtain I have drawn for you, but I)
And seemed as they would ask me, if they durst,
How such a glance came there; so, not the first
Are you to turn and ask thus. Sir, 't was not
Her husband's presence only, called that spot
Of joy into the Duchess' cheek: perhaps
Frà Pandolf chanced to say, "Her mantle laps
Over my lady's wrist too much," or "Paint
Must never hope to reproduce the faint
Half-flush that dies along her throat:" such stuff
Was courtesy, she thought, and cause enough
For calling up that spot of joy. She had
A heart—how shall I say?—too soon made glad,
Too easily impressed; she liked whate'er
She looked on, and her looks went everywhere.
Sir, 't was all one! My favor at her breast,
The dropping of the daylight in the West,
The bough of cherries some officious fool

Broke in the orchard for her, the white mule
She rode with round the terrace—all and each
Would draw from her alike the approving speech,
Or blush, at least. She thanked men,—good! but thanked
Somehow—I know not how—as if she ranked
My gift of a nine-hundred-years-old name
With anybody's gift. Who'd stoop to blame
This sort of trifling? Even had you skill
In speech—(which I have not)—to make your will
Quite clear to such an one, and say, "Just this
Or that in you disgusts me; here you miss,
Or there exceed the mark"—and if she let
Herself be lessoned so, nor plainly set
Her wits to yours, forsooth, and made excuse,
—E'en then would be some stooping; and I choose
Never to stoop. Oh sir, she smiled, no doubt,
Whene'er I passed her; but who passed without
Much the same smile? This grew; I gave commands;
Then all smiles stopped together. There she stands
As if alive. Will 't please you rise? We'll meet
The company below, then. I repeat,
The Count your master's known munificence
Is ample warrant that no just pretence
Of mine for dowry will be disallowed;
Though his fair daughter's self, as I avowed
As starting, is my object. Nay, we'll go
Together down, sir. Notice Neptune, though,
Taming a sea-horse, thought a rarity,
Which Claus of Innsbruck cast in bronze for me!
                                    —Robert Browning

Here are the attempts of some beginners in the art:

To a Poet

There's an odd little man at the end of our lane—
They say he's a miser and surely insane,
For he hoards all the queerest and silliest things—
A large amber sun, and the lilt a bird sings!
And right near the bottom his treasure chest sags
With myriad stars, tied in misty cloud bags.
A velvety butterfly, to a low tune,
Is nestling beneath a flat, crimsony moon.
And top of them lies, very lively and bright,
The saffron idea of a single mad night.
There's an odd little man at the end of our lane—
They say he's a miser and surely insane.
                                    —Georgia H. Cooper

Spring

This year is young and like a laughing child:
One moment gay, so easily beguiled

By teasing winds to loose the ready tears
Of April. Just as all the other years,

Young years, that danced away the fragrant days
In April dew and soft, white-blossomed Mays,

This year is young, and so, of course, will wear
May blossoms in the bright warmth of her hair.

—ESTELLE ROOKS

White Birch

She stands, a lonely maiden in the night,
Waiting for her master, Wind. How white
Her body gleams! She is a lovely thing—
Too fair a slave for such a blustering king!
She waits—yet I have seen her bending low
Upon the grasses from his furious blow
That marred the whiteness of her gleaming back;
And still she waits alone beneath the black
And diamond-studded splendor of the sky
To feel his cruel touch. I wonder why.

—NAOMI ROGIN

Market Day

I ran down the queerest and tiniest street,
Where lavender clover and daffodils meet;
Till I came to the village with youth in my hand
And saw in the market, a most unique stand!
An amethyst song and a saffron moonbeam,
Were sold at the price of my very best dream.
Directly above, was a large topaz thought
(All trimmed in bright red), which I instantly bought.
As soft as a moss rose, a lover's kiss lay,
But as I was turning, it blew right away.
Then I bought me the dearest, old, lopsided star
And a watery moon in a violet jar;
And I came home all loaded with packages gay—
But found that my youth had been spent in one day.

—GEORGIA H. COOPER

Envy

Stupid pigeon on my sill,
Pecking bread crumbs with your bill—

Wasting time, when you have wings,—
You could do such wondrous things!

Why are you content to gloat
Because you've rainbow on your throat?

Why not fly to distant lands;
There's romance on foreign sands.

Maybe one day you would feast
With sacred pigeons in the East,

Fed by some quaint slant-eyed maiden,
Who with barley corn is laden.

In old church eaves you might rest,
While friendly gargoyles watch your nest.

It's not sense to talk to you;
You'll peck bread crumbs all year through!

—JACQUELINE HOYT

Hill Magic

I am so high upon a hill
Where sea-green grass is tall and still,

Where vast blue sky and high hill meet,
White houses nestled at its feet,

And eagles drop, as they float by,
White feathers. Oh, I am so high!

I am so high where blue hills are
That I can almost reach a star,

And I can chat with clouds at will,—
I am so high upon a hill.

—ESTELLE ROOKS

To The Wind in the Leaves

You might cross the barren hill,
Spread the seed and run the mill,
Ease a sailboat of its load,
Clear the rubbish from the road.
I might find a fence to fix;
Nor delay here while you mix
Swirling red and yellow hues
Into paints you'll never use.
Your belief that when it's late
Gold October, work may wait
Makes us kin an hour; so
I'll just watch your artist-show.

—RUTH H. HAUSMAN

Sky Lady

The moon is a maiden, coquettish yet shy;
The clouds are her laces, the wind is her sigh,
The seas are her lovers who worship afar,
And following closer is one brilliant star.
The sky is her home; she hasn't another;
Though brighter and distant, the sun is her brother.
With lovers and laces, a brother, a sigh,
The moon is a maiden, coquettish yet shy.

—MIRIAM WOLFSON

The Woman of It

Spring
She laughed each time he brought his heart
And told him he had best depart.

Fall
But now she waits alone in vain
Hoping he'll bring it *once* again.

—LUCILLE SCHMEDTJE

Have you ever had to exercise restraint as the writer below did?

To a Bakery

In your window there are pies;
Tasty cookies greet my eyes.

There are rolls and berry tarts
And some cup-cakes shaped like hearts.

Cream puffs tempt me, and you bake
Such delicious coffee cake.

From them all I turn my head—
(Mother sent me out for bread!)

—ALICE LEVY

The Same Story

Behind a thick and cloudy door,
The moon was pacing on the floor.
The wind had locked her in that place
To keep her from the sea's embrace.
The sea had raged from night to morn,
But, when the cheerful sun was born,
He kissed her hair of flaming gold—
And thought "Oh, well—the moon was
old."

—FANNIE WILLIAMS

CHAPTER VI

WORDS AND THEIR EFFECTS

Words

Words with the freesia's wounded scent I know,
And those that suck the slow irresolute gold
Out of the daffodil's heart; cool words that hold
The crushed gray light of rain, or liquidly blow
The wild bee droning home across the glow
Of rippled wind-silver; or, uncontrolled,
Toss the bruised aroma of pine; and words as cold
As water torturing through frozen snow.

And there are words that strain like April hedges
Upward; lonely words with tears on them;
And syllables whose haunting crimson edges
Bleed: "O Jerusalem, Jerusalem!"
And that long star-drift of bright agony:
"Eli, Eli, lama sabachthani!"

—JOSEPH AUSLANDER

WORDS and silences are the instruments with which the poet fashions song. This chapter has to do with words. We have noted how the arrangements of accented syllables and unaccented syllables produce rhythms of various moods and meters, and how the identity of certain sounds produces various effects: musical, binding, structural. But besides this, words have an inherent magic that like the chameleon may change color with its surroundings. That the poet's music may be living, and not a mere echo of some "old sweet song," the words out of which it is blended should be living; that is, words which are crisp with the vitality of current usage. After all, it is the poet's purpose to communicate his feeling; his utterance should then be intelligible to his contemporaries. Expressions, which were alive in a past age but are dead today, should be tabooed. Some of these include *thee* and *thou, wilt, doth* and the like, *ne'er, o'er, e'en, 'gainst* and contractions of that kind; inverted expressions for the sake of rhyme, such as Spenser's "Unless she do him by the forelock take"; emphatic verb forms, used not for emphasis but to pad out the line: "Rough winds do shake the darling buds of May"; obsolete words and expressions:

quoth, saith, withal; slang, the meaning of which is clear today and gone tomorrow; and profane or other words not ordinarily used in polite society. *Damn's, hell's* and *devil's* sprinkled through a work do not lend the force which the writer often wishes them to convey. As a rule they are used by the versifier who is not a master of his craft as substitutes for exact expression. Crudities of this kind in a work of art will not do.

You understand, of course, that this advice applies to cultured utterance. When the nature of a poem demands uncouth expression as do some of Carl Sandburg's, Kipling's, Bret Harte's, and many others, then the use of it is another matter. No artist wants his little fishes to talk like whales. He does not, however, drag vulgarisms into verse as the voice of his own spirit. Some verse makers offend this way today. And young versifiers are influenced by them. Here is a case in point: In an imaginative poem about a bronze Buddha on the desk before him, a youthful poet referred to the maker in the far-off, shadowy Oriental workshop, as one "who didn't give a damn." The poem had moved with dignity up to that line; but that line was entirely out of keeping with the spirit of the rest of the poem as it was out of keeping with the conduct of the young verse maker toward his readers. Vulgar speech must not be used unless it is necessary to the matter in hand.

There is a time also for archaic speech, which we listed as tabooed. Authentic poets use it even today. In some of Thomas Hardy's poems archaisms become as alive as the ghosts of the past which flit through the lines, but this is when his emotion is speaking through a past age or through experience remote from what is familiar to a world of smoke and steel. It would be quite as inappropriate for him to use the speech of this machine world for his purpose, as it would be for us to communicate the feeling of our modern experiences through his archaisms. A beginner in the art of versification is not likely to be sufficiently sure of himself to handle such charged materials without first acquiring the art of living expression. He will want to make a collection of words suitable to the time and place out of which he is to hew his rhythms.

In the monosyllable there is a force which suits present-day rhythms. Many words of one syllable are Anglo-Saxon in origin. One critic has said that Anglo-Saxon words appeal to the heart instead of the head. Poetry is heart music; they should suit it well. Edna St. Vincent Millay is fond of the Anglo-Saxon word. In *The King's Henchman*, which is charming poetry as well as a delightful opera, there is no word which is not of Anglo-Saxon origin. In her lyrics also, she employs short words with striking effect. Read "Witch-Wife" and you will see how striking.

The verse maker may, however, use any living word that suggests his meaning. But it is not enough that words convey meaning. They should contribute to the music of utterance. Variety of sound within the sentence is one means of pleasing the ear. Successive words, too much alike in sound, are as unpleasant to the ear as is purposeless repetition of words, for which there are synonyms. Furthermore, if there be a choice between a word easily pronounced and one difficult to say, the poet will choose the one easily pronounced granted that he does not sacrifice his meaning. And what words are difficult to pronounce? Words in which there is a preponderance of consonant sounds, such as *stretched*. Words in which the vowel sounds are equally distributed with the consonants are easy to produce, hence, pleasing to the ear, as *lullaby, accolade, moonshine*.

As in the word, so in a succession of words, there must be a pleasing distribution both of vowel sounds and consonant sounds. To achieve a smooth flowing style the writer must have an ear to end sounds of words in relation to initial sounds of succeeding words. Only designed repetitions are pleasing. Obviously, the lines below need to be revised for a euphonious sequence of words, so that the sounds will slip together and run along smoothly.

1. Peace came on silken feet to meet the dawn of dusk.

"Meet" and "feet" are too close together. The ugly repetition of *eet* can be improved by using a word with a different vowel sound.

2. The stripling tree was stripped to its knees of its shining bark.

Repetition of *str, tr, str* and the many hissing sounds, *s*'s and *sh*'s, are most unpleasant to the ear. The close succession of short *i*'s in "stripling," "stripped," "its," "its," varied only by *ee* of "tree," which is quite similar to *i* and its shadings, and *ŏ* of "was," is unpleasant. John Keats believed that the open and closed vowels should be carefully blended to produce a melodious effect. The open vowels are shades and tones of *o, a, u*; that is, sounds made through an open mouth. *Ah* is the most open. The closed are *i, e*, and shades of those sounds.[1]

3. Down in Porto Rico a terrible hurricane came along, leveling the shacks of the poor and the mansions of the rich.

In hurri*cane came* we have a flat repetition of an almost identical ending. Furthermore, "came" is a weak verb; "swept" would be truer to the spirit. Then there are ugly *sh* and *ch* sounds coming too close together.

[1] Webster symbol for pronunciation is used.

Perhaps few scribes would be guilty of such gross misuse of beautiful sounds as appears in the succeeding prose passage. Exaggeration is merely to stress the point.

> 4. There will be but three showings of the varsity shows at the Hecksher theater. Those who wish seats are urged to purchase tickets as soon as possible. Tickets may be secured through agents' services in English classes.

Here you have careless repetition of words: *show*ing, *show*s; unpleasant repetition of *sh* and *g* sounds and a horrible clashing of sibilants: *sh*'s with *s*'s and *s*'s with *s*'s.

In poetry we are even more concerned with the music of sound, for through sound the poet must transmute the singing of his heart. He sings with his eye on the object, but his ear on both consonant and vowel sounds.

There are many devices for enhancing the music of verse. Perhaps the simplest to explain is the ancient one, alliteration. In our common speech there are many examples, left-overs from a far past: *r*hyme or *r*eason, *h*ale and *h*earty, *l*ast but not *l*east, *r*ough and *r*eady, *b*ed and *b*oard, out of *h*ouse and *h*ome, *k*ith and *k*in, *f*air, *f*at, and *f*orty. We have alliteration in "*s*ugar is *s*weet and *s*o are you," in the famous *v*eni, *v*idi, *v*ici of the Latin class, in the *b*ulls and *b*ears of Wall Street, in "Thy *K*ingdom *c*ome" of the Lord's prayer. It is the identity of the initial consonant sounds in words close together,—*r*ough and *r*eady, *s*ilent *s*eas; or the identity of the initial consonant sounds in the accented syllables of words close together,—de*p*endable *p*oor, *l*ife ever*l*asting.

In our tongue twisters we have alliteration done to excess:

> Peter Piper picked a peck of pickled peppers
> A peck of pickled peppers Peter Piper picked.

But judiciously employed, this consonant repetition enriches the melody of verse and binds words together in harmony or in contrast, by pressing the sounds upon the ear so that the impress is likely to remain. It is easy to remember names so coupled: Simple Simon; Herbert Hoover.

Anglo-Saxon poetry depended on alliteration to build the line and shape it. Rhyme was not used. A line from *Beowulf* will illustrate.

> Thence a *m*ile's *m*easure   lies the *m*ere

Each line was divided into two parts. The sound which was to be repeated through a line was generally used twice in the first part and once in the second. Rhyme has taken over this function.

Today alliteration is used chiefly for its melodic effect. Listen to the music in the lines below:

> With verses *d*ipt in *d*ew of Castalay
> —EDMUND SPENSER

> The *l*ong *l*ight shakes across the *l*akes
> And the wild cataract *l*eaps in glory
> —ALFRED, LORD TENNYSON

> The fair *b*reeze *b*lew, the white *f*oam *f*lew,
> The *f*urrow *f*ollowed *f*ree.
> —SAMUEL. T. COLERIDGE

Swinburne, whom Tennyson called a "reed through which all things blow into poetry," was very fond of alliteration, as he was of all devices for enriching the music of his verse. In the lines below, he went as far as any poet may dare:

> The *f*ields *f*all southward, a*b*rupt and *b*roken,
> To the *l*ow, *l*ast edge of the *l*ong, *l*one land.

He often cloyed his verses with sickening sweetness, the result of too much alliteration, but he had a sense of humor which prompted him to ridicule this fault of his, as he ridiculed his use of the too-long line in his satire, "Nyphalidia," which he opened with the lines:

From the depth of the dreamy decline of the dawn through a notable
    nimbus of nebulous moonshine,
Pallid and pink as the palm of the flagflower that flickers with fear of the
    flies as they float,
Are the looks of our lovers that lustrously lean from a marvel of mystic
    miraculous moonshine,
These that we feel in the blood of our blushes that thicken and threaten
    with throbs through the throat?

which is indeed what a critic has called it, miraculous moonshine! Through the mouth of Quince in the Prologue to *Midsummer Night's Dream*, Shakespeare laughs uproariously at the overdoing of alliteration,

> Whereat with blade, with bloody blameful blade,
> He bravely broached his boiling bloody breast,

and perhaps he laughed at vowel repetition also: "bl*a*meful bl*a*de he br*a*vely," of which more anon.

Music in words extends deeper than the initial sounds, however. Some words have the inherent magic of suggesting the sounds which they are intended to define. *Bell,* for instance, has a ring to it. *Tinkling* suggests a far different music from that in *clanking*. The very word *tinkling* suggests light musical sound, whereas *clanking* actually produces the metallic sound which the meaning suggests. No analysis of the word is necessary to sense this effect. Other such words are: *ding, dong; honk, honk; scat!; wheeze; whirr; scissors; scimiter; whet, whistle; thunder; lullaby; hiss; shrapnel; frigidaire; ripple; merrily; slippery; scrape.* Some critics contend that this sound quality of words is merely contributory to the meaning which we understand from them. Whether the magic be inherent or merely contributory, words have timbre.

Noise indicates sound; but in no sense does it suggest what *murmur, ripple, hum, drone, buzz, shriek, bellow* suggest. *Their* form is of their substance. This language device in which the sound of the word suggests its meaning has a large name, if you care to remember it: *onomatopœia* pronounced *on-o-mat-ō-pe'a.*

Poe's "The Bells" is a fine example of sustained onomatopœia. We quote the first stanza.

The Bells

I

Hear the sledges with the bells—
    Silver bells!
What a world of merriment their melody foretells!
    How they tinkle, tinkle, tinkle,
        In the icy air of night!
    While the stars that oversprinkle
    All the heavens, seem to twinkle
        With a crystalline delight;
        Keeping time, time, time,
        In a sort of Runic rhyme,
To the tintinnabulation that so musically wells
    From the bells, bells, bells, bells,
        Bells, bells, bells—
From the jingling and the tinkling of the bells.

In succeeding stanzas he suggests the varying metallic ring of golden bells, brazen bells, iron bells. You must read the whole of it aloud. In "The Eve of St. Agnes" by John Keats "the silver snarling trumpets 'gan to chide." Could trumpets speak to our ear more exactly than through "snarling" and "chide"?

Listen to the skaters in these lines from Wordsworth's "The Prelude":

                All shod with steel
        We hissed along the polished ice.

Note the living magic in that word "hissed." And Shakespeare gives you the song of the owl

> Then nightly sings the staring owl,
> *Tu-whit to-who!*

Here you have onomatopœia in its pristine state, "all the charm of all the Muses often flowering in a lonely word."

But there is a more subtle onomatopœia. Blent words may play in a major or a minor key, in tone with the meaning which gives them breath. Listen to these lines:

> And higher than the plover's whistling wing
> The silver arrow of his soul has fled.
> —THOMAS S. JONES, JR.

> Above the moaning wash of Cornish water,
> Cold upon Cornish rocks.
> —EDWIN ARLINGTON ROBINSON

> Thick as autumnal leaves that strow the brooks
> Of Vallombrosa
> —JOHN MILTON

Besides the sounds that we hear: the whistling wing, the cold wash of Cornish waters, the dry rustling of fall leaves, the poet has given us through some magic of his art the feeling of that rare height that never was—all paradise to hold; the melancholy sadness of that low moaning sea wash; the awe and mystery in the dead leaves along the brook side. The very word "Vallombrosa" is charged with the subtle magic of autumnal tone. And "strow" echoes mournfully. Sometimes overzealous modernists quote "strew," and the whole effect is lost.

On analyzing what it is in word combinations that so charges them with tone quality we find that it is the arrangement of vowel sounds and consonant sounds within them. Some words are constituted by their nature for the deeper, richer, fuller cadences and rolling rhythms of human speech, which reveal the deeper emotions. Others are constituted to suit the lighter inflections that voice the lighter moods. In combining words, the poet releases their latent magic.

In a copper wire there is sleeping power. Connect it with another wire and attach a bulb; what slept wakens into light. Without the connection there had been no awakening. So it is with words. Francis Thompson, a poet and very sensitive critic, said this of Coleridge's use of words: "He takes words which have had the life used out of them by the common cry of poets, puts them into relation, and they rise up like his own dead mariners, wonderful with a supernatural animation."

Is there any way of telling what word combinations will produce one effect and what another? Perhaps the poet's gift for magical phrasing may never be explained any more than other wondrous phenomena may be explained completely, but the phenomena, when questioned, may yield some answers, incomplete though they be.

Broadly speaking the long vowel sounds, $\bar{a}$, $\bar{e}$, $\bar{\imath}$, $\bar{o}$, $\bar{u}$, seem to be charged with power to suggest space, distance, depth, height, or any other effect that is large or dignified or solemn or intense. A preponderance of them makes the passage move with dignity or even solemnity. *O, u,* and *a,* have especial resonance quality. The solemnity of this passage seems to move upon the long *o*'s reinforced by a consonant that prolongs the vowel sound:

> While the great organ almost burst his pipes,
> Groaning for power, and rolling thro' the court
> A long melodious thunder to the sound
> Of solemn psalms, and silver litanies.
> —ALFRED, LORD TENNYSON

In the second line

> Groaning for power and rolling thro' the court

the *o*'s in "groaning" and "rolling" produce deep organ tones. And shades of the *o* tone echo the sound where $\bar{o}$ is not exactly repeated.

> Quoth the raven, "Nevermore."

The hollow echo of the *o* in "quoth" and the near-*o* in "more" was deliberately planned by Poe, master of sound effects. Describing how he came to produce "The Raven," he says in his *Philosophy of Composition,* that he chose the word "nevermore" because "the long *o* is the most sonorous vowel in connection with *r* as the most producible consonant." Phonetically, the *o* of "more" is slightly shorter than the *o* of "quoth," and not strictly long *o*; but it is near enough to long *o* to produce rich tone. Poe wanted a word which would roll. Suppose he had said, "Never again," would the effect have been the same?

Long *o* and long *u,* followed by a consonant sound which may be prolonged, have great sonorousness. Listen to the effect:

> Roll on, thou deep and dark blue Ocean, roll!
> —GEORGE GORDON, LORD BYRON

> Blow, bugle, blow, set the wild echoes flying
> —ALFRED, LORD TENNYSON

And again, the long vowels speak with the voice and the mood and the timbre of the bassoon:

> Then o'er sea-lashings of commingling tunes
> The ancient wise bassoons,

> Like weird
> Gray-beard
> Old harpers sitting on the high sea dunes,
> Chanted runes.
>
> —Sidney Lanier

The short vowel sounds, particularly ĭ and ĕ, seem well adapted to ideas suggesting lightness, grace, rapidity, and any other emotional effect on the lighter corners of the spirit. If they do not in themselves suggest these ideas, at least they lend themselves to the suggestion.

> With lisp of leaves and ripple of rain
> —Algernon Charles Swinburne

The lightness of the short i's in "lisp," "ripple," is in keeping with the delicacy of the sounds suggested. There is alliteration also to enhance the music.

> Little breezes dusk and shiver
> —Alfred, Lord Tennyson

Note the suggestion of light rapid movement in

> Come and trip it as ye go
> On the light fantastic toe
> —John Milton

The trochees which move rapidly intensify the effect of light grace. When Prospero finally frees Ariel, the gauzy sprite sings

> Merrily, merrily, shall I live now
> Under the blossom that hangs on the bough
> —Shakespeare

Almost all short vowels, carefully varied, in keeping with this gossamer thing of the air . . . And what a carefree mood lilts through the light vowels of

> Come hither, come hither, come hither:
> Here shall he see
> No enemy
> But winter and rough weather.
> —Shakespeare

In the consonant sounds also, there is life waiting to be quickened. The continuants: m, n, l, r, w, because they may be easily prolonged, aid the flow of a line; hence, their effect is soothing. They make for musical smoothness. They prolong the organ tones of the long vowels, particularly of o and u. Note the effects in these lines:

Then in a wailful choir the small gnats mourn
　　　　　　　　　　　　　　—JOHN KEATS

The coming musk-rose, full of dewy wine,
The murmurous haunt of flies on summer eves.
　　　　　　　　　　　　　　—JOHN KEATS

Save where the beetle wheels his droning flight,
And drowsy tinklings lull the distant folds:
　　　　　　　　　　　　　　—THOMAS GRAY

The *m*'s and *w*'s and *l*'s have their way in hushing and humming. They contribute to the onomatopœia of such passages.

Now listen to Coleridge:

Where Alph, the sacred river, ran
　Through caverns measureless to man
　　Down to a Sunless Sea.

Can't you hear the hollow of that river's voice through cavern on cavern? Haven't the *n*'s something to do with that echo: ra*n*, cave*n*s, ma*n*, dow*n*, su*n*less, with the reverberating *r*'s in seven words?

The stops: *b, p, d, t,* hard *g,* and hard *c,* create just the opposite effect. They slow up the movement or even obstruct the rhythm.

Little breezes dusk and shiver
　　　　　　　　　　　—ALFRED, LORD TENNYSON

Note how the *k* in "dusk" stops the onsweep of the winds. They are just little breezes. We have noticed the effect of the short vowels.

In this inimitable line of Keats's from "The Eve of St. Agnes"

The hare limp'd trembling through the frozen grass

you can feel the shiver of the little animal and the stiffness of the grass. You actually limp, feeling too how the limp halts the swift little creature's merry flight. And what a word is "trembling!" The *mbl*—say it! —actually performs the action. Every word in this line is rich in musical power.

The cataracts blow their trumpets from the steep
　　　　　　　　　　　—WILLIAM WORDSWORTH

Here the stops appropriately lend expressiveness to the ideas of rugged austerity in the steep. The hard *c*'s and the *b*'s, *t*'s and *d*'s slow the line into dignified pace in keeping with austere grandeur. The full vowels have something to do with the effect also.

Note how the repeated *d*'s generate power in the Nether Glooms. A son is wondering whether his dead father wants his violin down where

> The hours may be a dragging load upon him,
>   As he hears the axle grind
>   Round and round
>   Of the great world, in the blind
>   Still profound
> Of the night-time? . . .
>   —THOMAS HARDY: *To My Father's Violin*

One of the finest examples of sustained tone in which the stops contribute to the effect is the following poem by Thomas Hardy:

On Sturminster Foot-Bridge

(Onomatopœic)

> Reticulations creep upon the slack stream's face
>   When the wind skims irritably past,
> The current clucks smartly into each hollow place
> That years of flood have scrabbled in the pier's sodden base;
>   The floating-lily leaves rot fast.
>
> On a roof stand the swallows ranged in wistful, waiting rows,
>   Till they arrow off and drop like stones
> Among the eyot-withies at whose foot the river flows:
> And beneath the roof is she who in the dark world shows
>   As a lattice gleam when midnight moans.

Hear the softness in the last three lines—up beyond the withies, in his home.

Uncouth effects, appropriate to the thought, may often be achieved through the stops.

> Through the hot, black breath of the burnin' boat
>   Jim Bludso's voice was heard,
> And they all had trust in his cussedness,
>   And knowed he would keep his word.
>   —JOHN HAY

Ideas of harshness, brutality and the like may be suggested by appropriately harsh sound combinations up to a point. Taste and the ear must decide when to stop. The discord should not be prolonged to give pain. As in music, discord is introduced for the effect of richer music. If too many stops collide, the effect is unpleasant to the ear. Handled with restraint the stops may produce effects in keeping with the whole range of beauty, from grace to sublimity.

The austere dignity of the sublime seems well expressed through a

On Sturminster Foot-Bridge:
Reticulations = net forms; scrabbled = scraped; eyot = little island; withies = willows.

preponderance of stops carefully distributed, even when they are un-supported by long vowels. Ruggedness, boldness, sharpness, austerity on a large scale seem to find best expression through the rugged con-sonants.

> Our revels now are ended: these our actors,
> As I foretold you, were all spirits, and
> Are melted into air, into thin air:
> And, like the baseless fabric of this vision,
> The cloud-capp'd towers, the gorgeous palaces,
> The solemn temples, the great globe itself,
> Yea, all which it inherit, shall dissolve;
> And, like this insubstantial pageant faded,
> Leave not a rack behind: we are such stuff
> As dreams are made on, and our little life
> Is rounded with a sleep.
>
> —WILLIAM SHAKESPEARE

Too many of the stops cluttered together, like all other embellish-ments carried to excess, vitiate their purpose. Here is a line from the delicious nonsense of Swinburne:

Ah, how can fear sit and hear as love hears it grief's heart's craked grate's screech

Here are consonant combinations that screech indeed!

Note how the gutterals and hard *j* and *z* sounds can grate and how *r* can roll!

> . . . On a sudden open fly
> With impetuous recoil and jarring sound
> The infernal doors, and on their hinges grate
> Harsh thunder.
>
> —JOHN MILTON

If all this sounds like moonshine, contrast Milton's hinges with these:

> Then as was wont, his palace door flew ope
> In smoothest silence.
>
> —JOHN KEATS: *Hyperion*

How well oiled that "smoothest" is!

In this age of vertical expression the stops should find many oppor-tunities for contributory music.

Most conspicuous of our consonant sounds are our sibilants: *s, z, sh, zh,* and their relatives, *ch* and *j*. They may hiss like geese or hush like angels. To please, they must be carefully distributed. Shakespeare be-gins a sonnet

> When to the sessions of sweet silent thought
> I summon up remembrance of things past.

An exquisite lyric of Shelley's sings through its sibilants, supported by flowing *w*'s.

> Swiftly walk over the western wave,
>   Spirit of Night!
> Out of the misty eastern cave. . . .

In such song the sibilants are beautiful to the ear. When they are too insistent, however, or when they collide they are unpleasant. Tennyson never permitted an end *s* to collide with a beginning *s*. He went over his work carefully to remove any such defects. This he called "kicking the geese out of the boat." In his song: "You ask me, why tho' ill at ease," is a line

> And freedom slowly broadens down

which was frequently misquoted as

> And freedom broaden*s* *s*lowly down.

In this rendition the geese of "broaden*s* *s*lowly," which Tennyson was always so careful to kick out of the boat, are back in. He often protested against the misquotation.

Because Shakespeare dared

> The multitudinous seas incarnadine

it does not mean that a lesser than he may pile up *s*'s with immunity. On the rim of the Grand Canyon we are swept away by a oneness with grandeur. Little inconveniences, barrenness, lack of water, and the like do not matter. But where we are not overwhelmed by the sublime, details count. So the beginner had better look to his sibilants.

Pope, that consummate artist, whose polished verse made him, little suffering hunchback that he was, the dominating figure of the eight-eenth century, puts into practice the theory of contrasting tone effects through the repetition and distribution of vowel and consonant sounds:

> When Ajax strives some rock's vast weight to throw,
> The line too labors, and the words move slow;
> Not so, when swift Camilla scours the plain,
> Flies o'er th' unending corn, and skims along the main.

Why do the words "move slow" in line one, as Ajax strives to lift a great rock and throw it? Note how the *s* sounds coming together in "Ajax strives" and in "strives some," force you to stop; notice the stopping at the *ck* of "rock's," and the end *t*'s, "vast weight," with the two coming together, "weigh*t* *t*o." The line does indeed labor as Ajax

did with its obstructing *t*'s and *s*'s. And the long vowel sounds: *A* of
"Ajax," *i* of "strives," *a* of "weight," *o* of "throw," add to the weight.
Certainly they do not suggest lightness and speed as the short *i*'s in
"swift Camilla skims." And the consonant sounds, *w, n, l, r, s,* easily
prolonged, do not halt Camilla's movements.

The same difference in movement is suggested in Tennyson's "Lady
of Shalott." You have but to read the passage aloud to note the
contrast.

> By the margin, willow-veiled
> Slide the *h*eavy barges trail'd
> By slow horses; and un*h*ail'd
> The shallop flitte*th* silken-sailed
> Skimming down to Camelot.

The breath sounds, *h, th, wh,* seem to hush passages, or slow them
down for breath. In the passage above they both slow the barges and
hush the light movement of the shallop, un*h*ail'd; flitte*th*. They may
suggest the lightness of thistledown. The word "whisper" is significant
of the effect, as is Shakespeare's line

> Come *h*ither, come *h*ither, come *h*ither.

The labials *f* and *v* also lend themselves to ideas of brevity, intangi-
bility, mystery and even nothingness.

> Such stu*ff* as dreams are made on.

In Housman's poem printed below isn't something of the intangi-
bility and brevity of life suggested through the repetition of *f*'s and *v*'s
and breath sounds—a puff and we are here; a puff and we are on our
way! Both are well supported by liquids.

> From *f*ar, *f*rom eve and morning
> And yon twel*v*e-winded sky
> The stu*ff* o*f* life to knit me
> Blew *h*ither: here am I.

> Now—*f*or a brea*th* I tarry
> Nor yet disperse apart—
> Take my *h*and quick and tell me,
> *Wh*at *h*ave you in your *h*eart.

> Speak now, and I will answer;
> *H*ow shall I *h*elp you, say:
> Ere to the wind's twel*v*e quarters
> I take my endless way.

There are a great many other elements of beauty in this poem. No worth-while poem will have any single tone quality and nothing more. In any passage quoted in this chapter you will find other elements of beauty than the one pointed out, as well as contributory devices for creating the effect under discussion. In Wordsworth's skating passage, for instance, not only do you hear the hiss of the skates as was noted, but through a more subtle suggestion of the succeeding words, you *feel* the hardness of the ice and the very temper of good steel, as dear to the skater as an old brier is to the smoker. Passages and complete poems should be read with an ear to combined effects.

There are many subtleties of tone and word that have not been touched on here, but what has been suggested is enough for the first experiments.

A great many things have been pointed out as contributory to the tone quality of the poem—the timbre of the instrument through which the poet's imagination blows into emotion. We have thought about living words; onomatopœia; the quality of vowel tones; and the value of consonant sounds. These blend with rhythm, line length; with rhyme and assonance. And playing through all and directing all is the voice of the poet's heart.

And every time a poet sits down to write a poem does he think of *all* these things, you ask. Surely no. Perhaps he thinks of none of them. He may be carried away either by the beating of his song or the crying of his heart. His utterance may translate the fullness of both his heart and his song with little effort. After the first flush of creation, however, when the words are cold upon a page, the chances are that he will eye them critically, and if they do not sing his creation as his heart sang it to his mind, he will look to the cause. With words he has translated a feeling and a singing; to his words he must look. Guided by what he knows of the technique of musical effects he will delete here, substitute there, perhaps change whole passages. He may then experience the intellectual delight of pronouncing his own work good—good to his spirit, good to his ear. There is no less an imagination of the ear than of the eye. Indeed, to make his music the poet will find his ear imagination more potent than the other.

Great poets have left us some of their theories and their revisions to ponder. "Love reflects the things beloved." Out of our loving and our seeking we may enlarge our vision beautiful and thereby catch something of the poet's power over the haunting line, which, when all is said, can no more be fully explained than the quality of his voice or his unique personality can be explained. But inspiration hovers in the wake of art's bright agonies.

APPLICATION

1. Read "The Brook" and the "Song of the Chattahoochee" printed below. Compare them for their tone quality. What contributory devices do you find in each?

The Brook

I come from haunts of coot and hern
  I make a sudden sally,
And sparkle out among the fern,
  To bicker down a valley.

By thirty hills I hurry down,
  Or slip between the ridges,
By twenty thorps, a little town,
  And half a hundred bridges.

Till last by Philip's farm I flow
  To join the brimming river,
For men may come and men may go
  But I go on for ever.

I chatter over stony ways,
  In little sharps and trebles,
I bubble into eddying bays,
  I babble on the pebbles.

With many a curve my banks I fret
  By many a field and fallow,
And many a fairy foreland set
  With willow-weed and mallow.

I chatter, chatter, as I flow
  To join the brimming river,
For men may come and men may go,
  But I go on for ever.

I wind about, and in and out,
  With here a blossom sailing,
And here and there a lusty trout,
  And here and there a grayling,

And here and there a foamy flake
  Upon me, as I travel
With many a silvery water-break
  Above the golden gravel,

And draw them all along, and flow
  To join the brimming river,
For men may come and men may go,
  But I go on for ever.
      —ALFRED, LORD TENNYSON

Song of the Chattahoochee

Out of the hills of Habersham,
Down the valleys of Hall,
I hurry amain to reach the plain,
Run the rapid and leap the fall,
Split at the rock and together again,
Accept my bed, or narrow or wide,
And flee from folly on every side
With a lover's pain to attain the plain
  Far from the hills of Habersham,
  Far from the valleys of Hall.

All down the hills of Habersham,
  All through the valleys of Hall,
The rushes cried, *Abide, abide,*
The willful waterweeds held me thrall,
The laving laurel turned my tide,
The ferns and fondling grass said *Stay,*
The dewberry dipped for to work delay,
And the little reeds sighed, *Abide, abide,*
  Here in the hills of Habersham,
  Here in the valleys of Hall.

High o'er the hills of Habersham,
　Veiling the valleys of Hall,
The hickory told me manifold
Fair tales of shade, the poplar tall
Wrought me her shadowy self to hold,
The chestnut, the oak, the walnut, the pine,
Overleaning, with flickering meaning and sign,
Said, *Pass not, so cold, these manifold*
　Deep shades of the hills of Habersham,
　These glades in the valleys of Hall.

And oft in the hills of Habersham,
　And oft in the valleys of Hall,
The white quartz shone, and the smooth brook-stone
Did bar me of passage with friendly brawl,
And many a luminous jewel lone
—Crystals clear or acloud with mist,
Ruby, garnet and amethyst—
Made lures with the lights of streaming stone
　In the clefts of the hills of Habersham,
　In the beds of the valleys of Hall.

But oh, not the hills of Habersham,
　And oh, not the valleys of Hall
Avail: I am fain for to water the plain.
Downward the voices of Duty call--
Downward, to toil and be mixed with the main,
The dry fields burn, and the mills are to turn,
And a myriad flowers mortally yearn,
And the lordly main from beyond the plain
　Calls o'er the hills of Habersham,
　Calls through the valleys of Hall.
　　　　　　　　—SIDNEY LANIER

Select all the musical devices you can find. How does the musical movement suit the river? The brook? What differences do you note?

2. If a poet today were writing the poem below what would he eliminate as out of our living speech? Why is the poem as it stands a charming expression of the Elizabethan lyric?

Hymn to Diana

Queen and Huntress, chaste and fair,
     Now the sun is laid to sleep,
Seated in thy silver chair
     State in wonted manner keep:
          Hesperus entreats thy light,
          Goddess excellently bright.

Earth, let not thy envious shade
     Dare itself to interpose;
Cynthia's shining orb was made
     Heaven to clear when day did close:
          Bless us then with wishèd sight:
          Goddess excellently bright.

Lay thy bow of pearl apart
     And thy crystal-shining quiver;
Give unto the flying hart
     Space to breathe, how short soever:
          Thou that mak'st a day of night,
          Goddess excellently bright!

—BEN JONSON

3. Copy in your notebook passages of poetry in which liquids: *l, m, w,* fill the lines with music; passages in which various effects are produced by long vowels followed by a liquid; passages in which breath sounds interpret the thought. You cannot do this all at once. Be on the lookout for them as you read.

4. Read "The Raven," printed below, for artistic pleasure. Do you notice ways in which Poe's words have contributed to the eeriness of the atmosphere?

The Raven

Once upon a midnight dreary, while I pondered, weak and weary,
Over many a quaint and curious volume of forgotten lore—
While I nodded, nearly napping, suddenly there came a tapping,
As of some one gently rapping—rapping at my chamber door.
" 'Tis some visitor," I muttered, "tapping at my chamber door—
     Only this and nothing more."

Ah, distinctly I remember, it was in the bleak December,
And each separate dying ember wrought its ghost upon the floor.
Eagerly I wished the morrow;—vainly I had sought to borrow
From my books surcease of sorrow—sorrow for the lost Lenore—
For the rare and radiant maiden whom the angels name Lenore—
    Nameless here for evermore.

And the silken sad uncertain rustling of each purple curtain
Thrilled me—filled me with fantastic terrors never felt before;
So that now, to still the beating of my heart, I stood repeating
" 'Tis some visitor entreating entrance at my chamber door—
Some late visitor entreating entrance at my chamber door;—
    This it is and nothing more."

Presently my soul grew stronger; hesitating then no longer,
"Sir," said I, "or Madam, truly your forgiveness I implore;
But the fact is I was napping, and so gently you came rapping,
And so faintly you came tapping—tapping at my chamber door,
That I scarce was sure I heard you"—here I opened wide the door:—
    Darkness there and nothing more.

Deep into that darkness peering, long I stood there wondering, fearing,
Doubting, dreaming dreams no mortal ever dared to dream before;
But the silence was unbroken, and the stillness gave no token,
And the only word there spoken was the whispered word "Lenore!"
This I whispered, and an echo murmured back the word, "Lenore!"
    Merely this and nothing more.

Back into the chamber turning, all my soul within me burning,
Soon again I heard a tapping, somewhat louder than before.
"Surely," said I, "surely that is something at my window lattice;
Let me see, then, what thereat is, and this mystery explore—
Let my heart be still a moment, and this mystery explore;—
    'Tis the wind and nothing more."

Open here I flung the shutter, when, with many a flirt and flutter,
In there stepped a stately Raven of the saintly days of yore;
Not the least obeisance made he; not a minute stopped or stayed he;
But, with mien of lord or lady, perched above my chamber door—
Perched upon a bust of Pallas just above my chamber door—
    Perched, and sat, and nothing more.

Then this ebony bird beguiling my sad fancy into smiling,
By the grave and stern decorum of the countenance it wore,
"Though thy crest be shorn and shaven, thou," I said, "art sure no craven,
Ghastly grim and ancient Raven wandering from the Nightly shore—
Tell me what thy lordly name is on the Night's Plutonian shore!"
    Quoth the Raven, "Nevermore."

Much I marvelled this ungainly fowl to hear discourse so plainly,
Though its answer little meaning—little relevancy bore;
For we cannot help agreeing that no living human being
Ever yet was blessed with seeing bird above his chamber door—
Bird or beast upon the sculptured bust above his chamber door,
    With such name as "Nevermore."

But the Raven, sitting lonely on the placid bust, spoke only
That one word, as if his soul in that one word he did outpour.
Nothing further then he uttered—not a feather then he fluttered—
Till I scarcely more than muttered, "Other friends have flown before—
On the morrow *he* will leave me, as my hopes have flown before."
    Then the bird said, "Nevermore."

Startled at the stillness broken by reply so aptly spoken,
"Doubtless," said I, "what it utters is its only stock and store,
Caught from some unhappy master whom unmerciful Disaster
Followed fast and followed faster till his songs one burden bore—
Till the dirges of his Hope that melancholy burden bore
    Of 'Never—nevermore.' "

But the Raven still beguiling all my sad soul into smiling,
Straight I wheeled a cushioned seat in front of bird and bust and door;
Then, upon the velvet sinking, I betook myself to linking
Fancy unto fancy, thinking what this ominous bird of yore—
What this grim, ungainly, ghastly, gaunt, and ominous bird of yore
    Meant in croaking "Nevermore."

This I sat engaged in guessing, but no syllable expressing
To the fowl whose fiery eyes now burned into my bosom's core;
This and more I sat divining, with my head at ease reclining
On the cushion's velvet lining that the lamp-light gloated o'er,
But whose velvet violet lining with the lamp-light gloating o'er,
    She shall press, ah, nevermore!

Then, methought, the air grew denser, perfumed from an unseen censer
Swung by Seraphim whose footfalls tinkled on the tufted floor.
"Wretch," I cried, "thy God hath lent thee—by these angels he hath sent thee
Respite—respite and nepenthe from thy memories of Lenore;
Quaff, oh quaff this kind nepenthe and forget this lost Lenore!"
    Quoth the Raven, "Nevermore."

"Prophet!" said I, "thing of evil! prophet still, if bird or devil!—
Whether Tempter sent, or whether tempest tossed thee here ashore,
Desolate yet all undaunted, on this desert land enchanted—
On this home by Horror haunted—tell me truly, I implore—
Is there—*is* there balm in Gilead?—tell me—tell me, I implore!"
    Quoth the Raven "Nevermore."

"Prophet!" said I, "thing of evil!—prophet still, if bird or devil!
By that Heaven that bends above us—by that God we both adore—
Tell this soul with sorrow laden if, within the distant Aidenn,
It shall clasp a sainted maiden whom the angels name Lenore—
Clasp a rare and radiant maiden whom the angels name Lenore."
  Quoth the Raven, "Nevermore."

"Be that word our sign of parting, bird or fiend!" I shrieked, upstarting—
"Get thee back unto the tempest and the Night's Plutonian shore!
Leave no black plume as a token of that lie thy soul hath spoken!
Leave my loneliness unbroken!—quit the bust above my door!
Take thy beak from out my heart, and take thy form from off my door!"
  Quoth the Raven, "Nevermore."

And the Raven, never flitting, still is sitting, still is sitting
On the pallid bust of Pallas just above my chamber door;
And his eyes have all the seeming of a demon's that is dreaming,
And the lamp-light o'er him streaming throws his shadow on the floor;
And my soul from out that shadow that lies floating on the floor
  Shall be lifted—nevermore!

5. What musical devices does Poe use in "Annabel Lee"?

Annabel Lee

It was many and many a year ago,
 In a kingdom by the sea,
That a maiden there lived whom ye may know
 By the name of Annabel Lee.
And this maiden she lived with no other thought
 Than to love and be loved by me.

I was a child and she was a child,
 In this kingdom by the sea:
But we loved with a love that was more than love—
 I and my Annabel Lee;
With a love that the winged seraphs of heaven
 Coveted her and me.

And this was the reason that, long ago,
 In this kingdom by the sea,
A wind blew out of a cloud, chilling
 My beautiful Annabel Lee;
So that her highborn kinsman came
 And bore her away from me,
To shut her up in a sepulchre
 In this kingdom by the sea.

The angels, not half so happy in heaven,
    Went envying her and me—
Yes!—that was the reason (as all men know,
    In this kingdom by the sea)
That the wind came out of the cloud one night,
    Chilling and killing my Annabel Lee.

But our love it was stronger by far than the love
    Of those who were older than we—
    Of many far wiser than we—
And neither the angels in heaven above,
    Nor the demons down under the sea,
Can ever dissever my soul from the soul
    Of the beautiful Annabel Lee.

For the moon never beams without bringing me dreams
    Of the beautiful Annabel Lee;
And the stars never rise, but I feel the bright eyes
    Of the beautiful Annabel Lee;
And so, all the night-tide, I lie down by the side
Of my darling, my darling, my life and my bride,
    In the sepulchre there by the sea—
    In her tomb by the sounding sea.

6. Read Dryden's "Ode for St. Cecilia's Day" printed below. How is the spirit of the various instruments captured? What has the imagery to do with the suggestion of sounds?

Ode for St. Cecilia's Day

From harmony, from heavenly harmony,
    This universal frame began:
When nature underneath a heap
    Of jarring atoms lay,
    And could not heave her head,
The tuneful voice was heard from high,
    "Arise, ye more than dead!"
Then cold, and hot, and moist, and dry,
    In order to their stations leap,
        And Music's power obey.
From harmony, from heavenly harmony,
    This universal frame began:
    From harmony to harmony
Through all the compass of the notes it ran,
The diapason closing full in Man.

What passion cannot Music raise and quell?
  When Jubal struck the chorded shell,
    His listening brethren stood around,
      And, wondering, on their faces fell
  To worship that celestial sound:
Less than a God they thought there could not dwell
    Within the hollow of that shell,
      That spoke so sweetly, and so well.
What passion cannot Music raise and quell?

    The trumpet's loud clangour
      Excites us to arms,
    With shrill notes of anger,
      And mortal alarms.
The double double double beat
    Of the thundering drum
    Cries "Hark! the foes come;
Charge, charge, 'tis too late to retreat!"

    The soft complaining flute,
    In dying notes, discovers
    The woes of hopeless lovers,
Whose dirge is whisper'd by the warbling lute.

    Sharp violins proclaim
Their jealous pangs and desperation,
Fury, frantic indignation,
Depth of pains, and height of passion
    For the fair, disdainful dame.

    But O, what art can teach
    What human voice can reach,
    The sacred organ's praise?
Notes inspiring holy love,
Notes that wing their heavenly ways
    To mend the choirs above.

    Orpheus could lead the savage race;
And trees unrooted left their place,
    Sequacious of the lyre;
But bright Cecilia rais'd the wonder higher:
When to her organ vocal breath was given,
    An angel heard, and straight appear'd
      Mistaking Earth for Heaven.

GRAND CHORUS

As from the power of sacred lays
   The spheres began to move,
And sung the great Creator's praise
   To all the Blest above;
So when the last and dreadful hour
This crumbling pageant shall devour,
The trumpet shall be heard on high
The dead shall live, the living die,
And Music shall untune the sky!

7. Now read "Kubla Khan" two or three times, once at least aloud. What instances of subtle onomatopoeia can you find? What contribution to the music and to emotional effect is made by vowel repetitions? Liquids? Stops? Alliteration? What magic lines appeal to you?

Kubla Khan

In Xanadu did Kubla Khan
A stately pleasure-dome decree:
Where Alph, the sacred river, ran
Through caverns measureless to man
  Down to a sunless sea,
So twice five miles of fertile ground
With walls and towers were girdled round:
And there were gardens bright with sinuous rills
Where blossom'd many an incense-bearing tree;
And here were forests ancient as the hills,
Enfolding sunny spots of greenery.

  But oh! that deep romantic chasm which slanted
Down the green hill athwart a cedarn cover!
A savage place! as holy and enchanted
As e'er beneath a waning moon was haunted
By woman wailing for her demon-lover!
And from this chasm, with ceaseless turmoil seething,
As if this earth in fast thick pants were breathing,
A mighty fountain momently was forced:
Amid whose swift half-intermitted burst
Huge fragments vaulted like rebounding hail,
Or chaffy grain beneath the thresher's flail:
And 'mid these dancing rocks at once and ever
It flung up momently the sacred river.
Five miles meandering with a mazy motion
Through wood and dale the sacred river ran,

Then reach'd the caverns measureless to man,
And sank in tumult to a lifeless ocean:
And 'mid this tumult Kubla heard from far
Ancestral voices prophesying war!

The shadow of the dome of pleasure
Floated midway on the waves;
Where was heard the mingled measure
From the fountain and the caves.
It was a miracle of rare device,
A sunny pleasure-dome with caves of ice!
A damsel with a dulcimer
In a vision once I saw:
It was an Abyssinian maid,
And on her dulcimer she play'd,
Singing of Mount Abora.
Could I revive within me
Her symphony and song,
To such a deep delight 'twould win me
That with music loud and long,
I would build that dome in air,
That sunny dome! those caves of ice!
And all who heard should see them there,
And all should cry, Beware! Beware!
His flashing eyes, his floating hair!
Weave a circle round him thrice,
And close your eyes with holy dread,
For he on honey-dew hath fed,
And drunk the milk of Paradise.

—SAMUEL T. COLERIDGE

FIVE-FINGER EXERCISES

1. Rewrite the four passages criticized on pages 79 and 80 so that they will please the ear.

2. Make up a name which is musical through alliteration. Find some advertisements which seek to impress the consciousness through alliteration.

3. Write a sentence in which you suggest vastness, power, awfulness by your choice of words. Indicate how you tried to get your effect.

4. Write sentences in which your words contribute to the effect of lightness, rapidity, grace.

5. Go over the couplets you wrote in a previous lesson. Decide whether your choice of words pleases you in the light of this chapter on words and their music.

6. In the light of this chapter read this poem on words:

Crystals and Flame

The fused heat of words
Ignited by the mind
Flames high!

Yet clear as crystal, cool,
Composed, upon a page
Words lie.

—MARY CUMMINGS EUDY

A student felt this way about words:

Word Quest

You, whose delight was but to poise atilt
Some flower-cup in quivering ecstasy
Light as a happy song's rejoicing lilt,
Will not be etched in fragile tracery
Upon the sky again; for in blind zest
Some man has stilled your charm to soulless death,
Has made a butterfly his treasured quest,
Whose beauty fed upon the spring's warm breath.
Yet there are butterflies whose beckoning gleam
Is but a promise of a prize untold.
Chrysalis-bound, they do not live, but dream
Till captured; sleeping words cannot unfold
Their silken wings until the human mind
Becomes their store-house, where cramped prisons burst;
They flutter through its boundlessness to find
Star-seeking wings, that, tremulous at first,
Daily gain strength and surety of art
Till, in full splendor finally unfurled,
They lend their wings unto their captor's heart,
Whose flight, transcendent, thrills the watching world.

—RUTH H. HAUSMAN

Discipline Yourself

1. to use a living vocabulary: no o'er's, e'er's, remember not's, doth say's;
2. to express your own viewpoint rather than to echo some other writer's;
write with your eye on the object;
3. to develop your images logically: if the moon is a galleon let it act as a
galleon on the seas;

4. to strive for a rhythm that serves your emotion; to treat it logically;

5. to strive for an effect of naturalness in rhymes: no forced rhymes or too popular rhymes;

6. to invest your utterance with musical quality;

7. to pack every line with meaning—no adjectives, no adverbs merely to pad the line. Look to the noun and the verb.

8. to test everything you have created before you pronounce it done.

"Set down that work as good which, blurred and blotted, checked and counterchecked has stood all tests and issued forth correct."

—HORACE

ON READING POETRY

1. Become acquainted with poets through browsing in anthologies. When you find a poet who especially appeals to you, read his works until you know him well.

2. Learn to read poetry aloud. Verse should not be read like prose. On the other hand, the reader should do more than bring out the rhythm as a child does when he sing-songs his jingles. The reader of verse must take into account three things: the beat of the line, the beat of natural speech, the sense. Practice will show you how to harmonize the three. Bring out the music of the line by slowing up—not exactly stopping—at the end of each line just long enough to feel its vibrations yourself and to let your audience feel them, at the same time that you carry over the meaning from line to line. *Feel* the line, *feel* the sense, and you have it. Share what you are reading by looking at your listeners as you send them phrase on phrase. Do not be afraid that you may lose your place. (Better do that than read to yourself!) The pause takes care of that matter. It permits you to give out the thought, to receive acknowledgment of its receipt—this is flashed from the eyes of your listeners—and to gather from the page the sense of the next phrase.

CHAPTER VII

THE QUATRAIN

THE next simplest pattern to try is perhaps a four-line poem that has two rhymed lines and two unrhymed lines:

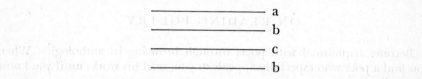

Such a form is called a quatrain. It may be in any rhythm. Iambic or trochaic meter is the simplest to try first, however. The beginner had best plan his quatrains in lines not longer than five feet, all one length or varying in length any way he chooses. His matter and his feeling must determine what arrangement to use.

When he has tried a quatrain, *a b c b*, in which he is restricted only slightly by the rhyming device, he may wish to experiment with any of many other combinations in which the restriction is slightly more binding. He will find that the most satisfactory arrangements for the device are perhaps

a a b b; a b c b; a b a b; a b b a.

A word here about the effect of the closing rhyme. It accents the pattern and emphasizes the idea, binding the four lines together. If this last line is left unrhymed, there is created a sense of falling apart which the versifier does not ordinarily intend when he uses rhyme.

Quatrains by recognized poets are reprinted here. They are followed by the experiments of beginners. There is rare beauty in this compact little form.

New Excavations

A workman with a spade in half a day
Can push two thousand lagging years away;
See, how the tragic villas, one by one,
Like drowsy lizards, creep into the sun.

—LEONORA SPEYER

Easter

The air is like a butterfly
With frail blue wings.
The happy earth looks at the sky
And sings.

—JOYCE KILMER

Pedigree

The pedigree of honey
Does not concern the bee;
A clover, any time, to him
Is aristocracy.

—EMILY DICKINSON

Auguries of Innocence

To see the world in a grain of sand;
  And a heaven in a wild flower;
Hold infinity in the palm of your hand,
  And eternity in an hour.

—WILLIAM BLAKE

Dirce

Stand close around, ye Stygian set,
  With Dirce in one boat conveyed,
Or Charon, seeing, may forget
  That he is old, and she a shade.

—WALTER SAVAGE LANDOR

On His Seventy-Fifth Birthday

I strove with none; for none was worth my strife,
  Nature I loved, and next to Nature, Art;
I warmed both hands before the fire of life,
  It sinks, and I am ready to depart.

—WALTER SAVAGE LANDOR

For a Pessimist

He wore his coffin for a hat,
  Calamity his cape,
While on his face a death's head sat
  And waved a bit of crape.

—COUNTEE CULLEN

The next two quatrains are from a sequence:

Quatrain V

Nothing is judged according to its size,—
  Between the great, the small, Love sets no bar,
And in the violet's purple incense lies
  All the immortal wonder of a star.

—THOMAS S. JONES, JR.

Quatrain XI

Here upon earth eternity is won,—
The soul that seeks God holds immortal fire,
As tiny dew that trembles on a brier
Reflects the radiance of the rising sun.
—THOMAS S. JONES, JR.

God's Likeness

Not in mine own, but in my neighbor's face,
Must I Thine image trace:
Nor he in his, but in the light of mine,
Behold thy Face Divine.
—JOHN B. TABB

Deep Unto Deep

Where limpid waters lie between,
There only heaven to heaven is seen:
Where flows the tide of mutual tears
There only heart to heart appears.
—JOHN B. TABB

Vestiges

Upon the Isle of Time we trace
The signs of many a vanished race:
But on the sea that laps it round,
No memory of man is found.
—JOHN B. TABB

QUATRAINS BY STUDENTS

Lace

All the field is white with lace;
Queen Anne just passed by this place,
Dropped her mantle as she ran,
Playing hide-and-seek with Pan.
—DORIS V. LECKY

Poet to His Love

You shall not lack for dainty words
To dine upon, and overhead
I'll build a roof of loving talk,
But ask me not for bread.
—ESTELLE ROOKS

April

April came: her eyes, opaquely gray,
Matched the color of her misty train;
Her footsteps as she pattered past my door,
Sounded strangely like the falling rain.
—NAOMI ROGIN

Spring Planting

The earth, still drowsy from its hibernation,
Stretches lazily within the shade.
It might fall back in frigid relaxation
If I were not to prod it with my spade.
—William Roehrick

To A Campus Oak

Very young and lovely, she
Unfurls green banners to the rain.
Thrill not so madly, little tree—
Spring will come again!
—Muriel F. Hochdorf

High Wind

There is nothing nearer heaven
Or farther from the ground
Than high wind on a hilltop,
Skybound.
—Estelle Rooks

Wish

All I ask is a night wind
To make the hemlocks shiver,
And a road that runs on silver toes
To meet a lonely river.
—Muriel F. Hochdorf

Solitaire

I am wedded to the greenwood,
And the mountains are my kin,
And my spirit's door is open
For the evening to come in.
—Muriel F. Hochdorf

Here are two on the same subject with very different imagery:

Spring

Come again to the city.
The song you sing so well
Will charm the frozen giant
And free me from his spell.
—William Roehrick

Spring

Obeying Nature's style decree,
The trees now don their finery;
And when arrayed in finest greens,
They put to shame our crêpe de chines.
—Gordon Howard

To Knute Rockne

Another reason why you have not died:
You are so resolute, so lacking fear,
That Death in his great house has frowned and said,
"Come, come! You can't stay here!"
—Estelle Rooks

IN LIGHTER VEIN

Confession

Last night I said I loved you,
Because I felt that way;
But this is even stranger:
I feel the same today.
　　　　—EVELYNE LOVE COOPER

Modern

"Do you love me, dear?" he cried
But feared a cold rejection.
"Of course I do," the maid replied,
"Why make *you* an exception?"
　　　　—EVELYNE LOVE COOPER

Winter

Dear sir, you've got the rheumatiz,
I fear you're growing old.
Your days are numbered, there's no hope,
You'll perish, with the cold.

　　　　—MARJORIE DeGRAFF

With Sympathy

The crowds must be an awful strain
Upon an empty subway train,
For when it comes into the station
It groans with grim anticipation.
　　　　—ALICE LEVY

Evaporation

Love is like tomato soup
Delicious when it's hot,
But losing all its flavor
As it cools off in the pot.
　　　　—ROSALIE MAHER

SUGGESTIONS

Now you write a quatrain packed with loveliness. If you have not something in your own heart just now, or if your notebook yields no fertile suggestion, perhaps you may find the germ of a poem in some idea below. Use also the suggestions under "The Couplet." Your imagination has not exhausted that list.

Deserted houses　　Empty lots　　Faces in the subway　　A stoker's hands　　A surgeon's hands　　Tenderness　　Radio　　Lights from windows　　Fog　　Jest　　Flight　　Silent wings　　Whim　　Orchard bloom　　Adventure　　Counting song　　Running song　　Dishwashing　　Desire　　Little human experiences: smiles, tears, pleasure at a gift, effect of absence　　Surprise　　A fleeting moment　　A dramatic moment　　A contrast　　A paradox　　Unsatisfied yearning　　A dream that flowers　　A longing　　A vision you hold　　Regret for a mistake　　Disappointment in what promised happiness　　Happiness in what promised disappointment

The simplest things are the loveliest. Let your expression be simple.

In writing your quatrains you may use the block form in which the first word of every line begins on the margin set by the first word of the poem, just as you wrote your couplet:

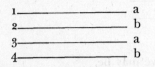

1————————— a
2————————— b
3————————— a
4————————— b

or you may indent. In prose you indent the first line of a paragraph. Rhyme governs the indention of poetry. Lines which rhyme together after the first line are equally indented.

1————————— a
2 ——————— b
3———————— c
4 ——————— b

Because 2 and 4 (above) are rhymed they are indented.

1————————— a
2 ——————— b
3 ——————— b
4———————— a

Because 2 and 3 (above) are rhymed they are indented; because 4 rhymes with 1 it has the same marginal beginning as 1.

When your quatrain is complete go over it carefully to see that it satisfies you artistically. Do your sentences fit neatly into the form with pleasant little surprises? Be sure that they do not all close at the end of the line. Perhaps the quatrain is one rich sentence.

If, however, you feel that your instrument needs tuning first, complete the lines below:

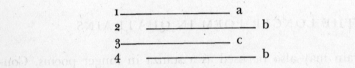

Down the fields of autumn   a   /./././.
   Over fields of flame   b   /././
—————————————   c   /./././.
—————————————   b   /././

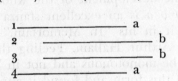

Lady, lady, listen: a   /././././.
———— I have to sell   b   /././
—————————————   c   /./././.
—————————————   b   /././

I met a fairy dressed in gold

One evening by the { river
                     lake
                     water

_____

_____

If you should ask how love may be,
I'd ask how stars may shine

_____

_____

THE LONGER POEM IN QUATRAINS

The quatrain may also be used as a stanza in longer poems. Continuity is established through repeating the pattern, each successive stanza contributing to the development of the whole poem and the large outer pattern. *a b b a* is an excellent stanza form for longer poems. Tennyson used it in his "In Memoriam," commemorating the death of his friend Arthur Hallam. Feeling that the jingle of alternate rhymes would be monotonous and not in keeping with his sorrow, he decided upon this form and found it appropriate for continuous varying effects. You see it is a couplet split by another couplet. This form is sometimes called the In Memoriam quatrain.

Because Omar Khayyám made a great poem in stanzas of the form *a a b a* this form is sometimes referred to as the Omar quatrain.

The most usual stanza quatrains are perhaps *a b c b* or *a b a b*.

In the poem of two or more quatrains you have a better opportunity for subtle balancing of varied sentences than you had in the couplet as a stanza pattern. It should give you pleasure to fit your sentences into the quatrain form with surprising variety. The sentences will not all end with the close of the line. The sentences fitted into stanza 2 will not fit in exactly the same way as those of stanza 1. The arranging of sentences to fit the form is like putting together the pieces of a puzzle to fit the form. Do not make a habit of filling the quatrain form this way:

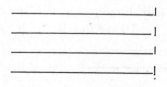

Rather fill the form like this:

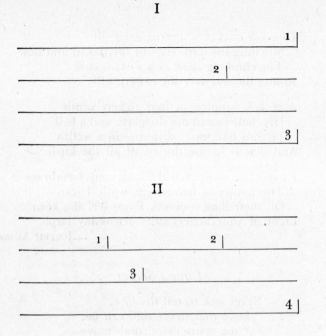

II

veliest of trees, the cherry now
 hung with bloom along the bough, ·
nd stands about the woodland ride
earing white for Eastertide.

ow, of my threescore years and ten,
wenty will not come again,
nd take from seventy springs a score,
 only leaves me fifty more.

nd since to look at things in bloom
ifty springs are little room,
bout the woodlands I will go
o see the cherry hung with snow.

—A. E. HOUSMAN

XXXIX

'Tis time, I think, by Wenlock town
 The golden broom should blow;
The hawthorn sprinkled up and down
 Should charge the land with snow.

Spring will not wait the loiterer's time
 Who keeps so long away;
So others wear the broom and climb
 The hedgerows heaped with may.

Oh tarnish late on Wenlock Edge,
 Gold that I never see;
Lie long, high snowdrifts in the hedge
 That will not shower on me.

—A. E. HOUSMAN

Touch

I hear a cricket at my window sill
  Stitching the dark edge of the dawn; and now
  The climbing siren of a distant cow
Rouses the sun over the eastern hill.

A cock is rapping in four rickety words
  His challenge to the sluggard; and a bell
  Jargons like water dripping in a well;
And dew is in the throats of all the birds.

I need but outstretched hands and I embrace
  The luxury of leaves: yet, while I lean
  On their long coolness, I can feel the keen
Light of your fingers drift across my face!
—JOSEPH AUSLANDER

Love's Secret

Never seek to tell thy love,
  Love that never told can be;
For the gentle wind doth move
  Silently, invisibly.

I told my love, I told my love,
  I told her all my heart,
Trembling, cold, in ghastly fears:—
  Ah! she did depart.

Soon after she was gone from me
  A traveller came by,
Silently, invisibly:
  He took her with a sigh.
—WILLIAM BLAKE

Sometimes

Across the fields of yesterday
  He sometimes comes to me,
A little lad just back from play—
  The lad I used to be.

And yet he smiles so wistfully
  Once he has crept within,
I wonder if he hopes to see
  The man I might have been.
—THOMAS S. JONES, JR.

La Belle Dame Sans Merci

O what can ail thee, knight-at-arms,
  Alone and palely loitering?
The sedge has wither'd from the lake
  And no birds sing.

O what can ail thee, knight-at-arms!
  So haggard and so woe-begone?
The squirrel's granary is full,
  And the harvest's done.

I see a lily on thy brow
  With anguish moist and fever-dew,
And on thy cheeks a fading rose
  Fast withereth too.

I met a lady in the meads,
  Full beautiful—a faery's child,
Her hair was long, her foot was light,
  And her eyes were wild.

I made a garland for her head,
  And bracelets too, and fragrant zone;
She look'd at me as she did love,
  And made sweet moan.

I set her on my pacing steed
  And nothing else saw all day long,
For sidelong would she bend, and sing
  A faery's song.

She found me roots of relish sweet,
  And honey wild and manna-dew,
And sure in language strange she said
  "I love thee true."

She took me to her elfin grot,
  And there she wept and sigh'd full sore;
And there I shut her wild wild eyes
  With kisses four.

And there she lullèd me asleep,
  And there I dream'd—Ah! woe betide!
The latest dream I ever dream'd
  On the cold hill's side.

I saw pale kings and princes too,
  Pale warriors, death-pale were they all:
They cried—"La Belle Dame sans Merci
  Hath thee in thrall!"

I saw their starved lips in the gloam
  With horrid warning gapèd wide,
And I awoke and found me here
  On the cold hill's side.

And this is why I sojourn here
  Alone and palely loitering,
Though the sedge is wither'd from the lake,
  And no birds sing.

              —JOHN KEATS

The Dark Song

She was sitting quiet
  In the quiet sun,
When suddenly she knew
  Her darkness had begun.

She was in the sunlight
  With fruit in her lap,
And light lay in her
  Like a golden sap.

Sitting where a sunlight
  Poured like wine
Through little young leaves
  Of a trumpet vine,

And stems like dark rivers,
  Staining the sun—
She knew, the way they widened,
  That darkness had begun.

Everything was fading
  In a gray blur,
And the sun and the trees
  Were growing dead to her.

Veils were spreading
  Over her eyes,
And she heard herself moaning
  Little soft cries.

Dark was stepping
  Into her mind.
Little soft cries
  Told her she was blind.

"I am blind. I am blind."
  And the rock of her chair
Was a slow chanting rhythm
  Sighing in the air.

"I am blind and the darkness
  Covers me;
Yet I think I touch the sun
  I cannot see.

"I think the sun is sifting
  Through the little leaves,
And the boughs make a music
  Over the eaves.

"And the wind is moving
  Over my hair—
It is like the hand
  Of a lover there.

"I can hear the grass creep;
  I can hear a bird
Draw the thinnest frailest note
  I have ever heard.

Here I am sitting
  In a cool dark,
With a thing in me
  Beautiful and stark;

With a thing in me
  That is a relief.
Oh, the many nights I hid
  My sorrow like a thief!

'All my nights a whisper,
  'Blind—soon blind!'
Lay unspoken in my heart,
  Buried from my kind.

'I could not tell my mother;
  The look in her eyes
Would be like a stricken thing
  That suddenly dies.

'I could not tell people
  Who cared for me,
And then be haunted by their eyes
  When I couldn't see.

"I hid it. I was furtive
  And heavy with this grief.
And now I am beautiful
  With relief.

"I think I can sit here
  Forever and ever.
I think I know a dark peace
  Clean of endeavor.

"I can sit here, quiet
  As I was before,
And listen to the wind flow
  Over the floor.

"I can feel the garden
  In its first bloom.
I can feel my mother
  In the next room.

"I can sit and listen
  To the clock on the shelf.
I can think little things
  To myself.

"I can listen to the clock—
  Tick, tick, tick—
Pierce the smooth silence
  With a star's prick.

"I can sit forever
  Still as can be,
Touched with darkness
  Fearlessly."

She sat in the sunlight
  With her hands folded.
The smile on her lips lay
  Peacefully molded.

She was breathing deeply,
  Carefully, there,
When her mother's full voice
  Sprang into the air:

"I am tired, Helen—
  It's nearly time for tea.
Helen, just see the time
  There for me."

Mother's voice, rich,
  And tall as a chime.
Mother's voice, "Helen,
  Just see the time."

She rose and the fruit fell
  Bumping on the floor.
She rose, and there was nothing
  Behind or before.

She rose and faced a darkness
  Clean as a stone,
And the clock was buried
  In a dark of its own.
                              —SHIRLEY BROWNRIGG

The quatrain form above is the most common stanza pattern for the ballad. The ballad, as you know, is a narrative poem, one that embodies a story or an incident. The old ballads sung by the minstrels dealt with death, feuds, love, intrigue, heroism—the elemental things that concerned primitive life. Invariably they were colored by superstition, and a note of tragedy often set the key. "Sir Patrick Spens," "The Twa Corbies," "Lord Randal," and the Robin Hood ballads are such familiar ballads.

In the ballads there is frequent repetition. The stanzas often add a line or two, making the overflow stanzas, as they are called, five or even six lines long. Those old ballads are supposed to be the expression of "unpremeditated art." And so they carry imperfections that mark folk poetry: wrenched accent, imperfect rhyme. Later poets have developed artistic ballads; that is, they consciously shaped them, using the old form and the old devices, even archaic words for archaic effect. Notable among the artistic type are "La Belle Dame Sans Merci" above; "The Pied Piper of Hamelin Town" by Browning; "The Rime of the Ancient Mariner" by Coleridge. In our own generation Edna St. Vincent Millay has created "The Ballad of the Harp Weaver," and Shirley Brownrigg, a very young poet, "The Dark Song" above—all in this quatrain pattern, some with the overflow stanza, elements of the supernatural, and the minor key of tragedy.

Not all ballads assume this form. Leonora Speyer did not use it for her "Ballad of Old Doc Higgins," which you may read on page 236, nor did Alfred Noyes for "The Highwayman," known and loved by every high-school pupil. But if you decide to write a ballad, it is the stanza that most likely will be best suited to your first experiment.

STUDENT VERSE IN QUATRAINS

Frost

A yellow leaf I saw last night
  Is like a distant star,
All silver brushed and crispy-white
  And daintier by far.

And where I step, the blue-white ground
  Crackles beneath my feet,
With nothing else to make a sound
  When frost and autumn meet.

—ESTELLE ROOKS

Beyond the Dunes

Here the dunes end,
    White gulls soar,
Singing high grass
    And one thing more—

Far and blue
    Where gulls are less:
A lone, unquiet
    Nothingness

That moans and tosses
    In passion—pain,
And then, exhausted,
    Sleeps again.

The hills of sea
    Keep coming on.
It does not matter
    That love is gone.

This sound drowns out
    A lover's name,
And memory
    Is quenched-out flame.

Blue waters' rush,
    Blue waters' fall,
This is enough
    And this is all.

Contentment lives
    Beyond a dune,
Sometimes a hazy
    Orange moon

To strew the sea
    With lazy gold,—
Oh, I'd be happy
    Growing old!
        —MURIEL F. HOCHDORF

To——

I have no soul; this evening I
Went walking down the long, dark sky,
And sleepy stars bade me "Hello,"
And asked me where I'd like to go.

"I'd like to see the moon," I said,
    (I did not know the moon was dead),
"And, oh, what shall I do, to wear
The ring of Saturn in my hair?"

I had my heavy soul with me,
But dropped it on a lilac tree,
And then I laughed, and sang and ran
Up where the milky way began.

And gathered stars to use for light,
And flung a kiss to the young god, Night,
Until the cold, white Dawn appeared
And brought this loneliness I feared.
        —GEORGIA H. COOPER

A Garden of Posies

I shall have a little house,
    On a crooked hill,
Where a million songs shall bloom
    Beneath my window-sill.

Fragrant songs, some soft, some bright
    Shot with rays of sun.
And my dreams shall water them,
    Not forgetting one.

Then, perhaps, when I am dull,
    Longing for a tune,
I'll pluck a single tiny bud,
    And hurl it to the moon.
        —GEORGIA H. COOPER

Reflections on a Sunday Morning

This cloudy sky above my April window
Has seen fresh blossoms that each new year brings
Because all flowers laugh and live one season
And so do we, and other living things.

So I shall spend today in some grand forest,
Where tall trees sway, and windy branches press
Upward and *up*, and if I die tonight,
I will have had my share of loveliness.

—ESTELLE ROOKS

Tribute—A Year Too Late

When I was up at Andree,
My eyes were always blind
To the curling grasses, tangled
By the fingers of the wind.

I never lay awake to hear
The sleepy song of rain
That murmurs low of nothingness
And hushes ghosts of pain.

I never saw the gold-eyed men
At dusk in every tree,
And the leaves were always talking
But they never talked to me.

Oh, I wear a mocking smile in town,
But to-night I hurried by
A field where crickets come to talk
For fear that I would cry.

At night the hills came closer,
And twilight was a sound
That everyone but me could hear
For miles and miles around.

The moon was a crumpled leaf blown
Against the midnight's breast—
Because I did not see it then,
It will not let me rest.

—MURIEL F. HOCHDORF

IN LIGHTER VEIN

A Would-Be Poet

Shall I write a sour rhyme
Or should I make it sweet?
Can it have three-quarter time
And must it have a beat?

I'd like to make a poem, dear,
Written just for you.
Trouble is an engineer
Can't be a rhymster too.

—CONSTANCE STERN

To B. C.

We said goodbye, 'tis true,
We both agreed to part—
And yet I don't feel blue
I have no broken heart.

I go about my way
And think of it no more;
I still feel young and gay—
It happened twice before.

—EVELYNE LOVE COOPER

CHAPTER VIII

SOME TERMS CLARIFIED

WERE it not for the limitations of book making, this chapter would not appear. In the natural course of his development the apprentice to the craft of poetry would ask the questions here raised. Then, and only then, would they be answered, in so far as there is an answer. What is beauty? What is art? What is spontaneous expression? What constitutes emotion? What is this pleasure that poetry should give? What is universality?

What is Beauty? We will not rush in where angels fear to tread, attempting to answer a question that philosophers have spent their lives debating. But perhaps no one ever attempted to write poetry or even to appreciate poetry without asking this question, if not with his lips certainly with his heart.

Every eye forms its own beauty. The young girl in a garden of roses will pluck a bud and holding it at arm's length exclaim, "Isn't it beautiful!" The straight, uncompromising lines of the Empire State building are beautiful to the modern architect. The surgeon who has removed the bandage from the place of an incision in a severe operation, seeing the white scar, commends the skill of his hands. "It's a beautiful wound," he says. The youngster versed in mechanics, lays his hand lovingly on his greasy black motor. To him it is a thing of beauty. Some peculiar insight, makes the motor, the rose bud, the Empire State building, the gleaming wound appeal to each of those temperaments. According to the nature of his insight each is impressed. The thing is familiar to him; significant; dear. It is beautiful. The beauty is in his own heart.

> Earth was not earth until her sons appeared,
> Nor Beauty Beauty ere Young Love was born.
> —GEORGE MEREDITH

Now, if he who has thus felt beauty can transfer this feeling through some artistic medium: sound, marble or paint, words, he has created artistic beauty. If the poet can so communicate his feeling toward life or any moment of life as to incite the same feeling in a sensitive reader —a reader who has taste and insight—he has created beauty. Out of this same moment every temperament versed in the craft might create a separate work of art.

The beauty which the poet creates is of a two-fold nature: of the substance and the form. His insight or mood has shown him the substance; his craft, the manner of his utterance, must translate the substance into a work of art. His creation is the result of a more complex process than that of the surgeon or the girl in the rose garden or the boy with the motor. He must distil the beauty of things and transfer delight in them to the reader out of a re-created thing of blended words.

If he be a romanticist he will seek beauty in that which uplifts the heart, transports it beyond the miserable present. He will lift you on a magic carpet out into "the light that never was on sea or land, the consecration, and the Poet's dream."

If he be a realist he will represent intense moments of life, so that you may weep "afresh love's long since cancell'd woe," as truth to reality calls forth the experience from its sleep in the tomb. "Beauty is truth, truth beauty." He will give you a glimpse of what you have not had courage enough to look upon with naked sight; what you have ceased to delight in or even see, because it has grown so familiar.

You may doubt at times that you are glimpsing beauty. But by its effects you shall know it. Beauty finds its way to the heart. We *feel* beauty. Its effect is pleasure.

But many a great poem—or what time has pronounced a great poem —wrings the heart, or fires our indignation, or fills us with horror. Is such an effect pleasurable? Let us see.

All human beings are more alike than they are different by appearance, by nature, by experience. It is in the common experience to love, to work, to suffer, to endure, to sacrifice, to aspire and finally to die. This likeness creates among human beings a bond of understanding, which though light as air is as strong as links of iron. Many complex elements may enter human consciousness to modify this understanding, but fundamentally we all understand another's feelings in the presence of death, at disappointment, in success, in struggle, in happiness, and so on. If we have not known these experiences actually ourselves, we have glimpsed them about us or we have known them through reading.

When the reader of poetry is moved through the horror, the irony of a situation, the injustice of circumstance, or the like, he is moved through sympathy for his human kin. This feeling of sympathy, which implies understanding of feeling, is pleasurable. We enjoy the tragedies of Shakespeare; we go to the motion pictures and have a good time weeping.

Through its form a poem may give esthetic pleasure besides emotional pleasure: "I've often felt just that way but never could express it like that"; "That is exactly what I think"; "Isn't that a beautiful poem!" are expressions that show we have been moved to pleasure. This feeling of pleasure is the effect of glimpsing beauty of some sort, beauty as the romanticist means it, or beauty as the realist means it. The more one knows of beauty the more beauty one will find, and therefore the more intense will be his pleasure.

The greatest poetry is likely to have as its substance that which touches the human experiences common to all mankind. Thus it makes what is called a universal appeal. Poems which deal with the fundamental, the elemental, are universal in their appeal. The beauty of poetry is elevated to the sublime when it impresses the spirit of man with the vastness, the power, the awfulness or the mystery of life. The Grand Canyon; the silence of death; the gigantic machine destroying to create; the firmament; the speed of a comet through space; the great unknown are subjects that may fill the soul with a sense of awe. When our brother out on the sea is overcome at the rhythmic endlessness of space, our heart understands.

But besides the fundamental likenesses in human beings there are fundamental differences. Temperament and insight will vary the response of readers as they vary the materials out of which the poet shapes his work of art. When a poem appeals to differences rather than to likenesses in the human race it is less universal but certainly none the less beautiful for its limited appeal.

It is ridiculous to suppose that a poem must appeal to everyone in the world to be a fine poem. So if all do not wax sympathetic over your artistic efforts, be of good cheer. The wound was beautiful to the surgeon; the greasy motor to the young mechanic. Robert Frost makes a strong appeal to those who understand New England and the New England mind, to those whose imagination responds to subtleties in the music of human speech; Edna St. Vincent Millay strikes a responsive chord in the heart of those who admire her impudence and those who exult in living. Those who delight in the music of words enjoy Coleridge and Swinburne. Understanding and temperament limit our likes and our dislikes. Pleasure which a poem may give will vary also with the purpose of the poem. A reader may enjoy the color, the truth, the force, the sheer music, the form of a poem, the magical use of words, or all of these things.

What are fit subjects to inspire pleasure? Any subject, any experience which you can handle with sympathy and imagination is a fit subject. The only subjects unfit would be those that evoke loathing or disgust, if enjoyment is your aim. Your insight and your taste can be the only guides to the selection of material. Since you are creating a work of art, the manner of your utterance should lift your experience above fact and invest it with the truth of your own mood. As your work genuinely interprets or suggests or re-creates a moment of life, you have created genuine beauty. An intense moment of life has stirred your imagination and with words and the music of sound you have solidified the impression. This stirs the reader's imagination to realize this moment. He is moved. His emotions are touched.

Here, perhaps, we should distinguish between genuine emotion and sentimentality in art. This poem makes a strong emotional appeal; that one is sentimental. There is an old saying, "She is too sweet to be wholesome." Any feeling carried to excess is unwholesome. When the verse maker dissipates his sympathies—bestows them without restraint, that is, when his feeling is uncontrolled by his mind or his expression, he is too sweet to be wholesome. When he shows lack of discrimination by bestowing his sympathy or his affection on something that has not the spiritual quality to deserve such feeling, he is too sweet to be wholesome—he is sentimental. His emotion, being evoked by something unworthy of it, is false. When a woman bestows on a lap dog the attentions due to a child we feel that she is sentimental.

The Mock Turtle of *Alice in Wonderland* sings "Turtle Soup" in a voice sometimes choked with sobs,

Beautiful Soup, so rich and green,
Waiting in a hot tureen!
Who for such dainties would not stoop?
Soup of the evening, beautiful Soup!
Soup of the evening, beautiful Soup!
  Beau-ootiful Soo-oop!
  Beau-ootiful Soo-oop!
Soo-oop of the e-e-evening.
  Beautiful, beautiful Soup!

Beautiful Soup! Who cares for fish,
Game, or any other dish?
Who would not give all else for two p
ennyworth only of beautiful Soup
Pennyworth only of beautiful Soup
  Beau-ootiful Soo-ôop!
  Beau-ootiful Soo-oop!
Soo-oop of the e-e-evening,
  Beautiful, beauti-FUL SOUP!

But a mock turtle is privileged to grow sentimental over beautiful soup!

Perhaps you have sung the lyric below. How vividly the images speak the lover's heart. And how much more is meant than is actually expressed.

O my Luve's like a red, red rose
That's newly sprung in June;
O my Luve's like the melodie
That's sweetly play'd in tune.

As fair art thou, my bonnie lass,
So deep in luve am I:
And I will luve thee still, my dear,
Till a' the seas gang dry:

Till a' the seas gang dry, my dear,
    And the rocks melt wi' the sun;
I will luve thee still, my dear,
    While the sands o' life shall run.

And fare thee weel, my only Luve!
    And fare thee weel awhile!
And I will come again, my Luve,
    Tho' it were ten thousand mile.
                    —ROBERT BURNS (1759-1796)

What popular love lyrics, sung over the radio, are poetry as genuine? Do you remember some that you would call sentimental? Some that you enjoy for the music rather than for the words?

Like the news reporter, the poet should not comment. He should present images. They will speak his feeling; through the imagination they will touch the listener's heart. Vague nouns, trite adjectives, "dear old's" and "sweet old's" will not supply imaginative deficiencies.

Professor Allan Abbott of Columbia University has devised an excellent scheme for testing a reader's ability to sense a true poem from a poor one. He gives four versions of a poem: the true poem, and the true poem treated sentimentally, prosaically, and unrhythmically. Everyone interested in poetry would do well to take the complete test; then, when he has made a study of poetry, to take a second. A leaf from the complete test is reprinted on page 124. You will have no difficulty in finding the sentimental version.

Sentimental treatment is like wearing the heart on the sleeve. It can create no tremendous effect, such as that of controlled passion: the cry of pain that is choked back; the service of those who stand and wait.

Keep back the one word more,
Nor give of your whole store;
For it may be, in Art's sole hour of need
Lacking that word, you shall be poor indeed.
                    —LIZETTE WOODWARD REESE

This is the advice of a true poet and teacher who practices restraint in her own work as she urges the need of discipline in the art of her pupils.

On the other hand an emotion may be genuine enough, the cause of it may be worthy, but the expression may be inadequate. In other words, the technique may make the emotion seem false. If the words and the movement of the rhythm are not in keeping with the nature of the substance the incongruity evokes laughter instead of tears. A

Read the poems, A, B, C, D, trying to think how they would sound if read aloud. Write "Best" on the dotted line above the one you like best as poetry.

SET 3. TO A SEA SHELL

A (..............)

Sea Shell, please sing me a song
Of ships and sailor-men;
Of strange kinds of birds and tree
On the Spanish Main:
Of fish and seaweed in the sea,
And whatever creature there may be,—
Sea Shell, please sing me a song!

B (..............)

Sea Shell, Sea Shell,
Sing me a song, Oh please!
A song of ships and sailor men,
Of parrots and tropical trees.
Of islands lost in the Spanish Main
Which no man ever may find again,
Of fishes and coral under the waves,
And sea-horses stabled in great green caves—
Sea Shell, Sea Shell
Sing me a song, Oh please!

C (..............)

Tender, tender Sea Shell,
Wilt thou sing me, please,
Of thy happy, happy home
'Neath the tropic trees?
Ah, the coral islands!
Ah, the wondrous fish!
For such a song I'd give thee, dear,
Whate'er a Shell could wish.

D (..............)

Sea Shell, I ask you will
You sing a song, please.
All about the ships and sailors
And the parrots in their tropical trees.
The islands I have read about on the Spanish Main
That no one will see again,
The fish and coral under the wave,
Sea horses that have their stables in caves;
Sea Shell, I ask you will
You sing a song, please.

large thought or a profound theme cramped into inappropriate form, like six-foot Willie in his little brother's coat, is funny.

> Jenny poisoned mamma's tea
> Mamma died in agonee
> Papa was quite cross and vexed
> "Jenny, my child," he said, "what next!"

With so much about restraint in artistic expression how can there be any spontaneity in poetry? Poetasters, who do not like the drudgery of discipline, bend the meaning of that word "spontaneity" to suit their own clumsy efforts. "That is the way the poem came to me," they will say. "There isn't another word that will take the place of the words I have used. I can't change it; it is just as I felt when I wrote it."

There is no art without discipline. If there is awkwardness in a line, it means that the maker is spontaneously a clumsy craftsman; not that his work is spontaneously beautiful. The wild strawberry over the wall has a charm that the cultivated garden fruit may lack. But if we reduce the wild strawberry to poetry we may have a difficult time taming words to its wildness. The *actual* wild strawberry is natural; poetry is art. If the wild strawberry *seems* natural in a poem, if the charm of its wildness is felt, the poem is spontaneous. In the highest sense of the word, to be spontaneous is to be free of all blemishes, to be new, yet inevitable. "The beauty of art is to conceal art." Strained effects, illogical development, repetitions, unpleasant sounds, slovenly rhyming, trite imagery, lack of imagination, may be the result of a first writing of a poem; but they are not art. They may be the clumsy work of a clumsy artisan; but there is little beauty in what calls attention to its blemishes. And a poem must be a creation of beauty.

Great masters have shown us how critically they examine their work; how they revise; how they develop their art with experience. There is no severer critic of himself than a genuine poet. Because he is an artist he burns with the artist's desire for perfection. Furthermore, "There is a pleasure in poetic pains that only poets know."

This bending of materials in which they work to the laws of the craft has evoked many exquisite passages. You saw how that was so, in Keats's line, "Yet did I never breathe its pure serene." Some of the revisions reproduced here should speak more forcefully for spontaneity than any arguments of lesser voices. To see the first drafts of a poet's manuscript is to see his mind at work. Ponder those reproduced on pages 127, 128, and 129.

Having seen Keats's revisions of "The Eve of St. Agnes," you may be interested in the remarks of his contemporary and friend, Leigh Hunt, editor of *The Examiner*.

Let the student of poetry observe, that in all the luxury of "The Eve of St. Agnes" there is nothing of the conventional craft of artificial writers; no heaping up of words or similes for their own sake or for the rhyme's sake; no gaudy common-places; no borrowed airs of earnestness; no tricks of inversion; no substitution of reading or of ingenious thoughts for feeling or spontaneity; no irrelevancy or unfitness of any sort. All flows out of sincerity and passion . . .

Subsequent editions of a poet's work are also often illuminating. The changes included are frequently the result of artistic growth in the years between.

Rossetti's "Blessed Damozel" as it appeared in *The Germ* in 1850 shows the need of the artist's touch.

> The blessed damozel leaned out
>   From the gold bar of heaven;
> *Her blue deep eyes were deeper much*
>   *Than a deep water, even.*
> She had three lilies in her hand,
>   And the stars in her hair were seven.

In *Poems* published in 1870 note the revision:

> *Her eyes were deeper than the depth*
>   *Of waters stilled at even.*

Walt Whitman's "Out of the Cradle Endlessly Rocking" is a magical revision of his first title, "Out of the Rocked Cradle."

In the *Craft of Poetry* Clement Wood tells how he revised his poem, "Winter Laughter." His exposition, headed "A Poem Criticized," is one of the most valuable contributions of a delightful book. Poe describes how he planned and wrote "The Raven" in his *Philosophy of Composition*. In *Convention and Revolt*, John Livingston Lowes gives instances of magical revisions, all of which prove that some of the artistry of the inspired poet is *conscious*. The vague thing called inspiration, for which some of our procrastinators sit down to wait, seems to hover about the alert craftsman. Indeed it is a common belief among artists that any work of art is nine-tenths perspiration and one-tenth inspiration.

Anyway, the labors of our most spontaneous poets should encourage and inspire all who would follow beauty and capture her moods in the meshes of verbal music.

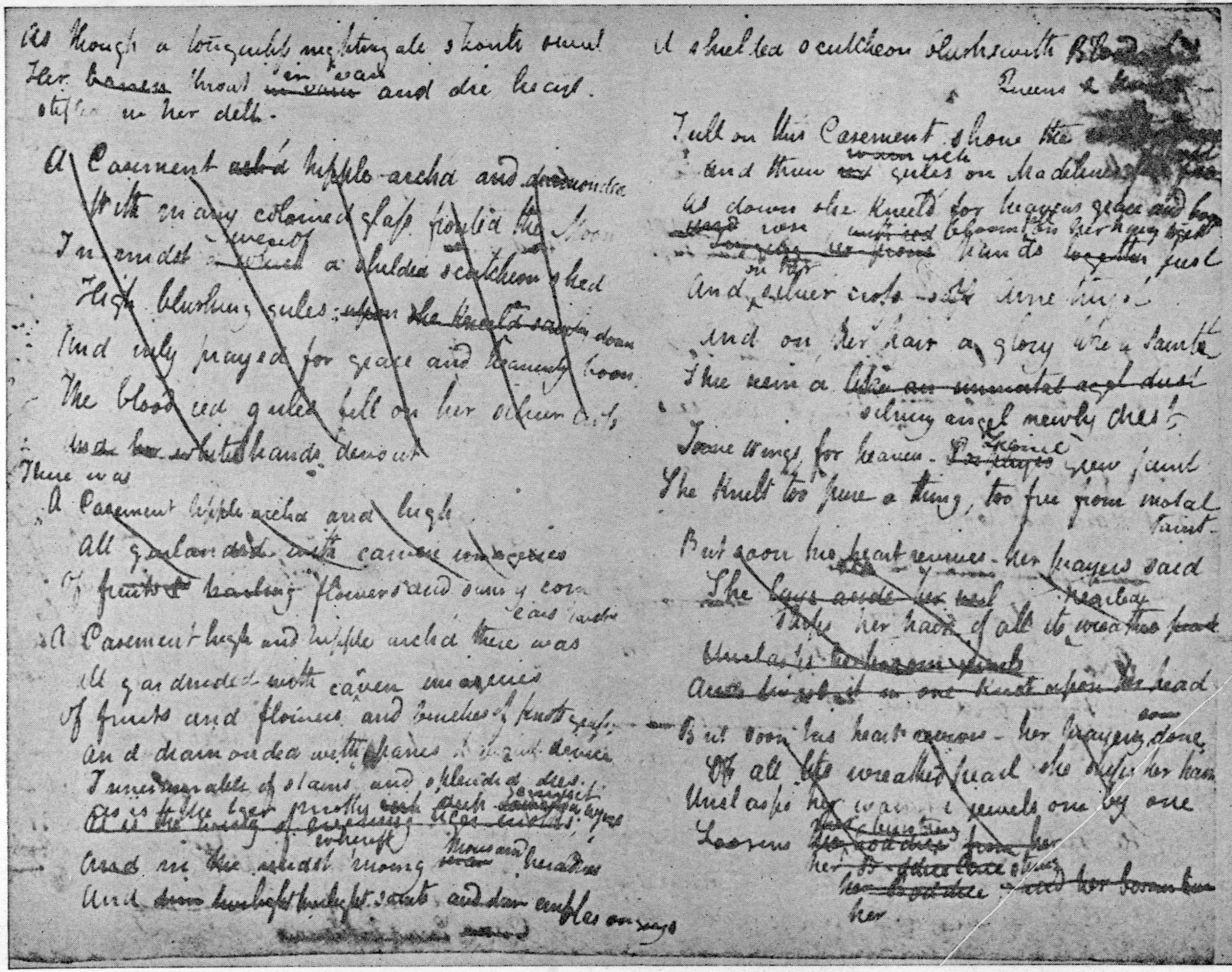

Two Pages of the First Draft of "The Eve of St. Agnes"

On the first looking into Chapman's Homer

Much have I travell'd in the Realms of Gold, ——
And many goodly States, and Kingdoms seen;
Round many Western islands have I been
Which Bards in fealty to Apollo hold. —
Of one wide expanse had I been told, —
Which deep brow'd Homer ruled as his Demesne;
Yet could I never judge what Men could mean
Till I heard Chapman speak out loud and bold. —
Then felt I like some Watcher of the Skies —
When a new Planet swims into his Ken,
Or like stout Cortez, when with wond'ring eyes
He star'd at the Pacific, and all his Men
Look'd at each other with a wild surmise —
Silent upon a Peak in Darien —

FIRST DRAFT OF THE SONNET "ON FIRST LOOKING INTO CHAPMAN'S HOMER"

Forescene.

The Overworld

Enter the Spirit & Chorus of the Years, the Spirit & Chorus
of the Pities, the Spirit of the Earth, the Spirits Sinister &
Ironic with their Choruses, ~~Chorus & Sinister Spirit~~, minor Spirits, Spirit-messengers
& Recording Angels.

Spirit of the Earth

What of the Immanent Will & Its designs?

Spirit of the Years.

It works unconsciously, as heretofore,
Eternal artistries in Circumstance,
Whose patterns, planned by rapt aesthetic rote,
Seem in themselves Its single listless aim,
And not their consequence.

Chorus of the Pities (aerial music.)

Still thus? Still thus? ~~Still thus?~~
                    ever
~~For aye~~ unconscious!
              An automatic sense ¶ Unweeting why or whence?
Then be the inevitable, as of old,
Although that so it be we dare not hold!

A PAGE FROM THE MANUSCRIPT OF "THE DYNASTS" BY THOMAS HARDY

SOMETHING TO DO

1. Below is a poem and part of another by the same poet. Both suggest beauty of an entirely different nature. Discover what contributes to the delicacy of the first; the sublimity of the second.

To a Snowflake

What heart could have thought you?—
Past our devisal
(O filigree petal!)
Fashioned so purely,
Fragilely, surely,
From what Paradisal
Imagineless metal,
Too costly for cost?
Who hammered you, wrought you,
From argentine vapour?—
"God was my shaper.
Passing surmisal,
He hammered, He wrought me,
From curled silver vapour,
To lust of his mind:—
Thou couldst not have thought me!
So purely, so palely,
Tinily, surely,
Mightily, frailly,
Insculped and embossed,
With His hammer of wind,
And His graver of frost."

—FRANCIS THOMPSON

The Hound of Heaven

I fled Him, down the nights and down the days;
  I fled Him, down the arches of the years;
I fled Him, down the labyrinthine ways
  Of my own mind; and in the mist of tears
I hid from Him, and under running laughter.
        Up vistaed hopes I sped;
        And shot, precipitated,
Adown Titanic glooms of chasmèd fears,
From those strong Feet that followed, followed after.
        But with unhurrying chase,
        And unperturbèd pace,

> Deliberate speed, majestic instancy,
>   They beat—and a Voice beat
>   More instant than the Feet—
> 'All things betray thee, who betrayest Me.'
> —FRANCIS THOMPSON

2. Thomas Hardy defined art as "the secret of how to produce by a false thing the effect of a true." Go through the poems or passages reprinted in this chapter and show how his definition applies.

3. Coventry Patmore believed that beauty of association is superior to the beauty of aspect, and a beloved relative's old battered tankard to the finest Greek vase. What poems can you find to support this belief? How does the poet communicate his feeling?

4. "The business of the poet and novelist is to show the sorriness underlying the grandest things, and the grandeur underlying the sorriest things." Is this the realist's point of view or the romanticist's? What modern poets have shown the sorriness underlying the grandest things? Read a passage aloud.

5. Read the poem, "When I was one-and-twenty," and answer the questions below it.

> When I was one-and-twenty
>   I heard a wise man say,
> "Give crowns and pounds and guineas
>   But not your heart away;
> Give pearls away and rubies
>   But keep your fancy free."
> But I was one-and-twenty,
>   No use to talk to me.
>
> When I was one-and-twenty
>   I heard him say again,
> "The heart out of the bosom
>   Was never given in vain;
> 'Tis paid with sighs a plenty
>   And sold for endless rue."
> And I am two-and-twenty,
>   And oh, 'tis true, 'tis true.
> —A. E. HOUSMAN

How do you know that two-and-twenty has brought "endless rue"? Does he say it has? What value has the restraint of those last lines?

6. Discuss the universality of this poem:

To Sleep

A flock of sheep that leisurely pass by
One after one; the sound of rain, and bees
Murmuring; the fall of rivers, winds and seas,
Smooth fields, white sheets of water, and pure sky;

I've thought of all by turns, and yet do lie
Sleepless; and soon the small birds' melodies
Must hear, first utter'd from my orchard trees,
And the first cuckoo's melancholy cry.

Even thus last night, and two nights more I lay,
And could not win thee, Sleep! by any stealth:
So do not let me wear to-night away:

Without Thee what is all the morning's wealth?
Come, blessèd barrier between day and day,
Dear mother of fresh thoughts and joyous health!
                                —WILLIAM WORDSWORTH

Have you ever had the experience described? Is the form of the poem sufficiently dignified for the ideas treated? Note the line length, the choice of
words in relation to the subject "Sleep."

7. Find a poem that you feel is lacking in universal quality. To what type
of person might it appeal?

8. To what type of person does T. S. Eliot's *Ash Wednesday* appeal?
His *The Wasteland*? If you cannot answer these questions, remember the
name. In your leisure time you may care to look him up.

9. Account for the appeal of Stephen Foster's "Old Folks at Home" (Swanee
River) and "Old Black Joe"; of "God Save the King" to an Englishman;
"The Marseillaise" to a son of France; "America" and "The Star-Spangled
Banner" to an American; the flag of one's native land; the hurdy-gurdy's
voice in spring; a worn first shoe.

10. What is lost to a radio audience when a reader of poetry announces
neither the work from which he reads an excerpt nor the author of the lines?
A moment ago the first stanza of "Endymion" by John Keats was so read.

11. The effect of a genuine lyric may be spoiled by sentimental reading. The
catch in the throat and the tear in the voice of the reader are misplaced.
They should be where the *author* placed them: in the silence between the
lines. Explain.

12. Discuss songs or messages on greeting cards that do for the higher emotions what the mock turtle did for soup. What papa did when he learned that "Jenny poisoned mamma's tea."

13. Apply the principle, that incongruity is a basis of humor, by making a parody of familiar lines.

14. Prepare an appreciation—in prose—of an old master of poetry or of a new one. Let the thread of unity be: By his works you shall know him. What evidence do you find of his sensitiveness to life? To beauty? Of his artistry? What do you find of significance to you in his poetry? What magic lines? Is he an artist of one or of many moods? Illustrate through parts of poems or entire poems. Do not take literally as the experience of the author the personal experience embodied in his verse. Through his poetry the great artist unlocks the heart of man rather than his own heart.

LEST WE FORGET

1. Write a line which has a feminine ending.
2. Match it with a suitable one in rhyme.
3. List some commonplace things which hold for you the beauty of association.
4. Whenever a phrase or a line sings itself into your heart, jot it down in your notebook. Indicate that it is your own by the word *original* or by your signature. Otherwise, after a lapse of time you may forget whether it is yours.

  Always write the name of the author and the source of quotations which you keep.
5. The daily papers feature poets and poetry in various ways. Start a clipping bureau and see what riches you may amass. Many poets of the past are *still* news. And there are always our flesh and blood contemporaries!

CHAPTER IX

THE TERCET

ANOTHER brief form to try is the tercet. Any complete poem of three lines, rhymed or unrhymed, is a tercet. But the most artistic effect is created by a single binder for the three-line endings in the way of one rhyme. The tercet, called also triplet, has a lyric grace appropriate to the single pointed idea. It is not so commonly used as the quatrain. Lines may be all one length and any length or of various lengths. For such a brief form five feet should probably be the limit. A heavier line would hardly suit the fragility of so slight a thing.

The scheme is *a a a*. Examples follow:

God

I see Thee in the distant blue
But in the violet's dell of dew
Behold! I breathe and touch Thee too.
—JOHN B. TABB

On Burns

In whomsoe'er, since Poesy began,
A Poet most of all men we may scan,
Burns of all poets is the most a Man.
—DANTE GABRIEL ROSSETTI

Fragment

Adapted from the "Vita Nuova" of Dante

What Mary is when she a little smiles
I cannot even tell or call to mind,
It is a miracle so new, so rare.
—PERCY BYSSHE SHELLEY

TERCETS BY STUDENT VERSIFIERS

Dream Garden

The garden where dreams flower is far
Tucked behind a twinkling star.
Can it be that's where you are?
—ROSALIE MAHER

Past and Future

He's married well, you say? . . . I see . . .
God grant him happiness, and me
An unretaining memory.
—JOYCE LANCASTER

Wind-Wolf

Clouds move like sheep across the stretch of cold
Bleak pasture-land and frightened, huddle close
As though a wolf had howled outside the fold.
—Estelle Rooks

Continuous flow may be insured by using the tercet as a stanza form. Instances may be found in the works of almost any poet. Here are a few:

John's Wife

No, no, I shouldn't call old Esther mad,
Though she would seem to think at times her lad,
The one that died at Loos, is living yet.

Only the other night she set a plate
For him, and wondered why he should be late
For supper: but at whiles we all forget

The dead are dead. How could I carry on,
If I must always bear in mind that John
Will never cross the threshold any more?

Why, only now, if I must tell you true,
I heard a step, and . . . well, it wasn't you
That I ran down to welcome at the door.
—Wilfrid Wilson Gibson

Whenas in silks my Julia goes
Then, then (methinks) how sweetly flows
That liquefaction of her clothes.

Next, when I cast mine eyes and see
That brave vibration each way free;
O how that glittering taketh me!
—Robert Herrick

Fireflies in the Garden

Here come real stars to fill the upper skies,
And here on earth come emulating flies,
That though they never equal stars in size,
(And they were never really stars at heart)
Achieve at times a very star-like start.
Only, of course, they can't sustain the part.

—ROBERT FROST

In March

Three lovely things today
I saw beat back the wind,
The March wind's bitter play.

A crocus shivering up,
Timorous, tremulous, frail,
Offering wan Spring its cup.

A ship through rack and rout
Slipping to port ice-sheeted,
Shrieking her triumph out.

A newly widowed wife
Bearing her proud grief high
Through the wrecked house of life.

Flower, boat and bride, all three,
Their beauty dazzles me,
Their freedom sets me free.

—HARRIET MONROE

See "Daphne," page 228, and "Forsythia," page 201.

High-school poets have fashioned poems in tercets:

Palm Sunday

We stroll toward home with palms in hand. The air
Is live with hum of talk and distant blare
Of horns; there is a shouting in the square.

Calvary lies silent, dreaming of the sea,
And sleepy flocks that graze upon the lea . . .
And roses blossom at Gethsemane.
—DORIS V. LECKY

Hawthorn for Hope

White hawthorn lingers by my door.
Love is a dream I'll know no more—
He brought me roses here before.

I have no hope. A soft wind blows
The hedge whereon my hawthorn grows.
It's scarce as fragrant as the rose.
—DORIS V. LECKY

To a Daguerreotype

Asenath Osgood, fair and straight,
Hair brushed back into a plait,
Were you ever, ever late?

Did you ever miss a date?
Did young Joseph have to wait
Long for you at the garden gate?
—JEAN DECKER

Das Zahlenlied

Flocks of days dark on the sky,
Whirring overhead, go by
Imperceptibly, and I

Count their wings in sudden fright—
Soon they will shut out the light. . . .
Hold me warm and close to-night.

Talk to me of moon-dark seas
Weaving far, faint melodies;
Silver, weighing down the trees.

Make me songs of windy dunes
Under lemon-colored moons
Pale as fairies' toy balloons.

Flocks are flying, flocks have flown,
Counting, counting, I have grown
Frightened. Don't leave me alone!
—MURIEL F. HOCHDORF

Forever
(To R. L. S.)

"Forever" is not much nor all
To say beside a garden wall
Just before the petals fall.

"Forever" is an honest word
Just before the dimly heard
Song of wind and migrant bird,—

Just before the summer goes,
Just before a petal blows,
Or a feather or a rose . . .
—JACK WILSON

CHAPTER X

IN THE JAPANESE MANNER

"Let your hokku resemble a willow-branch struck by a light shower and trembling a little in the wind."

—Bashō

A VERSE form used by the Japanese has an elusive charm all its own. It is a little atmosphere poem called *hokku*, "hokku" meaning *beginning phrase*. The tiny poem consists of a primary statement of thought, out of which grows a secondary thought, corollary to it. This duality is compressed into seventeen syllables—not feet—syllables, arranged in three lines of five, seven, and five. The whole creates an impression of elusiveness, of the feeling of things caught and solidified for a fleeting moment as a drop of water is solidified in the snow crystal.

Here is a classic one written by Bashō, the greatest hokku master of the seventeenth century. Every Japanese, it is said, learns it by heart.

> Furu ike ya
> Kawazu tobikomu
> Mizu no ato

Pronounce consonants as in English; vowels as in Italian.

> The old pond, aye! and
> The sound of a frog leaping
> Into the water.

What effect does this nameless little poem create? Notice what we hear: the sound of a single frog, not of many frogs. If we are aware of one such sound, the waters, the reeds and grasses, the shrubs, all the rich growth of the pond must be very still. We *feel* silence, or peace, or quiet through that single sound.

Many of these little poems are built on such an experience or environment rich in details, out of which one significant detail is selected. The finer the detail the more poignant the effect. Is it not so in moments of intense emotion? In an important crisis very often the thing that is impressed most deeply on our consciousness is some slight, almost irrelevant detail: the striking of the clock, the shape of a shadow on the rug, a fragrance, the falling of a flower petal. And ever afterwards that sound or shadow or fragrance or movement recalled precipitates the feeling of the whole experience again. Here we have a pond. Think of all the things associated with a pond: cattails, canoes, birds singing, sunset, picnics, the diving board, a bridge, water snakes, water rats, fishes, frogs, insects of many kinds, smells of many varieties, and sounds multitudinous, including wind, rain, thrush song. From that wealth of detail the poet selected one—the sound of a frog leaping. What he does not say affects us. Neither the Japanese artist nor the poet explains; he suggests. What he does not say is what speaks to the heart.

Every little Japanese hokku means more than the actual words convey. "Japanese poetry, at least the old Japanese poetry," writes Yone Noguchi, critic, essayist, autobiographer, and poet of rare quality in Japanese and English, "is different from western poetry in the same way as silence is different from a voice." The reader must be a poet, too, to read into the poem what is not there expressed.

"Indeed you are the outsider of our Japanese poems," adds Noguchi, "if you cannot read immediately what they do not describe to you." However, impressions may differ with the creative insight of the reader. We are told that many volumes have been written to interpret the classic frog poem above. One explanation is that the leaping of the frog is the symbol of the sudden illumination which may come to the soul in a period of silence and meditation. It will be remembered that the composer renounced the life of nobleman and courtier in his youth to become a pilgrim priest, poet, and teacher of poetry. He was something of a cavalier, something of a saint; a literary leader to whom the palace door was wide open; a lonely wanderer who chose the companionship of the poor and the lowly.

Even without the double significance the little pond fragment would have provocative charm as an atmosphere poem. *With* the double significance it has a profundity not expected in so slight a form.

To preserve both the spirit and the form of verse in translation is not an easy thing for the translator to do. Let us enjoy some translations by poets who preserved the inner spirit as nearly as possible but used English rhythms; then let us read some poems in the syllabic measure of the Japanese.

Unless otherwise stated the hokku translations in rhymed metrical pattern were made by Curtis Hidden Page. They preserve the elusiveness and incompleteness which are so characteristic of Japanese hokku in spite of his use of rhyme. He has succeeded in turning the little hokku into genuine poetry.

> Butterfly, awake, awake!
> Come let us take
> Our comrade way together!
>
> —BASHŌ

Bashō like Milton believed that purity and simplicity in living were necessary to purity and simplicity in writing. He believed that everything in the world might be caught in the meshes of the little hokku form provided the poet's attitude was constructive. One day while Bashō was out wandering with a favorite pupil, Kikaku, a red dragon fly darted past. Kikaku, who enjoyed his little joke, just as do pupils today, sang out

> A darting dragon-fly—but lo!
> Pluck off its wings, and so—
> A bright red pepper-pod!

"That isn't hokku!" remonstrated Bashō. "That is the wrong way, not to say it, but to see it. This is hokku:"

> A bright red pepper-pod—but lo!
> Put on it wings, and so—
> A darting dragon-fly.

Bashō believed that a true poet puts on wings; he does not take them off.

Another incident shows how this master's mind worked in creating hokku. This insight should be valuable to us, his pupils.

A number of town poets were gathered on the verandah of a tea house to feast and compose hokku in celebration of the full moon. Bashō accepted their invitation to join them and contribute.

> 'Twas the new moon's light . . .

he began. "No, it is the full moon!" interrupted the amused novices. But one, wishing to hear more of the fun, suggested that the unknown guest go on. The pilgrim teacher-poet began

> 'Twas the new moon's light . . .
> Since then I have watched it and waited . . .
> And lo!—to-night!

Astounded, and perhaps a little ashamed of their exhibition of cocksureness, they listened humbly to the principles of poetry from the great man's lips. Here is another by Bashō.

> Old battlefield, fresh with Spring flowers again—
> All that is left of the dream
> Of twice ten thousand warriors slain.

> There is a trinity of loveliest things:
> Moon, flowers—and now I go
> To find the third, the snow.

—RIPPO

"Snow," *Yuki* means also *the going*. There is a play on words.

You see how the general experience or the primary statement—old battlefield fresh with spring flowers, trinity of loveliest things—gives rise to the succeeding thought, which does not stop with the poem but actually begins in the heart of the reader to end, who knows where?

Indeed the incompleteness of the little form is a hereditary charm. For hokku was not always a verse unit. It was once the first stanza of a little ode called *tanka*. Its meaning, beginning phrase, gives its origin away. Two lines of seven syllables, *ageku*, completed the weighty five-line tanka of 31 syllables! One from the *Kokinshū* will illustrate.

Idete inaba
  Nushi naki yado to
Narinu to mo,
  Nokiba no ume yo
    Haru wo wasuru-na!

Though my dwelling
shall have become tenantless
when I am gone, do not
thou, O plum-tree by the eaves,
forget the spring!

Here is a tanka in the syllabic measure:

    The rippling sea-swell,
    Curling upon the gold sand,
    And, curving over,
    A bough of cherry blossoms,—
    Youth shielding eternal age.

Now in the thirteenth century poetical tournaments were at their zenith and "capping stanzas" was a favorite game. Contestants tried to complete a poem of which either the first or the second half was assigned in advance.

In the next century tanka sequences were the vogue as social games. Player 1 would give three initial lines. Player 2 would add two concluding lines. Player 3 would add three initial lines that could be read before the two by Player 2 but would also lend themselves to being completed into another tanka by player 4. So it went, in a chain of "linked sweetness." The Japanese passion for brevity soon led them to think of the beginning phrase as a unit of verse instead of a stanza. Before long they had discarded the 31-syllable form as too long.

Every conceivable experience was embraced in the smaller form. Nothing was too commonplace, even a drainpipe.

    O unremitting song of the roof-pipe drain
    Through long monotonous months of the season of rain . . .
    So life's long memories lull an old man's brain.
                        —REIKAN

Contrast is a favorite device of the hokku maker. You also may wish to use it when you experiment.

The nightingale has scarce begun his song . . .
And now alack!
That howling bean-cake peddler comes along!

—YAHA

Japanese poems abound in the things of nature: pines, cryptomerias, bamboos, azaleas, wisteria, lotus, iris, lespedeza. Because they have traditional significance to the Japanese, they are economical devices for suggestiveness. For instance, the wisteria and the cuckoo symbolize early summer; the plum blossom and the nightingale early spring; the plum blossom also means love; the fir tree, the heron, the tortoise mean anything long enduring: life, sorrow, loyalty, memory; dew, cherry-blossom, or separate joints of a bamboo stalk symbolize brevity, hence brief endurance of love, beauty, human life; the willow tree means a noble lady or graciousness. This poem on the cherry bloom of the mountain Yoshino made its author immortal.

Oh this, oh this!
Far beyond words it is!
Mountain of cherry-bloom, Yoshino-yama.

—YASUHARA TEISHITSU

To know the Sappho of Japanese song we should meet Chiyo who lived between 1703 and 1775. When she was a little girl a traveling teacher of poetry stayed overnight at her home and at the request of Chiyo's parents gave the little girl a lesson on hokku. Having given her as a subject for a poem "The Cuckoo"—you see they did it even there, even then—he rolled up in his blanket and went to sleep. Early the next morning the little girl greeted him with

Hototogisu   Cuckoo!
  Hototogisu tote   Again cuckoo!
Ake ni keri.   Again the daylight too!

She grew to be the most original of sweet singers. As a wedding gift to her husband she presented this hokku:

The persimmon, lo!
No one can tell till he tastes it!
Marriage is even so.

It was considered no mean wedding gift.

Poetry is held in highest esteem in Japan. The word for teacher, poet, lawyer is the same, *sensei*.

All things turned to poetry in Chiyo's hands. One morning when she went to her well to draw water she found a morning-glory twined around the well-sweep. Her poet's heart would not let her disturb it. This is a poem which immortalized the incident:

> The well-bucket taken away
> By the morning-glory—
> Alas, water to beg!
>
> —YONE NOGUCHI, *Translator*

In two poems Chiyo shows the suppressed grief of a mother at the death of her child. At play the little boy used to wander into the fields chasing dragon flies. She writes

> The hunter of dragon flies
> Today, how far away
> May he have gone!
>
> —YONE NOGUCHI, *Translator*

and

> Drear Autumn winds beat down the lingering leaves.
> Wet are the forest-ways, and wet my sleeves.
> O the sound of the wind, through the shoji . . .

One might go on quoting these elusive little poems. But surely, you have caught the spirit!

By using the Japanese method as Bashō taught it, and the Japanese restriction, *17 syllables of 5, 7, 5,* poets have created charming effects that keep the brevity, suggestiveness, and incompleteness of the old form even in English verse.

To the Japanese the seasons have special significance. More poetry has been inspired by the seasons than by any other subject.

Here is a season poem:

> The end of autumn
> And some rooks are perched upon
> A withered brown branch.

Nothing could be more characteristic of the bleakness of autumn than those rooks.

In constructing hokku the relative position of general and specific details is a matter of ingenuity. The general term and the specific term will not always be so clearly marked as in the pond poem and the end of autumn. Sometimes the significant detail is compressed into an adjective, an adverb, a phrase or a modifying clause. In the one below it appears before the general environment from which it was selected.

> Without a word of
> Warning, there in the autumn
> Sky, Mount Fugi stands.

The feeling of suddenness is what impresses the atmosphere of Fugi in autumn: "without a word of warning."

Other poems in the Japanese manner follow:

> More fleeting than the
> Flash of withered windblown leaf,
> This thing men call life.

Those below were done in English by Yone Noguchi. They are not translations.

1.

Suppose the stars fall
And break?—Do they ever **sound**
Like my own love song?

8.

Sudden pain of earth
I hear in the fallen **leaf**.
"Life's autumn," I cry.

3.

What is life? A voice,
A thought, a light on the dark,—
Lo, crow in the sky.

29.

Full of faults, you say.
What beauty in repentance!
Tears, songs . . . thus life flows.

30.

> Bits of song . . . what else?
> I, a rider of the stream,
> Lone between the clouds.

On the dedication page of *Iron Moths,* a collection of hokkus, is this by Isabel Fiske Conant.

Sakura

> Singing, we bring you
> A gift that will last through life;
> Pink cherry-blossoms.

Some others by the same poet follow:

Dead Friend

That my candle-light
Is quenched, you grieve . . . A new star
Shines on you tonight.

Homeless

These lighted windows,
And none for me? Look up; see
The constellation!

Kwannon, the Compassionate

This on a god's face?
But it is a woman-god . . .
Ah,—I understand!

Icarus

On tremulous wings
He soars above the maze of thought—
Alas! too near the sun . . .
—EVELYN AHREND

Glimpses

MAY   MANHATTAN

Tremulous blossoms   Tall, ugly buildings
Hang like butterflies upon   Tower over what was once
The young apple boughs.   A grassy meadow.

EL DORADO

Dew-drops in the grass
Look like brilliant diamonds
Yet my touch melts them.
—RUSSELL M. SPEAR

It is contended by some that syllabic measure in a language made of words of accented and unaccented syllables can have little music. With an ear to euphony one should be able to make music of a five-seven-five combination. Seventeen syllables may, in fact, be metrically arranged if one so has a mind. But freedom from regular meter seems to give an elusive charm peculiar to the syllabic measure. Here are some metrical patterns that one might try:

./././.   /./././
./././.   /././././
./././.   /././

./../   ././.
././/.   ./../.
./../   ././.

./../
../././   *(Vary the place of the anapest.)*
./../

It should be remembered that there were once quite as many objections to the introduction of the French forms, the French language also having little or no accent.

Presenting as it does so slight a restriction—no rhyme, no metrical requirement—and yet in the matter of compact thought and compact expression exacting so much care, the hokku form is well worth experimentation for sheer joy of creation as well as for the influence which the attempts will very likely exert on verse forms with more exacting strictures. Hokku makers are observers. Theirs must be the economy of thought; economy of expression.

The Japanese government maintains a Bureau of Poetry. Under its auspices competitions are held. A subject is given in advance and every one tries his hand at a hokku. In the early days only the court took part; today all classes—the contest is truly democratic! One year *Spring Breeze* was the subject assigned. In Japan the carpenter planes his wood in the open air. The wood shavings form the Japanese letter "no." Here is the prize poem:

Spring Breeze

As I walked past the
Carpenter's, the no-letters
Chased me down the lane.

In this poem the general term stands as the title, the specific one subordinated to it as the rest of the poem. Quite frequently the general term thus forms the title.

In the same spirit a young high-school student conveyed the feeling of our Western spring.

Spring

Tiers of tense faces
Watch a ball cut the air; then
Spat! into a glove.

—IDA YANOFSKY

Very few Americans would fail to catch the atmosphere of spring through the detail she selects to impress the feeling of the season.

Other experiments follow:

Evening at Home

Yesterday, her tear
Was wet salt upon my lips.
How sweet tomorrow?
—THEODORE NATHAN

Evening

Silver quietude
And the soft purr of a cat
Asleep by the fire. . . .
—AGNES DORDAN

Autumn

How did this broken
Leaf find its way about through
All the city dust?
—CAROL STEIN

Fall Leaves

Briskly and lightly
They dance around the flowers. . . .
Is death so lovely?
—JOSEPHINE FRANCO

Winter

Out of the north wind
One flake steps daintily on
A gray cobblestone.
—WILLIAM PEARLMAN

Winter

A whiff of camphor
Spices the dull atmosphere
Of a subway train.
—ALOIS HOPE

October

Middle of autumn. . . .
See! A golden pumpkin grins
Between withered stalks.
—HJALMER STEEN

October

Sharp rapier thrusts
Of the wind and a bloody
Spot on each brown leaf. . . .
—ARA TIMOURIAN

After Rain

The rain-drenched willow
Shivered. . . . Was it that the moon's
Kiss was so chilling?
—ADELE ZIMMERMAN

Words

Madly I chase bright
Feathered birds that fly lightly
Just beyond my grasp.
—OLIVE CLAIR

Impatience

I tossed away my
Dittany and poppies just
As the moon arose.
                    —OLIVE CLAIR

Betrothal

A dew diamond
Graces the slender finger
Of a lilac tree.
                    —ESTELLE ROOKS

Snow

Some birds flying high
Scatter the white notes of song
That fall fluttering.
                    —ONOLEE JONES

Poetaster

He catches a mood
In chains of gold, but the gold
Is only plated.
                    —MURIEL F. HOCHDORF

Despair

A silver twilight
With long, cold fingers of mist
Chokes back the lark's cry.
                    —MURIEL F. HOCHDORF

Steam Shovel

Yes, he does rest, this
Snorting giant, but does he
Dream of destruction?
                    —JULIUS GELBER

Beauty

The song of a thrush
Is tracing silver patterns
On the velvet night.
                    —NAOMI ROGIN

Insanity

Among polychromed
Songs of bird-like thoughts, I heard
A weird mutant note.
                    —WILLIAM ROEHRICK

City Dawn

A gay morning breeze
Danced to the rattling music
Of the milk bottles.
                    —NAOMI ROGIN

Creator

The shiny air drill
With its deafening shriek, does
It rip for progress?
                    —LEONARD COHEN

Frost

Magic craftsman, Frost!
The tangled mass of dull twigs,
A silver fountain!

And the green pine tree
Has become a pyramid
Of silver feathers.
                    —ALEX TALMADGE

INVITATION

Let us gather some
Cherry petals, for fragrance
Is long enduring. . . .

Do any of the following suggest poems in the Japanese manner? When
you have finished your lyric, test it for

Suggestiveness
Simplicity
Compactness of thought
Compactness of expression

Does it, a willow branch, tremble a little in the wind?

Peace   Evening   Loneliness   November   Autumn
      Inattention   Spring   The park   Fairy tale
Mist   Caprice   Knighthood   Power   Silence
A moonlight path   Sleeping song   Fog   Adventure
Slickers   Moon   Wind   City lights   Country lights
      Doubt   On the ferris wheel   Business   Conquest
Scherzo   Andante   Why?   Why are they glad?
      Where are they going?   What is it for?   When will it
end?   Who is the gainer?   What is loss?   What is suc-
cess?   The saddest thing   The most joyous   On the
ferry   Wounds   Any significant place: Niagara Falls, Grand
Canyon of the Colorado, the Mohave . . .   Zest   Toil
Progress   Summer (Any season)   Hunting   Treasure
      Dawn   Life   Play time   Little sister   Story
hour   Success   Steam drill   Air drill   Library
Sport   Joy   Sorrow   Pain   Expectation   Age
      Youth   Hokku on hokku   Wings   Flight   On
machinery   Radio   Orchard bloom   Whim   Jest

CHAPTER XI

THE CINQUAIN

CLOSELY related to the Japanese hokku is a little form invented by Adelaide Crapsey. She called it cinquain. *Verse* published after her death contains twenty-eight poems in this pattern. They too are exquisite little atmosphere poems. They suggest, as do the Japanese poems, the feeling of things and circumstances. Absence of rhyme gives them the same elusive charm. The scheme is five iambic lines arranged one foot on the first line, two feet on the second, three on the third, four on the fourth and one on the fifth. Substitutions frequently vary the music.

As an expression of the frail inventor's spirit, the cinquain form has special poignancy. Miss Crapsey was a victim of tuberculosis. She wrote most of the poetry which we have today at Saranac. In fact she gathered her poems together as her memorial.

Here are some of them, as incomplete in effect as her own life.

Snow

Look up . . .
From bleakening hills
Blows down the light, first breath
Of wintry winds . . . Look up, and
    scent
The snow!

November Night

Listen . . .
With faint dry sound,
Like steps of passing ghosts,
The leaves, frost-crisp't, break from the
    trees
And fall.

The Warning

Just now,
Out of the strange
Still dusk . . . as strange, as still . . .
A white moth flew: why am I grown
So cold?

The Guarded Wound

If it
Were lighter touch
Than petals of flower resting
On grass, oh. still too heavy it were,
Too heavy!

Night Winds

The old
Old winds that blew
When chaos was, what do
They tell the clattered trees that I
Should weep?

Release

With swift
Great sweep of her
Magnificent arm my pain
Clanged back the doors that shut my soul
From life.

Anguish

Keep thou
Thy tearless watch
All night but when blue-dawn
Breathes on the silver moon, then weep!
Then weep!

Trapped

Well and
If day on day
Follows, and weary year
On year . . . and ever days and years . . .
Well?

Roma Æterna

The sun
Is warm to-day,
O Romulus, and on
Thine olden Palatine the birds
Still sing.

Laurel in the Berkshires

Sea-foam
And coral! Oh, I'll
Climb the great pasture rocks
And dream me mermaid in the sun's
Gold flood.

In "Shadow" below, contrast creates the effect, but not that of the bean-cake peddler. Here is poignancy.

Shadow

A-sway,
On red rose,
A golden butterfly . . .
And on my heart a butterfly
Night-wing'd.

Blue Hyacinths

In your
Curled petals what ghosts
Of blue headlands and seas,
What perfumed immortal breath sighing
Of Greece.

Her pattern inspired young versifiers. When their first experiments appeared in print a reader remarked that they irritated her. "They promise so much," she complained, "touch the feelings and then leave one nowhere to think it all out for one's self!" That is exactly what Japanese poetry and cinquains are intended to do: they "tease one out of thought" as Keats says it.

Read them; then see what you can do. Use the "Invitation" under Hokku unless you have made provision for mental feasting at your own board.

To R. N.

Your voice
Still echoes in
My heart . . . What matter, then,
If you did not intend the song
For me?

—NAOMI ROGIN

To a White Narcissus

O white
Narcissus by
A still, clear pool, do you
Find joy in looking only at
Yourself?

—NAOMI ROGIN

From a Lover

What joy,
To fashion now,
A dainty chain of words,
To decorate the loveliness
Of you.

—JACQUELINE HOYT

Echo

I hear
You weeping still
Beside a mountain stream . . .
Where your proud love once gazed in
      pain . . .
Alone.

—LOUISE FISCHER

In Memoriam

The stars
Are not shining
Tonight. . . . Is it because
They know the grief that lies upon
My heart?

—JOSEPHINE FRANCO

November Tree

Old man,
Why do you bow
Your head so mournfully?
Is it because you take so long
To die?

—CONSTANCE STERN

Fire

The charred
And blackened grass
Is like tender feelings,
So easily bruised . . . But they will heal
Again.

—MARJORIE DEGRAFF

To Robert Frost

You
Distill all nature
In your charmed retort
And put the very essence into
Words.

—RICHARD HALLBERG

Summer Heat

The heat
Was like a huge
Obnoxious ape which strove
To crush and stifle me with breath
And weight.
—ROSLYN SOLLISCH

The Message

The lights
From out the fleet
Are magic silver words,
Telling how fair and cold a thing
Is death.
—JAMES GORHAM

The sudden death of a beloved teacher, Miss Kathryn E. Richardson, brought this spontaneous cinquain from a member of her official class.

To K. E. R.

Swallows
Dart southward, as
In other autumns . . . spring
Will come again, when cold is gone . . .
But you?
—JOYCE LANCASTER

Morse Code

Dot—dash. . . .
The signals light
From ship to ship. These sparks
That pierce the night, what do they say?
Dot—dash. . . .
—MIRIAM WOLFSON

Death House

They march
With drooping heads.
The shadow of the rope
Is on the wall. . . . With heavy feet
They march.
—MIRIAM WOLFSON

More Tangible

It would
Be nice to reach
The moon and kiss the man
Up there. But since you're here—oh, well,
You'll do.

—CONSTANCE STERN

In the cinquains below the young versifiers used trochees instead of iambs as an experiment.

Threat

Naughty,
Playful kitten,
If you scratch and bite . . . a
Fay will change you to a pussy
Willow.

—MURIEL SLATER

Counterfeit

Jazz,
Caught from tortured
Strings and passed as music,
Rings as false as any leaden
Coin.

—JAMES GORHAM

CHAPTER XII

PORTRAITS

EVERY one of us is interested in people. We enjoy this personality or find that unpleasant. Some people incite interest for their physical endowments; others for physical limitations. Some appeal through their spiritual qualities. It is the combination of the physical and the spiritual which makes most people appealing. However the appeal may be made, every individual is unique. Any observer may find in the characters passing in and out of his circle a great deal to stimulate his imagination.

Some portraits painted by authentic poets are collected here for your pleasure, followed by others drawn by students. Through a careful choice of details the artist attempts to create a single effect, that is, a definite impression; he omits what might interfere with that impression. Perhaps you will draw a portrait and enlarge the collection. Use whatever pattern suits your substance.

The Appraisal

Never think she loves him wholly,
Never believe her heart is blind,
All his faults are locked securely
In a closet of her mind;
All his indecisions folded
Like old flags that time has faded,
Limp and streaked with rain,
And his cautiousness like garments
Frayed and thin, with many a stain—
Let them be, oh, let them be.
There is treasure to outweigh them,
His proud will that sharply stirred
Climbs as surely as the tide,
Senses strained too taut to sleep,
Gentleness to beast and bird,
Humor flickering hushed and wide
As the moon on moving water,
And a tenderness too deep
    To be gathered in a word.

—SARA TEASDALE

Ianthe

From you, Ianthe, little troubles pass
   Like little ripples down a sunny river;
Your pleasures spring like daisies in the grass,
   Cut down and up again as blithe as ever.

            —WALTER SAVAGE LANDOR

My Star

All that I know
   Of a certain star
Is, it can throw
   (Like the angled spar)
Now a dart of red,
   Now a dart of blue;
Till my friends have said
   They would fain see, too,
My star that dartles the red and the blue!
Then it stops like a bird; like a flower, hangs furled:
   They must solace themselves with the Saturn above it.
What matter to me if their star is a world?
   Mine has opened its soul to me; therefore I love it.

            —ROBERT BROWNING

Aaron Stark

Withal a meagre man was Aaron Stark,
Cursed and unkempt, shrewd, shrivelled, and morose.
A miser was he, with a miser's nose,
And eyes like little dollars in the dark.
His thin pinched mouth was nothing but a mark;
And when he spoke there came like sullen blows
Through scattered fangs a few snarled words and close,
As if a cur were chary of its bark.

Glad for the murmur of his hard renown,
Year after year he shambled through the town,
A loveless exile moving with a staff;
And oftentimes there crept into his ears
A sound of alien pity, touched with tears,—
And then (and only then) did Aaron laugh.

            —EDWIN ARLINGTON ROBINSON

The Solitary Reaper

Behold her, single in the field,
  Yon solitary Highland Lass!
Reaping and singing by herself;
  Stop here, or gently pass!
Alone she cuts and binds the grain,
And sings a melancholy strain;
O listen! for the Vale profound
Is overflowing with the sound.

No Nightingale did ever chaunt
  More welcome notes to weary bands
Of travellers in some shady haunt,
  Among Arabian sands:
A voice so thrilling ne'er was heard
In spring-time from the Cuckoo-bird,
Breaking the silence of the seas
Among the fairest Hebrides.

Will no one tell me what she sings?—
  Perhaps the plaintive numbers flow
For old, unhappy, far-off things,
  And battles long ago:
Or is it some more humble lay,
Familiar matter of to-day?
Some natural sorrow, loss, or pain,
That has been, and may be again?

Whate'er the theme, the Maiden sang
  As if her song could have no ending;
I saw her singing at her work,
  And o'er the sickle bending;—
I listen'd, motionless and still;
And, as I mounted up the hill,
The music in my heart I bore,
Long after it was heard no more.
                    —WILLIAM WORDSWORTH

She is Overheard Singing

Oh, Prue she has a patient man,
  And Joan a gentle lover,
And Agatha's Arth' is a hug-the-hearth,—
  But my true love's a rover!

Mig, her man's as good as cheese
  And honest as a brier,
Sue tells her love what he's thinking of,—
  But my dear lad's a liar!

Oh, Sue and Prue and Agatha
  Are thick with Mig and Joan!
They bite their threads and shake their heads
  And gnaw my name like a bone;

And Prue says, "Mine's a patient man,
  As never snaps me up,"
And Agatha, "Arth' is a hug-the-hearth,
  Could live content in a cup,"

Sue's man's mind is like good jell—
  All one color, and clear—
And Mig's no call to think at all
  What's to come next year,

While Joan makes boast of a gentle lad,
 That's troubled with that and this;—
But they all would give the life they live
 For a look from the man I kiss!

Cold he slants his eyes about,
 And few enough's his choice,—
Though he'd slip me clean for a nun, or a queen,
 Or a beggar with knots in her voice,—

And Agatha will turn awake
 When her good man sleeps sound,
And Mig and Sue and Joan and Prue
 Will hear the clock strike round,

For Prue she has a patient man,
 As asks not when or why,
And Mig and Sue have naught to do
 But peep who's passing by,

Joan is paired with a putterer
 That bastes and tastes and salts,
And Agatha's Arth' is a hug-the-hearth,—
 But my true love is false!

    —EDNA ST. VINCENT MILLAY

Ruth

She stood breast-high amid the corn,
Clasp'd by the golden light of morn,
Like the sweetheart of the sun,
Who many a glowing kiss had won.

On her cheek an autumn flush,
Deeply ripen'd;—such a blush
In the midst of brown was born,
Like red poppies grown with corn.

Round her eyes her tresses fell,
Which were blackest none could tell,
But long lashes veil'd a light,
That had else been all too bright.

And her hat, with shady brim,
Made her tressy forehead dim;
Thus she stood amid the stooks,
Praising God with sweetest looks:—

Sure, I said, Heav'n did not mean,
Where I reap thou shouldst but glean,
Lay thy sheaf adown and come,
Share my harvest and my home.

    —THOMAS HOOD

The Merry Guide

Once in the wind of morning
 I ranged the thymy wold;
The world-wide air was azure
 And all the brooks ran gold.

There through the dews beside me
 Behold a youth that trod,
With feathered cap on forehead,
 And poised a golden rod.

With mien to match the morning
 And gay delightful guise
And friendly brows and laughter
 He looked me in the eyes.

Oh whence, I asked, and whither?
 He smiled and would not say,
And looked at me and beckoned
 And laughed and led the way.

And with kind looks and laughter
 And nought to say beside
We two went on together,
 I and my happy guide.

Across the glittering pastures
 And empty upland still
And solitude of shepherds
 High in the folded hill,

By hanging woods and hamlets
 That gaze through orchards down
On many a windmill turning
 And far-discovered town,

With gay regards of promise
 And sure unslackened stride
And smiles and nothing spoken
 Led on my merry guide.

By blowing realms of woodland
 With sunstruck vanes afield
And cloud-led shadows sailing
 About the windy weald,

By valley-guarded granges
 And silver waters wide,
Content at heart I followed
 With my delightful guide.

And like the cloudy shadows
 Across the country blown
We two fare on for ever,
 But not we two alone.

With the great gale we journey
 That breathes from gardens thinned,
Borne in the drift of blossoms
 Whose petals throng the wind;

Buoyed on the heaven-heard whisper
 Of dancing leaflets whirled
From all the woods that autumn
 Bereaves in all the world.

And midst the fluttering legion
 Of all that ever died
I follow, and before us
 Goes the delightful guide,

With lips that brim with laughter
 But never once respond,
And feet that fly on feathers,
 And serpent-circled wand.

—A E. HOUSMAN

Read also "John's Wife," Wilfrid Wilson Gibson, Chapter IX. Other portraits: "Portrait by a Neighbor" and "Witch-Wife" by Edna St. Vincent Millay; "Miss Loo" by Walter De La Mare; "Old Martin" by Joyce Kilmer; "Miniver Cheevy" by Edwin Arlington Robinson.

STUDENT EXHIBIT

Portrait

His hazel eyes
Were large and sad,
And little birds
Were the words he had,

That fluttered and beat
Against my soul;
His warm, red lips
Were sulky; whole

And shiny were
His brittle dreams;
He said "It *is*,"
And not "It *seems*."

His love was like
A fretful tune
That reached its climax
All too soon.

He burnt his heart
And liked the pain,
And so he fell
In love again.
　　　　　—GEORGIA H. COOPER

Tramp

A tattered coat,
A battered hat,
A cheery smile,
A nose that's flat.

An ambling gait,
Entangled hair,
Big dirty hands,
Quite free of care.

A jerky nod,
A shaggy brow,
A placid face—
He hates a plow.

Through sleet and snow,
Through wind and rain,
He shambles on,
Or hops a train.

A tattered coat,
A battered hat,
Lord of the road
For all of that.
　　　　　—EDNA MAYER

Lita

Lita is a winning lass,
　Light as a lilting tune;
Lita is a winning lass
　With a bit of the moon
Caught in her dark eyes;
　I have loved her long. . . .
Lita is a winning lass
　Light as a song.
　　　　　—ESTELLE ROOKS

Night Moth

She is a rose-garden lady
Made out of chiffon and lace.
Laughing and talking and dancing
With white moth grace.
She is most buoyant and lovely
When the moon is bright,—
A lie-abed lady by daytime,
Mirthful by night.
　　　　　—DORIS V. LECKY

To My Grandmother

My grandmother's hair
Is thistle-down white,
But her heart is as young
As a mountain sprite
Or a song just sung.
—Babette Kurtz

Portrait of a Lover

(In the Modern Manner)

Young and fair and wondrous wise,
Maiden, I would reach the blue;
Maiden, I would soar the skies
For a single kiss from you.

I would swim a sea world-wide,
If you'd watch me win the dare,—
Waiting on the other side,
Gray of eyes and gold of hair.

On the grate of hell I'd grin;
All the flames could never kill,
For the room that you are in
Finds me no-end hotter still.

Gold of hair and gray of eyes,
For a kiss, all this I'd do.
Young and fair one, just surmise
What I might perform for two.
—Theodore R. Nathan

Vision

I see her lying in the moonlight there;
A light, cool breeze caresses her and goes
Impressed with lily hands and golden
    hair
And beauty soft and fragile as a rose.
—Arthur Goebel

Foresight Saga

By the lordly Hudson River
Lived a scholar, Cy A. Wather.
Rode each morning in the subway,
Pushed and shoved with all his comrades,
Growled and grumbled at the slowness,
Ran each morning to the gateway,
Ran each morning up the stairway,
Ran each morning to his classroom
And each morning got a late slip.
Cut each day annoying classes,
Unprepared each day in P. T.,
Went from other rooms with passes.
All his thoughts were very cloudy.
Every afternoon detention;
Went through school on sixty-five and
Passed his four-year course in seven.
Now he's working in the subway;
Turns the heat off in the tunnel,
Turns the lights on when the sun sets,
Gets his fun from making punlets
With the younger generation
Which still strives for education.
—William Roehrick

Grandma

She sits beneath the linden tree,
And tells the children fairy tales.
A squirrel and a chickadee
Come closer, so they may hear too
The stories Grandma claims are true.

Her garden is a lovely place,
With roses climbing on the walls,
With marigolds and Queen Anne's lace,
And bluebells bordering all the walks
Around the lawn where Grandma talks.

Then when the sun has said "Good-day,"
She rocks before the fireplace
And listens to the crickets play
Until she thinks it's time for bed
And hustles off each sleepy-head.
—William Roehrick

Street Player

His aged face
Was lined with dirt.
His fingers hurt,
As he tried to play
A rusty flute . . .
His crusty lips
With dryness cracked;
And yet he blew
As though he thought
The world would pause
To hear his songs.
But as he stood
And wheedled out
A few bad notes,
A few wrong bars,
The only ones
To stop awhile
Were dirty children.
Silent . . . they stood,
Unconscious that

They gaped, wide-eyed,
On Pan, grown old.
Compelled to play
 (A man must eat)
He wanders on.
Picking pennies,
Limping along,
Blown by the wind,
Scorched by the sun
And fanned by the rain.
When the earth was young,
Aeons ago . . .
Pan must have sinned.
And since that day,
Throughout the ages
A man must go,
Blowing a flute.
Desolate, old,
And hungering.

—SYDNEY S. ABRAM

E. A. P.—A Portrait

You do not see deep, deep, into a mirror
Or into faces, either, or into words.
You take us up with gentleness so quiet;
With unlearned tolerance you always listen.

You do not understand, you do not know,
But in that ignorance you breed a love
That makes us happy for a little while.

Open the windows some summer evening,
Go to the piano and brush away the jazz.
Play "Hearts and Flowers" softly, "Home, Sweet Home,"
And touch us all with you and human music,
And hold us all within your heart of warmth.

—DELMORE SCHWARTZ

Cousin Zetta

She didn't ask
Too much of life.
She thought she'd make him
A decent wife.

"Elevator house—"
She told with pride.
(What was the reason
His first wife died?)

The first night he
Couldn't eat the steak
Her cheeks were red for
The neighbors' sake.

And then the time
She forgot the bread . . .
She never forgot what
Her husband said.

He couldn't sleep:
It was all her fault
Because the soup had
Had too much salt.

She wasn't rich,
And she wasn't wise,
So the years piled bags up
Beneath her eyes.

"A decent woman!"
(And she was such.)
She was so ugly,
And she cried so much.
—MURIEL F. HOCHDORF

Cousin Florrie

Her clothes were what
Are called genteel;
Her skin was freckled
Like cold oatmeal.

She crimped her hair and
Her chins were many,
She bought us cookies
At three for a penny.

She never could manage
To climb a bus;
Her eyes were tragic
When she envied us.

Her stockings were "service,"
Her high shoes tan. . . .
All she ever wanted
Was a good, kind man.
—MURIEL F. HOCHDORF

Brenda at Thirty

Level-eyed, serene and knowing,
Life to her is not the glowing
Thing it used to be. She has found
Beneath her feet the solid ground.
She races clouds no more.
Now she scrubs a too-clean kitchen floor
—GERTRUDE JOAN BUCKMAN

Merle

She's sophisticated, modern. Sighs
Are not for her, nor heartaches. Lies
Are spoken casually . . . "Life's a game
Of wits. No time for romance. Who's to blame?"
She laughs, shrugging her shoulders gaily. "Light
Me one of yours. . . . There is no right
Or wrong today. . . . Take all you can." She flaunts
Her creed in spite of countless taunts.
Her love is lightly given and as lightly cast away.
Suave to her fingertips, coolly, she goes her way.

—GERTRUDE JOAN BUCKMAN

HINTS TO THE PORTRAIT PAINTER

I. Draw a portrait suggested by any of the following:

A picture of yourself taken when you were younger   Wife   Husband   Father   Mother   Brother   Sister   Boy   Youth   King of household   Fruit vender   Old clothes man   Miner   Fisherman   Portrait of a lady   Plough boy   Abandon   Spring time   Old age   Stoker   Elevator man   Athlete   Street singer   Beggar   Spinster   Storybook girl, boy, etc.   Sir—   Helen   Will-o' the wisp   Middle age   Stripling   Electrician   Inventor   Tinker   Flirt   Mender   Tramp   Mary and Martha   Housewife   Lady with comb in her hair   Elfin girl

II. Draw a portrait bringing out a spiritual quality:

Serenity   Devotion   Inconstancy   Any other.

CHAPTER XIII

OBJECT POEMS

THINGS become significant through strange associations. The things on our table at home; a chair that a dear one sits in; our dog's special cushion; a hand bag worn at the corners may almost have the gift of words, so alive is it with significance. There is human interest in many an inanimate object. Our hobbies and our special pursuits and special interests invest objects with something of ourselves. The essence of a poem may be found in the history of an object; in its association; in its special physical or spiritual significance.

Beauty lingers in strange places; her finger has left an impress on many an object, which the unseeing or unknowing may call ugly. See where you can find it and preserve it in a poem.

Some of the purest poetry has been stimulated through objects. Keats's *Ode on a Grecian Urn* is an example. Keats had long brooded upon a Greek frieze—called in his day the Elgin Marbles, which his friend Haydon, the artist, had been instrumental in getting England to buy. You may see it if you go to the British Museum in London. This frieze from the Parthenon, carefully pieced together, impressed Keats, as anything classical impressed him. On it in relief are cavalcades of men on horseback, men driving chariots, cattle being brought to sacrifice. Out of his enjoyment of this Greek frieze Keats created another work of art. Instead of a frieze he made an urn. On its brede or border he drew, through his images, the spirit of Greek sculpture. The pictures on the urn were alive with the breath of ancient Greece mingled with Keats's own imagination.

Keats could do this because he was saturated with the spirit of the Greeks: he had read Greek history; had pondered Greek drawings; had handled and studied Haydon's Greek casts and had made tracings of his own. No artist makes a copy; he re-creates.

No wonder that his work is enduring. Here it is. You can see what else he put into it to make it live.

Ode on a Grecian Urn

Thou still unravish'd bride of quietness,
   Thou foster-child of silence and slow time,
Sylvan historian, who canst thus express
   A flowery tale more sweetly than our rhyme:
What leaf-fringed legend haunts about thy shape
   Of deities or mortals, or of both,
      In Tempé or the dales of Arcady?
What men or gods are these? What maidens loth?
What mad pursuit? What struggle to escape?
      What pipes and timbrels? What wild ecstasy?

Heard melodies are sweet, but those unheard
   Are sweeter; therefore, ye soft pipes, play on;
Not to the sensual ear, but, more endear'd,
   Pipe to the spirit ditties of no tone:
Fair youth, beneath the trees, thou canst not leave
   Thy song, nor ever can those trees be bare;
   Bold Lover, never, never canst thou kiss,
Though winning near the goal—yet, do not grieve;
   She cannot fade, though thou hast not thy bliss,
      For ever wilt thou love, and she be fair!

Ah, happy, happy boughs! that cannot shed
   Your leaves, nor ever bid the Spring adieu;
And, happy melodist, unwearièd,
   For ever piping songs for ever new;
More happy love! More happy, happy love!
   For ever warm and still to be enjoyed,
      For ever panting, and for ever young;
All breathing human passion far above,
   That leaves a heart high-sorrowful and cloy'd,
      A burning forehead, and a parching tongue.

Who are these coming to the sacrifice?
   To what green altar, O mysterious priest,
Lead'st thou that heifer lowing at the skies,
   And all her silken flanks with garlands drest?
What little town by river or sea shore,
   Or mountain-built with peaceful citadel,
      Is emptied of this folk, this pious morn?
And, little town, thy streets for evermore
   Will silent be; and not a soul to tell
      Why thou art desolate, can e'er return.

O Attic shape! Fair attitude! with brede
   Of marble men and maidens overwrought,
With forest branches and the trodden weed;
   Thou, silent form, dost tease us out of thought
As doth eternity: Cold Pastoral!
   When old age shall this generation waste,
     Thou shalt remain, in midst of other woe
Than ours, a friend to man, to whom thou say'st,
   "Beauty is truth, truth beauty,"—that is all
     Ye know on earth, and all ye need to know.
                    —JOHN KEATS

Long before he wrote this urn poem he had commemorated his
first sight of the frieze. Haydon had taken him to the British Museum
to see it. This is the poem, not so flawless as the later one, but still
containing some unsurpassable passages, notably parts of the last two
lines.

On Seeing the Elgin Marbles

My spirit is too weak—mortality
   Weighs heavily on me like unwilling sleep,
   And each imagin'd pinnacle and steep
Of godlike hardship tells me I must die
Like a sick Eagle looking at the sky.
   Yet 'tis a gentle luxury to weep
   That I have not the cloudy mind to keep,
Fresh for the opening of the morning's eye.
Such dim-conceivèd glories of the brain
   Bring round the heart an indescribable feud;
So do these wonders a most dizzy pain,
   That mingles Grecian grandeur with the rude
Wasting of old Time—with a billowy main—
   A sun—a shadow of a magnitude.
                    —JOHN KEATS

You may see from the other poems how very simple things have
been a source of poetical treatment.

Magic

Within my hand I hold
A piece of lichen-spotted stone—
Each fleck red-gold—
And with closed eyes I hear the moan

Of solemn winds round naked crags
Of Colorado's mountains. The snow
Lies deep about me. Gray and old
Hags of cedars, gaunt and bare,
With streaming, tangled hair,
Snarl endlessly. White-winged and proud,
With stately step and queenly air,
A glittering, cool and silent cloud
    Upon me sails.
    The wind wails,
And from the cañon stern and steep
I hear the furious waters leap.

                 —HAMLIN GARLAND

Porcelaine de Saxe

Petite Madame, your smiling face
Serenely scorns the commonplace,
And you, Monsieur, your bow is quite
The fine quintessence of polite!

In seventeen seventy you showed
Your garments as the latest mode,—
Panniers and puffs and fine plumed hat,
Buckles and bows and lace cravat—

But he who made you never guessed
That Time, who loves a sorry jest,
Destroying kings and monarchies,
Would spare you, gay futilities.

How many a timely circumstance
Has saved you from the swift mischance
Which would have left your pieces scattered,
And all your china graces shattered!

The busy housewife, in a fluster,—
A maid's far flung, impetuous duster,—
Twixt you and these still intervenes
The god of foolish figurines.

I shrug, but ruefully. Alas!
When I, and all of mine, shall pass,
Still in the best ceramic style
Monsieur shall bow, Madame shall smile!

             —VIRGINIA LYNE TUNSTALL

The Paisley Shawl

What were his dreams who wove this coloured shawl—
The grey, hard-bitten weaver, gaunt and dour
Out of whose grizzled memory, even as a flower
Out of bleak winter at young April's call
In the old tradition of flowers breaks into bloom,
Blossomed the ancient intricate design
Of softly-glowing hues and exquisite line—
What were his dreams, crouched at his cottage loom?

What were her dreams, the laughing April lass
Who first, in the flowering of young delight,
With parted lips and eager tilted head
And shining eyes, about her shoulders white
Drew the soft fabric of kindling green and red,
Standing before the candle-lighted glass?

—WILFRID WILSON GIBSON

Remembrance

Your hands have curved about this bowl,
 Your lips
Have left a kiss upon this teacup's rim.
Frail and inanimate things that can outlast
 Your beauty—
Have they no memory of you singing still
About them, echoes of your melody,
If I might catch my breath and bow my head
 To hear?
Do their bright surfaces remember not
So faint and tremulous flutter of the wings
Of light and shade and color that were you?
No print of touch, no perfume lingering
That beauty's ghost joined hand to hand might serve
As beauty's self, refashioning your loveliness for me.
 Mute bowl—
 Mute cup—
I might as vainly ask
The scent of some late jonquil to recall
 Lost April.

—ANNE SPENCER MORROW
in *Smith College Monthly*

EXPRESSION OF YOUNG CREATORS

To an Heirloom

It squats in awkward fashion on a china dish,
A patient, still reminder of another day;
A million crimson lights retrace its queer designs
As if in play with dreams that drift from far away.

What skilful craftsman wrought this glass in some thatched hut
In far Roumania, the oriental land,
And roamed the wild Carpathians in search of trade,
And round the fire bartered with a gypsy band?

What lovers' lips have touched its rim? What eyes have met
Above, in homage to a lady's winning grace?
What hands have lifted high the glass in fervent toast
To power, or to the fleeting smile of some fair face?

Clear, sparkling drops of wine were prisoned in its bowl
A hundred years ago; it held the lusty boast
Of stalwart guests who feasted in a banquet hall
And pledged a proud allegiance to their Balkan host.

I bow my head in reverence to my ancestors
Who drank their wine from you, oh ancient glass, that stand
Upon a rosewood table in my room. I bow
To you, bright symbol of a lost enchanted land!

—ETHEL GREENFIELD

Automobile

How can its clean and shiny stride be human,
Though human words and hands have formed its length?
A tiger, coiled inside a gear, responds
To prodding motions with a mobile strength.

Just tolerate our will, and cruise the streets,
O brutal plunge, stern prodigy of stuff
Too foreign to ourselves, and separate . . .
Your lithe, steel-cradled force is not enough:

For we will place ourselves in you each day,
And we will speak and touch and love and know.
How much you'll be of us we cannot say,
But human blood in cylinders will flow

Until the tawny coldness of your gleam
Is moulted, melted, changed to animal heat,—
Transfigured, to a body, pulsing, warm,
A bright extension of our human feet.

—DELMORE SCHWARTZ

Bayberry Candle

Fat green candle on a shelf alone,
Bayberry candle with your fragrance blown
Into the face of the small gold man
Who stands on the desk with the ostrich fan—
Your sharp, dry smell is a breath too strong
For the small gold man, or the tiny gong
That sings leaden hours in silver tone;
Bayberry candle on a shelf alone,
Your smell is the sand in a warm, blue noon;
The wash of the waves in the dark of the moon;
Your smell is the dawn on the sleeping docks,
And the uneven pathway across the rocks
Through the long sea-grass, when the tide is far,
That leads to the dunes where your gray fruits are,
Where the hours sleep on the sea's deep breast,
And the slowly ripening bud of rest
Is left unplucked. Oh, the tiny gong
Forgets the silver of its song,
And humbled, crushed, is the small gold man
Remembering how his days began.
Bayberry candle, think of me!
Why do you tell us of the sea?

—MURIEL F. HOCHDORF

Boulder

huge boulder!
ld! Far older
han anything or anyone.
orn back in the ages—
Vhat secrets it could tell
ying there in the twilight—
)f the glacier softened by the sun:
Iow it slipped and slid
cross the continent,
weeping forest and mountain before it
s it went.

—MORRIS ZWART

Absence

Tea cups
On a scarlet
Lacquered table; melted
Sunshine caught in two bright bits
Of china.

Tea cups
Drained of liquid
Yet brimful of fragrance,—
Tilted once by hands fragile as
Their lustre.

—JOYCE LANCASTER

To a Roof-Tile Horse

On the ridge poles of Chinese palaces and temples there is a parade of small porcelain animals, birds, and men, each denoting some emotion. The roof-tile horse is the symbol of gratefulness. This particular tile was one of a group exhibited at the recent Antiques Exposition held in the Grand Central Palace.

Foo, the little peach-bloom dog,
Sits upon a teakwood tray
And watches incense burn all day
Into a twirling fragrant fog.

He never feels the cold of night
Come creeping, creeping down the roof,
Chilling him from head to hoof.
He never feels the rain-flies light

And crawl along his pink-glazed back.
Summer's kiln will never bake
Him till he thinks his sides will break.
And sometimes in the prince's pack

He travels down to Lin Chin town.
When I watch them wind away
I want to shout to them, to say
"Wait, wait for me and I'll come down."

But if I left my ridge-pole place
To follow after little Foo
I can't think what the house would do.
For should I go I would disgrace

Our noble palace. When the Gods
Would see no horse-tile on the ridge,
They'd keep the sun from heaven's bridge,
They'd beat the foam clouds with their rods

And thrash the twisted pine trees, too.
I have to show we're grateful for
The good the Gods bring to our door.
I must be satisfied and true,
Else what would our great palace do?
                              —WILLIAM ROEHRICK

To a Plaster Owl

O owl, that perch there on my mantel shelf,
What thoughts go on behind your solemn face?
What secrets are you keeping to yourself
As you sit looking at the human race?

I wish that I might take a little peek
Into your mind; hear your soliloquies.
I'm sure I'd find what I must ever seek—
The piled-up wisdom of the centuries!
—RICHARD HALLBERG

Washington Bridge, December 1929

Now in the darkness of the year
When afternoons, grown still, more chill and drifting,
Voyage unseen to dusk and blue loose night,
The wind is voiding our dream of spring.

But all day long the rivets pulse, and cables
Crescent a river newly, cradle a word. . . .
—Will the gray sky gather the world to death?
Over the hush and sleep an iron breath

Tremendously *is*. . . . No wind nor snow
Refutes this fleshed geometry, this birth,
Curving the strength of life over the earth.
—DELMORE SCHWARTZ

SUGGESTIONS

Is there a poem in any object on this list?
Bayberry candles   Bell   Dipper at a well   Some heirloom   Old piece of furniture   An old manuscript   Oldfashioned jewel case   Prayer book   Pressed flower in an album   Anything you might see in a curio shop   Something in a museum   A musical instrument   Something relegated to the attic or the cellar   An old chest   A ship model   A walking stick   A bridge   Stone wall in your neighborhood   Hitching post   Any particular mark in the landscape, such as a church spire, weather vane, grain elevator

CHAPTER XIV

HOMELY EXPERIENCE

WHAT should we do without the homely things of the kitchen and the back yard; the cellar and the garden? And what a feeling of not-at-homeness in the world would be ours if the homely activities of life were suddenly all wiped away. Commonplace activities are vibrant with possibilities of poetic treatment. Poets have done rare things with the ordinary activities of washing clothes, hanging them on the line, cutting the grass, and the like. See for yourself.

Ellen Hanging Clothes

The maid is out in the clear April light
Our store of linen hanging up to dry;
On clump of box, on the small grass there lie
Bits of thin lace, and broidery blossom-white.
And something makes tall Ellen—gesture, look—
Or else but that most ancient, simple thing,
Hanging the clothes upon a day in spring,
A Greek girl cut out some old lovely book.
The wet white flaps; a tune just come in mind,
The sound brims the still house. Our flags are out,
Blue by the box, blue by the kitchen stair;
Betwixt the two she trips across the wind,
Her warm hair blown all cloudy-wise about,
Slim as the flags, and every whit as fair.
—LIZETTE WOODWORTH REESE

Breath of the Briar

O briar-scents, on yon wet wing
Of warm South-west wind brushing by,
You mind me of the sweetest thing
That ever mingled frank and shy:
When she and I by love enticed,
Beneath the orchard-apples met,
In equal halves a ripe one sliced,
And smelt the juices ere we ate.

That apple of the briar-scent,
Among our lost in England now
Was green of rind, and redolent
Of sweetness as a milking cow.
The briar gives it back, well nigh
The damsel with her teeth on it;
Her twinkle between frank and shy,
My thirst to bite where she had bit.

—GEORGE MEREDITH

Scythe Song

Mowers, weary and brown and blithe,
  What is the word, methinks, ye know,
Endless over-word that the Scythe
  Sings to the blades of the grass below?
Scythes that swing in the grass and clover,
  Something, still, they say as they pass;
What is the word that, over and over,
  Sings the Scythe to the flowers and grass?

Hush, ah, hush, the Scythes are saying,
  Hush, and heed not, and fall asleep;
Hush, they say to the grasses swaying;
  Hush, they sing to the clover deep!
Hush—'tis the lullaby Time is singing—
  Hush and heed not for all things pass;
Hush, ah, hush, and the Scythes are swinging
  Over the clover, over the grass!

—ANDREW LANG

Water

Water remembered, treasured up;
Water that has never touched an earthen cup;
Held only in the creased hollow of a hand . . .
Trickling through, flickering silver, furrowing black sand;
Water tapped at the source
Of damp cool precincts, moving without force:
Even and quiet and confident and clean
With all the beauty of some suave machine—
These things, these phrases wrenched themselves softly loose
Like young tulip bulbs or the inside grass spear whose
Rootless white green end is sweet to suck.
So the phrases filtered through, light struck,

Pulled loose from the intricate loam of thought and spaced
Themselves because you laughed; and got unlaced
Because you laughed at something that I said . . .
Your laughter was like water—not drink merely, but drink and dark-
grained deep-breathing bread.

—Joseph Auslander

Could any activity be more commonplace than putting the kitchen
in order? Yet see what an authentic poet may do with it. The author
actually began by sweeping her room!

The Monk in the Kitchen

I

Order is a lovely thing;
On disarray it lays its wing,
Teaching simplicity to sing.
It has a meek and lowly grace,
Quiet as a nun's face.
Lo—I will have thee in this place!
Tranquil well of deep delight,
All things that shine through thee appear
As stones through water, sweetly clear.
Thou clarity,
That with angelic charity
Revealest beauty where thou art,
Spread thyself like a clean pool.
Then all the things that in thee are,
Shall seem more spiritual and fair,
Reflection from serener air—
Sunken shapes of many a star
In the high heavens set afar.

II

Ye stolid, homely, visible things,
Above you all brood glorious wings
Of your deep entities, set high,
Like slow moons in a hidden sky.
But you, their likenesses, are spent
Upon another element.
Truly ye are but seemings—
The shadowy cast-off gleamings
Of bright solidities. Ye seem
Soft as water, vague as dream;
Image, cast in a shifting stream.

III

What are ye?
I know not.
Brazen pan and iron pot,
Yellow brick and gray flag-stone
That my feet have trod upon—
Ye seem to me
Vessels of bright mystery.
For ye do bear a shape, and so
Though ye were made by man, I know
An inner Spirit also made,
And ye his breathings have obeyed.

IV

Shape, the strong and awful Spirit,
Laid his ancient hand on you.
He waste chaos doth inherit;
He can alter and subdue.
Verily, he doth lift up
Matter, like a sacred cup
Into deep substance he reached, and lo
Where ye were not, ye were; and so
Out of useless nothing, ye
Groaned and laughed and came to be.
And I use you, as I can,
Wonderful uses, made for man,
Iron pot and brazen pan.

V

What are ye?
I know not:
Nor what I really do
When I move and govern you.
There is no small work unto God.
He requires of us greatness;
Of his least creature
A high angelic nature,
Stature superb and bright completeness.
He sets to us no humble duty.
Each act that he would have us do
Is haloed round with strangest beauty;
Terrific deeds and cosmic tasks
Of his plainest child he asks.
When I polish the brazen pan

I hear a creature laugh afar
In the gardens of a star,
And from his burning presence run
Flaming wheels of many a sun.
Whoever makes a thing more bright,
He is an angel of all light.
When I cleanse this earthen floor
My spirit leaps to see
Bright garments trailing over it,
A cleanness made by me.
Purger of all men's thoughts and ways,
With labor do I sound Thy praise,
My work is done for Thee.
Whoever makes a thing more bright,
He is an angel of all light.
Therefore let me spread abroad
The beautiful cleanness of my God.

VI

One time in the cool of dawn
Angels came and worked with me.
The air was soft with many a wing.
They laughed amid my solitude
And cast bright looks on everything.
Sweetly of me did they ask
That they might do my common task.
And all were beautiful—but one
With garments whiter than the sun
Had such a face
Of deep, remembered grace;
That when I saw I cried—"Thou art
The great Blood-Brother of my heart.
Where have I seen thee?"—And he said,
"When we are dancing round God's throne,
How often thou art there.
Beauties from thy hands have flown
Like white doves wheeling in mid air.
Nay—thy soul remembers not?
Work on, and cleanse thy iron pot."

VII

What are we? I know not.

—Anna Hempstead Branch

HOMELY THINGS THAT STUDENTS HAVE SUNG

Wash Day

Morning brought a clear cool sky,
So Monday thought it quite ideal
To get her laundry done.
She worked away with greatest zeal,

And soon her clothes were filmy white.
She took them out to dry, but found
No clothesline in the yard,
And spread them on the ground.

The early wind was passing by,
And stopped to have some fun.
He crept on hands and knees at first,
But soon began to run.

The clothes puffed up, and fell,
Then fluttered in the air, but were denied
Their play when Monday bustled out
Again and took them back inside.

—LUCILLE SCHMEDTJE

Thoughts While Washing Dishes

I wash the dishes every night at home;
And while I wash, my thoughts are far away.
I sail the seas in ships of gleaming gold,
And drop my anchor near the shore of dreams.
With wingèd feet I run across the sands
Until I stumble, drunk with joy. But still
I wash the dirty pots and pans, and think
I splash about in pools that rainbows made.
A plate slips. Crash! And back to work I speed.
But I don't stay, for when the chips are picked
I'm off again. . . . With Wordsworth at my side
I roam through fields of daffodils, and take the smell
Of soap for fragrant flowers. . . . The dish cloth is
A signal when I'm shipwrecked on the sea;
The pan, a hoodoo drum when I'm marooned
With savage tribes. But rescue comes with work,
And I must leave the isle of dreams; and sail
Back home to dishes, water, soap, and grease.

—BERNADETTA NICHOLS

It is a common experience to see the windows of a building touched by the light of the setting sun. Ruth Hausman found a latent poem there.

Incursio

(Inspired by sunset on the skyscrapers outside of Central Park)

Fusing the blaze of the red and the gold,
Millions of rectangles, giving by day
So much of light, meted out and controlled
By the shrewd plans that the demigods lay,
Magnify thousand-fold all the sun's fire,
Melt into one all-enveloping flame,
Leap to new brilliance now, higher and higher,
Daring the demigods ever to tame
Her whom their diagrams sought not to mention,
Her who is tending the flame in the west,
Her whom they thought by their skillful invention
Shamed to retreat from all shrines, man-possessed.
See her, you masters and vassals of duty,
Making the craft whose perfection you schemed
Into a temple where sunset's wild beauty
Burns with a rapture you never had dreamed
Ever could find your rock-fortified altar,
Ever could penetrate granite and steel.
See your precisely made reckonings falter;
There is one entrance you did not conceal . . .
Windows of skyscrapers, catch every ray,
Crimson the lake to reflect the occasion,
Shine into unseeing eyes, that they may
Learn the bright tidings of beauty's invasion.

—RUTH H. HAUSMAN

SUGGESTIONS

Do any of these homely things or homely activities connected with them suggest ideas for poems?

Putting in a frigidaire to take the place of the old ice box   Washing clothes   Ironing   Peeling vegetables   Preparing food of any kind   Dusting   Putting up preserves   Seed planting   Hoeing in the garden   Cutting the grass   Watering the garden   Mending a leak in faucet, hose, roof . . .   Mending a hole in the fence   Clipping a hedge   Carpentering: putting in book shelves, winding a window shade that does not spring

Upholstering an old chair   Hanging curtains   Winding
the clock   Painting the barn   Setting out strawberry plants
Shoveling snow from the sidewalk   Thawing a frozen
pipe   Answering the dumb-waiter   The incinerator
Burning out a fuse   Waiting for the apartment house elevator

CHAPTER XV

MORE OF THE WORD

QUITE as effective musically as the repetition of certain tones and echoes of tones in verse is the repetition of words themselves.

Turn again to the "Rime of the Ancient Mariner," which should be read from beginning to end with the ear tuned to its exquisite melody.

> The ice was here, the ice was there,
> The ice was all around.

Note the effect of the repetition of "ice." Chilled music and the effect chilling!

> Day after day, day after day,
> We stuck, nor breath nor motion.

Those four "days" are magical in their endlessness; and again

> Water, water, everywhere
> And all the boards did shrink;
> Water, water, everywhere
> Nor any drop to drink.

And what utter loneliness through the repetition of one word in

> Alone, alone, all, all alone,
> Alone on a wide wide sea!

No measurements are needed to suggest the sweep of the sea. Such repetition is very different from the slovenly repetition of the lazy versifier; it has a way of pressing unreality upon the ear, and impressing a mood upon the consciousness.

You see also how the swinging movement of the lines above is carried along on the repetition of a word or phrase; sometimes such iteration is binder to a sheaf of lines that would otherwise be nothing more than scattered fragments.

Refrains are an expansion of this word-repetition principle. Every school boy knows a song with a chorus. He knows that the chorus is repeated after each stanza of the song. This chorus might be called a burden or a refrain.

In poetry the refrain is a word, phrase, line or lines that are repeated at intervals.

The most important function of the refrain seems to be to impress a mood through repetition. In "Sea Fever" John Masefield gives us the nostalgic feeling of the sea-lover with "I must down to the seas again" with which he begins every stanza.

Tennyson strikes a note of sadness in his lines written in memory of his friend Arthur Hallam.

> Break, break, break
>   On thy cold gray stones, O Sea!
> And I would that my tongue could utter
>   The thoughts that arise in me.

Then after two stanzas he picks up the refrain

> Break, break, break,
>   At the foot of thy crags, O Sea!
> But the tender grace of a day that is dead
>   Will never come back to me.

Browning gives us the spirit of the cavalier in his repeated "Boot, saddle, to horse, and away!" which opens a poem and closes every stanza. And you all know the endless monotony suggested by Kipling's refrain "Boots, boots, boots, boots."

Sometimes the very mood which the refrain impresses was the inspiration of the poem.

Longfellow wrote in his diary November 12, 1845, "Began a poem on a clock, with the words 'Forever, never,' as the burden; suggested by the words of Bridaine, the old French missionary, who said of eternity, *C'est une pendule dont le balancier dit et rendit sans cesse . . . Toujours, jamais! Jamais, toujours! . . .*" And every one of the stanzas of the poem ends

> "Forever—never!
> Never—forever!"

At times refrains are meaningless except for the spirit which they infuse into the song: "Funiculi, Funicula" of the familiar "Some think the world is made for fun and frolic"; "Heigh nonino, no!"; and the soothing syllables of lullabies: "By-low, by-low," "Tura-lura-lura," and the like. Here is one followed by a line of meaning:

> Heigh ho! Sing heigh ho! Unto the green holly:
> Most friendship is feigning, most loving mere folly:
> Then heigh ho, the holly!
> This life is most jolly.
>
> —SHAKESPEARE, *As You Like It*

The refrain may have any position in a poem but most often it is placed at the close of the stanza, where like the rhyme of the last line, it serves as a binder to the lines of the stanza.

Charles Lamb's "The Old Familiar Faces" written in unrhymed verse is divided into stanzas which are held together by the refrain

All, all are gone, the old familiar faces.

To honor the approaching double marriage of Lady Elizabeth Somerset and her sister Lady Katharine, in 1596, Spenser composed ten stanzas of "Prothalamion" each one of which ends with the refrain:

Sweet Thames! run softly, till I end my song.

And sometimes words are repeated as refrains for the sheer joy of repeating them, it seems. The words "Highland Mary" seem dear to the lips of Robert Burns. In a lyric of that name each stanza closes with the words, though the complete refrain varies slightly with each repetition: the first with "O my sweet Highland Mary," which becomes "Was my sweet Highland Mary" in the second, "That wraps my Highland Mary" in the third, and finally "Shall live my Highland Mary."

This variation adds the element of surprise to that of familiarity which enhances pleasure.

The first three stanzas of the familiar "Charge of the Light Brigade" Tennyson closes with "Rode the six hundred," which becomes in the fourth, "Not the six hundred," and in the remaining stanzas "Left of six hundred" and "Noble six hundred!"

The echoes at the Irish Lakes of Killarney suggested the haunting refrain for the exquisite lyric which is quoted below in its entirety. No musical device may be fully enjoyed unless the poem in which it appears is read through.

> The splendor falls on castle walls
>   And snowy summits old in story:
> The long light shakes across the lakes
>   And the wild cataract leaps in glory.
> Blow, bugle, blow, set the wild echoes flying,
> Blow, bugle; answer, echoes, dying, dying, dying.
>
> O hark, O hear! how thin and clear,
>   And thinner, clearer, farther going!
> O sweet and far from cliff and scar
>   The horns of Elfland faintly blowing!
> Blow, let us hear the purple glens replying:
> Blow, bugle; answer, echoes, dying, dying, dying.
>
> O love, they die in yon rich sky,
>   They faint on hill or field or river:
> Our echoes roll from soul to soul,
>   And grow for ever and for ever.
> Blow, bugle, blow, set the wild echoes flying,
> And answer, echoes, answer, dying, dying, dying.
>   —ALFRED, LORD TENNYSON: *The Princess*

Every musical device has been fused into a richly modulated voice through which tones and overtones and undertones are flowing like the waters of the very cataracts at Killarney, which inspired this work of art.

In the French forms, which we will study later, no such variation in the refrain is permitted. There may be a subtle variation of *meaning*, but no change in the sound. Poe says that a refrain should be short and sonorous. That is why he chose "Nevermore" as the refrain for "The Raven," you may recall.

Magical as is the effect of word repetition, the silence of the unspoken word is often more impressive still. Who does not know the comfort of a friend with whom he does not have to keep up a steady flow of conversation? Who does not cherish the silence of understanding when eyes meet, and thoughts are exchanged with no words?

> Heard melodies are sweet but those unheard are sweeter.

The silences of poetry are rich in significance. In every line of any length somewhere there is a silent place, called the cæsura. "Cæsura" is derived from the Latin word *caedere* which means "to cut." The line is cut with a silence—the breath recovers its poise, so to speak, to continue because the meaning requires the stop. The cæsura is a sense pause which coincides with the metrical pause. Punctuation has nothing to do with it; though it naturally falls where a period or a semicolon falls in a line. To vary the position of this sense pause in successive lines enriches the music of verse. Let || represent the cæsura. See how the cæsuras shift position from line to line in the following:

> He spake;|| and to confirm his words, out flew
> Millions of flaming swords || drawn from the thighs
> Of mighty cherubim; || the sudden blaze
> Far round illumined hell: || highly they raged
> Against the Highest, || and fierce with grasped arms
> Clash'd on their sounding shields|| the din of war,
> Hurling defiance || toward the vault of heaven.
>   —JOHN MILTON

Sometimes there are two cæsuras in a line

> Lie there, my art.|| Wipe thou thine eyes; || have comfort.

Constant recurrence of cæsuras in the same position would make the rhythm monotonous. According to Pope, in a verse of ten syllables there is "naturally a pause either at the fourth, fifth, or sixth syllables." This is a bit too mechanical for any but his couplets.

But besides the sense pause, there is the musical pause.

> Break, break, break,
> On thy cold gray stones, O Sea!

Here the pause after each "break" has the effect of a rest in music. It suggests the receding of the waves, which break again with the word. And more: there is grief in those pauses.

In life, the moments of deepest emotion are wordless; the absence of words may deepen the emotion of poetry. Modern poets use leaders (dots) effectively to mark the silence of intense emotion. The poet must feel this silence in his own heart to transmit the effect to readers of his poetry.

> These be
> Three silent things:
> The falling snow . . . the hour
> Before the dawn . . . the mouth of one
> Just dead.
>
> —ADELAIDE CRAPSEY

Each silence is heavy with suggestion as though it waited for one heart to transfer its feeling to the other.

The silence precipitated by a shortened line may sharpen any emotional effect from exultation to despair.

Read these words of a despondent king

> Out, out, brief candle!
> Life's but a walking shadow; a poor player
> That struts and frets his hour upon the stage
> And then is heard no more. It is a tale
> Told by an idiot, full of sound and fury,
> Signifying nothing.
>
> —SHAKESPEARE, *Macbeth*

Note the effect of that "Signifying nothing." The line is left with a long pulsing silence—two beats are never filled.

See how the silence, which fills out the last line of each stanza in "The Lake Isle of Innisfree," gives time for the echoes to have their moments in the heart.

> I will arise and go now, and go to Innisfree,
> And a small cabin build there, of clay and wattles made;
> Nine bean rows will I have there, a hive for the honey bee,
>   And live alone in the bee-loud glade.
>
> And I shall have some peace there, for peace comes dropping slow,
> Dropping from the veils of the morning to where the cricket sings;
> There midnight's all a glimmer, and noon a purple glow,
>   And evening full of the linnet's wings.
>
> I will arise and go now, for always night and day
> I hear lake water lapping with low sounds by the shore;
> While I stand on the roadway, or on the pavements gray,
>   I hear it in the deep heart's core.
>
> —WILLIAM BUTLER YEATS

Note how "Easter" in the chapter, "The Quatrain," sings through the silence of that last line. Only two words are uttered. The rest is "unheard melody." In creating your own stanza patterns the effectiveness of the shortened line is something to remember. As much imagination may be brought to the combination of line lengths as to the creation of images.

In the chapter "Patterns To Try" at the back of this book, patterns are variously treated. You may wish to look at them before experimenting with your own.

SOMETHING TO DO

1. When you discover a poem which creates a breathless effect through the silence of a shortened line commit it to your notebook and share it with your writing fraternity.

2. Read these passages with a thought to the cæsuras in the line:

> Then, while I breathed in sight of heaven, he,
> Poor fellow, could he help it? recommenced
> And ran through all the coltish chronicle.
> —ALFRED, LORD TENNYSON

> These violent delights have violent ends,
> And in their triumph die; like fire and powder,
> Which, as they kiss, consume: the sweetest honey
> Is loathsome in its own deliciousness,
> And in the taste confounds the appetite:
> Therefore, love moderately; long love doth so;
> Too swift arrives as tardy as too slow.
> —WILLIAM SHAKESPEARE

3. Copy a passage from Shakespeare or Robert Frost. Mark the cæsuras by ||. Note how the poets vary the place in successive lines.

4. What effect have the repetitions in this passage?

> To-morrow and to-morrow and to-morrow
> Creeps in this petty pace from day to day

5. Write a word, a phrase or a line as a refrain to impress the mood of a poem. Later you may build upon this refrain as Longfellow constructed "The Old Clock on the Stairs" and Poe built "The Raven."

CHAPTER XVI

BIRDS AND FLOWERS

THE birds of the air and the flowers of the field have ever touched the heart of the poet. Maybe you too will give expression to the feelings inspired by one of them. Their accompaniments are flight, song, fragrance, grace, color and innumerable spiritual qualities, which the discerning heart may feel.

Try a poem on some bird or flower: a rose in a florist's window, iris, begonia on a window sill, scrawny half-dead stalk across the way, columbine nodding from a rock. Some bird you know intimately may suggest a song. Sparrows we have with us always. In different localities there will be many different birds to choose from. The coming of birds, their going, or the absence of bird or flower may suggest a poem. By flower, we mean any growing thing.

See what birds and flowers have inspired poets to create. Some are masterpieces.

The Throstle

"Summer is coming, summer is coming,
  I know it, I know it, I know it.
Light again, leaf again, life again, love again,"
  Yes, my wild little Poet.

Sing the new year in under the blue.
  Last year you sang it as gladly.
"New, new, new, new!" Is it then *so* new
  That you should carol so madly?

"Love again, song again, nest again, young again,"
  Never a prophet so crazy!
And hardly a daisy as yet, little friend,
  See, there is hardly a daisy.

"Here again, here, here, here, happy year!"
  O warble unchidden, unbidden!
Summer is coming, is coming, my dear,
  And all the winters are hidden.

—ALFRED, LORD TENNYSON

Song: *The Owl*

When cats run home and light is come,
  And dew is cold upon the ground,
And the far-off stream is dumb,
  And the whirring sail goes round,
  And the whirring sail goes round;
Alone and warming his five wits,
The white owl in the belfry sits.

When merry milkmaids click the latch,
  And rarely smells the new-mown hay,
And the cock hath sung beneath the thatch
  Twice or thrice his roundelay,
  Twice or thrice his roundelay;
Alone and warming his five wits,
The white owl in the belfry sits.

—ALFRED, LORD TENNYSON

Ducks and Heron

The ducks go down the pasture to the pond,
  Along their little path, one after one . . .
In file among the flowers and grass, a white
  Procession in the sun.

Like skiffs they launch into the water there
  With grace that is the birthright of a bird;
Their splashing has the softness of a sigh
  Or of a whispered word.

Once in the dusk a wild blue heron paused
  Among these ducks that dived and floated by . . .
His beauty was a song, his mystery
  A challenge and a cry!

A migrant to the marshes of the south
  From lands that felt the first thin whip of snow,
The heron lingered for an hour to learn
  The joys that ducks may know.

Then with the night, those wings that knew the sea,
  That knew the strength and splendor of the wind,
Spread forth their plumes above the ducks, and left
  The pond of peace behind.

—AGNES KENDRICK GRAY

Vespers

O Blackbird, what a boy you are!
How you do go it!
Blowing your bugle to that one sweet star—
How you do blow it!
And does she hear you, blackbird boy, so far?
Or is it wasted breath?
"Good Lord! She is so bright
To-night!"
The blackbird saith.

—THOMAS EDWARD BROWN

Clipped Wings

Why do you flutter in my arms and scream,
O frenzied bird, as my poised blue scissors gleam
Above your outstretched wings, and wait to clip
From your shining mallard plumes each buoyant tip?

As I prepare to groom you for the stool
Of shorn decoys who swim my barnyard pool,
Do you by some vague intuition sense
The subtle coming of your impotence?

Never again will you rapturously tilt
Your wings to the sun to wash them in its gilt,
To wheel, and dizzily eddy down the expanse
Of blue to earth like a whistling fiery lance.

And ended the nights when the bayou lies asleep
And stars like silver minnows swim its deep—
Of breathless waiting, as your wild mate swings
Over your head and spreads her satin wings.

O wildling, the rebellion in your blood and bone
Doubles the constant anguish of my own—
Your fear of dark earth-fettered days to be,
Of a world whose sky-lines are a mockery,

A world of shallow barricaded ponds
That holds for you no shining blue beyonds,
No flaming high horizons to fire your breast
And send you bugling on a blazing quest.

Find comfort in this: if your proud wings are shorn
By my faltering blades, you shall wax fat with corn,
Drowse in the sun, and never know the bite
Of adversity again in day or night.

Shielded from every skulking fox and hawk,
Contented on your puddle, you shall squawk
And find among my pens of placid geese,
Even as I, a sweet seductive peace.

But when wild mallards stretch their vibrant throats
Against the moon and fling their brazen notes
Earthward to challenge and stop the hearts of all
Who grovel on earth, in a proud strong trumpet-call;

And when the frosted silver bell of sky
Rings with the rush of wings and the joyous cry
Of mallards streaming home, home again—
What then, O wretched sky-born bird, what then!

—Lew Sarett

Ode to a Nightingale

My heart aches, and a drowsy numbness pains
  My sense, as though of hemlock I had drunk,
Or emptied some dull opiate to the drains
  One minute past, and Lethe-wards had sunk:
'Tis not through envy of thy happy lot,
  But being too happy in thy happiness,
    That thou, light-wingèd Dryad of the trees,
      In some melodious plot
  Of beechen green, and shadows numberless,
    Singest of summer in full-throated ease.

O for a draught of vintage! that hath been
  Cool'd a long time in the deep-delvèd earth,
Tasting of Flora and the country-green,
  Dance, and Provençal song, and sunburnt mirth!
O for a beaker full of the warm South!
  Full of the true, the blushful Hippocrene,
    With beaded bubbles winking at the brim;
      And purple-stainèd mouth;
  That I might drink, and leave the world unseen,
    And with thee fade away into the forest dim:

Fade far away, dissolve, and quite forget
  What thou among the leaves hast never known,
The weariness, the fever, and the fret
  Here, where men sit and hear each other groan;
Where palsy shakes a few, sad, last grey hairs,
  Where youth grows pale, and spectre-thin, and dies;
    Where but to think is to be full of sorrow
      And leaden-eyed despairs;
  Where beauty cannot keep her lustrous eyes,
    Or new Love pine at them beyond to-morrow.

Away! away! for I will fly to thee,
  Not charioted by Bacchus and his pards,
But on the viewless wings of Poesy,
  Though the dull brain perplexes and retards:
Already with thee! tender is the night,
  And haply the Queen-Moon is on her throne,
    Cluster'd around by all her starry Fays
      But here there is no light,
  Save what from heaven is with the breezes blown
    Through verdurous glooms and winding mossy ways.

I cannot see what flowers are at my feet,
  Nor what soft incense hangs upon the boughs,
But, in embalmèd darkness, guess each sweet
  Wherewith the seasonable month endows
The grass, the thicket, and the fruit-tree wild;
  White hawthorn, and the pastoral eglantine;
    Fast-fading violets cover'd up in leaves;
      And mid-May's eldest child,
  The coming musk-rose, full of dewy wine,
    The murmurous haunt of flies on summer eves.

Darkling I listen; and for many a time
  I have been half in love with easeful Death,
Call'd him soft names in many a musèd rhyme,
  To take into the air my quiet breath;
Now more than ever seems it rich to die,
  To cease upon the midnight with no pain,
    While thou art pouring forth thy soul abroad
      In such an ecstasy!
  Still wouldst thou sing, and I have ears in vain—
    To thy high requiem become a sod.

Thou wert not born for death, immortal Bird!
  No hungry generations trod thee down;
The voice I hear this passing night was heard
  In ancient days by emperor and clown:

Perhaps the self-same song that found a path
   Through the sad heart of Ruth, when, sick for home,
    She stood in tears amid the alien corn;
      The same that ofttimes hath
Charm'd magic casements, opening on the foam
   Of perilous seas, in faery lands forlorn.

Forlorn! the very word is like a bell
   To toll me back from thee to my sole self!
Adieu! the fancy cannot cheat so well
   As she is famed to do, deceiving elf.
Adieu! adieu! thy plaintive anthem fades
   Past the near meadows, over the still stream,
    Up the hill-side; and now 'tis buried deep
      In the next valley-glades:
Was it a vision, or a waking dream?
    Fled is that music:—do I wake or sleep?

—JOHN KEATS

To a Skylark

Hail to thee, blithe spirit!
   Bird thou never wert,
That from heaven, or near it,
   Pourest thy full heart
In profuse strains of unpremeditated art.

Higher still and higher
   From the earth thou springest
Like a cloud of fire;
   The blue deep thou wingest,
And singing still dost soar, and soaring ever singest.

In the golden light'ning
   Of the sunken sun,
O'er which clouds are bright'ning,
   Thou dost float and run,
Like an unbodied joy whose race is just begun.

The pale purple even
   Melts around thy flight;
Like a star of heaven
   In the broad daylight
Thou art unseen, but yet I hear thy shrill delight,

Keen as are the arrows
   Of that silver sphere,
Whose intense lamp narrows
   In the white dawn clear,
Until we hardly see—we feel that it is there.

All the earth and air
  With thy voice is loud,
As, when night is bare,
  From one lonely cloud
The moon rains out her beams, and heaven is overflow'd.

  What thou art we know not;
    What is most like thee?
  From rainbow clouds there flow not
    Drops so bright to see,
As from thy presence showers a rain of melody:

  Like a poet hidden
    In the light of thought,
  Singing hymns unbidden,
    Till the world is wrought
To sympathy with hopes and fears it heeded not:

  Like a high-born maiden
    In a palace tower,
  Soothing her love-laden
    Soul in secret hour
With music sweet as love, which overflows her bower:

  Like a glow-worm golden
    In a dell of dew,
  Scattering unbeholden
    Its aërial hue
Among the flowers and grass which screen it from the view:

  Like a rose embower'd
    In its own green leaves,
  By warm winds deflower'd,
    Till the scent it gives
Makes faint with too much sweet those heavy-wingèd thieves.

  Sound of vernal showers
    On the twinkling grass,
  Rain-awaken'd flowers,
    All that ever was
Joyous and clear and fresh, thy music doth surpass.

  Teach us, sprite or bird,
    What sweet thoughts are thine:
  I have never heard
    Praise of love or wine
That panted forth a flood of rapture so divine.

Chorus Hymeneal,
 Or triumphal chant,
Match'd with thine would be all
 But an empty vaunt,
A thing wherein we feel there is some hidden want.

What objects are the fountains
 Of thy happy strain?
What fields, or waves, or mountains?
 What shapes of sky or plain?
What love of thine own kind? what ignorance of pain?

With thy clear keen joyance
 Languor cannot be;
Shadow of annoyance
 Never came near thee;
Thou lovest—but ne'er knew love's sad satiety.

Waking or asleep,
 Thou of death must deem
Things more true and deep
 Than we mortals dream,
Or how could thy notes flow in such a crystal stream?

We look before and after,
 And pine for what is not:
Our sincerest laughter
 With some pain is fraught;
Our sweetest songs are those that tell of saddest thought.

Yet, if we could scorn
 Hate and pride and fear,
If we were things born
 Not to shed a tear,
I know not how thy joy we ever should come near.

Better than all measures
 Of delightful sound,
Better than all treasures
 That in books are found,
Thy skill to poet were, thou scorner of the ground!

Teach me half the gladness
 That thy brain must know;
Such harmonious madness
 From my lips would flow,
The world should listen then—as I am listening now.
      —Percy Bysshe Shelley

What in the flight of the skylark makes the last long line well suited
to it?

To a Skylark

Ethereal minstrel! pilgrim of the sky!
Dost thou despise the earth where cares abound?
Or, while the wings aspire, are heart and eye
Both with thy nest upon the dewy ground?
Thy nest which thou canst drop into at will,
Those quivering wings composed, that music still!

To the last point of vision, and beyond,
Mount, daring warbler!—that love-prompted strain
—'Twixt thee and thine a never-failing bond—
Thrills not the less the bosom of the plain:
Yet might'st thou seem, proud privilege! to sing
All independent of the leafy spring.

Leave to the nightingale her shady wood;
A privacy of glorious light is thine,
Whence thou dost pour upon the world a flood
Of harmony, with instinct more divine:
Type of the wise, who soar, but never roam—
True to the kindred points of Heaven and Home!
                                        —WILLIAM WORDSWORTH

Wordsworth wrote another poem, "To a Skylark" beginning, "Up with me, up with me into the clouds!" Some other bird poems are: "To a Waterfowl," by William Cullen Bryant; "The Sandpiper," by Celia Thaxter; "Philomela," by Matthew Arnold, page 229.

STUDENT ATTEMPT

The Ruby-Throated Humming Bird

Swift as a comet,
   Elusive as gold,
Vibrant with living;
   By man uncontrolled.

Flash of his colors,
   The low hum of wings
Whirring so quickly
   For that's how he sings;

Poised on a flower
   So gracefully shy,
Off in a flurry
   And lost to the eye.
                  —DOROTHY VIERTEL

Growing things concern the poet in the lines below:

Home-Thoughts from Abroad

Oh, to be in England
Now that April's there,
And whoever wakes in England
Sees, some morning, unaware,
That the lowest boughs and the brush-wood sheaf
Round the elm-tree bole are in tiny leaf,
While the chaffinch sings on the orchard bough
In England—now!

And after April, when May follows,
And the whitethroat builds, and all the swallows!
Hark, where my blossomed pear-tree in the hedge
Leans to the field and scatters on the clover
Blossoms and dewdrops—at the bent spray's edge—
That's the wise thrush; he sings each song twice over,
Lest you should think he never could recapture
The first fine careless rapture!
And though the fields look rough with hoary dew,
All will be gay when noontide wakes anew
The buttercups, the little children's dower
—Far brighter than this gaudy melon-flower!

—ROBERT BROWNING

The Primrose

Ask me why I send you here
This sweet Infanta of the year?
Ask me why I send to you
This primrose, thus bepearl'd with dew?
I will whisper to your ears:—
The sweets of love are mix'd with tears.

Ask me why this flower does show
So yellow-green, and sickly too?
Ask me why the stalk is weak
And bending (yet it doth not break)?
I will answer:—These discover
What fainting hopes are in a lover.

—ROBERT HERRICK

Daffodils

I wander'd lonely as a cloud
  That floats on high o'er vales and hills,
When all at once I saw a crowd,
  A host, of golden daffodils;
Beside the lake, beneath the trees,
Fluttering and dancing in the breeze.

Continuous as the stars that shine
  And twinkle on the Milky Way,
They stretch'd in never-ending line
  Along the margin of a bay:
Ten thousand saw I at a glance,
Tossing their heads in sprightly dance.

The waves beside them danced, but they
  Out-did the sparkling waves in glee:
A poet could not but be gay,
  In such a jocund company:
I gazed—and gazed—but little thought
What wealth the show to me had brought:

For oft, when on my couch I lie
  In vacant or in pensive mood,
They flash upon that inward eye
  Which is the bliss of solitude;
And then my heart with pleasure fills,
And dances with the daffodils.

—WILLIAM WORDSWORTH

The Rhodora

(On being asked whence is the flower)

In May, when sea-winds pierced our solitudes,
I found the fresh Rhodora in the woods,
Spreading its leafless blooms in a damp nook,
To please the desert and the sluggish brook.
The purple petals, fallen in the pool,
Made the black water with their beauty gay;
Here might the red-bird come his plumes to cool,
And court the flower that cheapens his array.
Rhodora! if the sages ask thee why
This charm is wasted on the earth and sky,
Tell them, dear, that if eyes were made for seeing,

Then Beauty is its own excuse for being:
Why thou wert there, O rival of the rose!
I never thought to ask, I never knew:
But, in my simple ignorance, suppose
The self-same Power that brought me there brought you.
—RALPH WALDO EMERSON

Some other flower poems are: "Trees" by Joyce Kilmer from *Trees and Other Poems*; "Loveliest of trees" by A. E. Housman (see page 111).

Late Chrysanthemums

This bloom is late, too late to stir my heart.
All through the heat of summer I have thought,
Returning to your cloistered garden spot
Each day to see a bud or blossom start;
But prim and stiff you held yourself apart
Until despair and disappointment fought
The fervent faith and hope I had been taught,
And nonchalantly let them both depart.
Then, after they had gone, when days were cold,
And I no longer looked for flowers to bloom,
Nor cared at all if from the sluggish mold
A bud might start, came blossoms to perfume
The barren garden with their acrid tang.
My heart had long forgotten how it sang.
—MARIE TELLO PHILLIPS

When the above poem appeared in the New York *Times* one November day, it stimulated lively discussion in the Poetry Class. The young members had different ideas about late-blooming chrysanthemums. They decided to answer Marie Tello Phillips in verses of their own. Here are a few of them:

Late Blossom

And if
This bit of new
October, blooms in rain
Or scattered snow, why is it then
Less joy?
—JOYCE LANCASTER

Chrysanthemums

What a joy to find you there
After all your friends have gone,
Knowing you're a flower rare,
All your petals still unshorn

By the cruel frost, who stays
Waiting, watching with a snare,
Killing what has taken days
To create—it is not fair!

Some warm magic in your bright
Sturdiness dispels the gloom
Of hopeless days; my heart is light
For your unexpected bloom.
　　　　　—Benedetta Civiletti

Late Chrysanthemums

Summer came with all her frills
And lacy leaves of green,
Forming from a barren place
A brightly colored scene.

Summer went, and left behind
Brown earth and withered grass,
A lonesome spot within my heart—
Why must her beauty pass?

But when at last the echoes
Had forgotten how she sang,
You came as a reminder
With your glowing autumn tang.
　　　　　—Marjorie DeGraff

The author of the next was interested in dramatics. See how her imagery reveals her taste.

Late Chrysanthemums

The garden was a frowsy mass
Of brittle browning leaves and twigs,
And I had no more thought to see
Your towsled yellow wigs.

My heart was drying to a lump,
Lifeless, like cracked and thirsty earth;
November, colourless and cold,
Had quite destroyed my mirth.

This morning, as I tried to clear
The funeral mounds of leaves away,
I saw your heads of dripping gold,
And felt a breath of May.
　　　　　—Ruth H. Klein

Late Chrysanthemums

Lovely autumn flower,
You are late in waking!
Busy Nature let you sleep
While she did her baking?
　　　　　—Muriel Slater

To C. L. P.

The stately cluster blooming there,
Imparts to all the autumn air
A scent of spring, and seems to be
A warmth for hearts that yearn to see
The growing leaves and budding trees,
And daisies waving with the breeze.
Oh flower, glowing bright in fall,
I know and like you best of all.
—GERTRUDE YONKE

Spring and summer yielded wealth also.

Forsythia

The sunlight runs a race outside my door
And throws a bar of light across the floor.
Spring, go away, I've need of you no more.

I have entirely too much work, you know,
To play: I've dishes, beds, and things to sew.
Spring, I forgot you many years ago.

Forsythia, your golden-fingered art
I fear. Begone, nor yet delay your start
Lest you should wind your sprays about my heart.
—DORIS V. LECKY

Apple Blossom

Is this
The moonlight on
A nightingale's full throat
Or but the dazzling whiteness of
New snow?
—ESTELLE ROOKS

Treasure

One day I thought I saw a coin
Glittering in the grass.
  And when I stooped to pick it up,
  Lo! it was a buttercup
Gleaming in the grass.

A little bud of yellow gold
Sparkling in the grass.
  A tender bit of melted sun—
  Lovely, and the only one
Shining in the grass.
—MURIEL WELCHER

CHAPTER XVII

OUR ANIMAL KIN

WITH all the beauty, the whimsicality, and grace of birds, perhaps the wingless creatures of earth and stream are closer to the human heart. Beast, fish, insect, reptile have spoken to the hearts that have understood them.

Perhaps you have a pet alligator, a turtle, a dog, a cat. Or better still, you may know the woods, the holes along a river bank, the waters of some stream or lake or even the deep sea. Their denizens are ready to leap into a poem, hewn from the wild by your sympathetic hand. Read what authentic poets have created out of experience with animals. Then search your own experience and attempt to cherish it in a poem.

Four Little Foxes

Speak gently, Spring, and make no sudden sound;
For in the windy valley, yesterday I found
New-born foxes squirming in the ground—
    Speak gently.

Walk softly, March, forbear the bitter blow;
Her feet within a trap, her blood upon the snow,
The four little foxes saw their mother go—
    Walk softly.

Go lightly, Spring, oh, give them no alarm;
When I covered them with boughs to shelter them from harm,
The thin blue foxes suckled at my arm—
    Go lightly.

Step softly, March, with your rampant hurricane;
Nuzzling one another, and whimpering with pain,
The new little foxes are shivering in the rain—
    Step softly.

—LEW SARETT

Through this lyric the tramp of oxen has been heard around the world, for it has been sung many times over the radio to exquisite music composed by Alma Steedman.

Oxen

"Gee . . Haw" . . . the furrow's deep,
And those who onward go must plod.
The day is long
And oxen have no song;
No sound is heard
Save "Gee . . . Haw!"
And curling lash
That cuts the raw
If step be taken wrong.

They know no plan
Of God or man,
Or how to weep;
They only know of furrows
Long . . . and . . . deep.

—MARY CUMMINGS EUDY

The Tiger

Tiger, tiger, burning bright
In the forests of the night,
What immortal hand or eye
Could frame thy fearful symmetry?

In what distant deeps or skies
Burnt the fire of thine eyes?
On what wings dare he aspire?
What the hand dare seize the fire?

And what shoulder and what art
Could twist the sinews of thy heart?
And, when thy heart began to beat,
What dread hand and what dread feet?

What the hammer? What the chain?
In what furnace was thy brain?
What the anvil? What dread grasp
Dare its deadly terrors clasp?

When the stars threw down their spears,
And water'd heaven with their tears,
Did He smile His work to see?
Did he who made the lamb make thee?

Tiger, tiger, burning bright
In the forests of the night,
What immortal hand or eye
Dare frame thy fearful symmetry?

—WILLIAM BLAKE

Old Hound

With paws in firelight dipped, and drowsy ears
He disregards the calling of the night.
The small fox runs, the hare his shadow fears,
Below the moon the wild geese wing their flight.
But under shelter now he seems content
With serene breath to lie in silken ease.
Back from the lonely forest's ferny scent,
His trail has ended at his master's knees.

He nods his proud head through a night of frost,
His twitching feet alone reveal his dream:
The whirling autumn cloud, the clear track lost,
The antlers gleaming in the mountain stream . . .
No inch of him betrays to morning skies
That hour—except his melancholy eyes.

—Florence Ripley Mastin

A Cow

Cows aren't clumsy—
My cow is slender
And lovely as a deer.
She is beautiful
When she lifts her head
Suddenly, in fear,
Nostrils distended,
Drinking the scent
The wind has blown.
Then it is, she looks
Like something chiseled
From a dark stone.

Once I heard her call
Into the silence
Of a summer's night.
When morning came,
The look of her eyes
Was a shining light.
Oh, the soft look
And the still look,
As she turned her head
To the little form
Of her calf, that lay
New-born—and dead.

—Julia Van der Veer

A Mother with Young Kittens

Torn between hunger and maternal cares,
She puts her nose beneath the fence to spy,
Reluctant to abandon to the night
The barrel where her sons and daughters lie.

The scented air awakes her gourmet's soul;
With upward shoving nose and agile claw
She pries the cover from the refuse can
And in the crack insinuates her paw.

Meticulous as any chatelaine
Choosing the courses when the king's to dine,
She worries out a well-picked knob of veal,
A crab claw and a haddock's sorry spine.

I move a step; she hears, and terrified
She seeks to bear away her grisly prize.
The bone is dropped in flight; upon my face
She turns reproachful grey madonna eyes.
                                                —RICHARD HART

Coyote Brood

What a bewildering world is yours, wild brood,
Cringing before the north wind's sullen mood,
And squirming as your mother's pink wet tongue
Licks the bedraggled fur of her new-born young.

Such eyes!—that come from darkness into day
Blinking and blinded by every sun-split ray,
Perplexed before the catastrophes of earth
That stalk you from the moment of your birth.

So overwhelmed by night, so round with wonder
When storm-clouds roll their drums in crashing thunder
To summon you, like a smiting challenge hurled,
To the battle for survival in this world.

Your span shall hold no respite from the pain
Of racking hunger, of stinging sleet and rain,
No loveliness but a moment of delight
Snatched in the sun or furtive in the night

Goaded by fear that prods you like a knife,
Oh, not for the complacencies of life;
Harried by belching steel and pitiless traps,
Your fondest hope is but a grim perhaps.

Into the world bewildered you were thrust,
To struggle bewildered with hate, disaster, lust;
Out of the world, defeated, driven, low,
To benevolent earth bewildered you will go.

—LEW SARETT

To a Mouse

(On turning her up in her nest with the plough, November, 1785)

Wee, sleekit, cowrin', tim'rous beastie,   *sleekit = sleek*
O, what a panic's in thy breastie!
Thou need na start awa sae hasty,
        Wi' bickering brattle!   *bickering = hastening*
I wad be laith to rin an' chase thee,   *brattle = scamper*
        Wi' murd'ring pattle!
                                                        pattle = plow-staff, or scraper

I'm truly sorry man's dominion
Has broken Nature's social union,
An' justifies that ill opinion
        Which makes thee startle
At me, thy poor, earth-born companion,
        An' fellow-mortal!

I doubt na, whyles, but thou may thieve;   *whyles = sometimes*
What then? poor beastie, thou maun live!
A daimen-icker in a thrave   *daimen-icker = occasional heaa*
        'S a sma' request;   *thrave = 24 sheaves*
I'll get a blessin wi' the lave,   *lave = rest*
        An' never miss't!

Thy wee bit housie, too, in ruin!
It's silly wa's the win's are strewin!
An' naething, now, to big a new ane,   *big = build*
        O' foggage green!   *foggage = herbage*
An' bleak December's winds ensuin,
        Baith snell an' keen!   *snell = sharp*

Thou saw the fields laid bare and waste,
An' weary winter comin' fast,
An' cozie here, beneath the blast,
        Thou thought to dwell,
Till crash! the cruel coulter past   *coulter = plow*
        Out through thy cell.

That wee bit heap o' leaves an' stibble
Has cost thee mony a weary nibble!
Now thou's turned out, for a' thy trouble,
     But house or hald,   *But = without; hald = abode*
To thole the winter's sleety dribble   *thole = endure*
     An' cranreuch cauld!   *cranreuch = hoar-frost*

But, mousie, thou art no thy lane   *lane = alone*
In proving foresight may be vain;
The best laid schemes o' mice an' men
     Gang aft a-gley,   *a-gley = awry*
An' lea'e us nought but grief an' pain,
     For promised joy.

Still, thou art blest compared wi' me;
The present only toucheth thee;
But och! I backward cast my e'e
     On prospects drear!
An' forward, though I canna see,
     I guess an' fear!

                                    —ROBERT BURNS

The next two sonnets have a little story. Leigh Hunt, editor of the
magazine, *The Examiner,* and the author of that poem which all school
children know, "Abou Ben Adhem," challenged Keats to write "On the
Grasshopper and the Cricket." Then and there, at Hunt's cottage, and
in a limited time, they each wrote a poem. Keats's was finished first.
Here is Hunt's:

The Grasshopper and the Cricket

Green little vaulter in the sunny grass
Catching your heart up at the feel of June,
Sole voice that's heard amidst the lazy noon,
When ev'n the bees lag at the summoning brass;
And you, warm little housekeeper, who class
With those who think the candles come too soon,
Loving the fire and with your tricksome tune
Nick the glad silent moments as they pass;
Oh sweet and tiny cousins, that belong,
One to the fields, the other to the hearth,
Both have your sunshine; both though small are strong
At your clear hearts; and both were sent on earth
To sing in thoughtful ears this natural song,—
In doors and out, summer and winter, Mirth.

Hunt saw how much better Keats's was than his, and was characteristically generous in his praise. Keats's sonnet follows:

On the Grasshopper and the Cricket

The poetry of earth is never dead:
　When all the birds are faint with the hot sun,
　And hide in cooling trees, a voice will run
From hedge to hedge about the new-mown mead;
That is the Grasshopper's—he takes the lead
　In summer luxury,—he has never done
　With his delights; for when tired out with fun
He rests at ease beneath some pleasant weed.
The poetry of earth is ceasing never:
　On a lone winter evening, when the frost
　　Has wrought a silence, from the stove there shrills
The Cricket's song, in warmth increasing ever,
　And seems to one in drowsiness half lost,
　　The Grasshopper's among some grassy hills.

Here are modern American crickets:

Autumn Crickets

A drowsy music drifts across the dusk
Where crickets fiddle fore wings out of tune
With half heard threnodies of grass and husk
And leaf-waves breaking on the low red moon.
This is the music that we heard below
The opened rose, in harmony with all
The fragrant rhythms of the night, the slow
Dance of the moonlight on a flowered wall.

Beneath the shadow-dances of the grass
Earth-pulses throbbed in these articulate wings.
They stay . . . though on this night the witch-clouds pass
Above the pathways of departing things.
We find, where shadow circles now are drawn,
The music playing . . . and the dancers gone.
　　　　　　　　　　　　　　　　—GLENN WARD DRESBACH

The Spider

With six small diamonds for his eyes
He walks upon the summer skies,
Drawing from his silken blouse
The lacework of his dwelling house.

He lays his staircase as he goes
Under his eight thoughtful toes
And grows with the concentric flower
Of his shadowless, thin bower.

His back legs are a pair of hands;
They can spindle out the strands
Of a thread that is so small
It stops the sunlight not at all.

He spins himself to threads of dew
Which will harden soon into
Lines that cut like slender knives
Across the insects' airy lives.

He makes no motion but is right,
He spreads out his appetite
Into a network, twist on twist,
This little ancient scientist.

He does not know he is unkind,
He has a jewel for a mind
And logic deadly as dry bone,
This small son of Euclid's own.
—ROBERT P. TRISTRAM COFFIN

Antelope with Cattle

Etching in a leap
Crags against the sky . . .
Bitterness and sleep
Wrestle in your eye.

Slow the rooted kine
Cull and taste repose.
Delicate the fine
Grace you never lose.

Arrogant to be
Quicksilver, not blood,
Printing daintily
Dainty hooves in mud.
—ROBERT McBLAIR

Snake

(Jardin Des Plantes)

He curled there quiescent
Imprisoned in the Garden,
Behind bars of metal
And thick walls of crystal
Apart in the stillness,
Withdrawn in the coils of
His own cryptic circles
That reach through the aeons—
Reach back to a Garden—
A mythical Woman
As slim as a birch-tree,
With hair spun of sunlight
And white naked body,
Arrested, transfixed by
His sinister splendour . . .

Through bright veils of clear glass
His diamond eyes glittered;
Then slowly his head raised
High over the circles,
The tip of the coils' end
Rose upright and sent forth
The death-rattle warning—
Defenced by ringed armour,
His fangs as his javelins,
He rattled his signal,
His drum-beat of battle . . .
Long, long since with languor
He stretched out his full length,
Each movement a silken
Slow rhythm of caressing,
Drew softly his sinuous
Voluptuous body
Against Earth's deep bosom—
Do his eyes hold visions
Of dimness of forests,
Of leaf-beds—tree arching—
Beyond bars of metal
And thick walls of crystal? . . .

—JESSIE LEMONT

Below is a high-school student's attempt:

The Black Panther

Deep within the jungle's darkness,
Waging a relentless duel
Among the wildest and the fairest,
Slinks the thicket's blackest jewel.

Merely one of many shadows,
Lighting to his lonely mind
By the fire of his hatred
All his burning eyes can find.

Soundless, though no sound escapes him,
Treading past on padded paw
With a lithe and flowing rhythm—
Feline beauty in the raw.

Fascinating is his motion,
Giving a satanic charm
To the ripple of smooth muscles,
Tensed at every breath of harm.

Thus the lord of awesome beauty
Bears the fierce feud of his race:
Power fleshed in vengeful sinew,
Craft concealed in bestial grace.

—JAMES MOONEY

CHAPTER XVIII

WORKS AND THEIR MAKERS

THE indebtedness which poets feel toward those who have influenced their art has not infrequently stimulated beautiful expression. Chapman's translation of Homer stirred Keats to write his exquisite "On First Looking Into Chapman's Homer." Ben Jonson paid a famous tribute "To the Memory of My Beloved Master, William Shakespeare," which you may read below. Coleridge said this: ". . . I regard, and ever have regarded the obligations of intellect, among the most sacred of the claims of gratitude. A valuable thought or a particular train of thought, gives me additional pleasure, when I can safely refer and attribute it to the conversation or correspondence of another." He was greatly impressed by the poetry of William Lisle Bowles, his contemporary. Only scholars read Bowles today, while the world reads Coleridge; but it was the greatness of Bowles that he influenced Coleridge to turn from metaphysics to poetry. Coleridge ever voiced his debt of gratitude. Bowles and Cowper, he wrote, were "the first who combined natural thoughts with natural diction: the first who reconciled the heart with the head."

In the same way Thomas Hardy, impressed by the poetry of William Barnes, was courageous in his praise. In "The Last Signal" he pays a beautiful tribute to Barnes in death. As the sun was setting, Hardy was trudging to a yew grove past the gate, wide-open, from which Barnes had so often set forth. The east was dark, but suddenly the sunlight flashed upon it and Hardy knew that Barnes was waving him farewell as he journeyed on his grave-way.

The works of an artist—writer, sculptor, painter, singer, architect— may speak in some unforgettable way, releasing something of magic from the listening heart. A poem may best convey the debt of gratitude which the influence has exerted.

Perhaps a line from a poem may sing itself in the memory, giving no peace until it has become the core of a new poem. The thoughts which it awakens are tribute enough to their original maker. His lines may appear quoted as the first line of the new poem or woven in skillfully some other way.

Perhaps inspiration may come to you, not through an artistic work but from some civic achievement or some historical event or a character connected with either. You may feel sorrow or joy over the achieve-

ment or failure, remembering that there is nothing so sad as a great
victory except a great defeat!

Some poems here show how poets have been moved to express
their debts of gratitude or appreciation for an influence which they
have cherished.

Socrates

He came coarse-cloaked, grotesque as shaggy Pan,
　　But kings of Homer and gray Hesiod
　　Gave place before that sturdy form bare-shod
From which the golden cord of reason ran;
And like Praxiteles, whose eye could span
　　In unhewn marble outlines of a god,
　　So he who leaned on logic as his rod
Moulded to majesty the mind of man.

The secret of the stars he left unsought,
　　Yet in the corner of a colonnade
　　He stood encircled by Athenian youth,
Shaking the guarded strongholds of their thought
　　With words that pierced each shallow barricade
　　Like silver trumpets challenging to Truth.
　　　　　　　　　　　　—Thomas S. Jones, Jr.

Copernicus

Above the gabled houses, blanched and bright,
　　When lanthorns vanish down a cobbled street,
　　He gazes from a watch-tower, gray with sleet,
To chart the secret pathways of the night.
In movements mystic as the spirit's flight
　　He hears a symphony of sandalled feet,
　　As silver dancers of the darkness meet,
Pale moon and meteor, sun and satellite.

New snow has fallen on the empty square,
　　Where safe and warm the fur-robed burghers dream
　　And bells hang silent in the frosty spire;
While he, through glittering areas of air,
　　Beholds the earth upon her orbit gleam
　　In choral dance around an ark of fire.
　　　　　　　　　　　　—Thomas S. Jones, Jr.

Memorabilia

Ah, did you once see Shelley plain,
    And did he stop and speak to you,
And did you speak to him again?
    How strange it seems and new!

But you were living before that,
    And also you are living after;
And the memory I started at—
    My starting moves your laughter!

I crossed a moor, with a name of its own
    And a certain use in the world no doubt,
Yet a hand's-breadth of it shines alone
    'Mid the blank miles round about:

For there I picked up on the heather
    And there I put inside my breast
A moulted feather, an eagle-feather!
    Well, I forget the rest.

—ROBERT BROWNING

To John Hall Wheelock

(On Receiving Two Books of His Early Poems)

I will turn away from all sweet-scented places
That have lured my soul with promises of sleep.
I will close my eyes on visionary faces,
I will lean above no dead thing on its bier;
No dear and tawdry relic will I keep
Of any festival of any year.
I will go without armor, breathless and alone,
Into the wood where once you wandered singing;
I will fear no voice that rises from any stone.
I will sing no song to keep my courage high,
No matter what sharp beauty may be springing
Between the spaces where your footprints lie.

—HELENE MULLINS

The Odyssey

As one that for a weary space has lain
   Lull'd by the song of Circe and her wine
   In gardens near the pale of Proserpine,
Where that Ææan isle forgets the main,
And only the low lutes of love complain,
   And only shadows of wan lovers pine—
   As such an one were glad to know the brine
Salt on his lips, and the large air again—
So gladly from the songs of modern speech
   Men turn, and see the stars, and feel the free
     Shrill wind beyond the close of heavy flowers,
     And through the music of the languid hours
They hear like Ocean on a western beach
   The surge and thunder of the Odyssey.

                    —ANDREW LANG

To the Memory of My Beloved Master, William Shakespeare

To draw no envy, Shakespeare, on thy name,
Am I thus ample to thy book and fame;
While I confess thy writings to be such
As neither man, nor muse, can praise too much.
'Tis true, and all men's suffrage. But these ways
Were not the paths I meant unto thy praise;
For silliest ignorance on these may light,
Which, when it sounds at best, but echoes right;
Or blind affection, which doth ne'er advance
The truth, but gropes, and urgeth all by chance;
Or crafty malice might pretend this praise,
And think to ruin, where it seemed to raise.
These are, as some infamous bawd or whore
Should praise a matron. What could hurt her more?
But thou art proof against them, and, indeed,
Above the ill fortune of them, or the need.
I therefore will begin. Soul of the age!
The applause, delight, the wonder of our stage!
My Shakespeare, rise! I will not lodge thee by
Chaucer, or Spenser, or bid Beaumont lie
A little further, to make thee a room:
Thou art a monument without a tomb,
And art alive still while thy book doth live
And we have wits to read and praise to give.
That I not mix thee so, my brain excuses,

I mean with great, but disproportioned Muses;
For if I thought my judgment were of years,
I should commit thee surely with thy peers,
And tell how far thou didst our Lyly outshine,
Or sporting Kyd, or Marlowe's mighty line.
And though thou hadst small Latin and less Greek,
From thence to honour thee, I would not seek
For names; but call forth thundering Æschylus,
Euripides, and Sophocles to us;
Pacuvius, Accius, him of Cordova dead,
To life again, to hear thy buskin tread,
And shake a stage; or, when thy socks were on,
Leave thee alone for the comparison
Of all that insolent Greece or haughty Rome
Sent forth, or since did from their ashes come.
Triumph, my Britain, thou hast one to show
To whom all scenes of Europe homage owe.
He was not of an age, but for all time!
And all the Muses still were in their prime,
When, like Apollo, he came forth to warm
Our ears, or like a Mercury to charm!
Nature herself was proud of his designs
And joyed to wear the dressing of his lines,
Which were so richly spun, and woven so fit
As, since, she will vouchsafe no other wit.
The merry Greek, tart Aristophanes,
Neat Terence, witty Plautus, now not please;
But antiquated and deserted lie,
As they were not of Nature's family.
Yet must I not give Nature all; thy art,
My gentle Shakespeare, must enjoy a part.
For though the poet's matter nature be,
His art doth give the fashion; and, that he
Who casts to write a living line, must sweat,
(Such as thine are) and strike the second heat
Upon the Muses' anvil; turn the same
(And himself with it) that he thinks to frame,
Or, for the laurel, he may gain a scorn;
For a good poet's made, as well as born.
And such wert thou! Look how the father's face
Lives in his issue, even so the race
Of Shakespeare's mind and manners brightly shines
In his well turnèd, and true filèd lines;
In each of which he seems to shake a lance,
As brandished at the eyes of ignorance.
Sweet Swan of Avon! what a sight it were
To see thee in our waters yet appear,
And make those flights upon the banks of Thames,

That so did take Eliza, and our James!
But stay, I see thee in the hemisphere
Advanced, and made a constellation there!
Shine forth, thou Star of poets, and with rage
Or influence, chide or cheer the drooping stage,
Which, since thy flight from hence, hath mourned the night,
And despairs day, but for thy volume's light.

—Ben Jonson

Shelley

Shelley, the ceaseless music of thy soul
  Breathes in the Cloud and in the Skylark's song,
  That float as an embodied dream along
The dewy lids of morning. In the dole
That haunts the West Wind, in the joyous roll
  Of Arethusan fountains, or among
  The wastes where Ozymandias the strong
Lies in colossal ruin, thy control
Speaks in the wedded rhyme. Thy spirit gave
  A fragrance to all nature, and a tone
  To inexpressive silence. Each apart—
Earth, Air, and Ocean—claims thee as its own;
  The twain that bred thee, and the panting wave
  That clasped thee, like an overflowing heart.

—John B. Tabb

YOUNG VERSIFIERS LAY THEIR GARLANDS AT THE FEET OF THE IMMORTALS

To Keats

("Beauty is truth, truth beauty.")

Your passion for a perfect phrase
Bewildered Beauty, and we hear
Not thought but subtle sound that plays
Upon the unsuspecting ear.
What wordly grace makes one unknown
Explain another? I have crossed
A hidden sea and swiftly flown
With Beauty, where sad Truth was lost.

—Gilbert O'Connor

When

When shall we three meet again?
When all of us are graying men?
When one is living in a shack,
A two-foot garden at the back?
When one rides in a limousine
And lives upon a French cuisine?
When you, or I, or maybe Bob
Is looking for another job?
In thunder, lightning, or in rain,
When shall we three meet again?

—William Roehrick

See "To Robert Frost" by Richard Hallberg on page 152 and "Someone There Is" by Naomi Rogin on page 364.

To Emily Dickinson

Crispy
Fragrant petals
Bright with wisdom, blossom
In a "little tippler's" singing
Rhythm:

Rhythm
Filled with love of
Beauty . . . rhythm praying
Not to live in vain . . . like her who
Sang it.

Dainty
"Debauchee of
Dew" . . . you'll always fill our
Weary hearts with ecstasy . . . quaint
Songster.
                —JOYCE LANCASTER

Peter Pan

You laugh,
And fairies peep
Out from the dimples in
Your cheek . . . and laughing too
I come.

I come,
Seeking to lose
Myself in wondrous depths
Of liquid pools, twin pools which are
Your eyes.

And when
In sprightly dance
Your toes twinkle and flash,
It seems my heart must pirouette
With joy.
                —HARRIET MEYER

Masefield

The sea
Does not unlock
Its secret words to all.
But it has given you the key
To them.
                —FANNIE WILLIAMS

History is an inspiring source to those who know how to find its lyric and dramatic moments.

Copper Kettle

(In memory of the Paul DuChaillu Expedition into Africa, 1856)

Across the tropic land, once more across
The twisted mangrove roots or mouldy logs,
DuChaillu plunged with his twelve men; the moss
And lush green weeds grew thick, and bogs
Bubbled with evil spirits; here the ants
Vied with the heat; there a lone crocodile
Half-swished in *Mondah* River, roused from his trance.

The aloe jungle stretched for mile on mile.
Then sundown in the woods no longer hot,
A rest from breaking paths through tangled trees,
And supper steaming in a copper pot—
Snake-stew and honey stolen from the bees;
The kettle glinting, glowing, braving the ire
Of a high-soaring *Njina*-country fire.

—ESTELLE ROOKS

Glory

Anne Hutchinson did not believe
    Word for word
The God of the Puritan meeting-house,
    And when they heard

Her disbelief, they banished her
    Into the cold;
And she was smiling, quiet-eyed,
    But she grew old

Before her time; yet with that same
    Stiff-necked pride
Of old New England, she preached *her* cause
    Until she died.

—ESTELLE ROOKS

Snow Moment

(New England, 1693)

Dawn-early though it was, they found much work
    For any girl to do; and least of all
Would Hannah shirk her task of bringing in
    The firewood. She gathered up her shawl;

Softly she crossed the doorstep, and the wind
    Lifted the snowflakes from their feather-hold
Upon the ground, to fling them in her face,
    And leave her laughing there, fragrant with cold.

—ESTELLE ROOKS

SUGGESTIONS

Have you read some work that has touched your imagination?

Does the characteristic of some poet suggest lines to you? Emily Dickinson's quiet reverence; Keats's poignant hope for achievement; Frost's unappreciated song for many years.

Is there some quiet singer to whom you would like to make a song?

Recently a lock of Keats's hair sold at an auction for $10; George Washington's for that sum multiplied by 50. Does that incident touch you?

Make a poem to some teacher to whom you are indebted.

Do any of these quotations suggest a theme? If so, incorporate part of it in a poem or use it as a title.

"When shall we three meet again?"
—WILLIAM SHAKESPEARE: *Macbeth*

"A thing of beauty is a joy forever."
—JOHN KEATS: *Endymion*

"Earth fills her lap with pleasures of her own."
—WILLIAM WORDSWORTH: *Intimations*

"For each age is a dream that is dying
  Or one that is coming to birth."
—ARTHUR O'SHAUGHNESSY: *Ode*

"Before the beginning of years,
    There came to the making of man
Time, with *a gift of tears*."
—ALGERNON CHARLES SWINBURNE: *Atalanta in Calydon*

"How are the mighty fallen, and the weapons of war perished!"
II SAMUEL, 2:27

"And eyes grown dim with gazing on the pilot-stars"
—ALFRED, LORD TENNYSON: *Choric Song*

". . . She had
A heart—how shall I say?—too soon made glad"
—ROBERT BROWNING: *My Last Duchess*

Is there a poem in any of these historical suggestions?
Grant's wife   Sherman's wife   An old sword or flag or medal
        Recent Antarctic Expedition   A historical landmark preserved by the Daughters of the American Revolution   Vergil's

Wood   Founding of Rome by Æneas   The human element in some historical situation that seems unreal   Thoughts of a deceased hero on a monument to him   The Unknown Soldier and visitors to his shrine—the perpetual light for him

Has some incident or some impression from American History the germ of a poem? *John Brown's Body* by Stephen Vincent Benét is the nearest thing to an American epic that Americans have. You are familiar with other epics: *Beowulf,* English; *The Song of Roland,* French; *The Iliad and The Odyssey,* Greek; *The Ænead,* Roman.

Go through an index to first lines or a title index in an anthology and see if some line or title does not suggest a poem.

CHAPTER XIX

INSCRIPTIONS

INSCRIPTIONS hold the intimacy of conversation. They let you in to the warmth of human communication. There is a tongue in an inscription. Dante's hell grows terrible through the words over the entrance:

Abandon Hope All Ye Who Enter Here

The inscriptions on the pyramids, speaking down the ages, have unlocked history. They have more human interest than the pyramids, which bear them. The pyramids testify to man's skill; the inscriptions to man's human kinship. His voice is in them.

Apt inscriptions in verse have their own special appeal. When touched with a personal note they hold something of the effect of fragrance.

Envoy

Go, little book, and wish to all
Flowers in the garden, meat in the hall,
A bit of wine, a spice of wit,
A house with lawns enclosing it,
A living river by the door,
A nightingale in the sycamore!

—ROBERT LOUIS STEVENSON

To My Wife

Take, dear, my little sheaf of songs,
   For, old or new,
All that is good in them belongs
   Only to you;

And, singing as when all was young,
   They will recall
Those others, lived but left unsung—
   The best of all.

—WILLIAM ERNEST HENLEY

This dainty tercet introduces *Japanese Poetry* from which many lines have been reprinted in this book:

> Inscribed: "To whom 'tis due"—
> Meaning, of course,
> My gentle reader, You.
>
> —CURTIS HIDDEN PAGE

What a profound reminder is this ancient inscription for a sun dial:

IT IS LATER THAN YOU THINK.

The last poem in Adelaide Crapsey's collection, from which many of her poems are reprinted in this book, closes the record of days when she walked in the shadow of death at Lake Saranac.

The Immortal Residue

> Wouldst thou find my ashes? Look
> In the pages of my book;
> And, as these thy hand doth turn
> Know here is my funeral urn.
>
> —ADELAIDE CRAPSEY

INSCRIPTIONS BY STUDENT VERSIFIERS

Inscription for a Garden Gate

> How does my garden grow?
> Open the gate—
> Rust on the lattice work,
> Hinges that grate
> Tell you, (though flourishing
> Be every rose)
> Barren my garden is,
> Sadly it grows.
>
> How does my garden grow?
> Hinges that glide,
> Gate swinging back at you
> When opened wide,
> Paths with the print of feet,
> (Though the wind blows
> Nothing but clover) sing,
> "Gayly it grows."
>
> —RUTH H. HAUSMAN

Inscription for a Garden Gate

Exhale your grief upon the scented air,
For it is thick with poppies; it will bear
Your woe and waft it gently out of reach
Of anyone who calls it back to teach
Solemnity to those who gather here
Petals of young delight and buds of cheer.

—RUTH H. HAUSMAN

Invitation

(An Inscription for a Garden Gate)

Step within this garden wall
If you've troubles, great or small.
Walk along this gravel path
To the pool where fountains play,
To the spot where lilies sway.
Drop your troubles as the leaves
Crisp and fall from branches near;
Toss your head where poppies blow
In the shining spots of sun.
Sing or dance or jump or run
Over grass that's wet with dew.
Pick a flower when you go
So that you will always know,
When you've troubles, great or small.
You may step within my wall.

—WILLIAM ROEHRICK

Inscription for a Garage Door

Behind this latticed door of ivied green
Lies happiness, a golden shadowed screen;
Here are quick memories of crimson trees,
Of blown flower fragrance flung upon the breeze,
Remembered wind and rain upon my hair,
Water on sand, and ferns in clusters; rare
Moments of wonder on some lonely road
Or still white ecstasy of forests, snowed.

—DORIS V. LECKY

Inscription for a Garden Wall

Little you know what ghosts are hidden here,
Of elves and fairies or some errant god,
Silent in distant, dark and shadowed paths . . .
Here through the fern and roses Pan has trod.

—DORIS V. LECKY

SUGGESTIONS

Plan an inscription for one of the following:

Fireplace	Garden gate	Knocker	Favorite woodland nook
	Book to a friend	Study door	Your own poetry collection
	Steamer chair on a city roof	Sea-shore umbrella	Sun
dial	Bookcase	Bookplate	Victrola record (a gift for a
friend)	Music for a friend	Baby's cup	Baby's first fork

CHAPTER XX

SOME GREAT SOURCES

FAMILIAR stories of the Bible, folk lore, myths and the like often suggest poetic treatment. The imaginative mind may transcend the bounds of the story and work out a poem on what has been left unsaid or what has been suggested.

A single verse in the Bible is the basis for Byron's famous "The Destruction of Sennacherib."

> And it came to pass that night, that the angel of the Lord went out, and smote in the camp of the Assyrians an hundred four-score and five thousand: and when they arose early in the morning, behold, they were all dead corpses.
>
> II KINGS 19:35

The Destruction of Sennacherib

The Assyrian came down like the wolf on the fold,
And his cohorts were gleaming in purple and gold;
And the sheen of their spears was like stars on the sea
When the blue wave rolls nightly on deep Galilee.

Like the leaves of the forest when Summer is green,
That host with their banners at sunset were seen:
Like the leaves of the forest when Autumn hath blown,
That host on the morrow lay withered and strown.

For the Angel of Death spread his wings on the blast,
And breathed in the face of the foe as he passed;
And the eyes of the sleepers waxed deadly and chill,
And their hearts but once heaved, and forever grew still!

And there lay the steed with his nostrils all wide,
But through it there rolled not the breath of his pride,
And the foam of his gasping lay white on the turf,
And cold as the spray of the rock-beating surf.

And there lay the rider distorted and pale,
With the dew on his brow and the rust on his mail;
And the tents were all silent, the banners alone,
The lances uplifted, the trumpets unblown.

And the widows of Ashur are loud in their wail,
And the idols are broke in the temple of Baal;
And the might of the Gentile, unsmote by the sword,
Hath melted like snow in the glance of the Lord.
—GEORGE GORDON, LORD BYRON

Genesis has this to say:

And Cush begat Nimrod: he began to be a mighty one in the earth
He was a mighty hunter before the Lord: wherefore it is said,
Even as Nimrod the mighty hunter before the Lord.
And the beginning of his kingdom was Babel, and Erech, and
Accad, and Calneh, in the land of Shinar.

In the succeeding chapter the building of the tower of Babel and the
confusion of tongues are recorded in nine short verses.

Anna Hempstead Branch takes this material and turns it into a thrilling poem illuminated by her mystical interpretation and imaginative
daring. It is too long to quote here. If you wish an exciting adventure
read "Nimrod" in *The Rose of the Wind*.

Here is a familiar figure from the Old Testament.

Solomon

They hewed him cedar trees of Lebanon,
And in his golden courts the people bowed
When through the seraphim a burning cloud
Covered the Temple of great Solomon;
But now the Glory of the Lord is gone—
Moloch and Ashtoreth, the ivory-browed,
Feast on the holy mountains which he vowed
To Jahveh from the horns of Gibeon.

Yet he whose wisdom turns to weariness
Has heard once more the mighty Voice that came
When Jahveh held the king's heart in His Hand;
And though about the throne his tribesmen press,
Over their heads he sees the sword of flame
And Israel scattered through an alien land.
—THOMAS S. JONES, JR.

And what follows is a condensed parable of the New Testament:

Opportunity

Once only did the Angel stir
The pool, whereat She paused in pain:
Another step outspeeded her;
The waters ne'er have moved again.

—JOHN B. TABB

You know the myth of Apollo and Daphne: how beautiful Daphne, fleeing from Apollo whose love she spurned, called upon her father the river god Peneüs to change her form when she felt her strength failing in the chase, and how he granted her prayer by transforming her to a laurel tree. See how Edna St. Vincent Millay treats that myth. Our modern Daphne has other ideas of being wooed.

Daphne

Why do you follow me?—
Any moment I can be
Nothing but a laurel-tree.

Any moment of the chase
I can leave you in my place
A pink bough for your embrace.

Yet if over hill and hollow
Still it is your will to follow,
I am off;—to heel, Apollo!

—EDNA ST. VINCENT MILLAY

In "A Fable for Critics" the irreverent James Russell Lowell handles the Daphne-Apollo myth like this:

Phœbus, sitting one day in a laurel tree's shade,
Was reminded of Daphne, of whom it was made,
For the god being one day too warm in his wooing,
She took to the tree to escape his pursuing;
Be the cause what it might, from his offers she shrunk,
And, Ginevra-like, shut herself up in a trunk;
And, though 't was a step into which he had driven her,
He somehow or other had never forgiven her;
Her memory he nursed as a kind of a tonic,
Something bitter to chew when he'd play the Byronic,
And I can't count the obstinate nymphs that he brought over
By a strange kind of smile he put on when he thought of her.

"My case is like Dido's," he sometimes remarked;
"When I last saw my love, she was fairly embarked
In a laurel, as *she* thought—but (ah, how Fate mocks!)
She has found it by this time a very bad box;
Let hunters from me take this saw when they need it,—
You're not always sure of your game when you've treed it.
Just conceive such a change taking place in one's mistress!
What romance would be left?—who can flatter or kiss trees?
And, for mercy's sake, how could one keep up a dialogue
With a dull wooden thing that will live and will die a log,—
Not to say that the thought would forever intrude
That you've less chance to win her the more she is wood?
Ah! it went to my heart and the memory still grieves,
To see those loved graces all taking their leaves;
Those charms beyond speech, so enchanting but now,
As they left me forever, each making its bough!
If her tongue *had* a tang sometimes more than was right,
Her new bark is worse than ten times her old bite."

Matthew Arnold listens to a nightingale in his native England. He recalls a Greek myth: Procne and Philomela were sisters. Procne was given in marriage to Tereus, King of Thrace (Daulis in Phocis). After the birth of their son Itylus, King Tereus grew tired of Procne. He plucked out her tongue to insure her silence, and pretending that she was dead, married Philomela. Through a web into which Procne wove her story she revealed her terrible plight to Philomela, and the sisters revenged the king's crime by killing Itylus and serving him as a dish to his father. In wrath the gods transformed Procne to a swallow, Philomela into a nightingale, and Tereus into a hawk. The song of the nightingale fills the night with clear, cold, melancholy music.

Here is the poem that Matthew Arnold created as an interpretation of the nightingale's song. Without a knowledge of the myth the lines are meaningless.

Philomela

Hark! ah, the Nightingale!
The tawny-throated!
Hark! from that moonlit cedar what a burst!
What triumph! hark—what pain!

O Wanderer from a Grecian shore,
Still, after many years, in distant lands,
Still nourishing in thy bewilder'd brain
That wild, unquench'd, deep-sunken, old-world pain—
    Say, will it never heal?

And can this fragrant lawn
With its cool trees, and night,
And the sweet, tranquil Thames,
And moonshine, and the dew,
To thy rack'd heart and brain
  Afford no balm?

  Dost thou to-night behold
Here, through the moonlight on this English grass,
The unfriendly palace in the Thracian wild?
  Dost thou again peruse
With hot cheeks and sear'd eyes
The too clear web, and thy dumb Sister's shame?
  Dost thou once more assay
Thy flight, and feel come over thee,
Poor Fugitive, the feathery change
Once more, and once more seem to make resound
With love and hate, triumph and agony,
Lone Daulis, and the high Cephissian vale?
  Listen, Eugenia—
How thick the bursts come crowding through the leaves!
  Again—thou hearest!
Eternal Passion!
Eternal Pain!

Pan hardly needs an introduction.

A Musical Instrument

What was he doing, the great god Pan,
  Down in the reeds by the river?
Spreading ruin and scattering ban,
Splashing and paddling with hoofs of a goat,
And breaking the golden lilies afloat
  With the dragon-fly on the river.

He tore out a reed, the great god Pan,
  From the deep cool bed of the river;
The limpid water turbidly ran,
And the broken lilies a-dying lay,
And the dragon-fly had fled away,
  Ere he brought it out of the river.

High on the shore sat the great god Pan,
  While turbidly flow'd the river;
And hack'd and hew'd as a great god can
With his hard bleak steel at the patient reed,
Till there was not a sign of the leaf indeed
  To prove it fresh from the river.

He cut it short, did the great god Pan
   \How tall it stood in the river!),
Then drew the pith, like the heart of a man,
Steadily from the outside ring,
And notch'd the poor dry empty thing
   In holes, as he sat by the river.

"This is the way," laugh'd the great god Pan
   (Laugh'd while he sat by the river),
"The only way, since gods began
To make sweet music, they could succeed."
Then dropping his mouth to a hole in the reed,
   He blew in power by the river.

Sweet, sweet, sweet, O Pan!
   Piercing sweet by the river!
Blinding sweet, O great god Pan!
The sun on the hill forgot to die,
And the lilies revived, and the dragon-fly
   Came back to dream on the river.

Yet half a beast is the great god Pan,
   To laugh as he sits by the river,
Making a poet out of a man:
The true gods sigh for the cost and pain—
For the reed which grows nevermore again
   As a reed with the reeds of the river.
            —ELIZABETH BARRETT BROWNING

Aucassin and Nicolete is a twelfth-century song-story of idyllic love.

      'Tis how two young lovers met,
      Aucassin and Nicolete,
      Of the pains the lover bore
      And the sorrows he outwore,
      For the goodness and the grace,
      Of his love, so fair of face.

Aucassin is the son of Count Garin de Biaucaire. Nicolete is a Sara-
cen maiden brought up a Christian in the home of the Count's captain.
When the love of the youthful pair is discovered Nicolete is made a
prisoner but escapes. Aucassin is imprisoned in a tower for releasing his
father's enemy upon his father's failure to keep his promise of a short
interview with Nicolete. Nicolete escapes into the woods where she
lives in hiding in a bower of boughs and leaves, which she has constructed, until Aucassin, released from prison, finds her. They journey
to Torelore only to be separated again—each on a different ship—
Aucassin back to his own land to rule in place of his father who has

died; Nicolete, to her father, King of Carthage, who soon arranges a marriage for her. But she will have none of it! Disguised as a jongleur, she makes her way to Aucassin's palace. In a lay, she describes the plight of Nicolete. The song ends in the reunion of the lovers. "So say they, speak they, tell they the Tale."

Perhaps you will read Andrew Lang's beautiful translation which has preserved the rare poetry of the idyll.

See how the two ballades below have caught something of the idyllic beauty of the fragrant old conte-fable.

Ballade of Aucassin

Where smooth the Southern waters run
   Through rustling leagues of poplars gray,
Beneath a veiled soft Southern run,
   We wandered out of Yesterday;
   Went Maying in that ancient May
Whose fallen flowers are fragrant yet,
   And lingered by the fountain spray
With Aucassin and Nicolete.

The grassgrown paths are trod of none
   Where through the woods they went astray;
The spider's traceries are spun
   Across the darkling forest way;
   There came no Knights that ride to slay,
No Pilgrims through the grasses wet,
   No shepherd lads that sang their say
With Aucassin and Nicolete.

'Twas here by Nicolete begun
   Her lodge of boughs and blossoms gay;
'Scaped from the cell of marble dun
   'Twas here the lover found the Fay;
   O lovers fond, O foolish play!
How hard we find it to forget,
   Who fain would dwell with them as they,
With Aucassin and Nicolete.

ENVOY

Prince, 'tis a melancholy lay!
   For Youth, for Life we both regret:
How fair they seem; how far away,
   With Aucassin and Nicolete.

                —ANDREW LANG

Ballade of Nicolete

All bathed in pearl and amber light
She rose to fling the lattice wide,
And leaned into the fragrant night,
Where brown birds sang of summertide;
('Twas Love's own voice that called and cried)
"Ah, Sweet!" she said, "I'll seek thee yet,
Though thorniest pathways should betide
The fair white feet of Nicolete."

They slept, who would have stayed her flight;
(Full fain were they the maid had died!)
She dropped adown her prison's height
On strands of linen featly tied.
And so she passed the garden-side
With loose-leaved roses sweetly set,
And dainty daisies, dark beside
The fair white feet of Nicolete!

Her lover lay in evil plight
(So many lovers yet abide!)
I would my tongue could praise aright
Her name, that should be glorified.
Those lovers now, whom foes divide,
A little weep,—and soon forget.
How far from these faint lovers glide
The fair white feet of Nicolete.

ENVOY

My Princess, doff thy frozen pride,
Nor scorn to pay Love's golden debt,
Through his dim woodland take for guide
The fair white feet of Nicolete.

—Graham R. Tomson

Then there are the folk tales of our northern lumber camps, all centering about one Paul Bunyan, wonderful in ingenuity. If you do not know Paul and his blue ox calf an adventure awaits your drawing *Paul Bunyan* from the library. In "Paul's Wife" Robert Frost tells how Paul "sawed his wife out of a white-pine log." That too is a long poem which you will want to read from his *Collected Poems*.

The poems following will show further how the Bible, the myth, and the folk tale or legend have stimulated song.

The legends of our North American Indians are rich material for poetry. Here is one.

A Dance for Rain

You may never see rain, unless you see
A dance for rain at Cochiti,
Never hear thunder in the air
Unless you hear the thunder there,
Nor know the lightning in the sky
If there's no pole to know it by . . .
They dipped the pole just as I came,
And I can never be the same
Since those feathers gave my brow
The touch of wind that's on it now,
Bringing over the arid lands
Butterfly gestures from Hopi hands
And holding me, till earth shall fail,
As close to earth as a fox's tail.

I saw them, naked, dance in line
Before the candles of a leafy shrine;
Before a saint in a Christian dress
I saw them dance their holiness,
I saw them reminding him all day long
That death is weak and life is strong
And urging the fertile earth to yield
Seed from the loin and seed from the field.
A feather in the hair and a shell at the throat
Were lifting and falling with every note
Of the chorus-voices and the drum,
Calling for the rain to come.
A fox on the back, and shaken on the thigh
Rain-cloth woven from the sky.
And under the knee a turtle-rattle
Clacking with the toes of sheep and cattle—
These were the men, their bodies painted
Earthen, with a white rain slanted;
These were the men, a windy line,
Their elbows green with a growth of pine.
And in among them, close and slow,
Women moved the way things grow,
With a mesa-tablet on the head
And a little grassy creeping tread
And with sprays of pine moved back and forth,
While the dance of the men blew from the north,
Blew from the south and east and west

Over the field and over the breast.
And the heart was beating in the drum,
Beating for the rain to come.

Dead men out of earlier lives,
Leaving their graves, leaving their wives,
Were partly flesh and partly clay,
And their heads were corn that was dry and gray.
They were ghosts of men and once again
They were dancing like a ghost of rain;
For the spirits of men, the more they eat,
Have happier hands and lighter feet,
And the better they dance the better they know
How to make corn and children grow.

And so in Cochiti that day
They slowly put the sun away
And they made a cloud and they made it break
And they made it rain for the children's sake.
And they never stopped the song or the drum
Pounding for the rain to come.

The rain made many suns to shine,
Golden bodies in a line
With leaping feather and swaying pine.
And the brighter the bodies, the brighter the rain
As thunder heaped it on the plain.
Arroyas had been empty, dry,
But now were running with the sky;
And the dancers' feet were in a lake,
Dancing for the people's sake.
And the hands of a ghost had made a cup
For scooping handfuls of water up;
And he poured it into a ghostly throat,
And he leaped and waved with every note
Of the dancers' feet and the songs of the drum
That had called the rain and made it come.

For this was not a god of wood,
This was a god whose touch was good,
You could lie down in him and roll
And wet your body and wet your soul;
For this was not a god in a book,
This was a god that you tasted and took
Into a cup that you made with your hands,
Into your children and into your lands—
This was a god that you could see,
Rain, rain in Cochiti!

—WITTER BYNNER

And here is a mermaid myth. This mermaid swam the Atlantic! The poem won a prize from the *Nation* where it first appeared.

Ballad of Old Doc Higgins

Old Doc Higgins shot a mermaid:
Vowed he'd ketch her, fish or woman, fiend or human;
Carryin' on along the river, caterwaulin' up the river,
Scarin' fish where they lay hid!
Swore he'd hev her, lights an' liver; (and what Doc Higgins swore, he did).

Old Doc Higgins cleaned his gun:
The proper fishin'-hook, he'd swan, fer mermaids' gills;
The slickest tackle! (Leaning on the pasture-wall, old Doc Higgins gave a
  cackle),
Watch him git her, pesky critter,
Tail an' all.

No one knew but old Doc Higgins:
No, an' none wuz goin' to know, 'twarn't no need fer folks to know.
He saw sister Mame's boy go swimmin' to her, natteral fool!
All uncovered wuz her breast, hair all streamin', shiny'z gold,
An' the rest—a fish's tail gormin' up his troutin' pool!

Higgins saw and never told:
Hev the hull town call *him* crazy? Sister Mame's boy, loony, lazy, heard
  him shoutin';
Turned an' laffed ez they went under, started kissin'—let 'em wonder,
Knowin' how the boy cud swim—
They'd make no laffin-stock uv him!

But here's the thing that riled him so:
Jest ez he wuz settlin' down to a peaceful mornin's fishin',
(How his baited line would hum up the stream to some swift eddy),
Settin' there enjoyin' things while the fish got good an' ready—he cud feel
  their noses pushin'—
Jest ez they wuz bitin' some—up she'd come!

Naked to the waist; an' sassy! Wavin' to him swimmin' by, shameless hussy;
Or jest singin' ez she floated, kind uv high,
No toon at all . . . (And he noted how her tail would flash and swish—
Gorry, how she scared the fish!) Old Doc Higgins on the shore
Yelled and swore.

And he'd watch her at the turning of the river, see her sink
Where the willow near the brink dipped to touch the mermaid's locks;
"Shucks," said old Doc Higgins, "Shucks!"
His ears didn't need no wax (thinking of the deafened crew,
And Odysseus, fettered fast), Oh he knoo a thing or two,

All the Higginses hed learnin'; needn't tie *him* to no mast!
Smilin' at him ez she passed—any lunk-head cud see through her—
Like to take a cow-hide to her!
Poor old Mame; her only son . . . (yes, but listen as you hasten,
Listen to the lonely singing, old man with a gun!)

> *Ah who will seek Muirish,*
> *The lost one, the sea-swan?*
> *Ah ripples, ah road*
> *Where the foolish, the frolicsome*
> *Strayed to her sorrow!*
> *Muireis is gone*
> *From the waters of Kerry,*
> *Ah tarry not, sisters,*
> *But speedily come!*
>
> *Beneath a strange willow*
> *She grieves with her sorrow,*
> *And all the bright sea-shells*
> *Are fall'n from her hair;*
> *Ah sisters, my friends,*
> *Where the ancient tide ends*
> *Will you fare,*
> *Will you follow*
> *The track of the tears?*
> *To Muirish the lost one,*
> *The sea-swan of Kerry,*
> *Ah tarry not, sisters,*
> *My loves and my dears!*
>
> *Ah . . . ah . . . ah . . .*

Heathen singin', fit fer Satan! Creeping close as she rose
From beneath her willow-bough, old Doc Higgins held his breath . . .
Now!
And singing turns to sighing, and a sighing pales to dying,
And a· dying lifts to death.

Ripples reddening as they float, rippling from a tender throat,
Reddening from a cry of pain . . .
Old Doc Higgins stood there blinking, and his thoughts were not all pretty
As he watched a whiteness sinking: wished he'd hed a good look at her,
Never'd git that chance again.

Gosh, it wuz a fust-rate shot!—Kissin' Mame's boy ez she drowned him,
Lips all pursed up when they found him,
Died uv kissin' like ez not—
Wal, there warn't no use in wishin';
An' tomorrer he'd go fishin'.

·　　·　　·　　·　　·　　·　　·

Mist can do strange things to rivers, make a ghost of any river:
Such a day is good for fishing; old Doc Higgins vowed he'd never
Seen the like, it did beat all, the way the pike
An' pickerel came a-crowdin' round; cat-fish too; and Lord, the trout
Jumpin' out!

Peter wuz a fisherman; guessed he'd hev to let *him* pass—
There wuz bass over there lyin' low—Higgins thot he'd like to go,
His time come to meet his God, with fishin'-rod an' basket spillin';
He'd be willin'! . . . *Say you so?*
Old Doc Higgins, say you so?

Mist that reaches thick and sallow up the ledges of the land:
Up to where a tired old man sits a while beneath a willow,
 (Willow-tree, you remember! But does he?)
And his pipe slips from his hand. . . . What's that creeping through the
    sedges?
Have a care, old Doc Higgins, sleeping there!

Mist that swirls . . . mist . . . mist . . .
Something holds him by the wrist: white and wet and cool and strong—
Fish or woman, fiend or human!
Oh, the shoal of leaping girls all about him, all about him,
Beautiful and baleful throng . . .

Muirish! Muirish! White Sea-swan!
Sister slain, sister slain! . . . And an answering crimson stain
Rises rippling where she sank.
Oh, the whimpering little man, fighting, frightened on the bank
As he wakes:

Sees a face—pale—pale—
Sees a tail—
Snatches at a bough that breaks!
 (Vengeful little willow-tree),
"God-a-mighty! Leave me be! Leave me be!"

    .   .   .   .

Thus they drowned him, old Doc Higgins, with their arms like wreaths
    around him,
Heavy silver wreaths around him,
Struggling, strangling, tightly pressed to a soft ironic breast.
Thus he lies . . .
In a grave of running water—who had slain a deep sea daughter.

Old Doc Higgins, old Doc Higgins, wishing so to die—a-fishing—
Thus he lies, till all things rise; if there still be aught to rise.

                                            —Leonora Speyer

For others see "Ruth" by Thomas Hood in Chapter XI; and "Blue Hyacinths" in Chapter X.

Of long poems you might enjoy Tennyson's *Idylls of the King; Tristram* by Edwin Arlington Robinson; and *Hyperion* by John Keats.

BEGINNERS HAVE GONE TO THE GREAT SOURCES

Two Muses

Tragedy:

> Melpomene ventures abroad this dark night,
> Drab, in soft mists of dull gray and ghost white.
> Sheathed in a shroud, like a man not long dead,
> The laurel is stiff, and the sky overhead
> Is dark as a casket; the lake is a pool
> Of blood from a corpse that was drained by a ghoul.
> Eerily, out of the silence she comes.
> At the back of my mind, a weird death chant she hums.

Comedy:

> Swift and light, Thalia whirls
> Round the willows, gypsy girls,
> Singing soft a wanton tune.
> Suddenly, a red balloon
> Floats from nowhere toward the sky—
> The dancer leaps and reaches high;
> She pricks her toy, and chuckles low
> To see its brilliance puff and go!

— GEORGIA H. COOPER

Night Muse

> The muse is as elusive, this gold night,
> As wingèd Pegasus in airy flight;
> She shouts to me from yellow aspen trees,
> Then, wearying, she sinks upon her knees
> Into a topaz pool, dripped from the skies. . . .
> As I give chase, on amber wings she flies
> Up to a saffron tree-top. . . . Looking down,
> She laughs to see my thoughts of sombre brown.

— GEORGIA H. COOPER

SUGGESTIONS

1. The follow-stories of our daily newspapers often play up something that was buried in the lead of the news story. A poem may be buried in a familiar Bible story or even a verse from the Bible as was Byron's "The Destruction of Sennacherib." Does one of the following items suggest a detail that might be the nucleus of a poem? You may have to do a little reading to develop your detail satisfactorily.

Visit of Queen of Sheba to King Solomon   Saul and David; envy of Saul   David and Goliath; the sword of Goliath   A carpenter or mason of Tyre in the days of King David   David and Jonathan   David's lament over Absalom at the time of his death; death of Absalom   Joseph and his brethren   Ruth   Esther and the golden scepter   Tablets of stone   A rod and a rock   Paul before King Agrippa

2. Is there a detail worthy of development in any of the following?

Roland's horn of ivory at Roncevals; Roland and Oliver; Roland and his sword, Durendal from *The Song of Roland*   An incident or character from the Norse tales: Baldur; the binding of Fenrir; Thor and his hammer   A Greek or a Roman myth: Jason and the golden fleece; wanderings of Odysseus, his return home, Penelope and Telemachus; Nausicaa, ten years later; Aeneas and Rome; Dido   A fashion or custom that dates to classic tradition   Cupid and Psyche   Daphne and Apollo   Narcissus and Echo   Naiad, dryad, satyr, siren

3. Consult the index of Gayley's *Classic Myths* or some other collection of classic myths and be prepared to tell briefly an incident centering about a character that interests you. Do you see possibilities of imaginative treatment? As an exercise, turn the narrative into verse.

4. Do you know any local legends that haunt the neighboring waters, mountains or hollows, such as the headless horseman of Sleepy Hollow, whaling off Nantucket, settling the West, the gulls of Salt Lake, redwoods of California, "Get along, little doagie"?

5. Memorize one of the psalms suggested below:

Psalm   19. The heavens declare the glory of God
         23. The Lord is my shepherd
         24. The earth is the Lord's, and the fulness thereof
         27. The Lord is my light and my salvation; whom shall I fear?
         42. As the hart panteth after the water brooks
        121. I will lift up mine eyes unto the hills
        127. Except the Lord build the house
        130. Out of the depths have I cried unto thee, O Lord
        137. By the rivers of Babylon, there we sat down

CHAPTER XXI

OCCASIONAL VERSE

Occasional verse is verse written to celebrate a special occasion, such as a fraternal meeting, Mother's day, Valentine's day, a birthday, the unveiling of a monument, or the like. Lowell's "Commemoration Ode" is an occasional poem. It was recited before the Harvard alumni, July 21, 1865, to honor those Harvard men who had given their lives in the Civil War. Frequently our newspapers carry occasional verse because newspapers feature what is of timely interest. For instance, when the world was commemorating the two thousandth anniversary of Vergil's birth in 1930, there appeared on the editorial page of the New York *Times* a sonnet "Vergil" by Thomas S. Jones, Jr. The day Dr. Fosdick's church on Riverside Drive, New York, was dedicated, there appeared in the same paper "The Riverside Church" by Louise Burton Laidlaw. Lindbergh's flight stimulated many poets—one hundred of their poems were collected by Charles Vale in *The Spirit of St. Louis*.

Some poets do not find the Muse ready to inspire them on occasion, for true poetry may not be forced. Robert Frost says that the only occasional poem he ever succeeded in writing was "The Tuft of Flowers,"

The Tuft of Flowers

I went to turn the grass once after one
Who mowed it in the dew before the sun.

The dew was gone that made his blade so keen
Before I came to view the levelled scene.

I looked for him behind an isle of trees;
I listened for his whetstone on the breeze.

But he had gone his way, the grass all mown,
And I must be, as he had been,—alone,

"As all must be," I said within my heart,
"Whether they work together or apart."

But as I said it, swift there passed me by
On noiseless wing a bewildered butterfly,

Seeking with memories grown dim o'er night
Some resting flower of yesterday's delight.

And once I marked his flight go round and round,
As where some flower lay withering on the ground.

And then he flew as far as eye could see,
And then on tremulous wing came back to me.

I thought of questions that have no reply,
And would have turned to toss the grass to dry;

But he turned first, and led my eye to look
At a tall tuft of flowers beside a brook,

A leaping tongue of bloom the scythe had spared
Beside a reedy brook the scythe had bared.

I left my place to know them by their name,
Finding them butterfly-weed when I came.

The mower in the dew had loved them thus,
By leaving them to flourish, not for us,

Nor yet to draw one thought of ours to him,
But from sheer morning gladness at the brim.

The butterfly and I had lit upon,
Nevertheless, a message from the dawn,

That made me hear the wakening birds around,
And hear his long scythe whispering to the ground,

And feel a spirit kindred to my own;
So that henceforth I worked no more alone;

But glad with him, I worked as with his aid,
And weary, sought at noon with him the shade;

And dreaming, as it were, held brotherly speech
With one whose thought I had not hoped to reach.

"Men work together," I told him from the heart,
"Whether they work together or apart."

—ROBERT FROST

If an occasion (it was written for a fraternal occasion) can be responsible for one such poem in a lifetime, our knee bends to *occasions*.

Part of the joy of living is to keep fresh the significant moments of our little drama. We have the birthday cake with its sixteen candles, the turkey at Christmas, the May-pole festival, the silver or gold anniversary. If we can intensify our joy through a poem so much the more our joy!

St. Valentine's Day

To-day, all day, I rode upon the down,
With hounds and horsemen, a brave company.
On this side in its glory lay the sea,
On that the Sussex weald, a sea of brown.
The wind was light, and brightly the sun shone,
And still we gallop'd on from gorse to gorse:
And once, when check'd, a thrush sang, and my horse
Prick'd his quick ears as to a sound unknown.
    I knew the Spring was come. I knew it even
Better than all by this, that through my chase
In bush and stone and hill and sea and heaven
I seem'd to see and follow still your face.
Your face my quarry was. For it I rode,
My horse a thing of wings, myself a god.
                              —WILFRID SCAWEN BLUNT

A Birthday

My heart is like a singing bird
    Whose nest is in a water'd shoot;
My heart is like an apple-tree
    Whose boughs are bent with thick-set fruit;
My heart is like a rainbow shell
    That paddles in a halcyon sea;
My heart is gladder than all these,
    Because my love is come to me.

Raise me a daïs of silk and down;
    Hang it with vair and purple dyes;
Carve it in doves and pomegranates,
    And peacocks with a hundred eyes;
Work it in gold and silver grapes,
    In leaves and silver fleurs-de-lys;
Because the birthday of my life
    Is come, my love is come to me.
                              —CHRISTINA GEORGINA ROSSETTI

This poem appeared in the New York *Times* for the occasion.

All Souls Night

Fetch the candles! Make a light!
  Let it search the growing gloom!
Shadows are abroad tonight—
  They shall enter every room.

This is the time for silence. Draw your chair
  Close to the hearth! The fragrant birchen log
  Smolders and shows a glowing eye. The dog
Lies stretched out motionless, save when with hair

Bristling along his back he cocks an ear
  To leaves that brush against the window frame
  Like tapping fingers of lost souls who came
From far-off regions, begging entrance here.

Draw close your chair! The guttering candles throw
  Strange shadows on the walls, and with the rain
  Come voices as of lost souls in their pain—
So was it in the time of Odilo.

Snuff the candles! Seek your bed!
  Down upon your bended knees!
As Saint Odilo once prayed,
  Pray you for the souls of these!

           —F. L. Montgomery

    There are occasions of special significance to youth. The graduation day is one.

Commencement: June 1929

All the lights are gleaming where the towns begin,
Men with quiet eyes there are, growing old within.
Here is rest and rest again,
Till the sun climbs west again.
Welcome, youth.

Horsemen of the storm roar by where the houses sleep;
Lightning strikes the foaming flanks, their stallions rear and leap.
Down the sky the thunders ride,—
Ghosts of violins inside
Softly weep.

They have sheathed the sickle moon where the towns begin,
They have pricked the sun's veins with a tiny pin.
They have clipped the wings of wind,
Flasks of midnight they have thinned,
Sweetened, cooled.

Shadows cast by grief and pain waited at their door.
They put all the lights out and crouched upon the floor;
Pulling down the window-shade,
Boasted they were not afraid.
They'd been good, they swore.

You have borne on cricket nights all the weight of June,
Heavy scent of rain-wet woods hidden from the moon;
You were seared by sunset fire,
Lashed by whips of quick desire,
You love life.

You are coming to the towns where the sun is cold;
Tell them that it once was warm, that the moon was gold.
Don't forget that early stars
Cut like sharp-edged scimitars.
Dare grow old!

—MURIEL F. HOCHDORF

Farewell, Friend

(*Commencement*, 1930)

Now we shall be transplanted once again,
Like saplings lifted from a crowded wood
And carried down the shadow-darkened glen
To live in open fields. It's very good

For saplings to be brought away from all
The vines and shrubs and bracken that secured
Them from the heedless wind when they were small,
For when their further life has been assured

By ample branches and determined roots,
The cluttered forest will not let them grow
Up tall and straight, but sends out hemlock shoots,
Sends oak boughs down, to cramp their branches so

That they are twisted till the tree trunks hurt . . .
In taking trees, let not one twig be bruised,
No single root be wrenched from homely dirt
Lest by that act resistance be refused,—

For untempered suns shrink tender leaves away . . .
When trees are planted in the field, there's room
To spread unhampered; reaching branches sway
Toward sky peak and sky rim. They bloom,

Such flowers as the wood has never known.
Growing in placid fields, they have a grace
And fullness, caught from living there alone,
That are nourished only by an open space.

You see that dogwood there beside the lake?
I brought it from the hill five springs ago
But no amount of growing here, will take
The curve it's kept since the time it used to blow

By wilder waters on a wilder site.
The charcoal trunk is bent, as if a flare
Of cliff still forced it out to seek the light.
Of course, it's changed, and yet the curve is there . . .

When we are taken off to live apart
In sun fields, we shall grow more full in heart;

Shall learn to sing and quiver in the breeze
Like sensitively cultivated trees.

Though we grow strong and flourish, under care,
The early forest bend will still be there.

—WILLIAM ROEHRICK

The Untrodden Road

(Written for Commencement, June 1931)

Green shadows quiver, restless, here
  On rows of ripening grain that show
Their tasselled heads from year to year
  In this bright valley that I know
  So well; where I have dug each row
With earthy hands; with heart and tread
  As strong as wind, as light as snow,—
The road untrodden lies ahead.

I have cleaned out the brook so clear
  That sun rays mingle to and fro
Down to the pebbled bed, and queer
  Shell-prisms capture them. I mow

The last grown patch, and prop my hoe
And rake neatly inside the shed,
　　Hearing farewell in the brook's flow.
The road untrodden lies ahead.

And I will follow it; no fear
　　Of rocky heights can ever grow
Within a singing heart, or drear
　　Gray shroud clothe the light spirit. Slow
　　First-fallen leaves drift down below
The maple tree . . . I look instead
　　For unknown peaks and now I go . . .
The road untrodden lies ahead.

ENVOY

Why must I question when I throw
　　The gate wide, where I shall be led,
To climb what hill, conquer what foe?
　　The road untrodden lies ahead.

—JOYCE LANCASTER

Students once made valentines of their first couplets and quatrains.
They were not very far advanced at the time.

Salesmanship

I'm not a crack salesman—I don't look the part;
Do you think for a kiss I could sell you my heart?

—NAOMI ROGIN

Invitation

Hearts and ribbons in the wind!
Can't you see they're only pinned?

—LUCILLE SCHMEDTJE

To My Valentine

I bind your heart with love-made twine
To hold it for my Valentine.

—AILEEN VOIGHT

Snow on Valentine's Day

The snow with skillful fingers, has traced upon the pane,
Two lacy hearts of snowdrops, and tied with Cupid's Bow.

—ROSLYN SOLLISCH

One in Hope

Now of course it's very trite
So say that you are my delight,
So I will say that you're divine.
Won't you be my Valentine?
    —CONSTANCE STERN

To Prince Charming

You woke my heart from slumber deep
I give it to you now to keep;
If you don't want to take it—then
Please put it back to sleep again.
    —NAOMI ROGIN

The president of the Poetry Club wrote the next lines to celebrate the appearance of the first anthology of student verse at George Washington.

For the Publication of "The Poets' Pack"

Each poem finely chiseled on a page,
    Black against white, is not alone
A verse, a line, a rhyming here or there,
    But something we have loved and known.

Spring walks the pages of this book,
    And ancient nights live long,
Gardens of triolets and rondels bloom,
    An elf-poem pipes a song.

These are not lines of verse that I see here,
These are dream children of another year.
    —ESTELLE ROOKS

OTHER OCCASIONAL VERSE BY YOUNG POETS

Cemetery

"The crosses are laid out in the order that the men stood in just before the attack."

The white battalions stand upon the grass,
Seeming to see the sky and breathe the air,
But really just remembering a time
When on a high green hill they watched the glare
Of bursting shells—and then—they plunged ahead
Into the darkness though they knew not where.
    —DORIS V. LECKY

On the Homeward Flight of the Graf Zeppelin

Sheer silver gray on a girdered core,
Swing off and sway toward your mother shore.
Some bearded mate at his midnight post,
Steering his freight for a distant coast,
Cries, "Look aloft!" and his gaze is far,
Tracing the course of a distant star.
Racing for day with exultant roar,
Sheer silver gray on a girdered core.

Crows stare afraid at the speeding light.
Strange prayers are made in the throbbing night.
Mariners, know, this extended sphere,
Men have made go. There is naught to fear.
Men launched this pale, shining meteor,
Sheer silver gray on a girdered core,
Closing a breach, flying swift and far.
When they can reach, they will stretch a star.

* * *

Swing off and sway toward your mother shore,
Sheer silver gray on a girdered core.
—THEODORE R. NATHAN

Two Worlds

Two worlds—today they shower him with fame.
He is a hero—he who was unknown.
With friendly smile, across the seas he came,
A conqueror, a superman—alone!

Two worlds—they say he linked them with a smile.
While others quarreled, the bravest youth had gone
In air, and mankind held its breath the while
A dauntless birdman raced the racing dawn.

Two worlds—and now the wide earth knows the phrase,
The magic words, "The Eagle of the Sea,"
And cheering him, the nations sing the praise
Of wingless eagles in eternity.

He flew—the living symbol of the score
Of thousand millions who can never fly,—
The dreaming birds whose bodies never soar,
Whose spirits seldom reach the distant sky.
—THEODORE R. NATHAN

To New Year Revellers

Sound the bronze bells
    To make the air ring;
Blow the great whistles,
    And dance and sing.

Brighten the night
    With tipsy cheer;
Welcome the heir
    Of yesteryear.

But Time, the sculptor
    Who carved the moon,
Will carve your headstones,
    Too soon, too soon.
                    —LIONEL DAY

Holiday

Off, away,
I leave today,
And I will be
Beside the sea.
The wind is there
To blow my hair,
And sun-baked sands
To warm my hands.
The waves will beat
Up at my feet
And I will rest
The honored guest
Of nature. In
The same soft din
Of crickets peeping,

Rollers sweeping
Cares away,
I soon will stay.
A laughing song
Will skip along
Within my heart,
Without a start,
Without an end,
And it will tend
To follow after
All the laughter
Of the grass
As I pass
On my way.
I'm off today.
                    —WILLIAM ROEHRICK

Anniversary for Armistice

The dry earth cracked,—men turned away, afraid
The truth that they had buried might arise,
Stripped naked of its winding-sheet of lies,
To point accusing fingers, cause to fade
The non-committal gods to whom they prayed.
Men thought it more polite to close their eyes
On truth stripped nude, than see why mankind dies.
For years were blood-soaked altars humbly laid.
And now we argue on effect and cause
And there is talk of brotherhood of men,
And lasting peace, and yet, when all is said,—
"Marines quell Nicaraugua . . ." loud applause,
And red gods make their medicine again.
It is so easy to forget the dead!
                                    —MURIEL F. HOCHDORF

A mangy cat strayed into the publication office one day. Spitz was a cat that had been a general pet when the school was a collection of shacks.

To a Stray Cat

Great Spitz's Ghost! Have you come back,
Returned from wanderings 'round the shack
Be-swizzled from a recent spree,
Returned to climb the "Cherry Tree"?
Amber-eyed, with feline grin,
With open arms we'll take you in,
But you must guard our cherries rare
And stalk Sir Mouse to his secret lair.
For she who makes this twig a tree
Swears by the gods, she'll none of thee.
                                    —RUBY MAE FISHER

SUGGESTIONS

Let us make a list of all the days that might inspire verse and try a poem for one.

General observance: New Year's Day　　　Lincoln's Birthday Washington's Birthday　　　St. Patrick's Day　　　Easter Day—for an easter card or to accompany a gift　　　April Fool's Day—for fun May Day　　　Memorial Day　　　Flag Day　　　Fourth of July (Independence Day)　　　Hallowe'en　　　Columbus Day Election Day　　　Thanksgiving Day　　　Christmas　　　Armistice Day

Public Occasions: Opening of new building, play center　　　Unveiling a monument　　　Dedicating a church　　　Naming a ship Passing of needed law, such as international copyright bill, etc.

Private Occasions: Birthdays　　　Wedding anniversaries　　　Graduation days　　　A first visit　　　Individuals will have others to add to the list

Social Occasion: Linen shower for bride　　　Welcoming a guest Bon voyage　　　On visiting a spot hallowed by associations: historical, religious, literary. . . .

CHAPTER XXII

VERSE FOR CHILDREN

To WRITE a poem for the younger members of the family or the younger members of some one else's family, if we have no little brothers or sisters or cousins of our own, is a great deal of fun. The important thing is to use imagery which will appeal to a child's taste. A little boy of six years would have no interest in a moon which was a sophisticated bride; but he might be intensely interested in a moon somersaulting in the lake. An observer will find many experiences of the children's especial own to put into verse.

Children's verse should sing. An editor of juvenile verse in a large publishing house once told the author that her chief test of juvenile verse submitted for a reading was, "Will the children go around the house repeating the lines?" Does it commit itself to memory? Suitable imagery, and singing quality, then, are two important requirements of verse for the little ones.

Besides writing *for* children, verse writers may enjoy writing about children with an eye upon the grown-up. Some flash missed by the child will be caught by the older person, who smiles with sympathetic understanding. Therein lies his delight. A. A. Milne is an artist at this kind of child-verse. Any grown-up may joy in it. The double appeal lets him as well as the child into the fun.

Before you plan your poem, decide whether you are writing to appeal to the children or to grown-ups. Children's poems must have all the fine qualities of poetry: no sentimentality; no mixed or vague images; no lack of unity.

Here are some children's poems that may stimulate your imagination.

Little

I am the sister of him
And he is my brother.
He is too little for us
To talk to each other.

So every morning I show him
My doll and my book;
But every morning he still is
Too little to look.
     —DOROTHY ALDIS

Where Go the Boats?

Dark brown is the river;
  Golden is the sand;
It flows along forever,
  With trees on either hand.

Green leaves a-floating,
  Castles of the foam,
Boats of mine a-boating—
  Where will all come home?

On goes the river
  'And out past the mill,
Away down the valley,
  Away down the hill.

Away down the river,
  A hundred miles or more,
Other little children
  Shall bring my boats ashore.
      —ROBERT LOUIS STEVENSON

Singing

Of speckled eggs the birdie sings
And nests among the trees;
The sailor sings of ropes and things
In ships upon the seas.

The children sing in far Japan;
The children sing in Spain;
The organ with the organ man
Is singing in the rain.
      —ROBERT LOUIS STEVENSON

Joe Pye's Counter

Joe Pye Weed runs a soda fountain;
His raspberry special he serves by the cone.
He doesn't keep straws in a silver-covered holder,
For his customers all carry straws of their own.
      —MARY J. J. WRINN

Miss T.

It's a very odd thing—
  As odd as can be—
That whatever Miss T. eats
  Turns into Miss T.;
Porridge and apples,
Mince, muffins and mutton,
Jam, junket, jumbles—
  Not a rap, not a button
It matters; the moment
  They're out of her plate,
Though shared by Miss Butcher
  And sour Mr. Bate,
Tiny and cheerful,
  And neat as can be,
Whatever Miss T. eats
  Turns into Miss T.
      —WALTER DE LA MARE

Alas, Alack!

Ann, Ann!
  Come! quick as you can!
There's a fish that *talks*
  In the frying-pan.
Out of the fat,
  As clear as glass,
He put up his mouth
  And moaned 'Alas!'
Oh, most mournful,
  'Alas, alack!'
Then turned to his sizzling,
  And sank him back.
      —WALTER DE LA MARE

The Owl and the Pussy-Cat

I

The Owl and the Pussy-Cat went to sea
  In a beautiful pea-green boat,
They took some honey, and plenty of money,
  Wrapped up in a five-pound note.

The Owl looked up at the stars above,
  And sang to a small guitar,
"O lovely Pussy! O Pussy, my love,
  What a beautiful Pussy you are,
          You are,
          You are!
What a beautiful Pussy you are!"

II

Pussy said to the Owl, "You elegant fowl!
  How charmingly sweet you sing!
O let us be married! too long we have tarried:
  But what shall we do for a ring?"

They sailed away for a year and a day,
  To the land where the Bong-tree grows,
And there in a wood a Piggy-wing stood,
  With a ring at the end of his nose,
          His nose,
          His nose,
With a ring at the end of his nose.

III

"Dear Pig, are you willing to sell for one shilling
  Your ring?" Said the Piggy, "I will."
So they took it away, and were married next day
  By the Turkey who lives on the hill.

They dinèd on mice, and slices of quince,
  Which they ate with a runcible spoon;
And hand in hand, on the edge of the sand,
  They danced by the light of the moon,
          The moon,
          The moon,
They danced by the light of the moon.

—EDWARD LEAR

Radiator Romping

Hot!
What!
Brownies in the radiator.
Listen to them chuckle
As they dance in pairs.
His-s-s-t!
Whis-s-s-t!
Hear the second answer?
They're talking to the brownies
In the pipe down stairs.

—MARY J. J. WRINN

Once, a class of young verse makers took the experiences of children as subjects for poems and wrote a collection of their own, which they called *Pegasus a Pony*. One of the members made a gingham cover for it and decorated it throughout with silhouettes, which she had cut out of magazine advertisements.

Here are some poems from *Pegasus a Pony*:

Spring

Spring's here; because it's almost time
For brother's birthday cake,
The sun comes now instead of nurse
To tell me when to wake,
I can stay out till six at night,
The sun's still shining then,
Long stockings have been put away—
I have my knees again.

—RUTH H. HAUSMAN

Disappointment

Nurse said I had a sister,
And if I wasn't bad,
They'd let me go and see her,
And, gee, but I was mad.
'Cause after I'd been very good—
A little naughty, maybe—
They showed me sister in a crib
And she was just a baby.

—WILLIAM ROEHRICK

Achievement

Oh, I've learned how to dress myself
And brush my hair, and tie my shoe;
Why, I can even clean my teeth
And wash my ears, can you?

—MILTON PURDY

Sagacity

I had a little kitten-cat
But all she did was sat and sat,
So now I've got a doggy too
To chase her round and make her mew

—HARRIET DOKTOR

Peril

When I ride on the wagon
And it is full of hay,
I sit right in the middle
So I won't slip away.
When it goes over bridges
And jounces down the road,
It squeaks and squeals but never
Upsets its dusty load.
—WILLIAM ROEHRICK

Fairyland

In fairyland are purple cats,
    And frogs with jeweled eyes,
And all the turtles wear high hats.
    (In fairyland are purple cats)
And also lemon-colored bats,
    Even a dog that flies.
In fairyland are purple cats
    And frogs with jeweled eyes.
—DORIS V. LECKY

The Well

You mustn't ever go too near
The well that's in our yard,
'Cause if you do, you might fall in
And getting out is hard.
Last summer when my cousin
Came visiting from town
He went right to the edge and
Started to look down.
But just as he leaned over,
(Although I can't quite tell) ,
He must have lost his balance,
'Cause in the well he fell.
At first I heard an awful splash
And then I heard a yell,
And when I ran to look, why there
He was down in the well.
His Ma she almost fainted but
My dad threw him a chain,
And when they pulled him out he looked
'Sif he'd been in the rain.
His hands and face were awful clean,
But he was awful wet;
The water running off his clothes
Made puddles where he set.
His Ma she took a Turkish towel
And rubbed him till he screamed.
She made him red, and worse off than
He was before, it seemed.
—WILLIAM ROEHRICK

Compensation

A girl sits next to me at school;
She doesn't ever miss:
She knows that five and four are nine,
And *that* goes into *this*;

A scrawly letter or a scratched
Out figure never mars
Her copy book, and it is full
Of little golden stars.

But when I get the answer wrong,
I let her sniff and laugh.
When Johnny brought a pear to school,
He didn't give *her* half!
—RUTH H. HAUSMAN

Playing in the Rain

Rain-kissed and rain-wet,
Playing in the rain;
For what child can stay within
When on his window pane
Rain drops and rain drops
Are singing a refrain?
—ESTELLE ROOKS

New Quarters

When callers come to our new house
My mother shows them in.
She shows them where the parlor ends
And where the halls begin.

The ice-box is electric
And she shows them how it runs,
And lets them see the shiny stove,
Big pots and little ones.

The old house hasn't anything
To show a guest in pride,
But it has banisters with posts
To stop you if you slide.
—RUTH H. HAUSMAN

The Road

A road leads past our doorway
To the summit of the hill
With People passing every day;
It isn't ever still.

I watch them pass and wonder
Why none of them will stay;
I am so very lonely
And I'm sure they'd love to play.

But Mother says they haven't time
To stop: they've work to do.
Someday I shall be grown-up—
Then I shall travel too.
—DORIS V. LECKY

Another time, each member of the class selected an animal as the subject of a poem, from a list submitted so that there would be no duplication, and made a box of *Animal Crackers*. Some of them are reprinted below.

Mother Duck and Her Ducklings

Old mother Duck
And her ducklings three
Waddled down past
The willow tree.

Said mother Duck
To her ducklings three,
"This is a pond;
Plunge in and see

What your webs are for!
Be quick; be bold!"
They answered, "Quack,
The water is cold!"

Since the ducklings three
Have learned to swim,
They spend all day
In the ducklings' gym.
—ONOLEE JONES

Meditation

I wonder, does the breath
That an elephant breathes out,
Have to travel all the way
From his breather to his snout!
Well, no doubt!
—JOYCE LANCASTER

Difference

A little bear lives in the zoo
He looks just like my "Teddy" do
He has a little flatty nose
But he has clawses in his toes.
—WILLIAM ROEHRICK

Onward and Upward

There was a horse in days of yore,
Who had his food but wanted more;
Not content with necessities,
He sought dessert from tops of trees.

And so to reach the top at all
He had to stretch his neck quite tall
Until one day with perfect ease
He found he reached the highest trees.

Now we just had to give a name
Because he was no more the same,
Because his neck had grown by half,
And so we christened him giraffe.
—SYLVIA ADELMAN

Wanderlust

My daddy went a-travelling
    When he was young and free.
He said once far away he saw
    A bear that looked like me.

Now Nanny says that little bears
    And seals and reindeer too
Are from Antarctica and not
    From cages in the zoo.

So now, how can I be content
    Till I myself can see
Those bears in cold Antarctica
    That look so much like me?
—LUCILLE SCHMEDTJE

Explain Please

Oh Mister Goat,
I haven't heerd
You tell me why
You got a beard.

Is it because
You were quite bad
When you were young
And just a lad?

Or can it be,
When you eat hay,
You save some for
A rainy day?

Or is it that
By some sad theft
Your chin was took
An' that's what's left?

Oh, Mister Goat,
I haven't heerd
You tell me why
You got a beard.
—LUCILLE SCHMEDTJE

Opportunity

Who has made my little pony
Keep his finger nails so shony?
His mother isn't near him
And neither is his daddy
So he could have a lovely time
But he just won't be baddy.
—GEORGIA H. COOPER

SUGGESTIONS FOR POEMS

Experiences of childhood: Bed time　　Food that is good for him or not!　　Putting on rubbers, galoshes, etc.　　Activities—skipping rope, hop-scotch　　The song of the peanut stand　　Wonders of children about the world around them: moon, wind, sprouting of plants, holes at seashore filling with water—any observation through the eye of childhood; imagery to be that of childhood.

Animals children enjoy: Elephant　　Goat　　Donkey　　Duck　　Cat　　Rooster　　Dog　　Pony　　Monkey　　Bear　　Hippopotamus　　Squirrel　　Lion　　Giraffe　　Fish　　Sheep　　Zebra　　Tiger　　Rabbit　　Alligator　　Crocodile　　Peacock　　Rhinoceros　　Pig

Animals as pets: Dog　　Cat　　Bird　　Horse　　Pony

Lowly creatures: Field mouse　　Spider and fly　　Butterfly　　Moth　　Ant　　Mole

CHAPTER XXIII

THE TRIOLET

Easy is the Triolet,
  If you really learn to make it!
Once a neat refrain you get,
Easy is the Triolet.
As you see!—I pay my debt
  With another rhyme. Deuce take it,
Easy is the Triolet,
  If you really learn to make it!

                     —WILLIAM ERNEST HENLEY

A NUMBER of verse patterns which originated in medieval France and in Provence will please young versifiers who would master rigid rules of structure. Many of these patterns have grown increasingly familiar, if not exactly popular, in English since Edmund Gosse wrote for the *Cornhill Magazine*, 1877, "A Plea for Certain Exotic Forms of Verse," meaning the rondel, the rondeau, the triolet, the villanelle, the ballade, and the chant royal. "Each has a fixed form," he says in this article, "regulated by traditional laws and each depends upon richness of rhyme and delicate workmanship for its successful exercise."

The French are very fond of the refrain, so fond of it that they have used it as the basis of many verse forms. The refrain, you may recall, is a word, a phrase, a line or group of lines repeated at intervals in a poem. The English refrain is sometimes marked by slight variations which add the element of surprise to the pleasure of recognition. Unlike the English refrain the French is unvaried in form. Words may not be altered in any way whatever, but the meaning may be artfully modified. In fact the French, like the Japanese, enjoy punning.

In a poem by Michael Lewis, the refrain is "My lady's eyes," which becomes at the first repetition "My lady sighs," and finally "My lady's size." The humor of the poem lies in this play upon words in the refrain. While the sound remains exactly the same, the words have been altered to give a new meaning with each repetition. Masters of the French forms try to bring in the refrain with a different application each time. While it is more difficult in English to achieve this delicate *nuance* of change of meaning, it should be attempted. The laughing lyrist may use his ingenuity with spelling or word or emphasis.

In the succeeding pages we shall take up some of these forms in the order of their difficulty. Our problem being to write verse, we are not concerned with the chronology of the forms or their significance to history. For a delightfully readable history of these forms and many more models than these pages will permit, we recommend to the curious verse maker Helen Louise Cohen's *Lyric Forms from France.*

The triolet is a simple form with which to experiment as an introduction to expression through the French forms. It is a single stanza of eight lines with only two rhymes. It is built on a refrain of the two lines which begin and end it. Line 1 is repeated as line 4. Letting capital letters represent the refrain, we may indicate the rhyme scheme of the triolet as *A B a A a b A B.*

The Kiss

1.	Rose kissed me to-day.	A
2.	Will she kiss me to-morrow?	B
3.	Let it be as it may,	a
4.	Rose kissed me *to-day;*	A
5.	But the pleasure gives way	a
6.	To a savor of sorrow;	b
7.	Rose kissed me to-day;	A
8.	*Will* she kiss me to-morrow?	B

—AUSTIN DOBSON

When the poet decided on his refrain the skeleton of his poem was like this:

1.	Rose kissed me to-day.	A
2.	Will she kiss me to-morrow?	B
3.		a
4.	Rose kissed me to-day	A
5.		a
6.		b
7.	Rose kissed me to-day;	A
8.	Will she kiss me to-morrow?	B

The writer then had to think about only three lines: two *a* lines and one *b* line.

A good way for the beginner to attempt the mastery of the form is first to write out the skeleton, filling in the refrain lines. He must be careful to bring in the refrain so skillfully each time that its recurrence seems natural.

In the triolet above there is charm in the artful modification of meaning through a shift in the accented word of the refrain: "kissed" in line 1; "to-day" in 4; "will" in 8.

While the earliest triolets dealt with grave subjects, the brevity of the triolet seems better to suit humorous, flippant, or light themes. Its chief charm lies in its lightness and grace. For that reason the lines should be short. The poem above has only two feet on a line.

Triolet sequences, that is, a chain of triolets on a single theme, have been attempted with considerable success. Harrison Robertson's below is one of two triolets; Thomas Hardy has written some. Austin Dobson, the most deft English poet of the French forms, has written a charming triolet-sequence "Rose-Leaves," from which the triolet first quoted is taken. Here is another of that sequence:

> I intended an ode
> And it turned into triolets.
> It began à la mode.
> I intended an ode,
> But Rose crossed the road
> With a bunch of fresh violets;
> I intended an ode,
> And it turned into triolets.

This he later changed to

"Urceus Exit"

> I intended an Ode
> And it turned to a Sonnet.
> It began à la mode,
> I intended an Ode;
> But Rose crossed the road
> In her latest new bonnet—
> I intended an Ode;
> And it turned to a Sonnet.
>
> —AUSTIN DOBSON

Others follow.

Love Planted a Rose

> Love planted a rose
> And the world turned sweet;
> Where the wheat field blows
> Love planted a rose.
> Up the mill-wheel's prose
> Ran a music beat.
> Love planted a rose
> And the world turned sweet.
>
> —KATHERINE LEE BATES

Two Triolets

What he said:
    This kiss upon your fan I press—
        Ah! Sainte Nitouche, you don't refuse it!
    And may it from its soft recess—
    This kiss upon your fan I press—
    Be blown to you, a shy caress,
        By this white down, whene'er you use it.
    This kiss upon your fan I press,—
        Ah! Sainte Nitouche, you *don't* refuse it!

What she thought:
    To kiss a fan!
        What a poky poet!
    The stupid man
    To kiss a fan
    When he knows—that—he—can—
        Or ought to know it—
    To kiss a fan!
        What a poky poet!

—Harrison Robertson

Not all triolets are in playful vein.

Song

    I made my shroud but no one knows,
        So shimmering fine it is and fair,
    With stitches set in even rows.
    I made my shroud but no one knows.
    In door-way where the lilac blows
        Humming a little wandering air,
    I made my shroud and no one knows,
        So shimmering fine it is and fair.

—Adelaide Crapsey

As a metrical exercise, the experience of attempting the form may be manipulated to fill the pattern. The next handling may produce something more poetic. Here are such experiments followed by other student attempts.

These Triolets!

It's difficult to write
These tricky triolets,
For even if they're light—
It's difficult to write—
They're so elusive—quite
Like woodland violets!
It's *difficult* to write
These tricky triolets!

—NAOMI ROGIN

Alas!

My little songs, ye are too young,
And no Great Pain inspires ye.
From Breaking Heart shouldst ye be wrung,—
My little songs; ye are too young
To know: "Experience must be sung."
Go! Hide your Immaturity!
My little songs, ye are too young,
And no Great Pain inspires ye.

—MURIEL F. HOCHDORF

In a Garden

There she was, and there was I,
Below, a flower, above, a tree;
The moon was gold, and full, and high—
There she was, and there was I.
She breathed a tiny, perfumed sigh
That somehow caught itself in me—
There she was, and there was I,
Below, a flower, above, a tree.

—LESLIE RUBIN

Triolet

Larkspur, thistle, these her eyes,
Eloquent of moving water—
Winged, unquiet—butterflies;
Larkspur, thistle, these her eyes,
Maybe if Apollo tries,
He can give them to her daughter.
Larkspur, thistle, these her eyes,
Eloquent of moving water.

—MURIEL F. HOCHDORF

Something in Common

I love the pretty things you say
Although they aren't true.
Your words grow sweeter every day,—
I love the pretty things you say;
You see, I understand the way
You feel because I'm like that too;
I love the pretty things you say
Although they aren't true.

—IRMA TERR

Guest

Every morn at break of day
    A sunbeam visits me;
Through drowsy eyes I see it play
Every morn at break of day;
On my nose it likes to stray,
    Hopping about with glee;
Every morn at break of day
    A sunbeam visits me.

—EVELYNE LOVE COOPER

Triolet

Apple trees reveal their souls
In the spring.
Shading soft enchanted knolls,
Apple trees reveal their souls—
Tenderly the sun enfolds
And glorifies each scented wing.
Apple trees reveal their souls
In the spring.

—GILBERT O'CONNOR

To D. M.

Autumn leaves in flaming flight
    Burn the heart.
With devouring feigned delight
Autumn leaves in flaming light
Mock the winter's weary night
    And depart—
Autumn leaves in *flaming* flight
    Burn the heart.

—GILBERT O'CONNOR

Some students found the triolet a vehicle for soft laughter.

The Only Poet

It would be lots of fun to be
The only living poet,
And if the honor fell on me
It would be lots of fun to be
Provider of all poetry,
Quite bad, and only me to know it!
It would be lots of fun to be
The only living poet.

—RUTH H. HAUSMAN

Reproof to the Advertiser

Though I smoke "Luckies" every day
I never made a hole in one;
I never acted in a play
Though I smoke "Luckies" every day.
I've made no statues out of clay;
A tennis match I never won.
Though I smoke "Luckies" every day
I never made a hole in one.

—WILLIAM ROEHRICK

Triolet

keep quite thin,
at no lunch.
, dietin'
keep quite thin.
1 Might I sin
just a munch!
keep quite thin,
at no lunch.

—Sylvia Lapidus

Reflections on the Moon

ne say the moon is made of cheese,
  But I know well it's ice
th glassy brooks and crystal trees.
ne say the moon is made of cheese;
ae touch of its cold cruelties
  Froze all my wishes twice.
ne say the moon is made of cheese,
  But I know well it's ice.

—Ethel Greenfield

Resolution

ocrastination is my sin:
  Tomorrow I shall stop it;
find it so hard to begin,
ocrastination is my sin,
at I shall call out from within
  My soul, the strength to drop it.
ocrastination is my sin—
  Tomorrow I shall stop it.

—Richard Hallberg

The Three Sneezes

Sneeze I

Quietly within my nose,
The small bacteria dwell;
A harmless germlet comes and goes;
Quietly within my nose,
The little coccus stays and grows.
I sneeze and wheeze and look like—well
Quietly within my nose
The small bacteria dwell.

Sneeze II

Oh what can I do
For a cold in the head?
I've taken hot brew
  (Oh what can I do?)
With lemon—katchoo!—
Ere going to bed.
Oh what can I do
For a cold in the head?

Sneeze III

A cold in the chest
And a nose like a cherry,
A handker—choo!—quest—
A cold in the chest
In red flannel dressed
Like a winter strawberry—
A cold in the chest
And a nose like a cherry.

—Muriel F. Hochdorf

TRY YOUR OWN PIPE

Before inventing your own triolet, you may find it limbering to develop a ready-made beginning:

Not about a rose   A
_____   B

Students of the forms have found it stimulating to develop such beginnings on the co-operative plan! One adds a line to complete the refrain, another carries the nonsense—for it is sheer nonsense—a bit farther until the end is in sight. To keep the contributions in tone, the mood is determined at the outset: Gay, quiet, subdued . . .

The two lines above were developed; then the other side of the question was considered:

Not about a rose	A	Here's about a nose
Shall we write a pome,	B	That grows on Schmedtje's face:
Nor about a nose,—	a	Nose looks like a rose.
Not about a rose	A	Here's about a nose—
Beneath the garden hose	a	To honor it in prose
Nor about a gnome.	b	Would be quite out of place.
Not about a rose	A	Here's about a nose
Shall we write a pome.	B	That grows on Schmedtje's face!

Play with any of these beginnings, altering as you please.

Happy is each poet   A
Coming here to play   B

Let us try a triolet
Just for practice sake

Spring is here and we're in school;
Isn't that a blessing?

There stood Eben Sweetzer
And there sat Mary Ann

Let us make a little song
Out of tears and laughter

Dancing down the hollow
Before the break of day

A cricket saws its violin
Beneath an autumn stone

CHAPTER XXIV

THE RONDEL

CLOSELY related to the eight-line triolet is the rondel. It consists of thirteen lines in any length built on a refrain. The lines are tipped with only two rhymes, no one of which may be repeated. The poem is divided into three stanzas. Since it is not quite so slight in form as the triolet it is capable of more serious service. The scheme is *A B b a; a b A B; a b b a A*. The refrain at the end should vary in meaning from the refrains above.

The Wanderer

1. Love comes back to his vacant dwelling—	A
2. The old, old Love that we knew of yore!	B
3. We see him stand by the open door,	b
4. With his great eyes sad, and his bosom swelling.	a
5. He makes as though in our arms repelling,	a
6. He fain would lie as he lay before;—	b
7. Love comes back to his vacant dwelling—	A
8. The old, old Love that we knew of yore.	B
9. Ah, who shall help us from over-spelling	a
10. That sweet, forgotten, forbidden lore!	b
11. E'en as we doubt in our heart once more,	b
12. With a rush of tears to our eyelids welling,	a
13. Love comes back to his vacant dwelling.	A

—AUSTIN DOBSON

Alons au Bois le May Cueillir

We'll to the woods and gather may
  Fresh from the footprints of the rain;
  We'll to the woods, at every vein
To drink the spirit of the day.

The winds of spring are out at play,
  The needs of spring in heart and brain.
We'll to the woods and gather may
  Fresh from the footprints of the rain.

The world's too near her end, you say?—
  Hark to the blackbird's mad refrain!
  It waits for her, the vast Inane?—
Then, girls, to help her on the way
We'll to the woods and gather may.

      —WILLIAM ERNEST HENLEY
    Original by Charles d'Orleans 1391-1465

    You will run across other forms than that above. An earlier form is one line longer, the whole refrain of two lines forming lines 13 and 14.

Rondel

Kiss me, sweetheart, the Spring is here,
  And Love is lord of you and me!
  The bluebells beckon each passing bee;
The wild wood laughs to the flowered year;
There is no bird in brake or brere
  But to his little mate sings he,
"Kiss me, sweetheart, the Spring is here,
  And Love is lord of you and me."

The blue sky laughs out sweet and clear;
  The missel-thrush upon the tree
  Pipes for sheer gladness loud and free;
And I go singing to my dear,
"Kiss me, sweetheart, the Spring is here,
And Love is lord of you and me!"

        —JOHN PAYNE

    In the above the first two stanzas are printed as one because that form suits the unit of thought which they express. You will see this arrangement again.

Another familiar rhyme scheme is *A B a b; b a A B; a b a b A B.*

"Awake, Awake!"

Awake, awake, O gracious heart,
   There's some one knocking at the door!
The chilling breezes make him smart;
   His little feet are tired and sore.
Arise, and welcome him before
   Adown his cheeks the big tears start:
   Awake, awake, O gracious heart,
There's some one knocking at the door!

'Tis Cupid come with loving art
   To honor, worship, and implore;
And lest, unwelcomed, he depart
   With all his wise, mysterious lore,
Awake, awake, O gracious heart,
   There's some one knocking at the door!
                    —FRANK DEMPSTER SHERMAN

Rondel for September

You thought it was a falling leaf we heard:
I knew it was the Summer's gypsy feet,
A sound so reticent it scarcely stirred
The ear, so still a message to repeat,—
"I go, and lo, I make my going sweet."
What wonder you should miss so soft a word?
You thought it was a falling leaf we heard:
I knew it was the Summer's gypsy feet.

With slender torches for her service meet
The golden-rod is coming; softer slurred
Midsummer noises take a note replete
With hint of change; who told the mocking-bird?
I knew it was the Summer's gypsy feet—
You thought it was a falling leaf we heard.
                    —KARLE WILSON BAKER

In the above poem the last six lines are tipped with rhymes in reversed order: *b a b a B A.*

The *B* line in the last refrain is omitted in this one:

Rondel

To his Mistress, to succour his heart that is beleaguered by jealousy.

Strengthen, my Love, this castle of my heart,
　And with some store of pleasure give me aid,
For Jealousy, with all them of his part,
　Strong siege about the weary tower has laid.
　Nay, if to break his hands thou art afraid,
Too weak to make his cruel force depart,
Strengthen at least this castle of my heart,
　And with some store of pleasure give me aid.
Nay, let not Jealousy, for all his art
　Be master, and the tower in ruin laid,
　That still, ah Love! thy gracious rule obeyed.
Advance, and give me succour of thy part;
Strengthen, my Love, this castle of my heart.

　　　　　　　　　　　—ANDREW LANG
　　　　　　　Original by Charles d'Orleans

The next rhyme pattern is still another variation: *A B b a   b a A B
a b a b A B.*

Rondel

I love you dearly, O my sweet!
　Although you pass me lightly by,
　Although you weave my life awry,
And tread my heart beneath your feet.

I tremble at your touch; I sigh
To see you passing down the street;
I love you dearly, O my sweet!
　Although you pass me lightly by.

You say in scorn that love's a cheat,
　Passion a blunder, youth a lie.
I know not. Only when we meet
　I long to kiss your hand and cry,
"I love you dearly, O my sweet,
　Although you pass me lightly by."

　　　　　　　—JUSTIN HUNTLEY MCCARTHY

Here again a young versifier found that the experience of trying the form made a good metrical exercise.

Foolishness

Rondel, rondel, a, b, a,
  Moving gayly, fast and light,
  Like a red and yellow kite,
Soaring high, as if to say,

"I'm a symbol of the day,"
  While I sit and lamely write,
"Rondel, rondel, a, b, a,
  Moving gayly, fast and light."

How I'd like to be a jay,
  Fly away from human sight,
  And a versifier's plight.
Do I really have to stay,
Rondel, rondel, a, b, a?

—LUCILLE SCHMEDTJE

Other student rondels follow:

Preference

The rain is dancing overhead
  With step as light as thistledown.
  The wind is in her whirling gown
And silence singing in her tread.

With laughter is my house fire fed—
  But pine logs are so dried and brown—
The rain is dancing overhead
  With step as light as thistledown.

Walls close me in, but I am fled
  Into the rain . . . Comfort, renown,
  Protection? No, I'll wear a crown
Of raindrops, and be free instead . . .
The rain is dancing overhead.

—JOYCE LANCASTER

Rondel of Yellow

Oh, yellow decks the field today,
And yellow glints the rill.
And drowsily against the hill
Like dreamy children leans the hay.

A brown bird's joy bursts clear; a spray
Of buttercups in his yellow trill.
Oh, yellow decks the field today,
And yellow glints the rill.

Two lady slippers flash as they
Trip, and point, and toe, until
Wind-sprite, in sundust yellow frill,
Puts his yellow flute away.
Oh, yellow decks the field today.

—LOUISE FISCHER

Autumn

Patient stacks of whispering hay
Stand out upon the sloping crown
Of Turkey Hill all shaggy brown.
They watch the swelling barn and weigh

Their chance of getting in. Who'll stay
The winter here above the town?
Patient stacks of whispering hay
Stand out upon the sloping crown

And see their brothers pitched away.
They watch with envy, and they frown,
For heartless storms will tear them down.
But now they stand throughout the day—
Patient stacks of whispering hay.

—WILLIAM ROEHRICK

Rondel

Come with flute and violin,
Hushing Time's slow feet.
Hours echo down the street
Where love's noiseless step has been.

Soon the hungry days begin
To scale the walls of my retreat.
Come with flute and violin,
Hushing Time's slow feet.

Draw the notes out taut and thin,
Stabbing,—bleeding,—arrow-fleet,
Dying, painfully complete.
Here is Eden, purged of Sin:
Come with flute and violin.

—MURIEL F. HOCHDORF

Rondel for Light Words

Skip them on lily ponds, limpid and clear,
Let them dance lightly for me and for you,
Sparkling where trees guard us from the world's view;
Let them skim silver and then disappear.

They were not made for the awed host to fear,
Made but to sparkle unseen save by two.
Skip them on lily ponds, limpid and clear,
Let them dance lightly for me and for you,

Pleasantly ripple the still waters here.
What if your aim is more graceful than true?
Pebbles can glisten, rose, orange, and blue.
Unmourned they go to a shallow green bier;
Skip them on lily ponds, limpid and clear.

—RUTH H. HAUSMAN

Night Mood

A cloud has drifted down to rest
  Upon the silent river shore,
  And through the black square of my
      door
The night has shuddered in and pressed

Upon my quiet, fearful lest
  The spreading fog engulf her, for
A cloud has drifted down to rest
  Upon the silent shore.

I welcome her, this friend in quest
  Of comfort and repose much more
  Than brilliant nights. I can't deplore
My loneliness; I have a guest.
A cloud has drifted down to rest.

—JOYCE LANCASTER

When You Went Back

When you went back, and autumn flame
  Was blazing from each tree,
  Did any thought of me
Recall some often murmured name?

Did sleeping echoes, waked, exclaim
  "Alone—why where is he?"
When you went back, and autumn flame
  Was blazing from each tree?

Alone, was moon-kissed night the same
  Along the silent quay,
  Where breezes, vagrant-free,
Breathed woodland fragrance as they
      came—
When you went back, and autumn flame
  Was blazing from each tree?

—LIONEL DAY

The Consequences of Being a Poet

(to R. N.)

Somehow, it's always been a poet's fate,
To love an ideal "Someone" quite in vain.
The thing has gone and happened once again—
This time to me. I've found my perfect mate . . .

I wouldn't mind it so if he would *hate*!—
But he's indifferent—cold, like autumn rain.
Somehow, it's always been a poet's fate,
To love an ideal "Someone" quite in vain.

I hope someday—before it's very late . . .
But I've had dreams for years, and only pain
Has come of them! Two things alone remain!
To write my sonnets, and to wait . . . and wait . . .
Somehow, it's *always* been a poet's fate!

—NAOMI ROGIN

Rondel to the Untiring Voice

Tell me that blue skies must follow the gray,
Bluebirds, not blackbirds, will be on the wing,
Tell me to clown it, to laugh and to sing;
How Alabama is calling in May.

How the old homestead is fragrant with hay,
Tell, and that beggars are richer than kings.
Tell me that blue skies must follow the gray,
Bluebirds, not blackbirds, will be on the wing.

Trill down the length of the keyboard and play
"Under the moonlight we'll meet in the spring"—
(How many dollars that short sob must bring!) —
Neighbors' victrola, the tenth time today
Tell me that blue skies must follow the gray.

—RUTH H. HAUSMAN

PRACTICE!

I am hungry for oakum and tar
And the smell of a salt wind blowing

* * * * * *

In a rondel the turn of the phrase
Is the flower of a singer's wit

* * * * * *

Many a tale grows sprightlier
When ladies meet for tea

* * * * * *

What's a citizen to do
When the circus takes the town?

* * * * * *

Just as of old Ben Jonson sang
"Drink to me only with thine eyes,"

* * * * * *

On the old ramparts above the Rhone

_____

* * * * * *

The page was sent to Naples   *Unless you can manage rhymes*
But the mule did not forget   *for "Naples," fill out the line*

* * * * * *

The page was sent to Naples, runs the tale

_____

* * * * * *

The narrow street climbed step on step
Up to the town and so did we

CHAPTER XXV

THE VILLANELLE

"A dainty thing's the Villanelle
Sly, musical, a jewel in rhyme."
—WILLIAM ERNEST HENLEY

THIS graceful form consists of nineteen lines, arranged in six stanzas, of any meter and any line length, though preferably a short line. It is built on two refrains, turning on only two rhymes.

Henley's complete villanelle on the villanelle with its pastoral suggestion of fluting shepherds and the sweetness of the ancient meadows which recall its origin will explain the structure.

The Villanelle

1.	A dainty thing's the Villanelle;	A¹
2.	Sly, musical, a jewel in rhyme,	b
3.	It serves its purpose passing well.	A²
4.	A double-clappered silver bell	a
5.	That must be made to clink in chime,	b
6.	A dainty thing's the Villanelle;	A¹
7.	And if you wish to flute a spell,	a
8.	Or ask a meeting 'neath the lime,	b
9.	It serves its purpose passing well.	A²
10.	You must not ask of it the swell	a
11.	Of organs grandiose and sublime—	b
12.	A dainty thing's the villanelle;	A¹
13.	And, filled with sweetness, as a shell	a
14.	Is filled with sound, and launched in time,	b
15.	It serves its purpose passing well.	A²
16.	Still fair to see and good to smell	a
17.	As in the quaintness of its prime,	b
18.	A dainty thing's the Villanelle,	A¹
19.	It serves its purpose passing well.	A²

As you may have observed, the first five stanzas are of three lines each; the sixth stanza of four lines. The first and the third lines form two refrains. Beginning with the first, each refrain is alternately repeated as the last line of each succeeding 3-line stanza. Both refrains are repeated in order: line 1 and line 3, as the final couplet which closes the last stanza. Let A^1 represent line 1 which is refrain 1. Let A^2 represent line 3 which is refrain 2. The scheme follows:

$$A^1\ b\ A^2;\quad a\ b\ A^1;\quad a\ b\ A^2;\quad a\ b\ A^1;\quad a\ b\ A^2;\quad a\ b\ A^1\ A^2$$

As in all the fixed forms, care must be taken to make the refrain seem spontaneous. "The beauty of art is to conceal art." Deftness and grace should characterize the Villanelle whether the mood be gay or serious. Because the refrain recurs so frequently and at such short intervals it demands special care. The following suggestion may prove helpful to the beginner.

First plan the couplet on which you will build your Villanelle; that is, A^1, A^2. In the poem above, it would be

> A dainty thing's the Villanelle
> It serves its purpose passing well.

These lines will come together at the end of the poem anyway; one should grow out of the other. Then split the couplet with a b line. Above, the line that split the couplet, that is the b line, is

> Sly, musical, a jewel in rhyme,

Try to vary the set of rhymes; that is, have the a rhymes differ from the b rhymes in vowel and consonant following. Do not have "ell" in the couplet and "et" in the line between.

Be sure also, before you go too far in your poem that you have words to supply your needs. You will need 7 a rhymes and 6 b's. There must be no strained effects in a villanelle. To serve its purpose passing well, it must indeed be

> Sly, musical, a jewel in rhyme.

How lightly a rare lyrist pays tribute to one of the last of great Greek lyric poets and recaptures something of the idyllic effect which the singer of the Golden Age achieved with exquisite simplicity.

In *The Idyls* Theocritus presents pastoral scenes in which shepherds
—Daphnis, Menalcas, Lacon—hold frequent singing or fluting matches
for rustic prizes: a goat, a pipe, a sheep. Flitting through the scenes are
Amaryllis, a rustic maiden; Simætha, another, who seeks Hecate's magic
for a spell against her faithless lover. Polyphemus, the cyclops, mourns
the loss of Galatea. Persephone is a goddess of nature; hence, "O Singer
of Persephone!" The references in Wilde's poem are all to Sicilian
scenes from the thirty idyls.

Theocritus

O Singer of Persephone!
　In the dim meadows desolate,
Dost thou remember Sicily?

Still through the ivy flits the bee
　Where Amaryllis lies in state;
O Singer of Persephone!

Simætha calls on Hecate
　And hears the wild dogs at the gate;
Dost thou remember Sicily?

Still by the light and laughing sea
　Poor Polypheme bemoans his fate;
O Singer of Persephone!

And still in boyish rivalry
　Young Daphnis challenges his mate;
Dost thou remember Sicily?

Slim Lacon keeps a goat for thee;
　For thee the jocund shepherds wait;
O Singer of Persephone!
Dost thou remember Sicily?

　　　　　　　　　　—OSCAR WILDE

In sprightlier vein, if less classical, are these lines inspired by a dainty lady. With such an inspiration any poet-lover might be moved to create as airy a trifle.

Villanelle of His Lady's Treasures

I took her dainty eyes, as well
  As silken tendrils of her hair:
And so I made a Villanelle!

I took her voice, a silver bell,
  As clear as song, as soft as prayer:
I took her dainty eyes as well.

It may be, said I, who can tell,
  These things shall be my less despair?
And so I made a Villanelle!

I took her whiteness virginal
  And from her cheeks two roses rare:
I took her dainty eyes as well.

I said: "It may be possible
  Her image from my heart to tear!"
And so I made a Villanelle!

I stole her laugh, most musical:
  I wrought it in with artful care;
I took her dainty eyes as well;
And so I made a Villanelle.

          —ERNEST DOWSON

This was published in the *Athenaeum* in 1874 and reprinted in "A Plea for Certain Exotic Forms of Verse," the *Cornhill Magazine*, 1877:

Wouldst thou not be content to die
  When low-hung fruit is hardly clinging,
And golden Autumn passes by?

Beneath this delicate rose-gray sky,
  While sunset bells are faintly ringing,
Wouldst thou not be content to die?

For wintry webs of mist on high
  Out of the muffled earth are springing,
And golden Autumn passes by.

O now when pleasures fade and fly,
  And Hope her southward flight is winging,
Wouldst thou not be content to die?

Lest Winter come, with wailing cry
  His cruel icy bondage bringing,
When golden Autumn hath passed by,

And thou, with many a tear and sigh,
  While life her wasted hands is wringing,
Shalt pray in vain for leave to die
When golden Autumn hath passed by.

—EDMUND GOSSE

How totally different is the effect of the next villanelle. It sings in minor key. The mood is in keeping with the desolation of an empty house when those who were its very life have all gone away. Notice how the restraint of the lines intensifies the effect of ruin and decay.

The House on the Hill

They are all gone away;
  The House is shut and still,
There is nothing more to say.

Through broken walls and gray
  The winds blow bleak and shrill:
They are all gone away.

Nor is there one to-day
  To speak them good or ill:
There is nothing more to say.

Why is it then we stray
  Around that sunken sill?
They are all gone away.

And our poor fancy-play
  For them is wasted skill:
There is nothing more to say.

There is ruin and decay
  In the House on the Hill:
They are all gone away,
There is nothing more to say.

—Edwin Arlington Robinson

A couplet by Robert Louis Stevenson suggested the next poem. You will find it at the close of the villanelle.

Villanelle, with Stevenson's Assistance

The world is so full of a number of things
  Like music and pictures and statues and plays,
I'm sure we should all be as happy as kings.

We've winters and summers and autumns and springs,
  We've Aprils and Augusts, Octobers and Mays—
The world is so full of a number of things.

Though minor the key of my lyrical strings,
  I change it to major when pæaning praise:
I'm sure we should all be as happy as kings.

Each morning a myriad wonderments brings,
  Each evening a myriad marvels conveys,
The world is so full of a number of things.

With pansies and roses and pendants and rings,
  With purples and yellows and scarlets and grays,
I'm sure we should all be as happy as kings.

So pardon a bard if he carelessly sings
  A solo indorsing these Beautiful Days—
The world is so full of a number of things,
I'm sure we should all be as happy as kings.

—FRANKLIN P. ADAMS

While the perfect model, as Jean Passerat (1534-1602) popularized it, consists of six stanzas, you will come across varieties. Here is one of nine stanzas—dangerously long—even for so charmingly graceful a work.

The air is white with snowflakes clinging;
Between the gusts that come and go
Methinks I hear the woodlark singing.

Methinks I see the primrose springing
On many a bank and hedge, although
The air is white with snowflakes clinging.

Surely, the hands of Spring are flinging
Wood-scents to all the winds that blow:
Methinks I hear the woodlark singing.

Methinks I see the swallow winging
Across the woodlands sad with snow;
The air is white with snowflakes clinging.

Was that the cuckoo's wood-chime swinging?
Was that the linnet fluting low?
Methinks I hear the woodlark singing.

Or can it be the breeze is bringing
The breath of violets? Ah, no!
The air is white with snowflakes clinging.

It is my lady's voice that's stringing
Its beads of gold to song; and so
Methinks I hear the woodlark singing.

The violets I see upspringing
Are in my lady's eyes, I trow:
The air is white with snowflakes clinging.

Dear, whilst thy tender tones are ringing,
Even whilst amid the winter's woe
The air is white with snowflakes clinging,
Methinks I hear the woodlark singing.

                                        —JOHN PAYNE

VILLANELLES BY HIGH-SCHOOL POETS

Moonlight Sonata

From blown seeds of ecstasy memories grow
  That blossom in moonlight to moments again,
While the mood of the midnight sings to me low.

The cherry tree, laden with armfuls of snow,
  Offers her sweetness once more in the lane;
From blown seeds of ecstasy memories grow.

When moonlight is stabbing lake waters I know,
  It throbs to the touch of a vanished moon's rain,
While the mood of the midnight sings to me low,

Sings to me, croons to me, hauntingly, slow. . . .
  Seven blue stars breathe a far-off refrain;
From blown seeds of ecstasy memories grow.

Bruised dreams and a heart-ache are hushed when I go
  To a lonely lake haunt to hear silence complain,
While the mood of the midnight sings to me low.

And my heart whispers peace in a slumber song, so
  That drowsiness closes the wide eyes of pain.
From blown seeds of ecstasy memories grow,
  While the mood of the midnight sings to me low.
                  —MURIEL F. HOCHDORF

Summer Wind

ll the sunlit fields are gay,
  Daisies dance in happy show,
or they hear the pan-pipes play.

istening to that sprightly fay,
  As he rushes to and fro,
ll the sunlit fields are gay.

rasses ripple, hedges sway,
  Pines no longer wish for snow,
or they hear the pan-pipes play.

till, above the trees you may
  Hear his whistling note, and ho!
ll the sunlit fields are gay.

hey forget about the day
  When the sleety wind will blow,
or they hear the pan-pipes play.

oding troubles float away;
  Flowers smile to see them go.
ll the sunlit fields are gay,
or they hear the pan-pipes play.
                —WILLIAM ROEHRICK

Plea to a Burglar

Robber, take my worldly things;
I will give them all to you;
Only leave my heart that sings.

Take my watch, my brooch, my rings;
Take my diamond bracelet too;
Robber, take my worldly things.

Rob me of my precious springs,
Bits of sunshine, drops of dew;
Only leave my heart that sings.

Hear my pleading voice. It flings
Far from me the joys I knew;
Robber, take my worldly things.

Take my palace, fit for kings;
A palace one can build anew;
Only leave my heart that sings.

Oh! the joy that freedom brings!
I'll be happy if you do,
Robber, take my worldly things;
Only leave my heart that sings.
                —IRMA TERR

Villanelle to My Dad

Who feels scarce thirty yet is full forty-two

(To accompany a lounging robe)

Ahoy there dad! and how are you
  On this portentous, solemn day?
You're fully forty years and two!

You're growing old—you know it's true
  Yet who would guess? Again I say
Ahoy there dad! and how are you?

Hm! you don't look the least bit blue
  And yet, you have three hairs of gray?
You're fully forty years and two!

I've heard that when you came to woo
  You were a gallant beau and gay;
Ahoy there dad! and how are you

This fine crisp morn in vestments new?
  We chose that robe, sedate and gray,—
You're fully forty years and two!

You know that it's fair time you drew
  A line between your youth and play.
Ahoy there dad! and how are you?
You're fully forty years and two!

—ETHEL GREENFIELD

Barriers

The marsh weeds grow outside the door
  That sheltered beauty, down the lane
Where love had worn a path before.

But now the grass peeps through the floor
  And watches while I wait in vain.
The marsh weeds grow outside the door

And cover footsteps that were more
  Than prints of feet, or marks of pain,
Where love had worn a path before.

The laughing wavelets on the shore
  Sigh for my house, so sad, so plain.
The marsh weeds grow outside the door

And bind me in to hear their lore
  Of memory, that chills my brain,
Where love had worn a path before.

That, hoping done, I can't ignore
  For it will never come again.
The marsh weeds grow outside the door
Where love had worn a path before.
                                —JOYCE LANCASTER

BORROW THE PIPES OF PASSERAT

Supply the blanks and develop:

If Passerat should come again	A¹
	b
He'd find new subjects for his pen	A²

* * * * *

Oh leave the shepherds and their sheep
  For granite canyons of the town;
Theocritus has need of sleep.

* * * * *

Oh leave the city's cavalcade,
  Jostling beneath the noonday heat,
And pipe with shepherds in the shade.

You bid me shape a villanelle
   In tempo light ——————
A lyric in an airy shell

     * * * * *

Drifting in pattern the snowflakes appear
——————————————————
Whispering white mystery lonely hearts hear

A poem built on these refrains appears below.

Snow Ghosts

Drifting in pattern the snowflakes appear;
   Slippered of silence from pathways unknown,
Whispering white mystery lonely hearts hear.

Gathering closely to cover the bier
   Of autumn close shrouded in death, lying prone.
Drifting in pattern the snowflakes appear.

Where are the tantrums of stormy last year?
   Out of pale nothingness calm peace has grown,
Whispering white mystery lonely hearts hear,

Touching with light powdered fingers the sere
   Dead leaves, and kissing the burr and the cone.
Drifting in pattern the snowflakes appear,

Building tall castles with turrets austere,
   Etching a magic that spring does not own,
Whispering white mystery lonely hearts hear.

In the hush of their footsteps, slow pulses with drear
   Ghost chants are rhythmed to chill monotone.
Drifting in pattern the snowflakes appear,
Whispering white mystery lonely hearts hear.
                       —JOYCE LANCASTER

CHAPTER XXVI

THE RONDEAU

A FIRST cousin to the rondel is the rondeau. "In Flanders Fields," which almost every school boy knows, is written in this pattern. The rondeau consists of fifteen lines in any meter and any line length with only two rhymes. It is divided into three stanzas of 5—4—6 lines. Lines 9 and 15 repeat the refrain which is made of the first few words of the first line,—strictly speaking the first four syllables. It does not rhyme with any line.

The rondeau lends itself to every mood. With X representing the refrain, here is the scheme: *Xa a b b a; a a b X; a a b b a X.*

In Flanders Fields

1.	In Flanders fields the poppies blow	Xa
2.	Between the crosses, row on row,	a
3.	That mark our place; and in the sky	b
4.	The larks, still bravely singing, fly	b
5.	Scarce heard amid the guns below.	a
6.	We are the Dead. Short days ago	a
7.	We lived, felt dawn, saw sunset glow,	a
8.	Loved and were loved, and now we lie	b
9.	In Flanders fields.	X
10.	Take up our quarrel with the foe:	a
11.	To you from failing hands we throw	a
12.	The torch; be yours to hold it high.	b
13.	If ye break faith with us who die	b
14.	We shall not sleep, though poppies grow	a
15.	In Flanders fields.	X

—JOHN McCRAE

In After Days

In after days when grasses high
O'ertop the stone where I shall lie,
   Though ill or well the world adjust
   My slender claim to honored dust,
I shall not question or reply.

I shall not see the morning sky;
I shall not hear the night-wind's sigh;
   I shall be mute, as all men must
     In after days!

But yet, now living, fain were I
That some one then should testify,
   Saying—"He held his pen in trust
   To Art, not serving shame or lust."
Will none?—Then let my memory die
     In after days!

                —AUSTIN DOBSON

If I Were King

If I were king—ah, love, if I were king!
What tributary nations would I bring
To stoop before your sceptre and to swear
Allegiance to your lips and eyes and hair.
Beneath your feet what treasures I would fling:—
The stars should be your pearls upon a string,
The world a ruby for your finger ring,
And you should have the sun and moon to wear
If I were king.

Let then wild dreams and wilder words take wing,
Deep in the woods I heard a shepherd sing
A simple ballad to a sylvan air,
Of love that ever finds your face more fair.
I could not give you any godlier thing
If I were king.

             —JUSTIN HUNTLEY MCCARTHY

McCarthy has divided his rondeau as John Payne divided his "Kiss me, sweetheart."

The Rondeau

You bid me try, Blue Eyes, to write
A Rondeau. What! Forthwith?—To-night?
  Reflect. Some skill I have, 'tis true;
  But thirteen lines!—and rhymed on two!—
"Refrain," as well. Ah, hapless plight!

Still, there are five lines—ranged aright.
These Gallic bonds, I feared, would fright
  My easy Muse. They did, till you—
      You bid me try!

That makes them nine.—The port's in sight:
'Tis all because your eyes are bright!
  Now just a pair to end in "oo,"—
  When maids command, what can't we do!
Behold!—the Rondeau, tasteful, light,
      You bid me try!

                              —AUSTIN DOBSON

The following is a beautiful example of a play on words that does not alter the *sound* of the refrain.

The Rondeau

Your rondeau's tale must still be light—
No bugle-call to life's stern fight!
  Rather a smiling interlude
  Memorial to some transient mood
Of idle love and gala-night.

Its manner is the merest sleight
O' hand; yet therein dwells its might,
  For if the heavier touch intrude
      Your rondeau's stale.

Fragrant and fragile, fleet and bright,
And wing'd with whim, it gleams in flight
  Like April blossoms wind-pursued
  Down aisles of tangled underwood;—
Nor be too serious when you write
      Your rondeau's tail.

                              —DON MARQUIS

Here is a sequence in rondeaux:

Rondeaux of Cities

It is commonly said that in affairs of the heart a Boston man asks, "What does she know?" a New Yorker, "What is she worth?" a Philadelphian, "Who is her father?" and a Baltimorean, "Is she good looking?"
—OLD PROVERB

I

A RONDEAU À LA BOSTON

A cultured mind! Before I speak
The words, sweet maid, to tinge thy cheek
    With blushes of the nodding rose
    That on thy breast in beauty blows,
I prithee satisfy my freak.

Canst thou read Latin and eke Greek?
Dost thou for knowledge pine and peak?
    Hast thou, in short, as I suppose,
        A cultured mind?

Some men require a maiden meek
Enough to eat at need the leek;
    Some lovers crave a classic nose,
    A liquid eye, or faultless pose;
I none of these, I only seek
        A cultured mind.

II

A RONDEAU À LA NEW YORK

A pot of gold! O mistress fair,
With eyes of brown that pass compare,
    Ere I on bended knee express
    The love which you already guess,
I fain would ask a small affair.

Hast thou, my dear, an ample share
Of this world's goods? Wilt thy papa[1]
    Disgorge, to gild our blessedness,
        A pot of gold?

[1] Pronounced *papaire*.

Some swains for mental graces care;
Some fall a prey to golden hair;
   I am not blind, I will confess,
   To intellect or comeliness;
Still let these go beside, *ma chère,*
     A pot of gold.

III

A Rondeau à la Philadelphia

A pedigree! Ah, lovely jade!
Whose tresses mock the raven's shade,
   Before I free this aching breast,
   I want to set my mind at rest;
'Tis best to call a spade a spade.

What was thy father ere he made
His fortune? Was he smeared with trade,
   Or does he boast an ancient crest—
     A pedigree?

Brains and bright eyes are overweighed,
For wits grow dull and beauties fade;
   And riches, though a welcome guest,
   Oft jars the matrimonial nest;
I kiss her lips who holds displayed
     A pedigree.

IV

A Rondeau à la Baltimore

A pretty face! O maid divine,
Whose vowels flow as soft as wine,
   Before I say upon the rack
   The words I never can take back,
A moment meet my glance with thine.

Say, art thou fair? Is the incline
Of that sweet nose an aquiline?
   Hast thou, despite unkind attack,
     A pretty face?

Some sigh for wisdom; Three, not nine
The Graces were. I won't repine
  For want of pedigree, or lack
  Of gold to banish Care the black,
If I can call forever mine
     A pretty face.

—ROBERT GRANT

STUDENT ATTEMPTS

Advice to Red Leaves

Beautiful, brief, flame up and die,
The thousand-winged horde stampedes close by.
Make of your grief a blazing thing,
Shout it across to the farthest wing,
Burn it across the sky.

Fling downward; the pool with the golden eye
Long will remember a scarlet cry.
That is your name he is whispering,
Beautiful, brief.

Though the world grow gray and forget to sing,
This moment hangs tense on a web-spun string.
Now, when the hunter's moon is shy,
Smile at the death in whose arms you lie,
Pray now for all that his kiss can bring,
Beautiful, brief.

—MURIEL F. HOCHDORF

When I Am Grown

When I am grown shall loveliness still be
A crystal song that's whispered just to me?
Oh, shall the dusk be just a part of day,
Shall Titian-headed Sunset fade away
Into the faeryland of imagery?

Say, shall a tree be, ever, just a tree,
Where Wind, the gypsy fiddler, now makes free?
Shall leaves that dance lose all their naiveté
When I am grown?

Will gods prove false, and shall the pillars sway
In all the shrines where now I come to pray?
And Beauty too? Oh! say of her that she
Alone will always whisper poetry!
The rest may go if loveliness will stay
When I am grown.

—MURIEL F. HOCHDORF

To H. B. S.

(Who crashed with two others during Easter week, 1930)

A man has died. All must obey
When called, with neither stop nor stay.
He went so quickly (a plane crashed) . . .
It's hard to feel a life was dashed
Like that. It's just the first of May.

His dogs, his children, still will play,
And he not here. It's queer to say,
When spring's fair fields are golden-splashed—
"A man has died."

He whom we loved is cold and grey.
A death is strange; it makes you weigh
Your chances . . . if the cord were slashed
That holds you here . . . but, no, you're lashed
Too well for that; and yet today
A man has died.

—JAMES GORHAM

Geegee was one sister's name for the other. Note the playful irony of the writer's "Be quiet!"

Geegee Be Quiet!

Geegee, be quiet; I have work to do.
How many times must I ask you to?
Can't you stop jabbering just for a while?
When I am scolding don't stand there and smile;
I have only my English and then I'll be through.

I saw Florence Jones on the avenue—
She wanted to be remembered to you.
Her hair was done beautifully in that new style—
Geegee, be quiet.

What dress shall I wear to the "frat" dance, my blue?
Or maybe my velvet of violet hue.
While you are there, please hand me that file,—
My long nail just broke—my! this candy is vile.
Geegee, be *quiet*!

—Evelyne Love Cooper

The criticisms that all tyros know, of triteness and commonplace expressions, two young versifiers turned into delicately humorous rondeaux:

On Spring Poems

If I'm allowed, some day I'll write
A verse on spring: of its delight
  I'll tell: of flowers wet with dew,
    And springtime skies of clearest blue;
A sun that bathes the earth with light.

I'll picture rosebuds closed up tight,
And violets, half-hid from sight,
  And nature, clothed in green anew:
    If I'm allowed!

I'll even finish it up right
By writing of the yearly fight
  That spring and winter must go through;
    In fact, there's nothing I won't do
To make my poem very trite—
    If I'm allowed!

—Richard Hallberg

To You

Oh, is there nothing new to write?
When I've a thought, you say it's trite,
You say I'm not the only one
Who says your hair is like the sun,
That your black eyes defy the night.

I really think it quite all right,
To say that you're my heart's delight,
But there you go, 'ere I've begun.
"Oh, is there nothing new?"

I'll try with all my main and might,
To write a verse to you, despite
The fact that you are making fun.
". . . A robe of love your charms have spun . . ."
Again! I hear your voice so light,
"Oh, is there nothing new?"

—JACQUELINE HOYT

On Finishing the Day's Latin

Ten centuries hence, will others sigh
That such as we, should live and die
    To vaunt our fame or rue our fate
    In language that they must translate,
As irksome as this "qui" and "quae"?

Will Ph.D's be garnered by
The lofty-browed ones who dared try
    To glorify our ancient state,
        Ten centuries hence?

Posterity, I testify
That we your classicists could vie
    In living life, with you who date
    Your triumphs from a time too late
To know us. Pass not coldly by,
        Ten centuries hence.

—RUTH H. HAUSMAN

To a Weary Ford

You've led your life and now you're through;
The junk-heap says you're overdue.
　I wish you'd go, but still you stay
　Close by my side dreading the day
When you will stop and say adieu!

I'll not forget the days we knew
Up north, down south and westward too,
　But we must part, for people say
　You've led your life!

I hate to let you go, it's true,
But what's a fellow going to do?
　You cough and moan and sigh today
　At hills that used to be just play
So now I think (between us two)
　You've led your life.

—FERNAND BECK

LET'S TRY A RONDEAU

Complete the line and develop in accordance with the pattern:

　If I were you . . .
　It's sad but true . . .
　When I have time . . .
　Of cabbages and kings . . .
　When Barrymore played Hamlet . . .
　With Charlie Chaplin art . . .
　An undertone . . .
　Beneath tall towers . . .
　To hum of dynamos . . .
　With line and bait . . .
　Of thee I sing . . .
　To you, my sweet, . . .
　As Juliet would say . . .
　When Mary's lamb appeared . . .
　In sharps and flats . . .

CHAPTER XXVII

THE ROUNDEL

SWINBURNE invented still another pattern which he called by way of distinction a roundel. His flexible pen composed one hundred lyrics in this form. The Swinburne roundel consists of eleven lines of three stanzas of 4, 3, and 4 lines. Lines 4 and 11 are the refrain. The refrain is the first word or the first few words of line 1. It ends with a word which rhymes with the last word in line 2. With X standing for the refrain, the plan of Swinburne's roundel is

$$Xa\ b\ a\ X^b;\ \ b\ a\ b;\ \ a\ b\ a\ X^b.$$

Here is one:

The Way of the Wind

1. The wind's way in the deep sky's hollow	Xa
2. None may measure, as none can say	b
3. How the heart in her shows the swallow	a
4. The wind's way.	X^b
5. Hope nor fear can avail to stay	b
6. Waves that whiten on wrecks that wallow,	a
7. Times and seasons that wane and slay.	b
8. Life and love, till the strong night swallow	a
9. Thought and hope and the red last ray,	b
10. Swim the waters of years that follow	a
11. The wind's way.	X^b

"Way" which closes the refrain determines the b rhyme. Swinburne permits the repetition of a word—here "swallow"—in a different sense from that of the first use of it.

He wrote a series of three roundels on the death of Richard Wagner. Here is one, in which something of the depth and sweep of Wagner's solemn music is caught in the rhythm to mingle with Swinburne's own passionate love of the sea.

III

From the depths of the sea, from the wellsprings of earth, from the wastes
    of the midmost night,
From the fountains of darkness and tempest and thunder, from heights
    where the soul would be,
The spell of the maze of music evoked their sense, as an unknown light
      From the depths of the sea.

As a vision of heaven from the hollows of ocean, that none but a god
    might see,
Rose out of the silence of things unknown of a presence, a form, a might,
And we heard as a prophet that hears God's message against him, and
    may not flee.

Eye might not endure it, but ear and heart with a rapture of dark delight,
With a terror and wonder whose core was joy, and a passion of thought
    set free,
Felt only the rising of doom divine as a sundawn risen to sight
      From the depths of the sea.

"Marzo Pazzo"

Mad March, with the wind in his wings wide-spread,
  Leaps from heaven, and the deep dawn's arch
  Hails re-risen again from the dead
    Mad March.

Soft small flames on rowan and larch
  Break forth as laughter on lips that said
  Nought till the pulse in them beat love's march.

But the heartbeat now in the lips rose-red
  Speaks life to the world, and the winds that parch
  Bring April forth as a bride to wed
    Mad March.

("Marzo Pazzo" is Italian for *Mad March*, pronounced *martzo patzo*.)

Swinburne loved children. It is said that he used to walk daily over Putney Heath when the maids were out with their perambulators just to see the children. In the poem below he reveals this affection.

Etude Réaliste

A baby's feet, like sea-shells pink,
    Might tempt, should heaven see meet,
An angel's lips to kiss, we think,
    A baby's feet.

Like rose-hued sea flowers toward the heat
    They stretch and spread and wink
Their ten soft buds that part and meet.

No flower-bells that expand and shrink
    Gleam half so heavenly sweet
As shine on life's untrodden brink
    A baby's feet.

This is followed by roundels on a baby's hands and a baby's eyes.

The next closes the *Century of Roundels*.

Envoi

Fly, white butterflies, out to sea,
Frail pale wings for the winds to try,
Small white wings that we scarce can see
    Fly.

Here and there may a chance-caught eye
Note in a score of you twain or three
Brighter or darker of tinge or dye.

Some fly light as a laugh of glee,
Some fly soft as a low long sigh:
All to the haven where each would be
    Fly.

Joseph Auslander has used this form with exquisite effect in *Sunrise Trumpets*. Here is one:

A Sandal String

No more than this: a sandal string.
  Some little child of Egypt wore
The sandal, and has left—a string . . .
  No more.

  Yet fingers tied it when it tore
With too much dizzy frolicking
  Of warm brown feet across the floor.

And when death came in like a king
  Silently through the bolted door
Some mother kept a sandal string . . .
  No more.

A STUDENT ROUNDEL

The Rain

The rain more sweet than any scent
Is showering down on every lane—
To every part of earth is lent
  The rain.

The roses hear its low refrain
And every budding head is bent
To catch a secret word. The grain

Beyond the garden is intent
As all its golden fingers strain
For wealth before the earth has spent
  The rain.

—MATTIE GARRITY

TEST SWINBURNE'S ROUNDEL PATTERN

Play on one of the refrains below. Remember that the underlined word marks the *b* rhyme.

The gull's way . . .
Content . . .
Wave on wave . . .
From marble waste . . .
A worn brown stone . . .
When grasses grow . . .
Purple with heather . . .
Flame . . .
Sleep . . .
Speed . . .
King for a day . . .

CHAPTER XXVIII

THE BALLADE

THE ballade is the oldest of French forms. The simplest form consists of 28 lines distributed thus: three 8-line stanzas and a half-stanza, called the envoy, which in the old ballades was addressed to some superior power as prince, lord, or muse. Each stanza must be a unit of thought: there must be no break between the first four lines and the next four. And each succeeding stanza must contribute to the development of the central thought, embodied in the refrain.

The ballade turns on three rhymes and is built on a refrain which appears as the last line of every stanza. The scheme is as follows:

For stanzas 1, 2, 3: *a b a b b c b C;* envoy: *b c b C.*

No rhyme may be repeated.

In all, 6 *a*'s are used; 14 *b*'s; 5 *c*'s including a refrain, which is repeated three times.

It is obvious then, that before you leave your first stanza you must be sure that the words to be matched, especially your *b* words, have a sufficient number of mates. If your first line were to close with "silver," for which there is no rhyme in our language, you could not get even to the second rhyme. To test out rhyming groups, use your consonant chart, page 60. Do this before you get very far along. If you find that you have hit upon a rhyme family which is not prolific, alter your words. Fourteen lines are far to go!

As in the other forms, the refrain must seem spontaneous. If when you have tried it, it moves awkwardly, discard it. Do not go on until you know it is euphonious and musical. In any of these forms a good first exercise is to turn into verse the experience of constructing the form. The result will probably be nothing more than verse; sparkling verse has its charms.

Do not expect to create a true poem at the first attempt. Practice, however, should yield dexterity in handling rhymes and meters; and skill in technique is the first requisite in the mastery of any art. Some day when a great theme sings through your soul your instrument will be in tune for giving it suitable expression.

Here are some ballades constructed in the pattern described.

Ballade of Middle Age

1.	Our youth began with tears and sighs,	a
2.	With seeking what we could not find;	b
3.	Our verses all were threnodies	a
4.	In elegiacs still we whined;	b
5.	Our ears were deaf, our eyes were blind,	b
6.	We sought and knew not what we sought,	c
7.	We marvel, now we look behind:	b
8.	Life's more amusing than we thought!	C
9.	Oh, foolish youth, untimely wise!	a
10.	Oh, phantoms of the sickly mind!	b
11.	What? not content with seas and skies,	a
12.	With rainy clouds and southern wind,	b
13.	With common cares and faces kind,	b
14.	With pains and joys each morning brought?	c
15.	Ah, old, and worn, and tired we find	b
16.	Life's more amusing than we thought!	C
17.	Though youth "turns spectre-thin and dies,"	a
18.	To mourn for youth we're not inclined;	b
19.	We set our souls on salmon flies;	a
20.	We whistle where we once repined.	b
21.	Confound the woes of human-kind!	b
22.	By Heaven we're "well deceived," I wot,	c
23.	Who hum, contented or resigned,	b
24.	"Life's more amusing than we thought!"	C

ENVOY

25.	*O nate mecum,* worn and lined	b
26.	Our faces show, but *that* is naught;	c
27.	Our hearts are young 'neath wrinkled rind;	b
28.	Life's more amusing than we thought!	C

—ANDREW LANG

Supreme in the realm of the ballade is the name François Villon. Sinister and bitter are most of his songs. Even while waiting to be hanged this vagabond poet wrote ballades. Here is one of his most famous, perhaps his most beautiful, ballade adapted from the French by Rossetti. The refrain "Mais ou sont les neiges d'autan?" meaning "But where are the snows of yester-year?" fired other verse makers to use the question refrain until it became quite common in ballades.

The word *ballade* is sometimes written *ballad* as it is in the next lyric. It is less confusing and more precise, however, to say *ballade* for the French form.

The Ballad of Dead Ladies

(From the French of François Villon, 1450)

Tell me now in what hidden way is
  Lady Flora the lovely Roman?
Where's Hipparchia, and where is Thais,
  Neither of them the fairer woman?
  Where is Echo, beheld of no man,
Only heard on river and mere,—
  She whose beauty was more than human?
But where are the snows of yester-year?

Where's Héloise, the learned nun,
  For whose sake Abelard, I ween,
Lost manhood and put priesthood on?
  (From love he had won such dule and teen!)
  And where, I pray you, is the Queen
Who willed the Buridan should steer
  Sewed in a sack's mouth down the Seine?
But where are the snows of yester-year?

White Queen Blanche, like a queen of lilies,
  With a voice like any mermaiden,—
Bertha Broadfoot, Beatrice, Alice,
  And Ermengarde the lady of Maine,—
  And that good Joan whom Englishmen
At Rouen doomed and burned her there,—
  Mother of God, where are they then? . . .
But where are the snows of yester-year?

ENVOY

Nay, never ask this week, fair lord,
  Where they are gone, nor yet this year,
Except with this for an overword,—
  But where are the snows of yester-year?
           —Dante Gabriel Rossetti

In this ballade Rossetti allowed himself the freedom of departing from the strict three-rhyme scheme. He was limited by the meaning of

Villon's ballade which he was trying to preserve in his English translation.

Here is another question refrain in the strict French pattern:

Where Are the Ships of Tyre?

Hark, how the surges dash
   On Tyrian beaches hoar!
With far-resounding crash,
   And unremitting roar,
   The white foam-squadrons pour
Their ranks with sullen ire
   Along the sandy floor;
"Where are the ships of Tyre?"

Within her walls the clash
   Of arms is heard no more;
No supple bough of ash
   Is hewn for mast or oar;
   Through no tall temple's door
Now gleams the altar fire,
   But winds and waves deplore,
"Where are the ships of Tyre?"

By night no torches flash
   From porches as of yore;
'Neath sword or stinging lash
   No slave now lies in gore;
   No voice that men adore
Lifts song to lute or lyre;
   With all the freight they bore
"Where are the ships of Tyre?"

ENVOY

Prince, with those "gone before,"
   We, whom these days inspire,
Must seek that unknown shore
   "Where are the ships of Tyre."

          —CLINTON SCOLLARD

Ballade of Ladies' Names

Brown's for Lalage, Jones for Lelia,
   Robinson's bosom for Beatrice glows,
Smith is a Hamlet before Ophelia.
   The glamor stays if the reason goes!
   Every lover the years disclose
Is a beautiful name made free.
   One befriends, and all others are foes.
Anna's the name of names for me.

Sentiment hallows the vowels of Delia;
   Sweet simplicity breathes from Rose;
Courtly memories glitter in Celia;
   Rosalind savors of quips and hose,
   Araminta of wits and beaux,
Prue of puddings, and Coralie
   All of sawdust and spangled shows;
Anna's the name of names for me.

Fie upon Caroline, Madge, Amelia—
   These I reckon the essence of prose!—
Cavalier Catherine, cold Cornelia,
   Portia's masterful Roman rose,
   Maud's magnificence, Totty's toes,
Poll and Bet with their twang of the sea,
   Nell's impertinence, Pamela's woes!
Anna's the name of names for me.

ENVOY

Ruth like a gillyflower smells and blows,
   Sylvia prattles of Arcadee,
Sybil mystifies, Connie crows,
   Anna's the name of names for me!
                         —WILLIAM ERNEST HENLEY

Louis Untermeyer does not agree with Henley!

Austin Dobson

Recites a Ballade by Way of Retort

("Anna's the name of names for me.")
— W. E. HENLEY

"Anna"! Insipid and weak as gruel—
   "Anna"! As flat as last night's beer—
Plain as a bed-post and stiff as a newel,
   Surely there's nothing of glamour here!
   Names by the hundred enchant the ear,
Stirring the heart with melodious claims;
   Arrogant, timid, impulsive, and dear—
Rose, after all, is the name of names.

Sally gleams like a laughing jewel,
   Bella's jovial, Maud's austere;
Rachel's complacent, Lydia's cruel,
   Laura is classical, Fanny is queer.
   Peggy reminds one of rustic cheer,
Lucy of lilies and lofty aims,
   Lola of fancies that shift and veer—
Rose, after all, is the name of names.

Sara's a fire for all men's fuel,
   Mary's a comfort for all men's fear,
Helen's the smile that invites the duel,
   Chloë's the breath of a yesteryear,
   Margaret somehow invokes the tear,
Lilith the thought of a thousand shames;
   Clara is cool as a lake and clear—
Rose, after all, is the name of names.

ENVOY

Hannah's for home and the 'woman's sphere';
   Vivian's all for dances and games;
Julia's imperious, Kate is sincere—
   Rose (after all) is the Name of Names!

Ballade of the Wasted Moon

Soon, all too soon, the moon will wane,
　And all too soon the stars that spray
The coast of night will slink again
　Back to the rising sea of Day,
　In fright before a morning ray.
The air breathes promise of a boon,
　But you, who'd grant, are far away . . .
And meanwhile, what a waste of moon.

To make it worse, the distant strain
　Of Philomela's roundelay
Comes near, to aggravate my pain;
　On silvered lawns the moonbeams play,
　The moon's a lost sun, gone astray
To make of night a higher noon;
　You will not join this bright array?
Ah, lady, what a waste of moon.

The lake's a field of silver grain,
　Each lawn a lake of waving gray,
And Cynthia's ensilvered train
　Sheds tattered fragments of the day
　In patches, where its edges fray.
This could be perfect made, and soon,
　If you were here . . . then must I say
"Ah, lady, what a waste of moon."

L'ENVOI

Princess, pity me; I pray
　I yet may sing another tune;
We'll meet,—but on some distant day,
　And meanwhile, what a waste of moon.
　　　　　　　　　　—EDWARD STASHEFF

A Ballade of Suicide

The gallows in my garden, people say,
  Is new and neat and adequately tall.
I tie the noose on in a knowing way
  As one that knots his necktie for a ball;
  But just as all the neighbors—on the wall—
Are drawing a long breath to shout "Hurray!"
  The strangest whim has seized me . . . After all
I think I will not hang myself to-day.

To-morrow is the time I get my pay—
  My uncle's sword is hanging in the hall—
I see a little cloud all pink and gray—
  Perhaps the rector's mother will *not* call—
  I fancy that I heard from Mr. Gall
That mushrooms could be cooked another way—
  I never read the works of Juvenal—
I think I will not hang myself to-day.

The world will have another washing day;
  The decadents decay; the pedants pall;
And H. G. Wells has found that children play,
  And Bernard Shaw discovered that they squall;
  Rationalists are growing rational—
And through thick woods one finds a stream astray,
  So secret that the very sky seems small—
I think I will not hang myself to-day.

ENVOI

Prince, I can hear the trumpet of Germinal,
  The tumbrils toiling up the terrible way;
Even to-day your royal head may fall—
  I think I will not hang myself to-day.
                    —GILBERT KEITH CHESTERTON

Chesterton restricted himself even more narrowly in this poem. Instead of *c* rhymes he uses *a*. His whole poem turns on two rhymes instead of three.

Another variety of the 8-line stanza ballade is the ballade à double refrain. As the name implies it employs two refrains. Austin Dobson's "The Ballade of Prose and Rhyme" printed below will explain the structure, *a b a B b c b C;* envoy, *b B c C.*

The Ballade of Prose and Rhyme

1.	When the ways are heavy with mire and rut,	a
2.	In November fogs, in December snows,	b
3.	When the north wind howls, and the doors are shut,—	a
4.	There is place and enough for the pains of prose;	B
5.	But whenever a scent from the whitethorn blows,	b
6.	And the jasmine-stars at the casement climb,	c
7.	And a Rosalind-face at the lattice shows,	b
8.	Then hey!—for the ripple of laughing rhyme!	C

1.	When the brain gets dry as an empty nut,	a
2.	When the reason stands on its squarest toes,	b
3.	When the mind (like a beard) has a "formal cut,"	a
4.	There is place and enough for the pains of prose;	B
5.	But whenever the May-blood stirs and glows,	b
6.	And the young year draws to "the golden prime,"	c
7.	And Sir Romeo sticks in his ear a rose,—	b
8.	Then hey!—for the ripple of laughing rhyme!	C

1.	In a theme the thoughts have a pedant-strut	a
2.	In a changing quarrel of "Ayes" and "Noes"	b
3.	In a starched procession of "If" and "But,"—	a
4.	There is place and enough for the pains of prose;	B
5.	But whenever a soft glance softer grows,	b
6.	And the light hours dance to the trysting-time,	c
7.	And the secret is told "that no one knows,"	b
8.	Then hey!—for the ripple of laughing rhyme!	C

ENVOY

1.	In the work-a-day world,—for its needs and its woes,	b
2.	There is place and enough for the pains of prose;	B
3.	But whenever the May-bells clash and chime,	c
4.	Then hey!—for the ripple of laughing rhyme!	C

To secure charm of effect in the use of the double refrain, the poet used the simple device of contrast. Notice how "There is place and enough for the pains of prose," the B refrain, contrasts with "Then hey!—for the ripple of laughing rhyme!" Since each stanza is constructed on two opposing refrains, which appear as line 4 and line 8, the whole stanza is a balanced contrast. Even the envoy is a contrast, the first refrain forming the second line, while the second refrain closes the final couplet.

Here are other ballades in this pattern:

Ballade à Double Refrain

Keeper of promises made in spring,
  Guilder of squalor in lowly cot—
Ever true and unwavering—
  These are the things that Love is not!
  This is pretty to round the plot
Of a play, for the playwright knows he must
  Tickle our fancies to boil his pot—
For Love is a liar we love to trust!

Passion immortal that poets sing,
  Highest of gifts that the gods allot!
Healing balm of affliction's sting—
  These are the things that Love is not!
  Ay, we would it were so, God wot!
Snatch we at apples that turn to dust!
  Learn we wisdom, then? Not a jot,
For Love is a liar we love to trust!

Poets and dramatists! Ye who cling
  Still to the old romantic rot,
Though I am telling a bitter thing,
  These are the things that Love is not!
  Love is a breeze blowing cold and hot,
A young man's fancy—a withering gust,
  Yet, let Love call and we rush to the spot,
For Love is a liar we love to trust!

L'ENVOI

Princess, I love you! I've quite forgot
These are the things that Love is not;
  'Tis bitter bread, but I beg a crust,
  For Love is a liar we love to trust!
                    —EDWIN MEADE ROBINSON

Ballade of Youth and Age

(Double Refrain)

Spring at her height on a morn at prime,
  Sails that laugh from a flying squall,
Pomp of harmony, rapture of rhyme—
    Youth is the sign of them, one and all.
    Winter sunsets and leaves that fall,
·An empty flagon, a folded page,
  A tumble-down wheel, a tattered ball—
These are a type of the world of Age.

Bells that clash in a gorgeous chime,
  Swords that clatter in outsets tall,
The words that ring and the fames that climb—
    Youth is the sign of them, one and all.
    Old hymnals prone in a dusty stall,
A bald blind bird in a crazy cage,
  The scene of a faded festival—
These are a type of the world of Age.

Hours that strut as the heirs of time,
  Deeds whose rumour's a clarion-call,
Songs where the singers their souls sublime—
    Youth is the sign of them, one and all.
    A staff that rests in a nook of wall,
A reeling battle, a rusted gage,
  The chant of a nearing funeral—
These are a type of the world of Age.

ENVOY

Struggle and sacrifice, revel and brawl—
Youth is the sign of them, one and all.
  A smouldering hearth and a silent stage—
  These are a type of the world of Age.
          —WILLIAM ERNEST HENLEY

There are more intricate forms of the ballade which you may wish to recognize or even try if you become deeply interested in this form. The ten-line ballade has stanzas of four rhymes, *a b a b b b c c d c D* followed by a 5-line envoy rhyming *c c d c D*; sometimes the envoy is omitted. There is the *double ballade* consisting of six stanzas of eight or ten lines rhymed either *a b a b b c b C* or *a b a b b c c d c D*. Usually the envoy is omitted.

Students usually have to do three ballades before they feel at home with the form. The left one below was a first exercise.

Ballade to Patience and You

Rhythm, rhythm, dee da dee.
Twenty-seven lines to go.
What sad fate will come to me
If I say I do not know
How to write it thus, or so,
In a most confined ballade?
Rhyming "b c" goes quite slow.
This trouble Dobson never had!

First a rhyme to end in "ee"
(Followed by a secret "oh"!)
Poetaster kin agree
That the task is full of woe,
Trying faithfully to show
That their verse is not so bad
As is argued to and fro—
This trouble Dobson never had!

Twelve lines stare unceasingly
As I search for words, and though
I have probed all history
For a striking clause to glow
In my theme, my forceful foe—
Prosaic Phrase—has rendered sad
And tasteless, all my work to be—
This trouble Dobson never had!

ENVOY

Oh, Muse, what can I do to throw
My thoughts before you? Am I mad
To wish for help from you—for ho!
This trouble Dobson never had.
                    —GEORGIA H. COOPER

Cusses

'Tis the Song of Sorrows I sing,
  With a lachrymosal eye,
For Life is a flimsy thing,
  A smile that ends in a sigh,
  A well that is growing dry.
End it, you say? Well, I would,
  I'd leave without a goodbye,
But—cusses!—what is the good?

No new kick experience can bring,—
  There's nothing that I didn't try;
I'd a girl that was fit for a king,
  She'd of good looks an over-supply.
  I loved her—my hope mounted high.
Omnia vincit—love should,
  But she loved another guy,
So—cusses! What was the good?

Beauty returns in the spring,
  To the hill and the wood and the sky.
When the ribbons of sunset still cling
  To the hair of the Evening—I cry
  For the color and light that must die
And the loveliness not understood.
  A song! but the Muse is shy,
So—cusses! What is the good!

L'ENVOI

Muse, Beauty is hurrying by,
  And I'd weave her a song if I could,
But for that one needs brains, so why—
  Oh, cusses! What is the good?
                    —MURIEL F. HOCHDORF

I Shall Go Back

I shall go back to see
  That twisting bit of unmown hill
Where poplar trees set free
  Long shadows reaching toward the rill,
  Where summer twilight flames until
The sky is charred and black,
  Where laboring waters turn the mill—
Some day I shall go back.

Beside the brook there'll be
  Our trailing clematis like chill
Pure snow this month. Our tree,
  The "beanstalk" one, must be there
    still
And waiting to be climbed. I thrill
Remembering the track
  Where once we heard the red-heads
    drill.
Some day I shall go back,

For there I left the key
  That youth must use to force the grill
Of humdrum bars, and flee
  The cage of reason, to fulfill
  Old whimsied hopes. I shall be Jill
While you are laughing Jack,
  Or Robin Hood in scarlet quill . . .
  Some day I shall go back.

ENVOY

If time will let the blackbird shrill
  His impudent attack,
And leave unchanged our youthful
  will . . .
  Some day I shall go back.
          —JOYCE LANCASTER

Romance Is Gone

The gallant figure of the past
  Has made his bow and left the floor,
The glamorous wit that braved the blast
  Of wind-swept seas for love, no more
  Will sigh and flatter and adore.
The pallid youths who carry on
  Have not the vigor *I* implore;
It's obvious romance is gone.

Why was my brief existence cast
  In this hard age, when I would soar
Amid Olympian clouds, high, fast
  Beside Apollo, who would pour
  Sweet words into my ears, not bore
Me with loud boasting of his brawn
  And how it helped the football score?
It's obvious romance is gone.

The pirate heaped about his mast
  Rich treasures and delights galore
For *her*. Though he was classed
  A reprobate, one can't ignore
  His gallantry. Won't fate restore
That glorious beau, from whom is
    drawn
  The modern man that I abhor!
It's obvious romance is gone.

ENVOY

Ye modern gods, bring back the roar
  Of quick-doomed dragons, and the
    dawn
That helped *him* plot abduction, for
  It's obvious romance is gone.
          —JOYCE LANCASTER

See "Occasional Verse," Chapter XXI, "The Untrodden Road" by
Joyce Lancaster.

FILL THE FORM

Is there a ballade in a refrain suggested below? Or does one below suggest a refrain that you want to develop?

Where are the buds of spring?
If girls are hoydenish today, now wasn't Eve?
Where are the simple girls that $\begin{cases} \text{grandma} \\ \text{grandpa} \end{cases}$ knew?
When Chivalry boards the rapid transit
Room for the generous hoop and bustle!
Did Adam ever have the influenza?
I'll find a subject for my lay tomorrow.
O son, beware of woman's charms!
If jests won't work, then try a solemn ditty.
Tomorrow I will start to diet.
I think I shall not wash myself today.
Perhaps she'll say "yes," and perhaps she'll say "no!"
Perhaps she'll say "no," but perhaps she'll say—"yes!"
That well may be, but I'm a modern $\begin{cases} \text{man!} \\ \text{girl!} \end{cases}$
I am not up to opera, you see.
When $\begin{cases} \text{father} \\ \text{Lula undertakes to be the guide} \\ \text{mother} \end{cases}$
Lucretius gave the same advice two thousand years ago.

(If above line is too long for your purposes, take only the end of it as the refrain.)

CHAPTER XXIX

OTHER FIXED FORMS

PANTOUM

THE French fondness for the refrain has caused them to assimilate a Malay form, the pantoum, which like the villanelle turns on the recurrence of two refrains. Instead of a definite number of three-line stanzas, however, it consists of an unlimited number of four-line stanzas rhymed *a b a b* with definite restrictions: lines 2 and 4 of each stanza in entirety become lines 1 and 3 of each succeeding stanza ad infinitum. The final quatrain usually picks up lines 1 and 3 of the first stanza in reversed order as 4 and 2 so that the chain ends with the first line as it began.

The scheme is as follows:

$A^1 B^1 A^2 B^2;$ $B^1 C^1 B^2 C^2;$ $C^1 D^1 C^2 D^2;$ $D^1 E^1 D^2 E^2;$ Final $E^1 A^2 E^2 A^1.$

A suggestion of monotony is inevitable. The repetition of lines throughout has been seized on by various poets to suggest the monotonous recurrence of one thing or another, such as the buzzing of a fly, incessant chatter, the misery of summer railroad travel.

In the "Malay Shopping Carol" which follows, a shopper who has returned a Christmas gift overhears the chatter of the store as she waits for attention at the book counter near the elevator. Every line appears twice. Other pantoums that you may care to read are "First Performance" by Michael Lewis in Untermeyer's *Forms of Poetry*; "An Election Night Pantoum" by Franklin P. Adams in *Tobogganing on Parnassus*; "Pantoum of Procrastination" and "A Malay Love-Song" by Louis Untermeyer in *Selected Poems and Parodies*; "Of Modern Books" by Carolyn Wells in *Baubles*; and "En Route" by Brander Matthews in *Fugitives from Justice*.

Malay Shopping Carol

Fifth Avenue Department Store, the Week After Christmas

"But I didn't exp ct such a crowd,	A¹
All we're lack ig are tape and confetti;	B¹
Still I'm rid of hat useless white shroud!	A²
Will you hand me that leather Rossetti?	B²
All we're lacking are tape and confetti—"	B¹
"Up! Going up—this way, please."	C¹
"Will you hand me that leather Rossetti?	B²
—Why *can't* people cover a sneeze!"	C²
"Up! Going up—this way, please."	C¹
"Vill you tell me vhere gald vishes are?"	D¹
"Why *can't* people cover a sneeze!"	C²
"Kindly step to the rear of the car."	D²
"Vill you tell me vhere gald vishes are?"	D¹
"Booths ahead. Seventh floor, clothes for men—	E¹
Kindly step to the rear of the car.	D²
Face the gate. The Adjustment? On ten.	E²
Booths ahead. Seventh floor, clothes for men—"	E¹
"The tax? Goodness, where is my purse?"	F¹
"Face the gate. The Adjustment? On ten—"	E²
"Can Woolworth's or Kress's be worse!"	F²
"The tax? Goodness, where is my purse?"	F¹
"How money's changed hands, you can see."	G¹
"Can Woolworth's or Kress's be worse!	F²
I'm next—will you *please* wait on me!"	G²
"How money's changed hands! You can see—"	G¹
"A button! An 1 there, she has torn it!—	H¹
I'm next—will you *please* wait on me!"	G²
"—Car's full." "Oh, I shouldn't have worn it.	H²
A button—and there, she has torn it!	H¹
Still, I'm rid of that useless white shroud—"	A² *Third line of stanza 1*
"Car's full!" "Oh, I shouldn't have worn it,	H² *of stanza 1*
But I didn't expect such a crowd!"	A¹ *First line of stanza 1*

—J. J.

In "In Town" below, Dobson, trying to work in the heat of town, is annoyed first by a hawker of strawberries, then by the buzz of a bluebottle fly that keeps eluding his swatter. Who has not had his nerves set on edge by just such an experience!

In Town

1.	Toiling in town now is "horrid"	A[1]
2.	(There is that woman again!) —	B[1]
3.	June in the zenith is torrid,	A[2]
4.	Thought gets dry in the brain.	B[2]

1.	There is that woman again	B[1]
2.	"Strawberries! fourpence a pottle!"	C[1]
3.	Thought gets dry in the brain;	B[2]
4.	Ink gets dry in the bottle.	C[2]

1.	Strawberries! fourpence a pottle	C[1]
2.	O for the green of a lane!—	D[1]
3.	Ink gets dry in the bottle	C[2]
4.	"Buzz" goes a fly in the pane!	D[2]

1.	O for the green of a lane	D[1]
2.	Where one might lie and be lazy!	E[1]
3.	"Buzz" goes a fly in the pane;	D[2]
4.	Bluebottles drive me crazy!	E[2]

1.	Where one might lie and be lazy,	E[1]
2.	Careless of town and all in it!—	F[1]
3.	Bluebottles drive me crazy:	E[2]
4.	I shall go mad in a minute!	F[2]

1.	Careless of town and all in it,	F[1]
2.	With some one to soothe and to . ll you;	G[1]
3.	I shall go mad in a minute:	F[2]
4.	Bluebottle, then I shall kill you!	G[2]

1.	With some one to soothe and to still you,	G[1]
2.	As only one's feminine kin do,—	H[1]
3.	Bluebottle, then I shall kill you:	G[2]
4.	There now! I've broken the window!	H[2]

1.	As only one's feminine kin do,—	H[1]
2.	Some muslin-clad Mabel or May!—	I[1]
3.	There now! I've broken the window!	H[2]
4.	Bluebottle's off and away!	I[2]

1. Some muslin-clad Mabel or May,   I¹
2.   To dash one with eau de Cologne: J¹
3. Bluebottle's off and away,   I²
4.   And why should I stay here alone?   J²

1. To dash one with eau de Cologne,   J¹
2.   All over one's eminent forehead;—   a
3. And why should I stay here alone!   J²
4.   Toiling in town now is "horrid."   A¹

Here Dobson does not repeat line 3 of stanza 1 as line 2 of the last stanza; he merely repeats *A¹* with an *a* rhyme for 2.

The pantoum below is a high school creation:

Dialogue Between a Proud Young Mother and a Neighbor

"I still think he looks like his father"—
"Oh, no, dear! He has my blue eyes,"
"But his eyes are a greenish-gray, rather"—
"Do you mean I don't know my own prize?"

Oh, no, dear! He has my blue eyes"—
"Well, you can't say that's not his Dad's nose"—
"Do you mean I don't know my own prize?"
"Just wait awhile, Mae, till he grows—

But you can't say that's not his Dad's nose"—
"What's a nose against hair, glowing Titian?"
"Just wait awhile, Mae, till he grows—
A nose means a lot when it's Grecian."

"What's a nose against hair, glowing Titian?
Whose dimples are those? And that grin?"
"A nose means a lot when it's Grecian"—
"But my folks all have that firm chin!

Whose dimples are those? And that grin?"
"But his eyes are a greenish-gray, rather"—
"But *my* folks all have that firm chin!"
"I still think he looks like his father!"

—JANE GRAY WARD

To avoid mistakes in blocking the pattern after the first stanza A^1 B^1 A^2 B^2 write in lines 2 and 4 as 1 and 3 of the next stanza before planning the new lines, 2 and 4, tipped with a new rhyme, and so on to the end. For example:

1. But I didn't expect such a crowd,	A^1	
*2. All we're lacking are tape and confetti;	B^1	* *to become 1*
3. Still I'm rid of that useless white shroud!	A^2	
*4. Will you hand me that leather Rossetti?	B^2	* *to become 3*

1. All we're lacking are tape and confetti	B^1
2.	
3. Will you hand me that leather Rossetti	B^2
4.	

Last stanza

1.	H^1
2. Still I'm rid of that useless white shroud	A^2
3.	H^2
4. But I didn't expect such a crowd!	A^1

LET MONOTONY COME INTO ITS OWN

Whatever recurs often should suggest possibilities for treatment as a refrain in a pantoum: the Fuller brush man, forgotten books, excuses, daily advertising, lateness—you will think of many others.
Is there a notion worth playing upon in any of the following?

They've tied up that mongrel again!
It's time to do the dishes
Laura can't find it
The promise of another loan
The largest _____ in the United States!
What's Amos up to now?
We guess we'll stay another year
Nothing like golf for reducing
We're moving again in the fall
Consult your dentist twice a year
The travel bureau needs another tourist

SESTINA

Most intricate of French patterns is the sestina. Anyone who likes to test his skill in putting together a verse puzzle should try making a sestina if only for the fun of the thing. The troubadour, Arnaut Daniel, invented it during the twelfth century; both Dante and Petrarch used it.

In its early form it was composed of six stanzas, each of six unrhymed lines of equal length, and a half stanza; that is, thirty-nine lines. Modern usage permits the words to rhyme in either two or three rhymes.

The six terminal words of the first stanza end the lines of every stanza in fixed order, no word appearing in the same position more than once. The last word of the stanza always ends the first line of the new stanza. The six words are repeated in the envoy, or tornada, three at the end of the lines with three somewhere in the first half of the lines; that is, two words to each line. Originally these words had to be two-syllabled nouns. Modern usage discards this restriction as is evident from models below. The order of repetition is as follows:

Stanza I	1 2 3 4 5 6
" II	6 1 5 2 4 3
" III	3 6 4 1 2 5
" IV	5 3 2 6 1 4
" V	4 5 1 3 6 2
" VI	2 4 6 5 3 1

Envoy:

Line 1—	2 Somewhere in first half; 5 end
" 2—	4 " " " " ; 3 "
" 3—	6 " " " " ; 1 "

In the next sestina, which Kipling has made a true poem, Tommy Atkins's dialect takes us a long way from the romance of Provence.

Sestina of the Tramp-Royal

Speakin' in general, I 'ave tried em all— 1
The 'appy roads that take you o'er the world 2
Speakin' in general, I 'ave found them good 3
For such as cannot use one bed too long, 4
But must get 'ence, the same as I 'ave done, 5
An go observin' matters till they die. 6

What do it matter where or 'ow we die, 6
So long as we've our 'ealth to watch it all— 1
The different ways that different things are done, 5
An' men an' women lovin' in this world; 2
Takin' our chances as they come along, 4
An' when they ain't, pretendin' they are good. 3

In cash or credit—no, it aren't no good; 3
You 'ave to 'ave the 'abit or you'd die, 6
Unless you lived your life but one day long, 4
Nor didn't prophesy nor fret at all, 1
But drew your tucker some'ow from the world, 2
An' never bothered what you might ha' done. 5

But, gawd, what things are they I 'aven't done; 5
I've turned my 'and to most, an' turned it good, 3
In various situations round the world— 2
For 'im that doth not work must surely die; 6
But that's no reason man should labor all 1
'Is life on one same shift, life's none so long. 4

Therefore, from job to job I've moved along; 4
Pay couldn't 'old me when my time was done, 5
For something in my head upset me all, 1
Till I 'ad dropped whatever 'twas for good, 3
An', out at sea, be'eld the dock-light die, 6
An' met my mate the wind that tramps the world; 2

It's like a book, I think, this bloomin' world, 2
Which you can read and care for just so long, 4
But presently, you feel that you will die 6
Unless you get the page you're readin' done, 5
An' turn another—likely not so good; 3
But what you're after is to turn 'em all. 1

Gawd bless this world; whatever she 'ath done— 2, 5
Excep' when awful long—I've found it good. 4, 3
So, write, before I die, " 'E liked it all." 6, 1
—RUDYARD KIPLING

After you have written the first stanza, to avoid needless mental effort, indicate the word order on blank lines and write down the proper words throughout the poem. For instance:

Stanza II				
		die	6	
		all	1	
		done	5	
		world	2	
		long	4	
		good	3	

Envoy					
	world	2	done	5	
	long	4	good	3	
	die	6	all	1	

The restriction may challenge undreamed of ingenuity.

Another in the same pattern follows.

Sestina

Fra tutti il primo Arnaldo Daniello
Gran maestro d'amor.

—PETRARCH

In fair Provence, the land of lute and rose,
Arnaut, great master of the lore of love,
First wrought sestines to win his lady's heart,
Since she was deaf when simpler staves he sang,
And for her sake he broke the bonds of rhyme,
And in this subtler measure hid his woe.

"Harsh be my lines," cried Arnaut, "harsh the woe
My lady, that enthorn'd and cruel rose,
Inflicts on him that made her live in rhyme!"
But through the metre spake the voice of Love,
And like a wild-wood nightingale he sang
Who thought in crabbed lays to ease his heart.

It is not told if her untoward heart
Was melted by her poet's lyric woe,
Or if in vain so amorously he sang;
Perchance through cloud of dark conceits he rose
To nobler heights of philosophic love,
And crowned his later years with sterner rhyme.

This thing alone we know: the triple rhyme
Of him who bared his vast and passionate heart
To all the crossing flames of hate and love,
Wears in the midst of all its storm of woe,—
As some loud morn of March may bear a rose,—
The impress of a song that Arnaut sang.

"Smith of his mother-tongue," the Frenchman sang
Of Lancelot and of Galahad, the rhyme
That beat so bloodlike at its core of rose,
It stirred the sweet Francesca's gentle heart
To take that kiss that brought her so much woe
And sealed in fire her martyrdom of love.

And Dante, full of her immortal love,
Stayed his drear song, and softly, fondly sang
As though his voice broke with that weight of woe;
And to this day we think of Arnaut's rhyme
Whenever pity at the labouring heart
On fair Francesca's memory drops the rose.

Ah! sovereign Love, forgive this weaker rhyme!
The men of old who sang were great at heart,
Yet have we too known woe, and worn thy rose.

—Edmund Gosse

If the sestina has two rhymes the pattern is as follows

Stanzas I, III, V	*a b a b a b*
Stanzas II, IV, VI	*b a b a b a*
Envoy	*a b a* (mid-line) ; *b a b* (end)

To keep the rhymes alternating throughout the sestina and at the same time to follow the rule of the game which requires that no word appear in the same position more than once, Swinburne worked out the following scheme.

Stanza I	1 2 3 4 5 6	Stanza IV	2 5 6 1 4 3
	a b a b a b		*b a b a b a*
" II	6 1 4 3 2 5	" V	3 2 1 6 5 4
	b a b a b a		*a b a b a b*
" III	5 6 1 4 3 2	" VI	4 3 2 5 6 1
	a b a b a b		*b a b a b a*

Envoy:

Line	1—	1 *a*; 4 *b*
"	2—	2 *b*; 3 *a*
"	3—	5 *a*; 6 *b*

Sestina

I saw my soul at rest upon a day	1a
As the bird sleeping in the nest of night,	2b
Among soft leaves that give the starlight way	3a
To touch its wings but not its eyes with light;	4b
So that it knew as one in visions may,	5a
And knew not as men waking, of delight.	6b
This was the measure of my soul's delight;	6b
It had no power of joy to fly by day,	1a
Nor part in the large lordship of the light;—	4b
But in a secret moon-beholden way	3a
Had all its will of dreams and pleasant night,	2b
And all the love and life that sleepers may.	5a
But such life's triumph as men waking may	5a
It might not have to feed its faint delight	6b
Between the stars by night and sun by day	1a
Shut up with green leaves and a little light;	4b
Because its way was a lost star's way.	3a
A world's not wholly known of day or night.	2b
All loves and dreams and sounds and gleams of night	2b
Made it all music that such minstrels may,	5a
And all they had they gave it of delight;	6b
But in the full face of the fire of day—	1a
What place shall be for any starry light,	4b
What part of heaven in all the wide sun's way?	3a
Yet the soul woke not, sleeping by the way,	3a
Watched as a nursling of the large-eyed night,	2b
And sought no strength nor knowledge of the day,	1a
Nor closer touch conclusive of delight,	6b
Nor mightier joy nor truer than dreamers may,	5a
Nor more of song than they, nor more of light.	4b
For who sleeps once and sees the secret light	4b
Whereby sleep shows the soul a fairer way	3a
Between the rise and rest of day and night,	2b
Shall care no more to fare as all men may,	5a
But be his place of pain or of delight,	6b
There shall he dwell, beholding night as day.	1a
Song, have thy day and take thy fill of light	1a; 4b
Before the night be fallen across thy way;	2b; 3a
Sing while he may, man hath no long delight.	5a; 6b

—ALGERNON CHARLES SWINBURNE

The Conqueror Passes

"Non dormatz plus! les messatges de douz pascor"
—RAIMBAUT DE VAQUEIRAS

Awaken! for the servitors of Spring
Proclaim his triumph! ah, make haste to see
With what tempestuous pageantry they bring
The victor homeward! haste, for this is he
That cast out Winter, and all woes that cling
To Winter's garments, and bade April be!

And now that Spring is master, let us be
Content, and laugh as anciently in spring
The battle-wearied Tristram laughed, when he
Was come again Tintagel-ward, to bring
Glad news of Arthur's victory—and see
Ysonde, with parted lips that waver and cling.

Not yet in Brittany must Tristram cling
To this or that sad memory, and be
Alone, as she in Cornwall; for in spring
Love sows against far harvestings,—and he
Is blind, and scatters baleful seed that bring
Such fruitage as blind Love lacks eyes to see,

Love sows, but lovers reap; and ye will see
The loved eyes lighten, feel the loved lips cling,
Never again when in the grave ye be
Incurious of your happiness in spring,
And got no grace of love there, whither he
That battered life for love no love may bring.

No braggart Heracles awaits to bring
Alcestis hence; nor here may Roland see
The eyes of Ande; nor here the wakening of spring
Vex any man with memories: for there be
No memories that cling as cerements cling,
No force that baffles Death, more strong than he.

Us hath he noted, and for us hath he
An hour appointed; and that hour will bring
Oblivion.—Then laugh! Laugh, dear, and see
The tyrant mocked, while yet our bosoms cling,
While yet our lips obey us, and we be
Untrammeled in our little hour of spring!

Thus in the Spring we jeer at Death, though he
Will see our children perish, and will bring
Asunder all that cling while love may be.
—JAMES BRANCH CABELL

From time to time in the columns of our daily newspapers appear the intricate forms of verse. The young versifier will do well to watch columns edited by masters of the craft of poetry, such as F. P. A., New York *Herald Tribune*; H. I. Phillips, New York *Sun*; Edwin Meade Robinson, Cleveland *Plain Dealer*; and R. H. L., Chicago *Tribune*.

A little story hinges on the sestina below, written by a high-school student. The author had passed from the Poetry Class into his seventh term English class. One day he came to his poetry teacher with: "Did you ever teach us the sestina?" "No," she laughed, "I never teach the sestina. Why?" His new teacher, it seems, had expected him to know the scheme, but in trying to illustrate it on the blackboard had got "balled up." What wonder! "Why don't you write him one," suggested his former poetry teacher, and directed him to Clement Wood's *The Craft of Poetry*. He took the suggestion and had some fun wrestling with the pattern.

His verse though rhymed follows the pattern of unrhymed sestinas. As a result the arrangement of rhymes is anything but uniform in the six stanzas.

Musa Invita

(A Pupil to Teacher)

You said, "SESTINA—try and see
If you can do that form for me."
And so SESTINA it shall be.
To write a poem in the way
That Petrarch did?—Well, I must say
That simply isn't done today.

Just take a look about today.
How many poems do you see
Written so? But still you say
In subtle tones that challenge me,
"Come, now, your poem done this way
A relic of old skill would be!"

Oh, where would modern poets be
If, when they wrote their verse today,
They had to write it in the way
That Dante did? . . . You surely see
How hastily you spoke to me.—
SESTINA . . . did you mean to say—

That geometric form? Well, say!
How did such verse form come to be?
If no one can explain to me
The reason for the form today,
Then here's the thing I do not see—
WHY use the darned thing, anyway?

And when I watch the easy way
That free verse singers say their say,
I must admit I cannot see
What use decrepit forms can be
To any amateur today—
To any rhymster, much less me.

And now a thought occurs to me:
This surely cannot be the way
To write poetic verse today;
So, since I've nothing more to say,
I'll end this plagued line with "be,"
And finish with a moral, see?

ENVOY

To me, O teacher, never say
To try the way you did, but be
Forewarned by what today you see . . .
—WILLIAM ROEHRICK

The next is by a later student who mastered the rhymed form:

Sestina

Maria Jones was telling me one day
A friend of hers had had her fortune read.
"Do you believe in what those fakers say?"
I asked. With quick assent she shook her head,
"Of course I do, and this one also may
At times bring back the spirits of the dead."

That made me think how through the years the dead
Have had an influence; even today
The fortune-teller proudly boasts his head
A meeting-place for ghosts to come and say
A spectral word or two. When he has read
Your birth date on the zodiac in May

He tells you how your Aunt Louella May,
Who loved you once but has been long since dead,
Is hankering to speak to you today.
Most certainly he then will shake his head
As if to throw off weighty thoughts. He'll say,
"But she has fled from lack of coin; I've read

The minds of Greek and Roman ghosts, and read
The palms of mummies too, and if I may
Have just a paltry sum, I'll wake the dead
Remains that were your aunt. You'll rue this day
Unless you hear her message through my head."
But if you're wise, you'll stop him there and say,

"I'd rather leave my aunt in peace. They say
My uncle paid to silence her. I've read
Her will. She left a fortune, yet today
You ask a fee to make her talk. The dead
Would rather rest in Stygian Caves. You may
Have cause some time to rue your meddling head

For torturing the spirits with that head."
Your mystic Brooklyn Hindu murmurs, "Say!
What's that? The spirit's rap! Your aunt—she's read
Your thought! And now, with lowered lights, I may
Read hers." But you disturb his trance, "The dead
Have hands to reach my purse! You rogue, good day!"

Alack-a-day! Trust no prophetic head,
No sign that lures in red, "Let Abdul say
The magic words that may bring back the dead!"
                        —JANE GRAY WARD

WITH THE TROUBADOURS

Before you invent your own sestina, see what you can make of these lines, using them as stanza I:

Lay the task aside and rest a moment	1
Out here in the deep cool of the twilight;	2
Loose the spirit in you to the evening:	3
Dark will give it back, refreshed and quiet,	4
All its fever lost in dew that touched it	5
Lightly as a moth wing on a flower.	6

Terminal words in order of appearance:

II—flower; moment; touched it; twilight; quiet; evening
III—evening; flower; quiet; moment; twilight; touched it
IV—touched it; evening; twilight; flower; moment; quiet
V—quiet; touched it; moment; evening; flower; twilight
VI—twilight; quiet; flower; touched it; evening; moment

Envoy:

Line 1. In first half: *twilight;* at end: *touched it*
"   2. "   "   "   : *quiet;*   "   "   : *evening*
"   3. "   "   "   : *flower;*   "   "   : *moment*

CHANT ROYAL

Closely related to the ballade is the rarer chant royal. It consists of five eleven-line stanzas in a restricted pattern and a five-line envoy, which repeats the rhyme scheme of the last five lines of the stanza. Like the other French forms (except the sestina) the chant royal is constructed on a refrain, which becomes the last line of each stanza including the envoy. Thus, in the development of the poem the refrain is sung six times. The most usual rhyme scheme is as follows:

Each stanza *a b a b c c d d e d E*
Envoy   *d d e d E*

No rhyme sound may be repeated.

As constructed by the early French poets, the chant royal was an allegory, the solution of which was embodied in the envoy. Verse writers of today disregard this rule.

The form is difficult but it *may* be the vehicle for high seriousness as well as mere nonsense.

As in the ballade the writer of the chant royal must have a care to his rhyme families. He will need:

    10 *a*'s
    10 *b*'s
    10 *c*'s
    18 *d*'s
    7 *e*'s including the Refrain *E*

If his envoy repeats the rhyme scheme of the last seven lines instead of the last five, he will need 12 *c*'s instead of 10.

The Chant Royal of Pure Romance

Romance is dead, say some, and so, to-day,	a
Honour and Chivalry are faint and cold;	b
And now, Adventure has no modern way	a
To stir the blood, as in the days of old.	b
They mourn the times of Gallantry as done,	c
Knighthood has seen the setting of its sun,	c
And fairy, nymph and genie, grown too shy,	d
No more, in these new lands, hold revel high;	d
There lives no mystery, now, and they cry woe	e
To this old world, so twisted and awry!	d
Romance is dead, say some; but I say No!	E

Haroun-al-Raschid, so the sceptics say,   a
  Would seek in vain for sights his book has told—   b
Crusoe could find no island far away   b
  Enough, his life with glamour to enfold—   b
Ulysses now might rove, nor fear to run   c
The risks of perils Homer's fable spun—   c
And Hiawatha's white canoe would try   d
In vain to find some beach, whence to descry   d
  The hunting-grounds where once he bent his bow.   e
Gone are the Halcyon Days, they sadly sigh;   d
  Romance is dead, say some; but I say No!   E

Not while the ancient sea casts up its spray   a
  Upon the laughing beach, and I behold   b
The myriad dancing ripples of the bay   a
  Speed out to meet the sunset's robe of gold;   b
Not till the last ship's voyage has begun;   c
Not till the storm god's lightnings cease to stun!   c
Not till the mountains lift no more to sky   d
Their secret fastnesses, and forests vie   d
  No more with winds and mists, with sun and snow,   e
And rustling fields no more to streams reply!   d
  Romance is dead, say some; but I say No!   E

Not while the Night maintains her mystic sway,   a
  And conjures, in the haunted wood and wold,   b
Her eerie shadows, fanciful and fey,   a
  With priests of Darkness, pale and sombre-stoled;   b
Not while upon the sea of Dreams are won   c
Strange ventures, escapades, and frolic fun;   c
Where tricksy phantoms, whimsically sly,   d
Order your deeds, you know not how or why;   d
  Where Reason, Wit and Conscience drunken go.   e
Have you e'er dreamed, and still can question? Fie!   d
  Romance is dead, say some; but I saw No!   E

Not while Youth lives and Springtime bids be gay!   a
  Not while love blooms, and lovers dare be bold!   b
Not while a poet sings his roundelay,   a
  Or men by maiden's kisses are cajoled!   b
You have not seen her, or you, too, would shun   c
The thought that in this world Romance there's none;   c
For oh, my Love has power to beautify   d
My whole life long, and all its charm supply;   d
  My bliss, my youth, my dreams, to her I owe!   e
And so, ye scornful cynics, I deny;   d
  Romance is dead, say some; but I say No!   E

ENVOY

God, keep my youth and love alive, that I	d
May wonder at this world until I die!	d
Let sea and mountain speak to me, that so,	e
Waking or sleeping, I may fight the lie;	d
Romance is dead, say some; but I say No!	E

—GELETT BURGESS

Versifiers who know anything about the restrictions of headline writing even of a school paper will appreciate the humor of this:

Chant Royal From a Copydesk
For Bob Garst,

The Best Copyreader I Know

I have written high school teachers down SAVANTS,
And poor unknowing husbands termed I MATES;
TROUSERS I've changed to be the homely PANTS,
I've used, for SAYS, AVERS and also STATES.
BEAUTY I've called full many a dame whose face
In even a bathing contest could not place.
RAP, HIT, ATTACK, FLAY, FIRE ON, aye, and SCORE
As synonyms I've used on times galore.
Many a sin against the lexicon
Have I performed, and ere I am no more
I would atone for headlines I have done.

HOP have I said, I fear me much, for DANCE,
And PROBES has doubled for INVESTIGATES;
And as for PLANS, there'd be quite little chance
But what my words was CARDS or BILLS or SLATES;
For NEGRO I have often writ OF RACE,
And BURNED TO DEATH was CHARRED in every case;
Instead of BLOOD I have relied on GORE,
And a TUNNEL usually was a BORE.
Defense for these atrocities have I none,
And though how I may do it puzzles me sore
I would atone for headlines I have done.

The home of the Governor I have called a MANSE,
GRILLS I employed to mean INTERROGATES;
PACHYDERMS often were my ELEPHANTS,
And CLEARS did duty for EXONERATES.
SILENT for MUM I ever would erase—

Likewise to BARE I would REVEAL abase—
GARB and not CLOTHING was the stuff one wore—
I named the President HERB, and there is no lower
Deed, I cannot think of even one.
Fervidly I the following boon implore:
I would atone for headlines I have done.

HIKE took I, noun and verb, to mean ADVANCE,
And WEIGHS or EYES to mean ADJUDICATES;
TRAGIC I've dubbed a fatal circumstance,
And PEACEMAKER termed one who arbitrates.
DETECTIVES called I SLEUTHS to save me space,
And every AVIATOR was an ACE.
HAIL was the WELCOME (v.) I knew of yore,
And crowds would not ARRIVE, but INWARD POUR.
This English language I have put upon
Grievously, and now I've thought it o'er
I would atone for headlines I have done.

Slang TAKEN FOR A RIDE and SWAG and PLANTS
I've used, although my soul it irritates;
And FIEND, at which the m. e. looked askance,
I have set down, and NOTES for CELEBRATES.
HEADQUARTERS spoke I of at times as BASE,
But only by the slotman's greatest grace:
ERE even have I used to mean BEFORE,
And TRAM for street car, though at every pore
My ignominy out in briny sweat would run.
By many a deep and awful oath I swore
I would atone for headlines I have done.

ENVOY

Boys, hair on hair from out my dome I tore
To fall upon the city room's cold floor
While I these noisome compositions spun;
But though it took entire my hirsute store,
I would atone for headlines I have done.

—RUFUS TERRAL
in "The Conning Tower" of the New York *World*

Perhaps the most famous chant royal in English is "The Dance of Death" by Austin Dobson. In his envoy he repeats the rhyme scheme of the last seven lines of the stanza instead of the last five.

The Dance of Death

(After Holbein)

"Contra vim Mortis
Non est medicamen in hortis."

He is the despots' Despot. All must bide,	a
Later or soon, the message of his might,	b
Princes and potentates their heads must hide,	a
Touched by the awful sigil of his right;	b
Beside the Kaiser he at eve doth wait	c
And pours a potion in his cup of state;	c
The stately Queen his bidding must obey;	d
No keen-eyed Cardinal shall him affray;	d
And to the Dame that wantoneth he saith—	e
"Let be, Sweet-heart, to junket and to play."	d
There is no King more terrible than Death.	E

The lusty Lord, rejoicing in his pride,	a
He draweth down; before the armèd Knight	b
With jangling bridle-rein he still doth ride;	a
He crosseth the strong Captain in the fight;	b
The Burgher grave he beckons from debate;	c
He hales the Abbott by his shaven pate,	c
Nor for the Abbess' wailing will delay;	d
No bawling Mendicant shall say him nay;	d
E'en to the pyx the Priest he followeth,	e
Nor can the Leech his chilling finger stay.	d
There is no King more terrible than Death.	E

All things must bow to him. And woe betide	a
The Wine-bibber, the Roisterer by night;	b
Him the feast-master, many bouts defied,	a
Him 'twixt the pledging and the cup shall smite;	b
Woe to the Lender at usurious rate,	c
The hard Rich Man, the hireling Advocate;	c
Woe to the Judge that selleth right for pay;	d
Woe to the Thief that like a beast of prey	d
With creeping tread the traveller harryeth:—	e
These, in their sin, the sudden sword shall slay.	d
There is no King more terrible than Death.	E

He hath no pity,—nor will be denied.   a
When the low hearth is garnishèd and bright   b
Grimly he flingeth the dim portal wide,   a
And steals the Infant in the Mother's sight;   b
He hath no pity for the scorned of fate:—   c
He spares not Lazarus lying at the gate,   c
Nay, nor the Blind that stumbleth as he may;   d
Nay, the tired Ploughman, at the sinking ray,   d
In the last furrow, feels an icy breath,   e
And knows a hand hath turned the team astray.   d
There is no King more terrible than Death.   E

He hath no pity. For the new-made Bride,   a
Blithe with the promise of her life's delight,   b
That wanders gladly by her Husband's side,   a
He with the clatter of his drum doth fright;   b
He scares the Virgin at the convent grate;   c
The Maid half-won, the Lover passionate;   c
He hath no grace for weakness and decay: d
The tender Wife, the Widow bent and gray,   d
The feeble Sire whose footsteps faltereth,—   e
All these he leadeth by the lonely way.   d
There is no King more terrible than Death.   E

ENVOY

Youth, for whose ear and 'monishing of late,   c
I sang of prodigals and lost estate,   c
Have thou thy joy of living and be gay;   d
But know not less that there must come a day,   d
Aye, and perchance e'en now it hasteneth,   e
When thine own heart shall speak to thee and say,   d
There is no King more terrible than Death!   E

A valiant pupil invented this one:

Chant Royal on the Fixed Forms

The French were first to use their mental might
Inventing forms to charm some troubadour
To sing in Provençal. I've known the plight
Of him who'd free his soul through staves of yore!
The tragic Muse, at seeing how I bent
Upon my task, warned, "You will soon be spent;"
And truth she spoke. Oh, I was wholly sane
Before I first picked up a lost refrain
And wondered what young Passerat would do
With this or that line singing in my brain.
These fixed forms have their spell upon me too!

It started with the triolet in light
And artless banter: eight short lines—no more,
A neat refrain, with rhymes not over trite;
I must have written two-and-twenty score.
I poured into a rondel, next, lament.
For plumèd knights whose gallant lives were lent
To love. As I progressed I would arraign
New hopes and plans for every fresh campaign.
Then Swinburne's roundel made its grand début,
With fan and lace mantilla from old Spain.
These fixed forms have their spell upon me too!

The gay ballade was wont soon to ignite
The fuel of my images. I wore
A look of dreamy bliss; I would recite
My finished lines to shadows on the floor.
The villanelle I wrote was sweetly blent
With thoughts of love and springtime's magic scent
Though you may call my lilting lines inane.
But, mind you now, I never was profane
Through stanzas, wild as Shakespeare's untamed shrew;
I was Petruchio, determined swain.
These fixed forms have their spell upon me too!

A pantoum lured me from light love; despite
My pleading friends I rushed in to explore
The tricky Malay mazes of its light
Repeated one and three, with two and four.
From dictionary to Roget I went,
Littering the room with paper. Omar's tent
Saw no more turmoil. Oh, I did not deign
To dull my whirling senses with cocaine,
For I had promised me that I'd go through
With all the strictest patterns. Not in vain,
These fixed forms have their spell upon me too!

I burned out Mazda globes pursuing bright
Rondeaux and lais and virelais galore
Until the rare sestina held me tight
Within its grim restrictions. I forswore
Its awesome end-words only to be pent
In halls, much narrower yet elegant,
In which the Chant Royal was to enchain
My similes. This king is wont to gain
Long service from his struggling subjects, who
Are well repaid if patience does not wane.
These fixed forms have their spell upon me too!

O Dobson, Villon, Arnaut! To attain
The topmost lookout in your walled domain
I do aspire. To genius, entre nous,
I know I need not struggle to explain,
These fixed forms have their spell upon me too!

—JANE GRAY WARD

EXERCISE—FOR TEN FINGERS AND ALL WITS

Take any refrain suggested for the Ballade and develop if you can. Better still, invent your own. By this time you must be skillful!

CHAPTER XXX

THE SONNET

THE sonnet is a lyric form of fourteen lines expressing a single thought or feeling or mood. Its natal land is Italy. It is built on two ideas, one deduced from the other, or closely related to it. As in geometry we have a demonstrated proposition with its corollary, so in this lyric form we have the development of a primary idea followed by a secondary idea which has grown out of the first. There is the same twofold development of ideas in the sonnet that there is in the tiny Japanese hokku, only there is more space for the development of each within the confines of the fourteen-line form.

This duality gives rise to two distinct but related parts in the construction of the sonnet, as closely related as the upper and lower lip of a sweet pea, each performing its separate function, but together giving identity to the bloom and attracting to its hidden fragrance. The primary development is conveyed in the first eight lines called the octave; the secondary development or corollary, in the final six called the sestet.

The Sound of the Sea

The sea awoke at midnight from its sleep,
    And round the pebbly beaches far and wide
    I heard the first wave of the rising tide
Rush onward with uninterrupted sweep;
A voice out of the silence of the deep,
    A sound mysteriously multiplied
    As of a cataract from the mountain's side
Or roar of winds upon a wooded steep.

Octave: Development of the sound of the sea

So comes to us at times from the unknown
    And inaccessible solitudes of being,
        The rushing of the sea-tides of the soul;
And inspirations, that we deem our own,
    Are some divine foreshadowing and foreseeing
        Of things beyond our reason or control.

Sestet: Spiritual significance of the sound to the meditative mind of the poet

—HENRY WADSWORTH LONGFELLOW

Roughly speaking, the octave develops the primary idea: presents a picture, states a problem, raises a question, from which grows the sestet: a six-line solution, application, comment, or the like. The two together produce a single emotional effect, through the single thread of thought that runs through the whole fabric. In *The Sonnet Today and Yesterday*, David Morton likens the movement of the sonnet to "the career of a rocket fired into the night sky—the accumulated momentum during ascendancy, the arrival at the zenith,—and the soft falling of many colored stars."

Somewhere between

> Or roar of winds upon a wooded steep

which ends the octave, and

> So comes to us at times from the unknown

the rocket breaks, and many stars fall softly through the succeeding lines.

Theodore Watts-Dunton has poured into the sonnet form the lesson of its metrical construction:

The Sonnet's Voice

(*A Metrical Lesson by the Seashore*)

> Yon silvery billows breaking on the beach
> Fall back in foam beneath the star-shine clear,
> The while my rhymes are murmuring in your ear
> A restless lore like that the billows teach;
> For on these sonnet-waves my soul would reach
> From its own depths, and rest within you, dear,
> As, through the billowy voices yearning here,
> Great nature strives to find a human speech.
> A sonnet is a wave of melody:
> From heaving waters of the impassioned soul
> A billow of tidal music one and whole
> Flows, in the "octave"; then, returning free,
> Its ebbing surges in the "sestet" roll
> Back to the depths of life's tumultuous sea.

Classified as to form, there are two general types of sonnet: the Italian or Petrarchan, which Petrarch perfected in the fourteenth century, and the English or Shakespearean, which Shakespeare brought to such perfection as to give it his name. The beginner, attempting his first sonnet, will find more leeway in the English form because the

rhyme scheme is slightly less restricted than that of the Italian mould:
seven rhymes as against either four or five. The Shakespearean form
is composed of fourteen lines of iambic pattern, five feet on a line.
The rhyme scheme is *a b a b c d c d e f e f g g*: three quatrains
and a couplet.

LXV

Since brass, nor stone, nor earth, nor boundless sea,   a
But sad mortality o'ersways their power,   b
How with this rage shall beauty hold a plea,   a
Whose action is no stronger than a flower?   b
O how shall summer's honey breath hold out   c
Against the wreckful siege of battering days,   d
When rocks impregnable are not so stout   c
Nor gates of steel so strong, but time decays?   d
O fearful meditation! where, alack!   e
Shall Time's best Jewel from Time's chest lie hid?   f
Or what strong hand can hold his swift foot back,   e
Or who his spoil of beauty can forbid?   f
   O! none, unless this miracle have might   g
   That in black ink my love may still shine bright. g

—WILLIAM SHAKESPEARE

Shakespeare's closing couplets are complete summaries emphasizing
in their pointed compactness the underlying thought of the poem.
Listen to some of them:

For thy sweet love remember'd, such wealth brings
That then I scorn to change my state with kings.

But if the while I think on thee, dear Friend,
All losses are restored, and sorrows end.

This thought is as a death, which cannot choose
But weep to have that which it fears to lose.

But flowers distill'd though they with winter meet,   *Leese =*
Leese but their show; their substance still lives sweet.   *lose*

Be not self-will'd, for thou art much too fair
To be death's conquest and make worms thine heir.

She carved thee for her seal, and meant thereby
Thou shouldst print more, nor let the copy die.

O, learn to read what silent love hath writ:
To hear with eyes belongs to love's fine wit.

For sweetest things turn sourest by their deeds;
Lilies that fester smell far worse than weeds.

Those attempting to plan an English sonnet would do well to think from the couplet backward.

The Italian or Petrarchan sonnet in its strictest form is slightly more exacting. The octave turns on two rhymes, *a b b a a b b a*, the middle *a*'s welding the two quatrains into close unity. In the early sonnet, the sestet which is derived from this octave took the form *c d e c d e* or *c d c d c d* so that the strict Italian form is

$$abba \quad abba \quad cde \quad cde$$
or
$$abba \quad abba \quad cd \quad cd \quad cd.$$

The following is a perfect example of the Italian sonnet:

On First Looking into Chapman's Homer

Much have I travell'd in the realms of gold	a
And many goodly states and kingdoms seen;	b
Round many western islands have I been	b
Which bards in fealty to Apollo hold.	a
Oft of one wide expanse had I been told	a
That deep-brow'd Homer ruled as his demesne:	b
Yet did I never breathe its pure serene	b
Till I heard Chapman speak out loud and bold:	a
—Then felt I like some watcher of the skies	c
When a new planet swims into his ken;	d
Or like stout Cortez, when with eagle eyes	c
He stared at the Pacific—and all his men	d
Look'd at each other with a wild surmise—	c
Silent, upon a peak in Darien.	d

While poets have taken no liberties to speak of with the rhyme scheme of the Italian octave they have played upon the sestet until it has assumed many varieties of rhyme scheme. Here are some of the three-rhyme combinations:

c d e c d e	*c d e e c d*
c d c d e e	*c d e e d c*
c d d c e e	*c d d e c e*
c d c e d e	*c d e d e c*
c c d e e d	*c d c e e d*

More frequent than the three-rhyme sestet is the two-rhyme sestet in the following combinations:

c d c d c d	c d c d d c
c d d c c d	c d c c d d
c d d c d c	c d c c d c

There are even other variations, but they need not concern the beginner.

The best way to achieve artistic power over the sonnet form, however, is first to master the conventional form; then after sufficient discipline—and without discipline no one has become a master—experiment with the varieties as your need dictates. Get the feeling and movement of the sonnet through a study of the masters old and new.

The voice in the heart crying out must determine the form of its expression. Spenser, the poet's poet, said this:

> For of the soule the bodie forme doth take;
> For soule is forme, and doth the bodie make.
> —*An Hymne in Honour of Beautie*

The sonnet has been an instrument for the expression of every conceivable emotion stirred by the depths and the shoals too of human experience. Its lines have voiced alike the complimentary grace of the Elizabethans, the majesty of Milton, the dignity of Wordsworth, the flippancy of Edna St. Vincent Millay, the portraiture of Elinor Wylie and Edwin Arlington Robinson, the conversational intimacy of Robert Frost, the reverence of Thomas S. Jones, Jr., the utter calm of David Morton. The mood that gives it timbre and the emotion caught in its mould are intensified in the stark compact process of its restrictions. It seems to be the law of compensation that for every accepted restriction the artist gains a feather in his wing of freedom.

Some sonnets follow, models in both the English and the Italian traditions with variations of these. Among them are sonnets on the form itself. Sonnets are presented with various groupings of lines. From the structural standpoint the most logical division is perhaps between octave and sestet if there is any division at all. As in other forms, lines may be indented to bring out the rhyme structure, or not, as the author pleases.

Here are some by Shakespeare himself:

XVIII

Shall I compare thee to a summer's day?
Thou art more lovely and more temperate:
Rough winds do shake the darling buds of May,
And summer's lease hath all too short a date:
Sometime too hot the eye of heaven shines,
And often is his gold complexion dimm'd;
And every fair from fair sometime declines,
By chance or nature's changing course untrimm'd;

But thy eternal summer shall not fade,
Nor lose possession of that fair thou owest;
Nor shall Death brag thou wander'st in his shade,
When in eternal lines to time thou grow'st:
So long as men can breathe, or eyes can see,
So long lives this, and this gives life to thee.

XXIX

When in disgrace with fortune and men's eyes
I all alone beweep my outcast state,
And trouble deaf heaven with my bootless cries,
And look upon myself, and curse my fate;
Wishing me like to one more rich in hope,
Featured like him, like him with friends possest,
Desiring this man's art, and that man's scope,
With what I most enjoy contented least;

Yet in these thoughts myself almost despising,
Haply I think on Thee—and then my state,
Like to the lark at break of day arising
From sullen earth, sings hymns at heaven's gate:
For thy sweet love remember'd, such wealth brings
That then I scorn to change my state with kings.

The master varies his own rhyme scheme to *a b a b   c d c d   e b e b
g g*

XXX

When to the sessions of sweet silent thought
I summon up remembrance of things past,
I sigh the lack of many a thing I sought,
And with old woes new wail my dear time's waste;
Then can I drown an eye, unused to flow,
For precious friends hid in death's dateless night,
And weep afresh love's long-since-cancell'd woe,
And moan the expense of many a vanish'd sight.

Then can I grieve at grievances foregone,
And heavily from woe to woe tell o'er
The sad account of fore-bemoanèd moan,
Which I new pay as if not paid before:
—But if the while I think on thee, dear Friend,
All losses are restored, and sorrows end.

CII

My love is strengthen'd, though more weak in seeming;
I love not less, though less the show appear:
That love is merchandized whose rich esteeming
The owner's tongue doth publish every where.
Our love was new, and then but in the spring,
When I was wont to greet it with my lays;
As Philomel in summer's front doth sing,
And stops her pipe in growth of riper days:

Not that the summer is less pleasant now
Than when her mournful hymns did hush the night,
But that wild music burthens every bough,
And sweets grown common lose their dear delight.
Therefore, like her, I sometime hold my tongue,
Because I would not dull you with my song.

LXXXVII

Farewell! thou art too dear for my possessing,
And like enough thou know'st thy estimate:
The charter of thy worth gives thee releasing;
My bonds in thee are all determinate.
For how do I hold thee but by thy granting?
And for that riches where is my deserving?
The cause of this fair gift in me is wanting,
And so my patent back again is swerving.

Thyself thou gav'st, thy own worth then not knowing,
Or me, to whom thou gav'st it, else mistaking;
So thy great gift, upon misprision growing,
Comes home again, on better judgment making.
Thus have I had thee as a dream doth flatter:
In sleep a king; but waking, no such matter.

CVI

When in the chronicle of wasted time
I see descriptions of the fairest wights,
And beauty making beautiful old rhyme
In praise of ladies dead and lovely knights,
Then, in the blazon of sweet beauty's best,
Of hand, of foot, of lip, of eye, of brow,
I see their antique pen would have express'd
Even such a beauty as you master now.

So all their praises are but prophecies
Of this our time, all you prefiguring;
And, for they look'd but with divining eyes,
They had not skill enough your worth to sing:
For we, which now behold these present days,
Have eyes to wonder, but lack tongues to praise.

LX

Like as the waves make towards the pebbled shore
So do our minutes hasten to their end;
Each changing place with that which goes before,
In sequent toil all forwards do contend.
Nativity, once in the main of light,
Crawls to maturity, wherewith being crown'd,
Crooked eclipses 'gainst his glory fight,
And Time that gave, doth now his gift confound.

Time doth transfix the flourish set on youth,
And delves the parallels in beauty's brow;
Feeds on the rarities of nature's truth,
And nothing stands but for his scythe to mow:—
And yet, to times in hope, my verse shall stand
Praising thy worth, despite his cruel hand.

LXXIII

That time of year thou may'st in me behold
When yellow leaves, or none, or few, do hang
Upon those boughs which shake against the cold,
Bare ruin'd choirs, where late the sweet birds sang:
In me thou see'st the twilight of such day
As after sunset fadeth in the west,
Which by and by black night doth take away,
Death's second self, that seals up all in rest:

In me thou see'st the glowing of such fire,
That on the ashes of his youth doth lie
As the death-bed whereon it must expire,
Consumed with that which it was nourish'd by:
—This thou perceiv'st, which makes thy love more strong,
To love that well which thou must leave ere long.

On Growing Old

Be with me, Beauty, for the fire is dying,
My dog and I are old, too old for roving,
Man, whose young passion sets the spindrift flying
Is soon too lame to march, too cold for loving.
I take the book and gather to the fire,
Turning old yellow leaves; minute by minute,
The clock ticks to my heart; a withered wire
Moves a thin ghost of music in the spinet.
I cannot sail your seas, I cannot wander
Your cornland, nor your hill-land, nor your valleys,
Ever again, nor share the battle yonder
Where the young knight the broken squadron rallies.
Only stay quiet while my mind remembers
The beauty of fire from the beauty of embers.

Beauty, have pity, for the strong have power,
The rich their wealth, the beautiful their grace,
Summer of man its sunlight and its flower,
Springtime of man all April in a face.
Only, as in the jostling in the Strand,
When the mob thrusts or loiters or is loud,
The beggar with a saucer in his hand
Asks only a penny from the passing crowd,
So, from this glittering world with all its fashion,
Its fire and play of men, its stir, its march,
Let me have wisdom, Beauty, wisdom and passion,
Bread to the soul, rain when the summers parch.
Give me but these, and though the darkness close
Even the night will blossom as a rose.

—JOHN MASEFIELD

Visitor

The long, blue evening brings the golden moon,
  From out the reaches of old, nameless lands,
To minds in need of beauty for a boon,
  And hearts in need of healing at her hands.
Wearing as any queen her shadowy gown,
  She comes in quiet to the grateful street,
A grave and thoughtful presence through the town,—
  And peace is with the passing of her feet.

Into the grieved and fretful hearts of men,
  The long-robed evening strays, a wanderer,
And there is rest and quietness again,
  And the cool, scented loveliness of her,—
Come, lately now, from old and weary lands,
Bearing this boon in beautiful, still hands.
                                                —DAVID MORTON

Guests

Browsing among old books long laid away
  In dusty corners and with none to care,
Nearly forgotten in our noisy day,—
  All suddenly there thronged about me there,
Fine ladies and such gentlemen of fashion,
  And such a stir of curtseying they made!
With quaint and stately speech and hinted passion
  Of tea-cup tints and delicate brocade.

And once—I swear—there drifted to my face,
  Across a century's disdainful span,
A wisp of perfume from a bit of lace,
  And once, the fainting rustle of a fan. . . . .
And only when I laughed my rude surprise,
They floated off with grave and startled eyes.
                                                —DAVID MORTON

Scars

The smell of ruin in the autumn air,
  When rusty twilights come too early down,
Will take the hearts of strong men unaware,
  And lure them from the friendly, lighted town,—
To walk old, lonely roadways where they learn
  Again of summers that have come to husk,
Where smoky stars like low-hung lanterns burn
  Above the crumbling borders of the dusk.

On littered ways where leaves are crisp and curled,
  And mist comes in between the passing shapes,
There go the proud and desolate of the world,
  Wrapped in their thoughtful silences like capes,
Walking dark roads beneath the autumn stars,
Each with his hidden and historic scars.

—David Morton

The following are in the Italian tradition:

Sonnets from the Portuguese

I

I thought once how Theocritus had sung	a
Of the sweet years, the dear and wished-for years,	b
Who each one in a gracious hand appears	b
To bear a gift for mortals, old or young:	a
And, as I mused it in his antique tongue,	a
I saw, in gradual vision through my tears,	b
The sad, sweet years, the melancholy years,	b
Those of my own life, who by turns had flung	a
A shadow across me. Straightway I was 'ware,	c
So weeping, how a mystic Shape did move	d
Behind me, and drew me backward by the hair;	c
And a voice said in mastery, while I strove,—	d
"Guess now who holds thee?"—"Death," I said. But, there,	c
The silver answer rang,—"Not Death, but Love."	d

—Elizabeth Barrett Browning

Sea-Sonnet

We have forgot, who safe in cities dwell,
The waters that a labouring planet bore;
Forgot to trace in their primeval lore
The shapeless epochs fluted to a shell.
Their old chaotic voices chronicle
The first confusion, and the dark, before
The first adventurer with spear and oar
Towards the unknown pushed out his coracle.

Yet, to the requiem of a dying earth,
When man has passed, his fever and his pride,
Still shall the constellations find a grave
In that Pacific whence the moon had birth,
And that same moon shall heap the desolate tide
Beneath the night's unchanging architrave.

—V. Sackville-West

Michelangelo

Upon the scaffolding where none may climb
  Wild powers and elemental passions surge;
    From chaos the colossal forms emerge—
Titans he summons from the womb of time.
The far bells of the campanile chime
  Unheeded, while dæmonic forces urge
    Sibyls that dream upon the twilight's verge
And brooding prophets, savage and sublime.

He toils alone: as yet no eye has seen
  The sombre visions on the vault above,
    The giants towering up the gloomy nave.
But ever at his side two spirits lean—
  Dante, who whispers of immortal Love;
    Plato, of Beauty found beyond the grave.

—Thomas S. Jones, Jr.

Clonard

By lost Clonard the river meads still hold
  Forgotten dreams, white memories pure as dew,
  Of fragrant days when scholars wandered through
The marshy grass, and hearts had not grown old;
Beneath her purple hills a saint once told
  A starry tale, a story strange and new
  Brought from the dawn-lands—and all Eiré drew
Around his moat to hear the words of gold.

There stands no cross, or tower, or ancient wall
  Mellow with simple peace men used to know,
    And from the fields no courtly town has sprung:
Only along green banks the blackbirds call,
  Just as they did a thousand years ago
    In morning meadows when the world was young.
                              —THOMAS S. JONES, JR.

Tears

When I consider Life and its few years—
A wisp of fog betwixt us and the sun;
A call to battle, and the battle done
Ere the last echo dies within our ears;
A rose choked in the grass; an hour of fears;
The gusts that past a darkening shore do beat;
The burst of music down an unlistening street—
I wonder at the idleness of tears.
Ye old, old dead, and ye of yesternight,
Chieftains, and bards, and keepers of the sheep,
By every cup of sorrow that you had,
Loose me from tears, and make me see aright
How each hath back what once he stayed to weep:
Homer his sight, David his little lad!
                              —LIZETTE WOODWORTH REESE

The strict Italian rule was to give pause after each quatrain of the octave, as Longfellow does in "The Sound of the Sea": 1) the sea awakes; 2) it was a voice. The meaning was not carried over from the octave to the sestet. But in truth the lines of demarcation are not usually so exactly defined as this. Milton, in whose hands the sonnet became a trumpet, carries the thought from quatrain to quatrain and even from octave to sestet. And so you hear of the Miltonic sonnet.

The general structure, however, remains the same whether a period interrupts the flow or not.

On His Blindness

When I consider how my light is spent
Ere half my days, in this dark world and wide,
And that one' talent which is death to hide
Lodged with me useless, though my soul more bent
To serve therewith my Maker, and present
My true account, lest He returning chide,—
"Doth God exact day-labour, light denied?"
I fondly ask:—But Patience, to prevent

That murmur, soon replies, "God doth not need
Either man's work, or His own gifts: who best
Bear His mild yoke, they serve Him best: His state
Is kingly; thousands at His bidding speed
And post o'er land and ocean without rest:—
They also serve who only stand and wait."

—JOHN MILTON

These sonnets have variations in the sestet:

Expedition

Now, in wood coverts, blue windflowers are waking,   *English*
Blue as a girl's eyes, staring even so—   *octave*
And you and I, these stony streets forsaking,
Might leave the town, might walk a wood I know,
And take a path and come upon them, there,
So suddenly it were a blue surprise
What fragile ecstasies the earth may bear,
What happiness may still look out of eyes.

And you would turn to me, and I to you,   *Variation*
Strangely bewildered, since we have not learned,   *in sestet:*
In all our tortured ways, and' never knew   *e f e f f e*
A happiness that is so lightly earned
As that we came on when our path had turned
To scattered windflowers and their delicate blue.

—DAVID MORTON

II

What other name had half expressed the whole   *Italian*
Of that incomparable and touching grace
Which spells the shape of danger in your face?
It is the very pattern of your soul;
The eagle's home, above the moon's control,
Above the seas, the high precipitate place;
The stairway cut from planetary space;
The crystal steps which climb a steeper goal.

The shadow of its light is only this: *Variation*
That all your beauty is the work of wars   *in sestet*
Between the upper and the nether stars;
Its symmetry is perfect and severe
Because the barbarous force of agonies
Broke it, and mended it, and made it clear.

                       —ELINOR WYLIE

The Sonnet

A sonnet is a moment's monument,—   *Italian*
Memorial from the Soul's eternity   *octave*
To one dead deathless hour. Look that it be,
Whether for lustral rite or dire portent,
Of its own arduous fulness reverent:
Carve it in ivory or in ebony,
As Day or Night may rule; and let Time see
Its flowering crest impearled and orient.
A Sonnet is a coin: its face reveals   *English*
The soul,—its converse, to what Power 'tis due:—   *sestet*
Whether for tribute to the august appeals
Of Life, or dower in Love's high retinue,
It serve; or, 'mid the dark wharf's cavernous breath,
In Charon's palm it pay the toll to Death.
                  —DANTE GABRIEL ROSSETTI

"Scorn Not the Sonnet"

Scorn not the Sonnet; Critic, you have frowned,   *Italian*
Mindless of its just honors; with this key
Shakespeare unlocked his heart; the melody
Of this small lute gave ease to Petrarch's wound;
A thousand times this pipe did Tasso sound;
With it Camöens soothed an exile's grief;
The Sonnet glittered a gay myrtle leaf
Amid the cypress with which Dante crowned
His visionary brow; a glow-worm lamp,   *Variation*
It cheered mild Spenser, called from Faery-land   *in sestet:*
To struggle through dark ways; and, when a damp   c d c d e e
Fell round the path of Milton, in his hand   *(Rare)*
The Thing became a trumpet, whence he blew
Soul-animating strains—alas, too few!

—WILLIAM WORDSWORTH

In this sonnet is compressed a history of the form.

The Sonnet

I

The Sonnet is a fruit which long hath slept   *Italian*
And ripened on life's sun-warmed orchard-wall;
A gem which, hardening in the mystical
Mine of man's heart, to quenchless flame hath leapt;
A medal of pure gold art's nympholept
Stamps with love's lips and brows imperial;
A branch from memory's briar, whereon the fall
Of thought-eternalizing tears hath wept:
A star that shoots athwart star-steadfast heaven;   *No variation*
A fluttering aigrette of tossed passion's brine;
A leaf from youth's immortal missal torn;
A bark across dark seas of anguish driven;
A feather dropped from breast-wings aquiline;
A silvery dream shunning red lips of morn.

II

There is no mood, no heart-throb fugitive,   *Italian*
No spark from man's imperishable mind,
No moment of man's will, that may not find
Form in the Sonnet; and thenceforward live
A potent elf, by art's imperative
Magic to crystal spheres of song confined:
As in the moonstone's orb pent spirits wind
'Mid dungeon depths day-beams they take and give.
Spare thou no pains; carve thought's pure diamond   *Variation*
With fourteen facets, scattering fire and light:—   *in sestet:*
Uncut, what jewel burns but darkly bright?   **c d d c e e**
And Prospero vainly waves his runic wand,   *(Rare)*
If, spurning art's inexorable law,
In Ariel's prison-sphere he leave one flaw.

III

The Sonnet is a world, where feelings caught   *Italian—*
In webs of phantasy, combine and fuse   *Variation*
Their kindred elements 'neath mystic dews   *in both*
Shed from the ether round man's dwelling wrought; *octave*
Distilling heart's content, star-fragrance fraught   *and*
With influences from the breathing fires   *sestet*
Of heaven in everlasting endless gyres
Enfolding and encircling orbs of thought.
Our Sonnet's world hath two fixed hemispheres:
This, where the sun with fierce strength masculine
Pours his keen rays and bids the noonday shine;
That, where the moon and the stars, concordant powers,
Shed milder rays, and daylight disappears
In low melodious music of still hours.

                  —JOHN ADDINGTON SYMONDS

SONNETS BY STUDENTS

Unnamed Sonnet

I have been fed on honeyed dreams so long
That I have grown to lose the taste for bread,
And though I parch for truth, I drink instead
The beaded wine of hope that cools my tongue,
But does not quench my thirst. If I were strong,
I would have done with you, nor bow my head
Beside the grave where part of me lies dead,
Nor would I seek an anodyne in song.
And yet—and yet—a dream is god-like fare,
While love is fragile fruit, wind-born of June,
Whose sharp delight is withered in July.
Because I love you more than I can bear,
I weave, all out of petals of the moon,
A love that never lived, that shall not die!
      —MURIEL F. HOCHDORF

Sonnet

Oh, you and I are pitifully small
To look up at the stars. They seem to shake
With distant mirth for us, yet after all,
We are the warp and woof of stuffs that make
A trail of frozen fire down the sky.
That is our dust grown infinite we see
That laughs at us, remote and far and high
Above horizons of eternity.

The hands of earth upon the brow star-fired
Are sweet to feel, and human dust may know
A warmth and nearness by the stars desired
When they forget to laugh. Oh, let us grow
To hold each other close on starry nights,
To love the city's thousand tiny lights!
      —MURIEL F. HOCHDORF

Monticello

"All men created equal"—black and bold
The words stand in my mind, but near this chair,
I like to think what textbooks never told:
You added one word here, took out one there.
"Pursuit of happiness"—though this will ring
Through eager ears for centuries, in some
Tense moment did you stop your work to fling
A spoiled sheet out, or watch the evening come?
"Inalienable rights"—this is your phrase
And born perhaps within these stately halls,
But I prefer to think of summer days,
When in the shadow of your ivied walls,
You sat to watch your flower garden grow,
Or smoked a pipe, like any man I know.
                                        —RUTH H. HAUSMAN

To the Passing of Sail

From here upon the wind-bleached rocks, as dark
Swims out across the river, I can see
A clipper hull, with swinging topmast stark
Against the dimming sky. Her shrouds fly free
Like broken, tangled threads of some huge skein
That spiders made about her yards. And now
A looming lumber ship, tall-sided Dane,
Aloof and proud, throbs by my clipper's bow.

Though prideful youth will ever scorn the old,
My ancient ship, your clan was once the best
In all the world. From laden clipper hold
A nation drew her strength for freedom's quest,
And you, smug Dane, were Fulton's boyhood dream
When steam was young and wind-taut sail supreme.
                                        —LIONEL DAY

To the Clipper Ship, Benjamin F. Packard

Not long ago you roamed the seven seas
And back, with canvas booming from the Horn
To icy Tunanak. You moored at quays
Where coolies brought you guano, teak, and thorn,
Or brown men loaded copra for the West.
A famous master loved your oaken beams,
And on his lonely midnight watch, would rest
Against your spume-bright rail, and dream great dreams.

You well deserve the wind-swept, ancient grave
Of faithful ships, but lolling like a hound,
Too old to join the hunt, not stirring save
To groan and roll upon the swelling sound,
You mourn the past—justly. Your cargo now
Is dancing feet and lovers in the bow!

—LIONEL DAY

Dejection

This day is damp and close and darkly-cast.
I never saw so sad a day before.
Like ghosts or shades or wraiths from out the past
The mists are drifting through the little door
Between the hills, that lets the valley out
To touch the river. There the clouds intwine
Their fingers in the smoky hair about
The city where the lights begin to shine.
I find this evening suited well to me.
It meets my need of smoke and mist and shades.
Until I find that I've forgotten she
Was faithless, till the insult dims and fades,
I, like a rain-drenched carnival, must go,
My spirits quenched, my pennants drooping low.

—JAMES GORHAM

Someone There Is—

(to Robert Frost)

Someone there is who doesn't love the stone
Of cities, and their skies of opaque glass;
Who cannot listen to the wind's low moan
As she laments the death of trees and grass
But flees in horror from the hideous sound
To seek the softer singing of a jay
In some far field.—A simple heart has found
Its happiness among the mellowed hay.

Someone there is who knows how much I long
To leave the noisy clank of steel that blends
With harsh-voiced motors in discordant song—
Victorious; and from his fields he sends
A host of wingèd words that bear me high
Into a silence, and a wide, wide sky. . . .

—NAOMI ROGIN

Chance

The book I read by no design or plan,
The bar of swift, unconscious music heard,
The lightly spoken casual, treasured word,
Should be rebukes to nature, that she can,
Being the guardian of the hopes of man,
Intrust such precious gifts to the absurd,
The flippant messenger of chance, preferred
For their delivery since time began.
I have no cause to doubt, that as the light,
Piercing a prism in a wavering ray,
Flames not to color if the watcher be
On any spot but one, you also might
Never have met my eyes, and that one day
Might just as well have been denied to me.

—RUTH H. HAUSMAN

Forgotten Children

The garden is a cool expanse of green,
  And very lonesomely the children stand
High on a pedestal behind a screen
  Of shrubs; the small boy holds the dainty hand
The little girl extends, with wistful eyes.
  At rise of day, a robin pipes a song
Star-clear and brief, but all too soon he flies
  Up into heaven, and the day is long.

So let the garden feel small feet that run,
  And children early up and quick about,
Who love wild roses and the morning sun,
  Who fling their spirits skyward with a shout.
Oh, fill the garden with young joy and strife,
And the marble children, too, will spring to life!

—ESTELLE ROOKS

SUGGESTION

Life is filled with subjects for sonnets. Consult your notebook. Warning! Take no liberties with the line length of the sonnet. Write five iambic feet to the line.

CHAPTER XXXI

BLANK VERSE

STRICTLY speaking blank verse is any metrical verse unrhymed. *Hiawatha* is written in blank verse, four-foot trochaic meter.

> At the door on summer evenings
> Sat the little Hiawatha
> Heard the whispering of the pine-trees,
> Heard the lapping of the waters,
> Sounds of music, words of wonder;
> "Minne-wawa!" said the pine-trees,
> "Mudway-aushka!" said the water.
> —HENRY WADSWORTH LONGFELLOW

Evangeline is written in blank verse—dactylic hexameter:

This is the forest primeval. The murmuring pines and the hemlocks,
Bearded with moss, and in garments green, indistinct in the twilight,
Stand like Druids of old, with voices sad and prophetic,
Stand like harpers hoar, with beards that rest on their bosoms.
Loud from its rocky caverns the deep-voiced neighboring ocean
Speaks, and in accents disconsolate answers the wail of the forest.
—HENRY WADSWORTH LONGFELLOW

Collins's "Ode to Evening" is in stanzas of four lines unrhymed, two in iambic pentameter followed by two in iambic trimeter:

> If aught of oaten stop, or pastoral song,
> May hope, chaste Eve, to soothe thy modest ear,
> Like thy own solemn springs,
> Thy springs and dying gales. . . .

There are others. But blank verse is generally understood to mean the heroic blank verse of Shakespeare's plays. Before Shakespeare, Marlowe used it in his plays:

> Was this the face that launched a thousand ships
> And burnt the topless towers of Ilium?
> —*Dr. Faustus*

And Milton used it after him in his *Paradise Lost* when he sang

> Of man's first disobedience and the fruit
> Of that forbidden tree, whose mortal taste
> Brought death into the world, and all our woe.

It consists of any number of unrhymed lines written in iambic meter, five feet on a line. Usually it is not divided into stanzas, but when it is the first line of each stanza may be indented. It is characterized by the imaginative and emotional qualities of all well written poetry. The dignity and continuity of its measure are admirably suited to grave poetry.

It lends itself alike to meditative and to dramatic movements. Hence the great plays of Shakespeare in blank verse and their impressive soliloquies such as Hamlet's "To be or not to be"; Prospero's "We are such stuff as dreams are made on"; Macbeth's meditations on sleep and on the brevity of life. It is effective as a vehicle for narrative, and it is effective as a vehicle for dialogue, so necessary a part of the drama. It is the most artistic medium for reproducing the subtleties of conversational tones. Perhaps no living poet gives greater proof of how effective it is in this way than Robert Frost. He has bent it to his will, or shall we say his ear, and what an instrument it is in his poetic hands!

The most important things for the beginner to remember in writing blank verse are these: have a care for the end of the line; have a care for the cæsura.

Monotony would be the result if the sense-close of a passage coincided too often with the metrical-close of the line; in other words, if the sentences came to a stop too often at the end of the line. Such lines are called end-stopped lines. As Shakespeare developed his art he used fewer and fewer end-stopped lines. Break the monotony by carrying over the sense of the passage from one line to the next, forming what you know as run-on lines. This is nothing new to you. You did this in your first experiments with continuous couplets. But the continuous nature of blank verse demands perhaps greater attention to this point.

Furthermore, many lines of five feet, all ending on an accented syllable might grow monotonous. The skillful writer of blank verse occasionally introduces an extra syllable at the end of the line

> My hands are of your color, but I shame
> To wear a heart so white. (Knocking within) I hear a knock*ing*
> At the south entry: . . .
>   —WILLIAM SHAKESPEARE

> And some are loaves and some so nearly balls
> We have to use a spell to make them bal*ance*;
>   ·   /   · / · / ·   /   ·   /   ·
>   —ROBERT FROST

Next, the placing of the cæsura in blank verse is most important. A cæsura or sense pause, cuts every five-foot line of verse. A very rare line may not have one. Occasionally, there are two cæsuras in a line. The artist displays his skill by shifting the position of the cæsura as line is added to line. If too many fall after any one foot the rich music of blank verse is impaired. The marked passage below will illustrate this shifting of the cæsura.

1. But how to take last leave// of all I loved?
2. O golden hair,// with which I used to play
3. Not knowing!// O imperial-moulded form,
4. And beauty// such as never woman wore,
5. Until it came// a kingdom's curse with thee—
6. I cannot touch thy lips,// they are not mine,
7. But Lancelot's;// nay, they never were the King's.
8. I cannot take thy hand;// that too is flesh
9. And in the flesh thou hast sinn'd;// and mine own flesh,
10. Here looking down on thine polluted,// cries
11. 'I loathe thee:'// yet not less, O Guinevere,
12. For I was ever virgin// save for thee,
13. My love thro' flesh// hath wrought into my life
14. So far,// that my doom is,// I love thee still
                    —ALFRED, LORD TENNYSON: *Guinevere*

Note also that sometimes the cæsura falls at the end of a foot, as in line 2: *O gold' en hair'//*; and sometimes it interrupts a foot as in line 7: *But Lance' lot's// nay'*. An extra unaccented syllable before the cæsura is another device for bringing surprise into a line of blank verse.

$$/ \quad / \quad . \quad . \quad / \quad . \quad . \quad / \quad . \quad /$$
Wake Duncan with *thy* knocking!// I would thou couldst

The third foot seems like a substituted amphibrach with the cæsura following. Or considering it from another angle, if we regard the first three feet as of two syllables each, the fourth foot is a substituted anapest interrupted by a cæsura after the first syllable. Its place after the extra syllable is effective as a variation of what the pattern promises.

In blank verse there are the substitutions and the syncopations that you find in any other iambic pentameter verse. Listen to the rich orchestrated effect of these lines from Edwin Arlington Robinson's *Tristram*:

1.   . . . The last word fell
2. Like a last coin released unwillingly
3. By caution giving all. And while the King
4. Said what he said, Tristram was seeing only
5. A last look in two dark and frightened eyes
6. That always in the moonlight would be shining,
7. Alone above the sound of Cornish waves
8. That always in the moonlight would be breaking
9. Cold upon Cornish rocks.

See how in line 2 the second foot, *last' coin'*, with its two accents compensates for the foot ahead which has only light stresses. Note the effect in line 4 of the substituted trochee, *said' what*, and *Trist' ram* in the third foot. In lines 6 and 8 there are only three speech accents: *al, moón, shin; al, moon, break*. We should read the lines

> That *al'* ways in the *moon'* light would be *shin'* ing,
> That *al'* ways in the *moon'* light would be *break'* ing

There is a rush over *ways in the* and *light would be* as against the basic metronomic beat

> That al' ways in' the moon' light would' be shin' ing
> That al' ways in' the moon' light would' be break' ing

But the syncopation of line 6 followed by the regular beat of 7 and the syncopation of 8 throb with suspense. Then it breaks with a substituted trochee: *Cold' upo*n Cornish rocks.

An artist may vary from the norm ./././././ as much as he dares, provided that he compensates for frustrating the expectations that his pattern has aroused. Such subtleties in the handling of meter come with long practice. You may gradually acquire insight through a study of the masters and through your own experiments. When you have enjoyed the blank verse in this chapter and practiced the five-finger exercises, read the suggestions for creating your own.

The soliloquies from Shakespeare's plays are often complete poems.

To Be, Or Not To Be

(From *Hamlet*, Act III, Sc. I, Hamlet's Speech)

To be, or not to be: that is the question:
Whether 'tis nobler in the mind to suffer
The slings and arrows of outrageous fortune,
Or to take arms against a sea of troubles,
And by opposing end them? To die: to sleep;
No more; and, by a sleep to say we end
The heart-ache and the thousand natural shocks
That flesh is heir to, 'tis a consummation
Devoutly to be wish'd. To die, to sleep;
To sleep: perchance to dream: ay, there's the rub;
For in that sleep of death what dreams may come
When we have shuffled off this mortal coil,
Must give us pause. There's the respect
That makes calamity of so long life;
For who would bear the whips and scorns of time,
The oppressor's wrong, the proud man's contumely,
The pangs of dispriz'd love, the law's delay,

The insolence of office, and the spurns
That patient merit of the unworthy takes,
When he himself might his quietus make
With a bare bodkin? who would fardels bear,
To grunt and sweat under a weary life,
But that the dread of something after death,
The undiscover'd country from whose bourn
No traveller returns, puzzles the will,
And makes us rather bear those ills we have
Than fly to others that we know not of?
Thus conscience does make cowards of us all;
And thus the native hue of resolution
Is sicklied o'er with the pale cast of thought,
And enterprises of great pith and moment
With this regard their currents turn awry,
And lose the name of action.

—WILLIAM SHAKESPEARE

Hyperion

Deep in the shady sadness of a vale
Far sunken from the healthy breath of morn,
Far from the fiery noon, and eve's one star,
Sat gray-hair'd Saturn, quiet as a stone,
Still as the silence round about his lair;
Forest on forest hung about his head
Like cloud on cloud. No stir of air was there,
Not so much life as on a summer's day
Robs not one light seed from the feather'd grass,
But where the dead leaf fell, there did it rest.
A stream went voiceless by, still deadened more
By reason of his fallen divinity
Spreading a shade: The Naiad 'mid her reeds
Press'd her cold finger closer to her lips.
  Along the margin-sand large foot-marks went,
No further than to where his feet had stray'd,
And slept there since. Upon the sodden ground
His old right hand lay nerveless, listless, dead,
Unsceptred; and his realmless eyes were closed;
While his bow'd head seem'd list'ning to the Earth,
His ancient mother, for some comfort yet. . . .

—JOHN KEATS

In these opening lines of "Hyperion," which Keats never finished,
the fallen god and the landscape about him reflect the majesty of
despair. Blank verse is appropriate to the sublime.

An Old Man's Winter Night

All out of doors looked darkly in at him
Through the thin frost, almost in separate stars,
That gathers on the pane in empty rooms.
What kept his eyes from giving back the gaze
Was the lamp tilted near them in his hand.
What kept him from remembering the need
That brought him to that creaking room was age.
He stood with barrels round him—at a loss.
And having scared the cellar under him
In clomping there, he scared it once again
In clomping off; and scared the outer night,
Which has its sounds, familiar, like the roar
Of trees and crack of branches, common things,
But nothing so like beating on a box.
A light he was to no one but himself
Where now he sat, concerned with he knew what,
A quiet light, and then not even that.
He consigned to the moon, such as she was,
So late-arising, to the broken moon
As better than the sun in any case
For such a charge, his snow upon the roof,
His icicles along the wall to keep;
And slept. The log that shifted with a jolt
Once in the stove, disturbed him and he shifted,
And eased his heavy breathing, but still slept.
One aged man—one man—can't fill a house,
A farm, a countryside, or if he can,
It's thus he does it of a winter night.

—ROBERT FROST

How perfectly all the details blend to breathe age: the blank verse, the old man forgetting what he went for, the winter night, the old moon, its pale light on the snow and icicles. There is a sadness about this lonely old man that is taken up by every detail.

Mending Wall

Something there is that doesn't love a wall,
That sends the frozen ground-swell under it,
And spills the upper boulders in the sun;
And makes gaps even two can pass abreast.
The work of hunters is another thing:
I have come after them and made repair

Where they have left not one stone on a stone,
But they would have the rabbit out of hiding,
To please the yelping dogs. The gaps I mean,
No one has seen them made or heard them made,
But at spring mending-time we find them there.
I let my neighbor know beyond the hill;
And on a day we meet to walk the line
And set the wall between us once again.
We keep the wall between us as we go.
To each the boulders that have fallen to each.
And some are loaves and some so nearly balls
We have to use a spell to make them balance;
"Stay where you are until our backs are turned!"
We wear our fingers rough with handling them.
Oh, just another kind of outdoor game,
One on a side. It comes to little more:
There where it is we do not need the wall:
He is all pine and I am apple-orchard.
My apple trees will never get across
And eat the cones under his pines, I tell him.
He only says, "Good fences make good neighbors."
Spring is the mischief in me, and I wonder
If I could put a notion in his head:
"*Why* do they make good neighbors? Isn't it
Where there are cows? But here there are no cows.
Before I built a wall I'd ask to know
What I was walling in or walling out,
And to whom I was like to give offence.
Something there is that doesn't love a wall,
That wants it down!" I could say "Elves" to him,
But it's not elves exactly, and I'd rather
He said it for himself. I see him there,
Bringing a stone grasped firmly by the top
In each hand, like an old-stone savage armed.
He moves in darkness as it seems to me,
Not of woods only and the shade of trees.
He will not go behind his father's saying,
And he likes having thought of it so well
He says again, "Good fences make good neighbors."

—ROBERT FROST

Birches

When I see birches bend to left and right
Across the line of straighter darker trees,
I like to think some boy's been swinging them.
But swinging doesn't bend them down to stay.
Ice-storms do that. Often you must have seen them
Loaded with ice a sunny winter morning
After a rain. They click upon themselves
As the breeze rises, and turn many-colored
As the stir cracks and crazes their enamel.
Soon the sun's warmth makes them shed crystal shells
Shattering and avalanching on the snow-crust—
Such heaps of broken glass to sweep away
You'd think the inner dome of heaven had fallen.
They are dragged to the withered bracken by the load,
And they seem not to break; though once they are bowed
So low for long, they never right themselves:
You may see their trunks arching in the woods
Years afterwards, trailing their leaves on the ground
Like girls on hands and knees that throw their hair
Before them over their heads to dry in the sun.
But I was going to say when Truth broke in
With all her matter-of-fact about the ice-storm,
I should prefer to have some boy bend them
As he went out and in to fetch the cows—
Some boy too far from town to learn baseball,
Whose only play was what he found himself,
Summer or winter, and could play alone.
One by one he subdued his father's trees
By riding them down over and over again
Until he took the stiffness out of them,
And not one but hung limp, not one was left
For him to conquer. He learned all there was
To learn about not launching out too soon
And so not carrying the tree away
Clear to the ground. He always kept his poise
To the top branches, climbing carefully
With the same pains you use to fill a cup
Up to the brim, and even above the brim.
Then he flung outward, feet first, with a swish,
Kicking his way down through the air to the ground.
So was I once myself a swinger of birches;
And so I dream of going back to be.
It's when I'm weary of considerations,
And life is too much like a pathless wood
Where your face burns and tickles with the cobwebs

Broken across it, and one eye is weeping
From a twig's having lashed across it open.
I'd like to get away from earth awhile
And then come back to it and begin over.
May no fate wilfully misunderstand me
And half grant what I wish and snatch me away
Not to return. Earth's the right place for love:
I don't know where it's likely to go better.
I'd like to go by climbing a birch tree,
And climb black branches up a snow-white trunk
Toward heaven, till the tree could bear no more,
But dipped its top and set me down again.
That would be good both going and coming back.
One could do worse than be a swinger of birches.

—ROBERT FROST

WHAT YOUNG POETS HAVE SAID IN BLANK VERSE

The Unemployed Speak of Snow

(Their spokesman is a tall young man who once might have built a tower to the sun.)

I never dreamed such treasure lay in snow,
Not clean snow either. When I was a boy,
We with our sleds found joys a-plenty in
A dash downhill, or a swift and eager fight
With snowballs hard and white as moons might be
If moons were made of marble. Then, we ate
Our icicles for candy canes, and dipped
Each other's heads in drifts. That snow was clean!
The warmth of bodies mingled with the ice
And breath of wind, and left us all aglow.
Our hearts went dancing with the lightest flakes.
The snow I shoveled off today was scarce
Allowed to touch the ground. Still now it lies,
A patterned blanket on the roofs, to shape
The bleak and jagged outlines into softness;
Piles are left on some forgotten streets.
But we, the army of the unemployed,
Swooped with our shovels, picks, and fire-hose,
And swept the snow to slush and to destruction.
I never dreamed such treasure lay in snow.
Five dollars a day for walking ankle-deep
Through melted ice a-trickle down your boots.
If he were not so sick with crying nights
For food, I'd buy my youngest son a sled!

—ESTELLE ROOKS

Portrait of an Afternoon

How strange today has been, at least, today
Outside my window where the placid river
Stretches so flat and still; one end of it
Is pointed north between the sentinels
That will some day support the bridge,
While I, between two windows tall and gray
(Like sentinels too) look up awhile to see
This strangeness: twisting wind, and snow, and rain,
First one and then another, never just
A silent view of river, shore, and bridge.
But now there's only a drifting, aimless void
Of flakes, tugging at one another, loosing
Between my windows and the bridge a veil
Of velvet white. I have been sitting here,
One elbow on the desk, making a pattern
Of snow and words on paper, weaving a scarf
Of quietness, that I may put it on
And feel the vivid white about myself.
But when I lift my head to frame it all
Through the window, the veil and snow and peace
Have slipped away and left a blowing rain.
A rhythmic tapping takes the place of still
Slow whisperings. The Drive is gray with rain
And sings a whirring song of tires on wet
Asphalt—and rain—and ever falling rain,
That fills my heart with questionings . . . How strange
Today has been, or is it I am strange?

—JOYCE LANCASTER

Ann Curtis

Dramatic Monologue

You think Ann pretty? Well, I don't. Her hair
Is gold, but hair is just a little thing
To heart. Her soul is frozen stiff. The only
Two things she loves are Jane and her own self.
She makes me feel like crouching, nearly dead
With cold by snowy mountain peaks, but Jane
Is merry, sparkling water, leaping down
From sunny hills; she looks like roses at dawn
That seem to have a private joke with God.
I wonder that the icy peaks don't crush
The fragile roses! Ann's husband? Jane is

Like Peter. He had a dreamer's soul and fault.
He loved all beauty, nature, women, books . . .
Ann rose in all her strength and crushed out love
And Peter's life. . . . He died by his own hand.
He looked just like a birch that had been bent
By winds. . . . Then three weeks later Jane was born.
You think Ann pretty? Well, I don't, for Peter
Was my friend. . . .

—Babette Kurtz

Boats

She steams on up the river passing all
With haughty mien, not deigning to relinquish
The center of the stream for one who finds
The going difficult. This steamship seems
Just like my Aunt Maria, with her head
Tilted toward the sky. She cares not even
That! for people like you and me, who use
Our puny strength, like insignificant tugs
To help her on her way. She hands out money,
Thousands at a time, to help, she says
The poorer class, but like the smoke from funnels
Of huge and domineering ships, it goes,
But no one knows, and least of all does she,
The place to which it goes. And all it is
Is fuel to keep her conscience steaming strong
So she may hold her head above the tide.

—Dorothy Viertel

The Saxophone

This sobbing fits the city—can't you see,
Listening to that croon, a sprawling drunkard
Under the leprous light of dimming lampposts
As day flows in between the tall, tall buildings;
A street-car's hollowing of night's steep silence;
Old beggars, blind, scratching yellowish violins;
The subway's sound or any newsboy's call,
Or someone's weeping on a quiet street?
—I know the saxophone was born from this.
When people are asleep and darkness holds
The city with soft hands, I watch and listen—
Sometimes I think I see the city placing
Its mouth upon a saxophone and playing
—Almost as mothers kiss their little children.

—Delmore Schwartz

Blank Verse

Eyes are queer windows looking in,—not out,
Only sometimes have I been quick enough
To catch a glimpse, before the shade was drawn,
Of treasure buried at the very core
Of being: of one road that led to peace,
Of one green softness in an arid plot,
Of one gold bird that only woke to sing
On purple midnights when no moon swung low.
People are jealous of the secret deeps
Behind their eyes; they bar the windows well.
A little girl with auburn hair and eyes
Like brown and yellow pansies bears inside
A world of people with fantastic names
That come to talk with her if she but call.
She goes to school with Strunby, and plays tag
Along the way with Oosty-boon and Karl,
But Roma holds her hand when she is ill.

*   *   *

There is a boy whose eyes are blue with smoke
That rises from an altar down below.
One name rings sweet between the world and him.
His pulses chime it: "Lucy, Lucy—," oh,
Its sound pursues him, and he hears it sung
At sundown by the sea against the rocks,
And told by rain, and moaned by windy pines.

*   *   *

A woman that I know lives in a dream
Of hollyhocks beside a grey stone wall,
The feel of buttons on rough khaki cloth,
A bandaged head to hold in her two hands,—
The dream ends here—but hollyhocks bloom on.
—MURIEL F. HOCHDORF

Irrigation

See that field of green? Not long ago
It was a desert, barren and forsaken.
People used to shun its arid wastes,
And those few fools who tried to travel it,
Are lying somewhere—or their bones are lying—
Buried in the drifts that used to be
Where all this greenery is stretching now.

You ask, "How was the land made fertile, then?"
A very simple matter. Someone came,
A little wiser than the rest, and thought it out.
Instead of shying from the searing stretch of sand
And useless rock, he puzzled for a way
To cultivate it—make it beautiful.
He looked around, and found the means not far
To seek: a fairly good-sized river ran
Between two sloping hills a few miles from
The desert's edge; the rest was obvious—
It was not long before a deep-dug ditch
Allowed the energizing water to revive
That almost-corpse.
                          But all the years that went
To waste before a man arrived who knew
The thing to do! And yet, it was so simple!

I wonder if you think—as I have thought—
That one could irrigate an arid heart.

                                        —NAOMI ROGIN

Progress

The place where I go picking violets
Is in a wood, and so is damp and dark,
With glints of sunlight skipping in between
The leaves. The violets there stand boldly up
Or else they curl quite unexpectedly
Over a twig or under a shriveled leaf,
And smell of woods and rain-wet earth; and spring
Patches of pale mayflowers grow there too,
That look like tiny wisps of pink chiffon,
Scattered among the leaves . . . Sometimes as I
Lie there, I hear the sudden scream and shriek
Of passing subway trains below the hill
And then I think that just ten miles from here
People sit all day long at steel machines . . .

In time the city will creep up until
This spot is choked out by a factory—
Perhaps for artificial violets.

                                        —RUTH H. KLEIN

Vision

I thought I saw two starlings lightly fall,
And all the sky became as white as ivory;
Far purer than the rajah's sacred tusks,
Far calmer than the moon's reflected shadow—

I thought I saw two starlings lightly fall.
But, when I calmed my slowly-whirling senses
Enough to gaze without a frank betrayal,
I saw that Elsa lowered starling eyes.
I saw the lids as pure as sacred ivory,
As virginal as lilies at the altar,
As languid as the floating lotus scent.
I thought of how the knights went out to battle,
Content to die because of someone's eyes—
I thought I saw two starlings lightly fall.

—LESLIE RUBIN

Mexican Peasant

Twelve colored penny banks were done. The pack
Was made, and Indian Pedro, in his hut
Beside the mountain road which led to Taxco,
Prepared to take it to the town for market
Day in the age-old cobbled square beneath
The smiling church spires. Pedro now reviewed
His handiwork and with great pride, recalled
The six full days that he had spent on it.
First he had molded clay, in forms of pigs
And horses, then had laid them in the sun
To bake, the while he had mixed paint—bright red,
Yellow, and black. As he had colored each,
His thoughts had pictured some young customer
Who would delight in such a maze of colors.
The young Pepita, daughter of the town
Sombrero vendor, always begged for pigs
With yellow ears. She would have this one, too,
For Pedro often gave a bank away.
What matter that this generosity
Would bring to him no money for his *mole*,[1]
Or clothes, or clay to make more savings banks . . .
Twelve colored penny banks were done . . . old Pedro
Lifted the pack and trudged along the road.
He thought again of small Pepita. She,
Like him, would never own a bright centavo
To drop inside behind the yellow ears,
But that was life. . . . Old Pedro hurried on;
He had to reach the market place by eight.

—LUCILLE SCHMEDTJE

[1] Pronounced *mo' leh*—a highly seasoned sauce used with Mexican foods, particularly chicken and turkey.

Where Shall I Go?

In every little crooked path that leads
Across a meadow or into a wood
A sprite, Adventure, sings. Her murmured song
Is carried on light winds, and tangled here
And there in long green branches of tall trees.
But ah! my ears to mortals are attuned;
Adventure's voice is faint and indistinct.
I know not if she lies at this path's end.
Or shall I find her where the path begins?

—MIRIAM WOLFSON

Thoughts on Taking an Anaesthetic

I never knew I had a soul until
The day I left my body on the ground
And, rising, sailed away with wings unfurled
No longer hampered with my arms and legs
But feeling such a freedom as is known
To those who travel in a dark and gloomy
Tunnel, when suddenly the blackness splits
And leaves them once more free to breathe in light
And air. I used to wonder how I'd feel
When I was dead; have I discovered now?
But if it were like this, how foolish is
The fear and dread we mortals hold of going:
To leave the close confinement of this shell
In which our feelings jostle one another
And all succeed in growing badly bruised;
To rise into a purer atmosphere
And slowly spread our thoughts upon the air
Where, fanned by gentle currents, burning wounds
Are cooled and lose their pain. If this be death,
Why must we call it tragedy?

—MARJORIE DEGRAFF

Solitaire

Jack on my Queen . . . Oh dear, I will forget.
Not that it matters greatly if I do—
If I don't win who cares? Of small import
Whether I win or lose at cards—at life—
No, that's not true. I know quite well it does:
No matter what we say, or how we smile,
It hurts and always will until the end. . . .
Lord, how my eyes do ache. I sewed too long—
I suppose it's that. . . . She was so eager, though,
To wear the dress. And didn't she look sweet!
Her friends declare she's spoiled, but I know better;
No one as fine as my girl could be harmed
By having more things done for her than others.
Sally, Elaine—they're nice, but not my girl. . . .
Oh my, another play I didn't see.
But here's a move—this black six on that seven. . . .
It seems no more than yesterday that she
Brought her to me, a tiny mite with hair
Like gold—asking if I would take their child.
And even if it hadn't been my sister's,
The child was his, and nothing else quite mattered.
I didn't love her then. But she'd forgive
Me that, I'm sure, if she could understand
How bitter I was against them both just then. . . .
There! I knew that I'd forget the cream—
When she comes in, it will be much too late—
I'd better go and buy it now. . . . That movie
Last night was very good—I didn't like
The girl—a selfish brat, allowed her mother
To work her fingers to the bone, yet not
A single thought did she once give to her
Until the very end. . . . That's life, I guess. . . ,
Jack on my Queen—oh dear, I will forget.

—Florence Luft

FIVE-FINGER EXERCISES

1. Copy the passages below, numbering the lines in each passage for easy reference. Mark the position of the cæsuras by //. Underline extra end-line syllables. Underline twice a cæsura that follows an extra syllable. Find a syncopated line. Mark the metrical pattern above it and the speech accents below. What effect has the rush of the unaccented speech phrases?

What truth is carried into the heart in passage *b*?

> a. The ship was now a speck upon the water,
> And soon, from where she was, would not be that,
> And soon was not; and there was nothing left
> That day, for her, in the world anywhere,
> But white birds always flying, and still flying,
> And always the white sunlight on the sea.
> —Edwin Arlington Robinson: *Tristram*

> b. You live still in the night, and are not ready
> For the new dawn. When the dawn comes, my child,
> You will forget. No, you will not forget,
> But you will change. There are no mortal houses
> That are so providently barred and fastened
> As to keep change and death from coming in.
> Tristram is dead, and change is at your door.
> —Edwin Arlington Robinson: *Tristram*

2. From any of Shakespeare's plays select a passage that you like and read it aloud. In your reading bring out the music of speech but also the music of the line by stopping just long enough at the close of the line to free its metrical vibrations without halting the sense from line to line. Let there be a nice harmony of sense phrasing with musical phrasing. Remember the power of the pause. It may be filled with stage business; it may be the vehicle for carrying your meaning out across the distance into the heart of your listener.

3. Indicate which lines are complete five-foot lines and which have extra syllables at the end.

> a 1. But music for the time doth change his nature

> b 1. But scarce could hear each other speak for noise
> 2. Of clock and chimes like silver hammers falling

> c 1.   Common as light is love,
> 2. And its familiar voice wearies not ever.

> d 1. To know nor faith, nor love, nor law; to be
> 2. Omnipotent but friendless is to reign;

e 1. He follow'd, and she turn'd to lead the way
  2. Through agèd boughs that yielded like a mist
  3. Which eagles cleave upmounting from their nest.

f 1. "The blaze, the splendor, and the symmetry,
  2. I cannot see—but darkness, death and darkness."

4. Turn these passages into iambic lines of five feet with an extra syllable at the end of each line; then make one of your own.

a. Take a long look at the beauty of the blossoms you see on the tree.

b. Where are you going on such a fine morning? Do tell me.

c. It was not meant that I should possess this treasure.

5. Indicate which lines have the cæsura after an iambic foot; after the unaccented syllable of an iambic foot; in connection with an extra syllable:

a. Pray for my soul. More things are wrought by prayer
  Than this world dreams of. Wherefore, let thy voice
  Rise like a fountain for me night and day.

b. How many cowards, whose hearts are all as false

c. Good night, Sir Tristram, Prince of Lyonesse.

d. There drew me forth the brand Excalibur

e. Days after, vexed with doubt and indecision.

f. Besides the brain was like the hand, and grew
  With using; thence the man's if more was more;

g.   Untimely words
  Are not for love, and are like frost on flowers

h. Whereat the Baron saying, "I well believe
  Ye be of Arthur's Table," a light laugh

i. Ye congregated powers of heaven, who share

j. The Soul of Man, like unextinguished fire
  Yet burns towards heaven with fierce reproach, and doubt,

6. Construct three five-foot iambic lines with the cæsura placed as follows:

a. after an iambic foot.

b. within an iambic foot, that is, after the unaccented syllable.

c. after an extra syllable.

Use any model in this chapter as a help to you.
Your three lines need have no sense relation to one another.

SUGGESTIONS

Write at least twenty-five lines of blank verse, using any one of the following suggestions or any idea which any suggestion may stimulate.

Before you do any of these exercises, imagine your audience. Are you talking to several or to one? Make some point in your poem and stop when you have told enough. Unify your poem with a theme and test afterwards for logical sequence and single effect. Have in the poem no matter that does not contribute to the development of your idea and the effect which you want to create.

1. Set down your train of thought while you are doing something mechanical: tying your tie, lacing your shoes, combing your hair, washing the dishes, or the like.

2. Imagine you are one of the following and express your train of thought as you carry on your duties:

> Usher in a theatre   Doorman at a theatre, bank   Elevator man   Postman   Maid dusting the furniture, mopping the floor, running the vacuum cleaner   Taxi driver   Delivery boy Student on the morning of an examination

3. Think out loud as you play basketball, as you swim.

4. Give one side of a telephone conversation.

5. Overhear a conversation in a beauty parlor. It may or may not be light.

6. Write a dramatic monologue in which you comment on a person gone.

7. Speculate on what caused a change of attitude in some one you used to call friend.

8. Analyze the character of some one.

Test your blank verse for richness of quality.

1. Are the lines five-foot iambic lines?
2. If you substitute, have you recovered your iambic meter?
3. Do some lines run on?
4. Have you used an extra syllable at the end of a line?
(You do not have to; but in twenty-five lines an extra syllable might lend charm.)
5. Have you varied the position of the cæsura in successive lines?

6. Have you varied the position of the cæsura in relation to the foot: after the foot, after the first syllable of a foot, after an extra syllable added to a foot?

Never

break a hyphenated word at the end of a line.

divide a word at the end of a line; that is, do not have one syllable on line 4 and the rest of the word on line 5.

CHAPTER XXXII

A CLASSIC FORM: SAPPHICS

THE Greek and the Latin versifier deals with quantity: long and short stresses; whereas we deal with accented and unaccented syllables. There are critics who believe, therefore, that there can be no true English poetry in the classic meters. Nevertheless, to experiment with at least one Greek form is a stimulating exercise. The activity will give an insight into a classic song-pattern other than "the stateliest measure ever moulded by the lips of man," the dactylic hexameters of Homer's *Odyssey* and Vergil's *Æneid,* which American students sometimes regard as the only meter used by the Greeks and the Latins.

Sappho, whom the Greeks regarded as their greatest and sweetest singer, invented a rhythm of haunting beauty. We call it *Sapphics.* Translated into English meter, a sapphic line consists of five feet: the central one of three syllables, a dactyl; the other four of trochees. A sapphic stanza consists of three of these lines followed by a shorter line of two feet, the first of which consists of three syllables, a dactyl; the second, of two, a trochee. This fourth line is called an adonic. There is no rhyme. The nature of the terminal foot calls for feminine endings: two-syllabled words accented on the first syllable.

Here is the pattern:

1. /. /. /.. /. /.

2. /. /. /.. /. /.

3. /. /. /.. /. /.

4. /.. /.

A spondee may be used instead of a trochee in lines 1 and 2, foot 2 and 5; and in line 3, foot 5.

Some poems in the sapphic rhythm follow:

Sapphics

Leaps the little river, and laughs at fetters; /./././././.
Through the pebbled channel it flutes and flutters; /././././././.
Dances down the rapids where Autumn scatters /././././././.
    Gold on the waters. /../.

Something bends the sedge and the rushes over,
Something moves and gleams where the grasses waver,—
Can it be a nymph that has taken cover,
    Couched by the river?

May it be a naiad with breasts that glimmer,
Chased of satyrs, dreading their hoofèd clamor,
Finding strange delights in the fears that claim her,
    Joy in the tremour?

Maybe Pan himself in the ferny hollow
Peels a wand and notches a pipe of willow,
Perks an ear and nods as he harks the mellow
    Song of the shallow.

Who shall say 'twas only the leaves that glinted?
Gods of eld survive; it is faith has fainted—
Some shall see forever the forests haunted,
    Earth all enchanted;

Some shall heed the lyres in the winds that murmur,
Some shall see the Triton beneath the comber,
Some shall hear the loom of the pagan Summer
    Weaving her glamour;

Hearing wings that dream: 'Tis the mounting pigeon
Bearing Venus home to her own Ægean!
They are outcasts, strayed from a golden region,
    Drunk on old legend.

              —Don Marquis

To a Greek Statue

Through the years you stand always gravely smiling,
Warmth of earth yet snow of a driftless beauty:
Youth and joy forever as one brief moment,
Waiting in silence.

And for us, the moment you stopped to listen,
Rapt before a Voice that should tell you all things;
So for us, an image of life unbroken,
Youth made immortal!

—THOMAS S. JONES, JR.

Sapphics

All the night sleep came not upon my eyelids,
Shed not dew, nor shook nor unclosed a feather,
Yet with lips shut close and with eyes of iron
Stood and beheld me.

Then to me so lying awake a vision
Came without sleep over the seas and touched me,
Softly touched mine eyelids and lips; and I too,
Full of the vision

Saw the white implacable Aphrodite,
Saw the hair unbound, and the feet unsandalled
Shine as fire of sunset on western waters;
Saw the reluctant

Feet, the straining plumes of the doves that drew her,
Looking always, looking with necks reverted,
Back to Lesbos, back to the hills whereunder
Shone Mitylene;

Heard the flying feet of the Loves behind her
Make a sudden thunder upon the waters,
As the thunder flung from the strong unclosing
Wings of a great wind.

So the goddess fled from her place, with awful
Sound of feet and thunder of wings around her;
While behind a clamor of singing women
Severed the twilight.

Ah the singing, ah the delight, the passion!
All the Loves wept, listening; sick with anguish,
Stood the crowned nine Muses about Apollo;
Fear was upon them,

While the tenth sang wonderful things they knew not.
Ah, the tenth, the Lesbian! the nine were silent,
None endured the sound of her song for weeping;
Laurel by laurel,

*Lesbian-Sappho
of Lesbos was
called the tenth
muse.*

Faded all their crowns; but about her forehead,
Round her woven tresses and ashen temples
White as dead snow, paler than grass in summer,
Ravaged with kisses,

Shone a light of fire as a crown for ever.
Yea, almost the implacable Aphrodite
Paused, and almost wept; such a song was that song;
Yea, by her name too

Called her, saying, "Turn to me, O my Sappho";
Yet she turned her face from the Loves, she saw not
Tears or laughter darken immortal eyelids,
Heard not about her

Fearful fitful wings of the doves departing,
Saw not how the bosom of Aphrodite
Shook with weeping, saw not her shaken raiment,
Saw not her hands wrung;

Only saw the beautiful lips and fingers,
Full of songs and kisses and little whispers,
Full of music; only beheld among them
Soar, as a bird soars

Newly fledged, her visible song, a marvel
Made of perfect sound and exceeding passion,
Sweetly shapen, terrible, full of thunders,
Clothed with the wind's wings.

Then rejoiced she, laughing with love, and scattered
Roses, awful roses of holy blossom;
Then the Loves thronged sadly with hidden faces
Round Aphrodite,

Then the Muses, stricken at heart, were silent;
Yea, the gods waxed pale; such a song was that song.
All reluctant, all with a fresh repulsion,
Fled from before her.

All withdrew long since, and the land was barren,
Full of fruitless women and music only.
Now perchance, when winds are assuaged at sunset,
Lulled at the dewfall,

By the gray sea-side, unassuaged, unheard of,
Unbeloved, unseen in the ebb of twilight,
Ghosts of outcast women return lamenting,
Purged not in Lethe,

Clothed about with flame and with tears, and singing
Songs that move the heart of the shaken heaven,
Songs that break the heart of the earth with pity,
Hearing, to hear them.

—ALGERNON CHARLES SWINBURNE

PUPILS SING IN SAPPHIC MEASURE

Gone

Many times the wind, like an ancient hermit,
Swept the sandy floor of the beach in silence.
Many times before had I watched and listened,
Never so lonely.

—WILLIAM ROEHRICK

Departure

Breath of sweetgrass, blown through the aisles of evening
Wide before you, why does it waken music?
Now the songs that died in the throat of morning
Pour forth in moonlight.

You, that stopped to listen beneath her window,
Turn and go, your hat in your hand, go slowly
Down the scented, echoing aisles of evening
Heartsick and haggard.

Love-bereft, bereaving the lips that love you,
Well you know the dusk of the gods is on you,
That will gather never again the golden
Apples of Freya.

Not for long the thirst nor the flesh that hungers,—
Winter snows drift over the tallest burning;
Summer noons that quilted her sleeping body
Ride to their setting.

Summer nights will come that will reel with sweetgrass,—
Less than sun-drowned moonlight your love will be then.
Time with patient fingers will cool your forehead,
You will lie quiet.

Grieve not now that still the receding fever
Heats your baffled blood and constricts your breathing:
Grieve that troubled pulses should sleep, that even
Grief should be mortal.

—MURIEL F. HOCHDORF

CHAPTER XXXIII

THE EPIGRAM

> What is an Epigram? A dwarfish whole;
> Its body brevity, and wit its soul.
> —SAMUEL T. COLERIDGE

As COLERIDGE suggests, the epigram is a brief poem on a single idea with an ingenious turn of thought which gives point to the lines. Usually more is meant than meets the eye. While some epigrams are merely pointed sayings compactly expressed in rhyme, many contain a deep underlying idea that is sharply suggested to the reader through the compactness of construction.

Alexander Pope, poet of polished regularity, wrote the following epigram for the collar of a dog belonging to the Prince of Wales.

> I am his Highness' dog at Kew;
> Pray, sir, tell me,—whose dog are you?

In *The Sonnet Today and Yesterday*, David Morton points out that the Greek epigram embodies the same singleness of idea and duality in unity as does the sonnet, that is, "a primary statement, followed by a secondary one associated with and prompted by the first, where it is not positively derived from it." To illustrate:

> This house, where once a lawyer dwelt
> Is now a smith's. Alas!
> How rapidly the iron age
> Succeeds the age of brass!
> —WILLIAM ERSKINE

The primary statement is, "This lawyer's house is now a smith's." Out of this idea grows the thought, "How rapidly the iron age succeeds the age of brass!" Iron age parallels smith's house; brass age (with its *double entende*) the lawyer's.

Here are others:

> Great things are done where men and mountains meet;
> These are not done by jostling in the street.
> —WILLIAM BLAKE

A Reply

Sir, I admit your general rule,
That every poet is a fool:
But you yourself may serve to show it,
That every fool is not a poet.

—MATTHEW PRIOR

There is no rule as to the length or meter of the epigram, but the greatest number seem to be in couplet or quatrain form. Epitaphs— verses to honor (mock) the dead—are often epigrams. Here are some:

Life is a jest, and all things show it;
I said so once, and now I know it.

—JOHN GAY

Here lies my wife: here let her lie!
Now she's at rest—and so am I.

—JOHN DRYDEN

John Bird, a laborer, lies here,
Who served the earth for sixty year
With spade and mattock, drill and plough;
But never found it kind till now.

—SYLVIA TOWNSEND WARNER

A courtier prepares an epitaph for Charles II:

Here lies our Souvereign Lord the King,
Whose word no man relies on,
He never said a foolish thing,
Nor ever did a wise one.

—JOHN WILMOT, EARL OF ROCHESTER

Epitaph on Newton

Nature and Nature's laws lay hid in night:
God said, "Let Newton be!" and all was light.

—ALEXANDER POPE

This ancient epitaph is attributed to every cemetery in Scotland:

Here lie I, Martin Elginbrodde:
Hae mercy o' my soue, Lord God,
As I wad do were I Lord God
And ye were Martin Elginbrodde.

It is ironical that over the grave of Shakespeare, the poet of all time, this doggerel should appear, intended no doubt to prevent disturbance of his remains:

> Good friend, for Jesus' sake, forbear
> To dig the dust enclosed here;
> Blest be the man that spares these stones
> And curst be he that moves my bones.

The spelling here used is modernized.

On a slab at the grave of Keats in Rome are these words: "Here lies one whose name is writ in water." And Dante lies beneath, "Here am I, Dante, laid—shut out from my native shores." The history of a period is packed in those lines.

Here are some epigrams from the Greek Anthology, or "collection of flowers." This ancient collection covers more than a thousand years: from 490 B.C. to 1000 A.D. More than three hundred poets some unknown but immortalized by the signature "without a master" are among the contributors of more than four thousand epigrams or epigrammatic poems, rarely exceeding twelve lines in length.

Edgar Lee Masters used *The Greek Anthology* as a model for his *Spoon River Anthology*, a collection of more than two hundred epitaphs in which the dead of a Middle West village reveal the truth about themselves: their struggles, disappointments, intrigues, loves, and hates. "Anne Rutledge" and "Lucinda Matlock" are two that you may enjoy reading.

After the models below, the name of the ancient writer appears first. The name of the translator follows.

The Lion Over the Tomb of Leonidas

> Of beasts am I, of men was he most brave
> Whose bones I guard, bestriding this his grave.
> —Anonymous, Walter Leaf

A Farewell

> Venus, take my votive glass,
> Since I am not what I was:
> What from this day I shall be,
> Venus, let me never see.
> —Plato, Matthew Prior

Timon's Epitaph

Here lie I, Timon; who, alive, all living men did hate:
Pass by, and curse thy fill; but pass and stay not here thy gait.
                  —Herodotus, William Shakespeare

Spirit of Plato

Eagle! why soarest thou above the tomb?
To what sublime and star-ypaven home
     Floatest thou?
I am the image of swift Plato's spirit,
Ascending heaven—Athens doth inherit
     His corpse below.
               —Anonymous, Percy Bysshe Shelley

Dion of Tarsus

Dion of Tarsus, here I lie, who sixty years have seen.
I was not ever wed, and would my father had not been!
               —Anonymous, Alma Strettell

The Tomb of Diogenes

"Tell me, good dog, whose tomb you guard so well."
"The Cynic's." "True; but who that Cynic tell."
"Diogenes, of fair Sinope's race."
"What? He that in a tub was wont to dwell?"
"Yes: but the stars are now his dwelling-place."
             —Anonymous, John Addington Symonds

Anticipation

Far happier are the dead, methinks, than they
Who look for death, and fear it every day.
               —Lucilius, William Cowper

Saon of Acanthus

Here lapped in hallowed slumber Saon lies,
Asleep, not dead; a good man never dies.
            —Callimachus, John Addington Symonds

On a Fowler

With reeds and bird-lime from the desert air
Eumelus gather'd free, though scanty, fare.
Nor lordly patron's hand he deign'd to kiss:
Thrice thirty years he lived, and to his heirs
His reeds bequeath'd, his bird-lime, and his snares.
　　　　　　　　　　—ISIDORUS, WILLIAM COWPER

Menodotis

Menodotis's portrait here is kept;
　　　Most odd it is
How very like to all the world, except
　　　Menodotis.
　　　　—LEONIDAS OF ALEXANDRIA, RICHARD GARNETT

On an Old Woman

Mycilla dyes her locks, 'tis said,
　　But 'tis a foul aspersion;
She buys them black, they therefore need
　　No subsequent immersion.
　　　　　　　　　—LUCILIUS, WILLIAM COWPER

Go tell the Lacedæmonians, passer-by,
That here, obedient to their words, we lie.
　　　　　　　　　　—SIMONIDES OF CEOS,

　　　for tomb of the 300 Spartans who died defend-
　　　ing the pass of Thermopylæ vs. Persian army.

Epitaph for a Hound

Dead as thou liest now,
Sealed in this tomb,
I think the wild beasts tremble still
Before thy white bones,

O huntress Lycas;
And thy bravery great Pelion knows
And splendid Ossa
And the lonely peaks of Cethæron.

A few years ago *Vanity Fair* published four pages of epitaphs written by a group of artists for themselves. A few are reproduced below.

R.I.P.
F. P. A.

Beneath This Green And
Tear-Sprent Sod
The Bones of F. P.
Adams Lie.
He Had A Rotten Time,
But, God!
How He Did Hate To
Die!

Neysa McMein

Gaze Upon the Lovely, Green
Grave Of Neysa M. McMein,
If That Causes You No Tear,
Damn You, Go Away From Here.

Don Marquis

I Am Not Here! Nor Life Nor
Death Might Bind
The Scornful Pinions Of My
Laughing Mind!

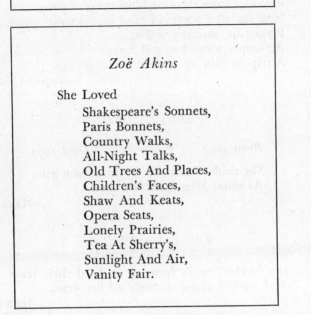

Here Lies The Body Of

May Wilson Preston

She Moved From New York
To Relieve The Congestion.

Zoë Akins

She Loved
  Shakespeare's Sonnets,
  Paris Bonnets,
  Country Walks,
  All-Night Talks,
  Old Trees And Places,
  Children's Faces,
  Shaw And Keats,
  Opera Seats,
  Lonely Prairies,
  Tea At Sherry's,
  Sunlight And Air,
  Vanity Fair.

For sharpening the wit and challenging terse expression, no form has greater potentialities than the epigram. Beginners should have many pleasant hours writing epitaphs for an old suit of clothes, a seven-years'-old felt hat, an old pipe, pair of shoes, a threadbare suit, frayed sweater, a textbook at the end of a not-too-enjoyable course, even a report card. It is a part of human nature to want to keep those personal articles that are dear to us regardless of appearances. This trait often causes humiliation to the more meticulous members of the family. Give the article a decent burial and honor it with a suitable epitaph.

Beginners may also enjoy writing humorous epitaphs for themselves and their friends.

Hilaire Belloc has done some sharp epigrams. Edwin Arlington Robinson has turned some famous epigrams into neat English verse. See "Variations of Greek Themes" in *Captain Craig* or *Collected Poems*. See also Thomas Hardy's *Collected Poems*.

NOVICES' ATTEMPTS

An Epitaph

(Dedicated to a man who died of thirst in the desert)

Death for you was eiderdown of rest,
Freedom from the clutching grasp of pain,
Who traveled wastes of sand in unknown quest,
Forgetting, as many will again,
An empty water bag will make
A trip in vain, no matter for what sake.

—GEORGE CHAMALIAN

Harriet Ames

Born 1834   *Died 1933*

She made Death wait at the garden gate;
As usual Miss Ames was late.

—MARY GRANT

Laura Ann Phillips

She soothed men's hearts and dried their tears
And walked alone through all her years.

—JUNE CURLEY

Beneath this sodden ground lies one
Who could not end an epitaph;
She wailed and shrieked and went to death
Still looking for the other half.

—ROSE ANN MURRAY

Miser

He kept for his own joy all things of any worth,
But now at last he gives himself to the rich earth.

—JOEL KENDLER

For a Flag-Waving Business Man

Within the ashes of this pot
Lies a well-paid patriot.

—HENRY STEPHENS

CHAPTER XXXIV

APPROACHING THROUGH THE THEME

EVERY poem has a thread of thought running through it. All the images and ornaments of the poem are strung upon it. Here is a package of assorted beads, varying in size, shape, texture, color. Each is a bead and nothing more. Select a few of them, grade them, slide them on to a waxed string and you have a necklace. It is the string running through, which transforms a handful of isolated stones into a thing of beauty for some fair neck. The string is invisible; no one is aware of it. Let the string break, and your necklace is gone. Beads you may still have, brilliant and sharply cut, but no necklace.

The waxed string is the invisible theme. The beads are the images. Not until they are properly placed along the theme do they become a poem.

For heavy rough-cut beads a stout thread is needed; a finer one will do for stringing the fragile beads. Certain threads are so durable that they may be used again and again: when you no longer enjoy the beads the thread will form the foundation for another string. The necklace will be new and lovely for the new beads though the thread is an old one.

Just how a poem begins no one can say. Perhaps no two poets begin in the same way. Sometimes, we are told, the insistent beat of the rhythm in the heart suggests the song; a fancy, a fragrance, a sound may be the beginning of an exquisite lyric. A line may sing in the brain, giving the creator no peace until he has set it down as a climax. In his *Philosophy of Composition* Poe explains how he consciously created "The Raven." We know what stimulated Keats to write "The Ode on a Grecian Urn" and "On First Looking Into Chapman's Homer." Out of one work of art, a Greek frieze, an Elizabethan translation of Homer, grew another: in the one case an ode, in the other a sonnet. Whatever the mystery of creation, in the works of great poets certain themes recur again and again. It seems to be in the nature of those who have the urge for poetic expression to brood on certain aspects of life, certain human experiences. In different ages they use different materials to develop these themes, or they consider the theme from different viewpoints. We often hear it said that there is nothing new to write about. This means that the basic truths of life and the fundamental experiences of humanity are the same in the beginning, now, and forever. It is the manner not the matter that changes. Robert

Frost uses farm materials, the experience of mending a wall between an apple orchard and a pine orchard, to develop the thought that men should think for themselves and not become the slaves of tradition; Carl Sandburg gives voice to the same wisdom through a piece of steel which would pry loose old foundations and become a nail in a skyscraper.

The young aspirant will do well to give himself the experience of approaching the construction of a poem through a theme. He will find it stimulating to take a thought which all men ponder at some time or other, turn it over in his mind, and see what comes of it. The outer structure will give it new life. His own way of looking at it will give it freshness.

A thought to the theme of the poem is valuable, perhaps most valuable, in another way. When a poem is done, the theme is an admirable instrument for measuring the unity of the poem. Perhaps one beautiful image is not in keeping with the theme. It may be irrelevant to the purpose,—and where is the purpose to be felt if not through the theme? The theme will show it up; it will have to go.

When you are developing your poem, reference to a theme will often show up disjointed members that should be smoothed out, explained, or discarded. One student in a verse writing class loved images so well that she would pile them up one on another without heed to the thread of thought that should bind them. This was a good fault in a beginner. It showed a fertile mind. But it was a fault which had to be corrected before any poem of hers would make a single impression. A wobbly theme gives the effect of cross eyes. So she used to write out her theme and refer to it many times in the course of revision, deleting regretfully and substituting suitable matter in the gaps. There was *no* other way to keep from getting lost in the labyrinth of her many ideas. Having slain the Minotaur, she was able, with her finger on the thread of her theme, to guide herself Theseus-like through the maze.

Extraneous matter, which does not point to the effect you desire to convey, may be saved for glorious use another time. A notebook is a safe deposit vault of inestimable security.

Thought to the theme will do something toward appreciation and understanding of poetry other than your own. If you can grasp the underlying thought of a difficult poem you may find it quite simple to interpret the surface details that obscure the inner meaning. It is like the friends we understand. Understanding them, we know they could not have meant this, or they certainly would not do that. Sometimes it is not too easy to reduce a theme to words, but in every poem worth anything a theme of some sort is present, as the spinal column is present in the co-ordinating body of healthy men.

Below are some poems showing various treatments of the same theme by different poets. When you have read these perhaps you will feel inclined to select one of the universal themes and give it new beauty through your treatment.

The strange experience of death is one that has interested poets from time immemorial. In death the concerns of life have no significance.

Dirge

Never the nightingale,
Oh, my dear,
Never again the lark
Thou wilt hear;
Though dusk and the morning still
Tap at thy window-sill,
Though love ever call and call
Thou wilt not hear at all,
My dear. my dear.

—ADELAIDE CRAPSEY

Unhearing

Shut softly in a stilly world,
Her days have fallen without sound,
Late roses dropped upon the ground.

Her childlike hair is lightly curled;
Her eyes are starry, still and deep
As Summer waters in their sleep.

Serenely beautiful and kind,
She smiles out from her separate star,
Where only quiet people are.

The widening casements of her mind
Swing outward to the morning's glow;
She hears the secrets of the snow.

The utter stillness draws more near;
The muted hours about her close.
She wears the silence as a rose.

She hears the things we may not hear.
A far wind stirs the sleeping strings;
Deaf to one world, another sings.

—ADA ALDEN

"Regret Not Me"

Regret not me;
 Beneath the sunny tree
I lie uncaring, slumbering peacefully.

 Swift as the light
 I flew my faery flight;
Ecstatically I moved, and feared no night.

 I did not know
 That heydays fade and go,
But deemed that what was would be always so.

 I skipped at morn
 Between the yellowing corn,
Thinking it good and glorious to be born.

 I ran at eves
 Among the piled-up sheaves,
Dreaming, "I grieve not, therefore nothing grieves."

 Now soon will come
 The apple, pear, and plum,
And hinds will sing, and autumn insects hum.

 Again you will fare
 To cider-makings rare,
And junketings; but I shall not be there.

 Yet gaily sing
 Until the pewter ring
Those songs we sang when we went gipsying.

 And lightly dance
 Some triple-timed romance
In coupled figures, and forget mischance;

 And mourn not me
 Beneath the yellowing tree;
For I shall mind not, slumbering peacefully.

—THOMAS HARDY

Legend

As you would speak of flowers, speak so of her;
　For she was young and lovely and adored,
Too frail a chalice, brimming and astir
　Where time's long sweets and wonderments were poured.
So say no names at all of flesh and blood,
　And tell no tale of sickness or distress,—
Only how light and colour's turbulent flood
　Was here a poised and captive loveliness.

And let there be a legend in this place,
　Of one who came . . . and passed . . . and was no more
Than a remembered fragrance and a face,
　A flower-like body swaying through a door
That closed forever on one radiant hour,
Whose passing was the passing of a flower.

　　　　　　　　　　　　　—David Morton

Requiescat

　　　Tread lightly, she is near
　　　　　Under the snow,
　　　Speak gently, she can hear
　　　　　The daisies grow.

　　　All her bright golden hair
　　　　　Tarnished with rust,
　　　She that was young and fair
　　　　　Fallen to dust.

　　　Lily-like, white as snow,
　　　　　She hardly knew
　　　She was a woman, so
　　　　　Sweetly she grew.

　　　Coffin-board, heavy stone,
　　　　　Lie on her breast;
　　　I vex my heart alone,
　　　　　She is at rest.

　　　Peace, peace; she cannot hear
　　　　　Lyre or sonnet;
　　　All my life's buried here,
　　　　　Heap earth upon it.

　　　　　　　　　　　　　—Oscar Wilde

To an Athlete Dying Young

The time you won your town the race
We chaired you through the market-place;
Man and boy stood cheering by,
And home we brought you shoulder-high.

Today, the road all runners come,
Shoulder-high we bring you home,
And set you at your threshold down,
Townsman of a stiller town.

Smart lad, to slip betimes away
From fields where glory does not stay,
And early though the laurel grows,
It withers quicker than the rose.

Eyes the shady night has shut
Cannot see the record cut,
And silence sounds no worse than cheers
After earth has stopped the ears:

Now you will not swell the rout
Of lads that wore their honours out,
Runners whom renown outran
And the name died before the man.

So set, before its echoes fade,
The fleet foot on the sill of shade,
And hold to the low lintel up
The still-defended challenge-cup.

And round that early-laurelled head
Will flock to gaze the strengthless dead,
And find unwithered on its curls
The garland briefer than a girl's.

—A. E. Housman

There are many variations of the theme death. One deals with death as a mighty leveler. It is no respecter of rank, riches, or talents.

On the Tombs in Westminster Abbey

Mortality, behold and fear
What a change of flesh is here!
Think how many royal bones
Sleep within these heaps of stones;
Here they lie, had realms and lands,
Who now want strength to stir their hands,
Where from their pulpits seal'd with dust
They preach, "In greatness is no trust."
Here's an acre sown indeed
With the richest royallest seed
That the earth did e'er suck in
Since the first man died for sin:
Here the bones of birth have cried
"Though gods they were, as men they died!"
Here are sands, ignoble things,
Dropt from the ruin'd sides of kings:
Here's a world of pomp and state
Buried in dust, once dead by fate.

—FRANCIS BEAUMONT

Of Death

The glories of our blood and state
  Are shadows, not substantial things;
There is no armour against fate;
  Death lays his icy hand on kings:
    Sceptre and crown
    Must tumble down,
And in the dust be equal made
With the poor crooked scythe and spade.

Some men with swords may reap the field,
  And plant fresh laurels where they kill;
But their strong nerves at last must yield;
  They tame but one another still:
    Early or late,
    They stoop to fate,
And must give up their murmuring breath,
When they, pale captives, creep to death.

The garlands wither on your brow,
   Then boast no more your mighty deeds;
Upon Death's purple altar now,
   See where the victor-victim bleeds:
     Your heads must come
     To the cold tomb;
Only the actions of the just
Smell sweet and blossom in their dust.

                  —JAMES SHIRLEY

Novices will probably not attempt to write a poem as long as "Elegy Written in a Country Churchyard" by Thomas Gray, but they will surely want to be familiar with it. It may be found in the works of Gray, in Palgrave's *Golden Treasury,* and in *The Oxford Book of English Verse.* It is read more widely perhaps than any poem in the English language.

When the Lord said, "Let there be light," He probably felt the shock of pleased surprise at realizing light. "And there was light." However eagerly we look forward to the coming of spring we are surprised at the first bursting of a bud, the first flowering tree after the long snow, just as though we had not known spring before. No amount of preparation for the death of a loved one will steel the anxious watchers to the actual coming of death. No amount of anticipating will quite destroy the shock of actual realization of life's happy little moments. Surprise is an ancient theme. In a thirteenth century song, one of our earliest lyrics, this theme is made articulate.

Cuckoo Song

Sumer is icumen in,
   Lhude sing cuccu!   *lhude = loud*
Groweth sed, and bloweth med,
   And springth the wude nu—
         Sing cuccu!

Awe bleteth after lomb,   *awe = ewe*
   Lhouth after calve cu;   *lhouth = loweth*
Bulluc sterteth, bucke verteth,   *sterteth = leaps*
   Murie sing cuccu!

Cuccu, cuccu, well singes thu, cuccu:
   Ne swike thu naver nu;   *swike = cease*
Sing cuccu, nu, sing cuccu,
   Sing cuccu, sing cuccu, nu!

Today surprise is sung as of old:

And Now These Jonquils

By night there came a clearing in the sky,
  And soft airs blowing since the rain was done,
Hushed in the dark, a warm, wet wind went by
  And—now, these jonquils shining in the sun!
Some secret, hurried rendezvous was held,
  Of hidden seed and airs in quest of mirth,
Some happy, hushed conspiracy that spelled
  This glittering line of laughter for the earth.

Who was aware of beauty in the night,
  Of blossom-breaking muffled through the dark,
Or any glimmering shafts of yellow light?—
  Too secret and too hushed for us to mark,
Up from the South a warm, wet wind had strayed,
And—now these jonquils, joyously arrayed!
                                   —David Morton

Is This the Lark?

Is this the lark
  Lord Shakespeare heard
Out of the dark
  Of dawn? Is this the bird
  That stirred
Lord Shakespeare's heart?

Is this the bird whose wing,
Whose rapturous antheming,
Rose up, soared radiant, became
Sharp flame
To Shelley listening
And made him sing,
Throbbing alone, aloof, fervently apart,
His profuse strains of unpremeditated art?

To think that I should hear him now
  Telling that single fiery rift of heaven a wild lark comes! . . .
The fresh cool scent of earth yearns at the plough;
  In short keen rapid flurries the woodpecker drums . . .
To think that I should hear that mad thing sliding
  Along a smoking opal ladder!

Hear the inevitable deluge of music riding
  Into the sun, richer now—fainter now—madder!
To think that I should hear and know
  The song that Shelley heard, and Shakespeare, long ago!
                                        —JOSEPH AUSLANDER

In the light of this chapter read again "On First Looking Into Chapman's Homer."

The evanescence of things has long concerned the poet.

Nothing Gold Can Stay

Nature's first green is gold,
Her hardest hue to hold.
Her early leaf's a flower;
But only so an hour.
Then leaf subsides to leaf.
So Eden sank to grief,
So dawn goes down to day.
Nothing gold can stay.

                                        —ROBERT FROST

To Daffodils

Fair daffodils, we weep to see
  You haste away so soon:
As yet the early-rising sun
  Has not attain'd his noon.
    Stay, stay,
  Until the hasting day
    Has run
  But to the even-song;
And, having prayed together, we
  Will go with you along.

We have short time to stay, as you,
  We have as short a spring;
As quick a growth to meet decay
  As you, or anything.
    We die,
  As your hours do, and dry
    Away
  Like to the summer's rain;
Or as the pearls of morning's dew
  Ne'er to be found again.
                    —ROBERT HERRICK

To the Virgins, To Make Much of Time

Gather ye rose-buds while ye may,
  Old Time is still a-flying:
And this same flower that smiles to-day,
  To-morrow will be dying.

The glorious lamp of heaven, the sun,
  The higher he's a-getting,
The sooner will his race be run,
  And nearer he's to setting.

That age is best which is the first,
  When youth and blood are warmer;
But being spent, the worse, and worst
  Times, still succeed the former.

Then be not coy, but use your time;
  And while ye may, go marry:
For having lost but once your prime,
  You may for ever tarry.
                    —ROBERT HERRICK

Here is a more modern view of evanescence:

If Robert Herrick Had Been Dorothy Parker

Gather your roses while you may,
  Old time is on the go;
And the same sweet bud that smiles to-day
  To-morrow dies, you know.

The time is best which is the first,
  When love is warm and bold;
Your figure, skin and charm are worst
  With age, when love is cold.

Then be not coy; get hot to-day
  Else you may ever tarry,
And gather your roses while you may—
  If you can't get Tom, take Harry.

—ERIC DIVINE
in "The Conning Tower" of the New York *World*

The brevity of human life is a theme often sung.

Sonnet

When I have fears that I may cease to be
Before my pen has gleaned my teeming brain,
Before high-pilèd books, in charact'ry,
Hold like rich garners the full ripened grain;
When I behold, upon the night's starred face,
Huge cloudy symbols of a high romance,
And think that I may never live to trace
Their shadows, with the magic hand of chance;
And when I feel, fair creature of an hour,
That I shall never look upon thee more,
Never have relish in the faery power
Of unreflecting love;—then on the shore
Of the wide world I stand alone, and think
Till love and fame to nothingness do sink.

—JOHN KEATS

Now turn to page 88 and read Shakespeare's immortal lines, "Our revels now are ended. . . ."

Moths

Where is it that these frail adventurers go
  That veer so lightly, with so brave a will,
So delicate and strange, that tremble so,
  For all the dusk is windless, now, and still . . . ?
Where is there left, in crashing worlds whose wake
  Is strewn with shards of kingdoms shocked and tossed,
A place for things so frail as well might break
  Their wings against a twilight, and be lost . . . ?

What kings of earth, no longer now renowned,
  Have gazed at dusk, beyond such shapes as these,
To shadowy empires whence their arms were bound,
  Blind to white moths gone straying through the trees,
Nor thought how all the kingdoms they might cull
Were brief as these—and not so beautiful!

—DAVID MORTON

The mystery of inheritance is one to challenge wonder.

Ancestral

Once on this porch a woman, with my name,
Tied up her morning-glories to the wall,
Smiled on her trumpet-vines' perennial flame,
And plied her trowel where the weeds were tall.

No living eye remembers how her hand
Fastened the fallen tendril to its twine.
But in her portrait, from a ruffled band,
Emerges still the replica of mine.

No living heart remembers how she smiled
With lowered lashes like my youngest child.

—JESSICA NELSON NORTH

The old order changeth giving place to new.

A Roman Road

A road shines through the forest of the years
  Where on swift wings the gods come charioted
  By sun and moon, until the earth is red
With Mars' mailed host and Woden's bleeding spears;
But down the burning wood of lonely fears
  A fair White God goes by with noiseless tread,
  The Thorns of Fire are stars that wreathe His Head,
And in His Heart is pity for men's tears.

The flaming Michael holds the haunted tor,
  And from the wildwood steals the thin sweet chime
    Of evening bells at monastery gates;
All silent now—the gods return no more,
  Yet buried deep beneath the drift of time
    The ruined roadway still endures and waits.

—Thomas S. Jones, Jr.

A Sea Dirge

Full fathom five thy father lies:
    Of his bones are coral made;
Those are pearls that were his eyes:
    Nothing of him that doth fade,
But doth suffer a sea-change
Into something rich and strange.
Sea-nymphs hourly ring his knell:
    Hark! now I hear them,—
    Ding, dong, bell.

—William Shakespeare

The epitaph on Shelley's grave is composed of lines 4 and 5. He was drowned, you remember.

Art will live when man and his institutions have passed into oblivion—the spiritual things endure beyond the material.

Ozymandias of Egypt

I met a traveller from an antique land
Who said: Two vast and trunkless legs of stone
Stand in the desert. Near them on the sand,
Half sunk, a shatter'd visage lies, whose frown
And wrinkled lip and sneer of cold command
Tell that its sculptor well those passions read
Which yet survive, stamp'd on these lifeless things,
The hand that mock'd them and the heart that fed;
And on the pedestal these words appear:
"My name is Ozymandias, king of kings:
Look on my work, ye Mighty, and despair!"
Nothing beside remains. Round the decay
Of that colossal wreck, boundless and bare,
The lone and level sands stretch far away.

—PERCY BYSSHE SHELLEY

The great cycle—life and death and life again—is another theme that poets brood on.

As a Star from the Dust

There is neither beginning nor end;
   No one is late or early.
   The mists of the dawn are pearly,
Pearly the moonlit night.

The first spring flowers that blow
   Are the fluttery white
Of the earliest flakes of snow.

The way we go is not clear,
   Nor clear the way we came;
Yet there is nothing to fear,—
   We, born of the ash and the flame,
Eaten by moth and rust,
Shall rise as a star from the dust.

—ADA ALDEN

Crystal Moment

Once or twice this side of death
Things can make one hold his breath.

From my boyhood I remember
A crystal moment of September.

A wooded island rang with sounds
Of church bells in the throats of hounds.

A buck leaped out and took the tide
With jewels floating past each side.

With his high head like a tree,
He swam within a yard of me.

I saw a golden drop of light
In his eyes turned dark with fright.

I saw the forest's holiness
On him like a fierce caress.

Fear made him lovely past belief;
My heart was trembling like a leaf.

He leaned towards the land and life
With need above him like a knife.

In his wake the hot hounds churned;
They stretched their muzzles out and yearned.

They cried no more, swam and throbbed;
Hunger drove them until they sobbed.

Pursued, pursuers reached the shore
And vanished. I saw nothing more.

So they passed, a pageant such
As only gods could witness much;

Life and death upon one tether
And running beautiful together.

—ROBERT P. TRISTRAM COFFIN

Man is ever the seeker, never finding what he seeks.

The Voyager

Columbus-like, I sailed into the night,
   The sunset gold to find:
Alas! 'twas but the phantom of the light!
   Life's Indies lay behind!

                  —JOHN B. TABB

Love has ever been a favorite theme with poets. Shakespeare wrote a sequence of one hundred fifty-four sonnets on this theme and he had this to say in defense of never varying it:

Why is my verse so barren of new pride,
So far from variation or quick change?
Why with the time do I not glance aside
To new-found methods and to compounds strange?
Why write I still all one, ever the same,
And keep invention in a noted weed,
That every word doth almost tell my name,
Showing their birth and where they did proceed?
O, know, sweet love, I always write of you,
And you and love are still my argument;
So all my best is dressing old words and new,
Spending again what is already spent:
For as the sun is daily new and old,
So is my love still telling what is told.

He sings of the constancy of love.

CXVI

Let me not to the marriage of true minds
Admit impediments. Love is not love
Which alters when it alteration finds,
Or bends with the remover to remove.
O, no! it is an ever-fixèd mark
That looks on tempests and is never shaken;
It is the star to every wandering bark,
Whose worth's unknown, although his height be taken.
Love's not Time's fool, though rosy lips and cheeks
Within his bending sickle's compass come;
Love alters not with his brief hours and weeks,
But bears it out even to the edge of doom.
   If this be error and upon me prov'd,
   I never writ, nor no man ever lov'd.

Edna St. Vincent Millay laughs at love's inconstancy:

> I shall forget you presently, my dear.

There are many variations of the theme. Here is one by George Dillon that captures the very freshness of youth in love with life and living.

April's Amazing Meaning

April's amazing meaning doubtless lies
   In tall hoarse boys, and slips
Of slender girls with suddenly wider eyes
   And parted lips.

For girls must wander pensive in the spring
   When the green rain is over,
Doing some slow inconsequential thing,
   Plucking clover.

And any boy alone upon a bench
   When his work's done will sit
And stare at the black ground, and break a branch
   And whittle it

Slowly; and boys and girls, irresolute,
   Will curse the dreamy weather
Until they meet past the pale hedge and put
   Their lips together.

The great social problems that have arisen with the evolution of our modern world suggest vital themes: the conflicts of self with self, man with man, nation with nation. Here are two poems that treat social problems:

The Man with the Hoe

Written after seeing Millet's world-famous painting of a brutalized toiler in the deep abyss of labor.

> God made man in His own image:
> in the image of God He made him.—Genesis.

Bowed by the weight of centuries he leans
Upon his hoe and gazes on the ground,
The emptiness of ages in his face,
And on his back the burden of the world.
Who made him dead to rapture and despair,
A thing that grieves not and that never hopes,

Stolid and stunned, a brother to the ox?
Who loosened and let down this brutal jaw?
Whose was the hand that slanted back this brow?
Whose breath blew out the light within this brain?

Is this the Thing the Lord God made and gave
To have dominion over sea and land;
To trace the stars and search the heavens for power;
To feel the passion of Eternity?
Is this the dream He dreamed who shaped the suns
And markt their ways upon the ancient deep?
Down all the caverns of Hell to their last gulf
There is no shape more terrible than this—
More tongued with cries against the world's blind greed—
More filled with signs and portents for the soul—
More packt with danger to the universe.

What gulfs between him and the seraphim!
Slave of the wheel of labor, what to him
Are Plato and the swing of Pleiades?
What the long reaches of the peaks of song,
The rift of dawn, the reddening of the rose?
Thru this dread shape the suffering ages look;
Time's tragedy is in that aching stoop;
Thru this dread shape humanity betrayed,
Plundered, profaned and disinherited,
Cries protest to the Powers that made the world,
A protest that is also prophecy.

O masters, lords and rulers in all lands,
Is this the handiwork you give to God,
This monstrous thing distorted and soul-quencht?
How will you ever straighten up this shape;
Touch it again with immortality;
Give back the upward looking and the light;
Rebuild in it the music and the dream;
Make right the immemorial infamies,
Perfidious wrongs, immedicable woes?

O masters, lords and rulers in all lands,
How will the future reckon with this Man?
How answer his brute question in that hour
When whirlwinds of rebellion shake all shores?
How will it be with kingdoms and with kings—
With those who shaped him to the thing he is—
When this dumb Terror shall rise to judge the world,
After the silence of the centuries?

—EDWIN MARKHAM

Steel

This man is dead.
Everything you can say
Is now quite definitely said:
This man held up his head
And had his day,
Then turned his head a little to one way
And slept instead.

Young horses give up their pride:
You break them in
By brief metallic discipline
And something else beside. . . .
So this man died.

While he lived I did not know
This man; I never heard
His name. Now that he lies as though
He was remembering some word
He had forgotten yesterday or so,
It seems a bit absurd
That his blank lids and matted hair should grow
Suddenly familiar. . . . Let him be interred.

Steady now. . . . That was his wife
Making that small queer inarticulate sound
Like a knife;
Steady there. . . . Let him slip easy into the ground;
Do not look at her,
She is fighting for breath. . . .
She is a foreigner . . .
Polak . . . like him . . . she cannot understand . . .
It is hard . . . leave her alone with death
And a shovelful of sand.

"O the pity of it, the pity of it, Iago!" . . .
Christ, what a hell
Is packed into that line! Each syllable
Bleeds when you say it. . . . No matter: Chicago
Is a far cry from Cracow;
And anyhow
What have Poles
To do with such extraneous things as hearts and souls?

There is nothing here to beat the breast over,
Nothing to relish the curious,

Not a smell of the romantic; this fellow
Was hardly your yearning lover
Frustrated; no punchinello;
But just a hunky in a steel mill. Why then fuss
Because his heavy Slavic face went yellow
With the roaring furnace dust? Now that he is in
The cool sweet crush of dirt, to hell with your sobbing violin,
Your sanctimonious cello!
Let the mill bellow!

If you have ever had to do with steel:
The open-hearth, the blooming-mill, the cranes
Howling under a fifty-ton load, trains
Yowling in the black pits where you reel
Groggily across the sluice of orange fire, a sheet
Tongued from the conduits that bubble blue green; if
Ever you have got a single whiff
Out of the Bessemer's belly, felt the drag
And drip and curdle of steel spit hissing against hot slag;
If ever you have had to eat
One hundred and thirty degrees of solid heat,
Then screwed the hose to the spigot, drowned in steam,
Darted back when the rods kicked up a stream
Of fluid steel and had to duck the ladle that slobbered over, and scream
Your throat raw to get your "Goddam!" through—
Then I am talking to you.

Steve did that for ten years with quiet eyes
And body down to the belt caked wet
With hardening cinder splash and stiffening sweat
And whatever else there is that clots and never utterly dries;
He packed the mud and dolomite, made back-wall,
Herded the heat, and placed his throw in tall
Terrible arcs behind smoked glasses, and watched it fall
Heavy and straight and true,
While the blower kept the gas at a growl and the brew
Yelled red and the melter hollered "Heow!" and you raveled
Her out and the thick soup gargled and you traveled
Like the devil to get out from under. . . . Well, Steve
For ten years of abdominal heft and heave
Worked steel. So much for that. And after
Ten years of night shifts, fourteen hours each,
The Bessemers burn your nerves up, bleach
Rebellion out of your bones; and laughter
Sucked clean out of your guts becomes
More dead than yesterday's feet moving to yesterday's drums. . . .
And so they called him "Dummy." The whole gang
From pit boss down to the last mud-slinger cursed
And squirted tobacco juice in a hot and mixed harangue

Of Slovene, Serb, Dutch, Dago, Russian, and—worst—
English as hard and toothless as a skull.
And Steve stared straight ahead of him and his eyes were dull.

Anna was Steve's little woman
Who labored bitterly enough
Making children of stern and tragic stuff
And a rapture that was hammered rough,
Spilling steel into their spines, yet keeping them wistful and human. . . .
Anna had her work to do
With cooking and cleaning
And washing the window curtains white as new,
Washing them till they wore through:
For her the white curtains had a meaning—
And starching them white against the savage will
Of the grim dust belching incessantly out of the mill;
Soaking and scrubbing and ironing against that gritty reek
Until her head swam and her knees went weak
And she could hardly speak—
A terrible unbeaten purpose persisted:
Colour crying against a colourless world!
White against black at the windows flung up, unfurled!
Candles and candle light!
The flags of a lonely little woman twisted
Out of her hunger for cool clean beauty, her hunger for white!—
These were her banners and this was her fight!

No matter how tired she was, however she would ache
In every nerve, she must boil the meat and bake
The bread—and the curtains must go up white for Steve's sake!
One thing was certain:
That John and Stanley and Helen and Mary and the baby Steven
Must be kept out of the mills and the mill life, even
If it meant her man and she would break
Under the brunt of it: she had talked it through with him
A hundred times. . . . Let her eyeballs split, her head swim—
The window must have its curtains!

Lately Steve had stopped talking altogether
When he slumped in with his dinner pail and heavily
Hunched over his food—
So Anna and the children let him be;
She was afraid to ask him any why or whether
As he sat with his eyes glued
On vacancy—
So Anna and the children let him brood.
Only sometimes he would suddenly look at them and her
In a ghastly fixed blur
Till a vast nausea of terror and compassion stood

Blundering in her throat and swarming in her blood—
And she shivered and knew somehow that it was not good.

And then it happened: Spring had come
Like the silver needle-note of a fife,
Like a white plume and a green lance and a glittering knife
And a jubilant drum.
But Steve did not hear the earth hum:
Under the earth he could feel merely the fever
And the shock of roots of steel forever;
April had no business with the pit
Or the people—call them people—who breathed in it.

And then it happened: nobody could tell whose
Fault it was, but a torrent of steel broke loose,
Trapped twenty men in the hot frothy mess. . . .
After a week, more or less,
The company, with appropriate finesse,
Having allowed the families time to move,
Expressed a swift proprietary love
By shoving the dump of metal and flesh and shoes
And cotton and cloth and felt
Back into the furnace to remelt.

And that was all, though a dispatch so neat,
So wholly admirable, so totally sweet,
Could not but stick in Steve's dulled brain:
And whether it was the stink or the noise or just plain
Inertia combined with heat,
Steve, one forenoon, on stark deliberate feet,
Let the charging machine's long iron finger beat
The side of his skull in. . . . There was no pain.

For one fierce instant of unconsciousness
Steve tasted the incalculable caress;
For one entire day he slept between
Sheets that were white and cool, embalmed and clean;
For twenty-four hours he touched the hair of death,
Ran his fingers through it, and it was a deep dark green—
And he held his breath.

This man is dead.
Everything you can say
Is now quite definitely said.

                                        —JOSEPH AUSLANDER

Students developed the following poems from themes which they brooded on and discussed. Some of them embody the themes illustrated above.

Black Rock

Here the mountain curves fade back and back
Until I cannot tell them from the sky.
The golden valley, swinging far below,
Has such a calm immensity that I
Am rested. Here the tired pine trees tow

The lazy forest up a slant of hill
And the sun is running sluggish rivers down
The cliff. There is some reason here for life.
This splendor, spreading from the mountain's crown,
Has made my soul forget the city strife.

When I am in the city, mockery
Is all I find in scattered squares of sky.
And as I crawl in tunnels there, my soul
Is crowded down and down in me. I
Become as blind as the ever night-eyed mole.

I listen to the wild metallic roar
Of screeching rails and grating parts of steel
That clank and grind each other, endlessly
Pounding a cynic's song until I feel
Harsh discord is the only harmony.

I learn why men are crowded to their work
And daily weave the thread into their shrouds
As they go welding, with a torch of pain,
The joints that hold the girders in the clouds;
The basic principles I can explain.

But here, upon the cooling crevassed rock,
As the smoky dusk turns softly into night,
I can look up, and take my being out,
Send it rising toward some far star's light
And watch it mounting till it loses doubt,

Traveling in and up the universe . . .
The sudden finding of this massive world
Has loosed in me bewildered, awed surprise;—
And now I feel how lavish beauty, hurled
Upon these giant hills, can sympathize.

I search the round horizon for the why.
I search the valley, tiny farms and fields,
The pasture lands, the mountain's tree-grown side,
But nowhere is there any sign that yields
The mystery these nature wonders hide.

. . . . .

I know that all this has for me
Some message from eternity.
Am I too small, too small to see?

—WILLIAM ROEHRICK

Harvest

Noon

A slash of sunlight fell upon the slope
    Sidewise, like Ceres' fingertip, to point
A prophecy of golden wheat, a hope
    Of harvest plenty. Patternlike, a joint

Of sunray fell where rows of seeds made lines
    Even and bright upon the hill. . . . He stood
Alone to view that fertile plain; the signs
    Of that year's crop, he saw, and found it good.

Then wandering down into the valley, passed
    His favorite poplar, passed the shed, discerned
That nearly every foot was sown, at last
    Arriving at one bit of field unturned.

He absently bent down and sifted soil
    To heal the gashes where the seed lay bare.
The sunlight slithered on that place where toil
    Had filled the plain with promises and prayer.

Night

The storm had crept upon the shrinking plain
    And bitten it with teeth of wind and fire,
Clawed and broken it, inflicted pain
    On all the land, strewn sedge and briar.

From each dim edge of valley to the hill,
    The tempest raged for one short night, then brush
And weeds in scrawny heap on heap stretched still
    And gray in utter desolation. Hush

And death lay on the storm-torn harvest field.
  Beside a stricken poplar tree, as gray
And torn as all this waste before him, kneeled
  A man, wide shoulders bent. The very way

He propped his form against the mangled tree
  Was pain. Four months before, he had stopped to lean
Against the poplar, finding it hard to see
  How anything could change that peaceful green.

Morning

The spring, that year, came soon and held good rain
  And wheat-field sun. The planting went ahead
With care and promise. The farmer sowed his grain
  And walked his field once more with hopeful tread.

                        —JOYCE LANCASTER

Field Plowing

I can plow upon the hill
Where the pines and birches stand;
I can hold the reins in hand
Though the valley, green and still,
Stretches from the mountain slope
Like a sagging crazy quilt.
White anemones may tilt
With the wind where shadows grope;
Dogwood blossom on the bough;
Still my hand is on the plow.
But when I am in the field
That runs along beside the stream,
And the shivering grasses gleam
With spray, then I must surely yield
My plow, and set the horses free;
For as I sing the field is gone.
Exotic visions, misty-born,
Rise around, enchanting me,
And I must answer to the call
That rumbles in the water-fall.

                        —WILLIAM ROEHRICK

In Grantan Wood

Why brood on death? You fill my searching mind,
My living heart with rebel disbelief.
I do not look with scorn upon your grief;
I only turn my steps away to find

Another road, where verdantly alive,
The infant grass defies the charred remains
Of autumn burning down; where steady rains
Have called the eager farmer out to drive

The plow in even stripes across the land
And make a widening pattern of the ranch.
The old leaf falls, pressed from the branch
By new green shoots. Far downward on the sand

There lies a bit of feathered tragedy:
A mother thrush, still warm, beneath her nest.
But in it, loud-billed, vital young are pressed
Close, side by side, and anxious to be free.

It is so small a part of all this breath,
This constancy in growth, this birth that sings
Of life revolving in and with these things
And all the earth. . . . Why do you brood on death?

—JOYCE LANCASTER

Confession

If hunger had not been so fierce in me,
And if my arms had ached a trifle less;
If I had known that you were mine to take
And waited for my sign in eagerness,
I'd not be looking wistful now,
Alive to catch your merest casual glance,
And, catching it, to tremble from sweet ache,
And cherish in my heart what any chance
Acquaintance might be showered with;
I'd not be seeing in this book
Your face, aloof, upon the printed words,
Your eyes that peck my heart like birds.

—GERTRUDE JOAN BUCKMAN

Monody

These I'll be missing
When I am old:
Lips warm for kissing
And a youth all gold;

Slim trees grown tender
In the dusk of Spring;
And a river, slender
As a silver string;

A frog's hoarse calling
Down a mossy lane,
And the dim, blue falling
Of an April rain,

Bold tulips growing
 (Molten cups of fire) ,
And the wind blowing
Round a tall church spire;

The silver tune
Of a young brook's chant,
And a saffron moon
In the sky aslant;

The crimson glow
Of the day's ending,
And the silent snow
Like stars descending;

The fog's cool fingers
On my tired eyes,
And the note that lingers
When a wild bird cries;

The strong sea heaving
In a mighty gale,
And willows grieving
Near an amber trail:

These I'll be missing
When Youth has fled—
But Death I'll be kissing
In his narrow bed.

—Rubye Mae Fisher

Song

Oh, I was young and proud and free
When Love in homespun came to me.

'Twas then I scorned the offered bread
And wanted angel cake instead.

My giddy head was filled with tales
Of shining swords and dragon scales,

Of princesses and milk-white steeds
And tournaments or noble deeds;

Forgotten was the simple joy
Of shepherd lass and shepherd boy;

I had not been the same girl since
The goosegirl met the youngest prince

And married him. My hope soared high
Until the king's son passed me by.

Now I am young and free. Today
I'll go a-hunting Love, to say

 (But not too eagerly, I trust) ,
"Oh, may I taste your golden crust?"
—Estelle Rooks

A very few lines may embody a profound theme. Like many poets before her, the author of "Nile" is impressed by nature's coldness to man's brief day of power.

Nile

The silent river flows along
As though no Pharaoh ever stood
Upon its shore, as though it had
Not heard a Cleopatra's song.
—Carol Stein

Tryst

Until tonight I have not flown so high
Nor soared so free for many earthy days.
Until chance wind swung me upon a star
I think I had forgotten all the ways

Of whirling off the earth a league or so—
Or far enough at least above the mist,
The dark, the cold, to see myself and you.
But now at last I keep belated tryst

With truth, and I am half afraid: I can
Reach out and lay my fingertip on all
The basic whys of earth since chaos was,
For truth and I myself have grown so tall

That I can see our love and can explain.
I am a wingèd seeker of each thing
Of beauty that the world and life create.
Below, the flaring dogwood blossoms sing

My heart a rhapsody in white. . . . And just
Last night a light-clad moonbeam shyly came
Across the sill to weave a pattern dance
With young leaf shadows near the window frame.

I lay and watched them till my eyelids burned. . . .
Today I found austerity: the strong
Sure curve that is the bridge stirred me, for I
Could feel a parted force bound by one long

Thin thread of power. . . . Far, far, beyond the edge
Of city rhythm is a cliff-bound shore
Where maddened breakers scream, and laugh, and scream,
And tear at rocks, surge back, and reach for more.

Their wildness fills me with such ecstasy
That it is near to pain. But I was stilled
Before the beauty of a love I sought
With arms too eagerly outstretched, fulfilled

I thought, in you who seemed to offer me
The one strange loveliness I had not found,
The one last joy I could not reach to hang
Upon my diadem. Now on the ground

I see your strength within a little wall
Of solid stone. You know not how to fly
Outside your neatly tended yard, and there
You stay, for you are you . . . and I am I.

—JOYCE LANCASTER

The Rum Ship

They found her helpless off the Banks, her crew
Of murdered men and captain's corpse asprawl
Upon the wheel-house deck. Strong men who knew
Her tale of daring never more will call
"Below!" at sight of gray patrol ships. One
More lawless craft is moored to rot at last
Beside a dock, her final cargo run,
With rum-kegs empty now before the mast.

A thousand others pondered here as I,
Upon the brine-encrusted dock at night
When no star lit the murky arch of sky,
And rain came slanting by her mast-head light.
Did hi-jack raid, or mutineering blow
Decide her fate? Black sides alone can know.

—LIONEL DAY

On Seeing the 175th Infantry Memorial

O men, oblivious to wind and sky,
O soldiers wrought in greening bronze, who know
No art but that of strife—what is this foe
At whom you scream your silent battle cry?
What awful tyranny would justify
The fear-born hate your straining faces show?
Your cause is dead that made false trumpets blow
Betraying notes, which sent men out to die.

Immortal Mars, who thrives in hearts of men,
Must fling his gauntlet in the peace-man's face,
With sneering dare. His madly bellowed word
Calls nations forth to needless war, but when
The god is served with battles' stark disgrace,
Men weep as reason's puny voice is heard.

—LIONEL DAY

SUGGESTIONS

1. Re-read some of the poems in other chapters with a thought to the
theme. Compare for theme "An Old Man's Winter Night" by Frost with

"On Growing Old" by Masefield; "Mending Wall" by Frost with "Prayers of Steel" by Sandburg; "The Dark Song" by Shirley Brownrigg with Milton's sonnet "On His Blindness"; "In Flanders Fields" by John McCrae with "Aftermath" by Sassoon.

2. Here are a few themes as old as poetry, even as old as mankind. You may wish to work out a poem on one of them, remembering that the fresh viewpoint and fresh images are what bring delight in the treatment of old themes. You will think of many others. Those below have been reduced to brief statements.

> What is life?
> Life is short.
> All lovely things are transitory.
> Spring is ever a wonder.
> All things proclaim the beauty of spring.
> Autumn suggests sadness.
> What is death?
> The things of earth do not trouble the dead.
> Death is a mystery.
> Where does death lead?
> According to the mood or temperament Death gives hope; fills the spirit with fear; fills the spirit with awe.
> Death is a mighty leveler.
> All is vanity.
> Empires pass away but art remains.
> The eternal things are those of the spirit.
> Nothing is impossible to youth.
> Youth passes, filling the spirit with regret.
> Age brings decay.
> Sacrifice exalts the spirit.
> Suffering ennobles the spirit.
> The spirit is willing; the flesh is weak.
> The sense and soul are constantly at war.
> According to the mood love is eternal; love is constant; love is ephemeral.
> What does science explain?
> Man yearns to overcome the forces of nature.
> "An honest man's the noblest work of God."—ALEXANDER POPE
> "Man's inhumanity to man
>   Makes countless thousands mourn."—ROBERT BURNS

FIVE-FINGER EXERCISES

Gather into your scrap books as many poems as you can showing a new treatment of an old theme. How does the spirit of the age influence the author's viewpoint?

CHAPTER XXXV

APPROACHING THROUGH THE MOOD

ANOTHER way to induce the Muse is through the mood. Which one of the nine may accept the invitation will depend upon the kind of mood that has taken possession of the writer's spirit. This mood will ultimately manifest itself in the atmosphere or feeling which the poem exhales.

You have only to enter a dimly-lighted chancel to feel the hush of worship, whether the place be empty or filled with a devout congregation; when you wake up on a Sunday morning, you *feel* Sunday: there is something in the sounds of the day that makes them differ from those of the bustling six dedicated to traffic in the mart. The minute you step into a large railroad station like the Grand Central of New York or the Gare de L'Est of Paris, through the motion, through the smells, the sounds, the images, and the suggestion of all these things, you *feel* travel.

This same feeling recalled—worship, Sunday stillness, travel—may suggest any or all of the images connected with it.

Because the beginner may find his own particular method of creating poetry only by experiment, he should give himself the experience of creating a poem out of a mood, intangible though it may seem. A gay mood will find its expression in gay movement, in images wrought of joy—daffodils, trumpeters of spring, or the like. The effect will be to move the heart of the reader to a feeling of joy. Any other mood may find its expression through suitable materials in suitable tempo.

In centering attention on the mood or atmosphere of a poem (they mean the same thing) we are merely repeating what we have done right along when we have selected all the materials for our poem with a thought to its effect on the reader, and when in revision we have removed all extraneous matter. But, as in short stories, sometimes the character is most prominent, and we say we have a character story; sometimes the plot is the thing, and we say we have an action story; sometimes the atmosphere predominates, and we say we have an atmosphere story, although in any one, plot, character, and atmosphere intermingle to create a single unified whole; so in the lyric, atmosphere may predominate. The poem then gives pleasure largely through an intangible impression. The reader enjoys it for its atmosphere. Such a poem is Walter de La Mare's "The Listeners" and Robert Frost's

"House Fear." It is not improbable that De La Mare began his poem with the feeling of weirdness evoked by a deserted house; and Robert Frost with the feeling of fear.

The Listeners

"Is there anybody there?" said the Traveller,
    Knocking on the moonlit door;
And his horse in the silence champed the grasses
    Of the forest's ferny floor.
And a bird flew up out of the turret,
    Above the Traveller's head:
And he smote upon the door again a second time;
    "Is there anybody there?" he said.
But no one descended to the Traveller;
    No head from the leaf-fringed sill
Leaned over and looked into his grey eyes,
    Where he stood perplexed and still.
But only a host of phantom listeners
    That dwelt in the lone house then
Stood listening in the quiet of the moonlight
    To that voice from the world of men:
Stood thronging the faint moonbeams on the dark stair,
    That goes down to the empty hall,
Hearkening in an air stirred and shaken
    By the lonely Traveller's call.
And he felt in his heart their strangeness,
    Their stillness answering his cry,
While his horse moved, cropping the dark turf,
    'Neath the starred and leafy sky;
For he suddenly smote on the door, even
    Louder, and lifted his head:—
"Tell them I came, and no one answered,
    That I kept my word," he said.
Never the least stir made the listeners,
    Though every word he spake
Fell echoing through the shadowiness of the still house
    From the one man left awake:
Ay, they heard his foot upon the stirrup,
    And the sound of iron on stone,
And how the silence surged softly backward,
    When the plunging hoofs were gone.

House Fear

Always—I tell you this they learned—
Always at night when they returned
To the lonely house from far away
To lamps unlighted and fires gone gray,
They learned to rattle the lock and key
To give whatever might chance to be
Warning and time to be off in flight:
And preferring the out- to the in-door night,
They learned to leave the house-door wide
Until they had lit the lamp inside.

How familiar are Frost's details to all of us. Who has not whistled to keep his courage high?

The thing that the young versifier must bear in mind as he builds up atmosphere is to include only congruous details. To explain this point: In an Autumn poem in which a student suggested the melancholy of the dying year she introduced a robin in such a way that the reader simply had to think of spring. This was a false note for the atmosphere: melancholy Autumn. "But you *do* see robins in autumn and the season isn't always melancholy," she said in defense of what she had done. True. But her autumn *was* melancholy and her robin contributed to the melancholy neither by contrast—it might have done that with proper handling—nor as a harmonious detail.

Besides her spring robin, there was a gay little breeze that danced lightly, and out of tune with melancholy. "Some days are that way," protested the writer. True again. But her poem had set out to give the impression of melancholy. If she had wished to show the *variability* of autumn—a pleasing effect to work for—she should have selected many other details with her eye on this variability of autumn. The effect would then have been variability, or inconstancy; not melancholy. The whole atmosphere might be summed up in the single word *variability*. The weather-cock might be its symbol. There would be no break in the mood.

The same experience viewed through different moods may be utterly changed. In exalted mood we may look upon a scene to find it the noblest work of nature; in another mood the same scene may impress us with only its ugliness. It is not the scene but the mood which has changed. Again, we may look upon a familiar line of trees against the sky and be overcome with its beauty. "Were they always there?" we ask ourselves. "How could we have missed them?" Our seeing mood has made a discovery.

Almost any experience has been interpreted variously by many poets, according to their moods. How differently the seasons impress them. Take autumn. A number of autumn poems have been assembled below for you to read and feel. The madness of Shelley speaks through the wild west wind, "breath of autumn's being"; the quiet reverence of Emily Dickinson through her Indian Summer; Keats's devotion to beauty in any form finds expression in the music of "To Autumn." The poet reveals his mood largely through his imagery, with the rhythm keeping time.

Indian Summer

These are the days when birds come back,
   A very few, a bird or two,
   To take a backward look.

These are the days when skies put on
   The old, old sophistries of June,—
   A blue and gold mistake.

Oh, fraud that can not cheat the bee,
   Almost thy plausibility
   Induces my belief,

Till ranks of seeds their witness bear,
   And softly through the altered air
   Hurries a timid leaf!

Oh, sacrament of summer days,
   Oh, last communion in the haze,
   Permit a child to join,

Thy sacred emblems to partake,
   Thy consecrated bread to break,
   Taste thine immortal wine!

—EMILY DICKINSON

Ode to the West Wind

I

O Wild West Wind, thou breath of Autumn's being
   Thou from whose unseen presence the leaves dead
Are driven like ghosts from an enchanter fleeing,

   Yellow, and black, and pale, and hectic red,
Pestilence-stricken multitudes! O thou
   Who chariotest to their dark wintry bed

The wingèd seeds, where they lie cold and low,
   Each like a corpse within its grave, until
Thine azure sister of the Spring shall blow

   Her clarion o'er the dreaming earth, and fill
(Driving sweet buds like flocks to feed in air)
   With living hues and odours plain and hill;

Wild Spirit, which art moving everywhere;
Destroyer and preserver; hear, O hear!

II

Thou on whose stream, 'mid the steep sky's commotion,
   Loose clouds like earth's decaying leaves are shed,
Shook from the tangled boughs of heaven and ocean,

   Angels of rain and lightning! there are spread
On the blue surface of thine airy surge,
   Like the bright hair uplifted from the head

Of some fierce Mænad, even from the dim verge
   Of the horizon to the zenith's height,
The locks of the approaching storm. Thou dirge

   Of the dying year, to which this closing night
Will be the dome of a vast sepulchre,
   Vaulted with all thy congregated might

Of vapours, from whose solid atmosphere
Black rain, and fire, and hail, will burst: O hear!

III

Thou who didst waken from his summer dreams
   The blue Mediterranean, where he lay,
Lull'd by the coil of his crystàlline streams,

Beside a pumice isle in Baiæ's bay,
And saw in sleep old palaces and towers
  Quivering within the wave's intenser day,

All overgrown with azure moss, and flowers
  So sweet, the sense faints picturing them! Thou
For whose path the Atlantic's level powers

  Cleave themselves into chasms, while far below
The sea-blooms and the oozy woods which wear
  The sapless foliage of the ocean, know

Thy voice, and suddenly grow gray with fear,
And tremble and despoil themselves: O hear!

IV

If I were a dead leaf thou mightest bear;
  If I were a swift cloud to fly with thee;
A wave to pant beneath thy power, and share

  The impulse of thy strength, only less free
Than thou, O uncontrollable! if even
  I were as in my boyhood, and could be

The comrade of thy wanderings over heaven,
  As then, when to outstrip thy skiey speed
Scarce seem'd a vision—I would ne'er have striven

  As thus with thee in prayer in my sore need.
O! lift me as a wave, a leaf, a cloud!
  I fall upon the thorns of life! I bleed!

A heavy weight of hours has chain'd and bow'd
One too like thee—tameless, and swift, and proud.

V

Make me thy lyre, even as the forest is:
  What if my leaves are falling like its own?
The tumult of thy mighty harmonies

  Will take from both a deep autumnal tone,
Sweet though in sadness. Be thou, Spirit fierce,
  My spirit! Be thou me, impetuous one!

Drive my dead thoughts over the universe,
  Like wither'd leaves, to quicken a new birth;
And, by the incantation of this verse,

Scatter, as from an unextinguish'd hearth
Ashes and sparks, my words among mankind!
Be through my lips to unawaken'd earth

The trumpet of a prophecy! O Wind,
If Winter comes, can Spring be far behind?
                    —PERCY BYSSHE SHELLEY

To Autumn

Season of mists and mellow fruitfulness!
    Close bosom-friend of the maturing sun;
Conspiring with him how to load and bless
    With fruit the vines that round the thatch-eaves run;
To bend with apples the moss'd cottage-trees,
    And fill all fruit with ripeness to the core;
        To swell the gourd, and plump the hazel shells
With a sweet kernel; to set budding more,
And still more, later flowers for the bees,
Until they think warm days will never cease,
    For Summer has o'er-brimmed their clammy cells.

Who hath not seen thee oft amid thy store?
    Sometimes whoever seeks abroad may find
Thee sitting careless on a granary floor,
    Thy hair soft-lifted by the winnowing wind,
Or on a half-reap'd furrow sound asleep,
    Drowsed with the fume of poppies, while thy hook
        Spares the next swath and all its twinèd flowers;
And sometimes like a gleaner thou dost keep
    Steady thy laden head across a brook;
    Or by a cider-press, with patient look,
        Thou watchest the last oozings hours by hours.

Where are the songs of Spring? Ay, where are they?
    Think not of them, thou hast thy music too,—
While barrèd clouds bloom the soft-dying day,
    And touch the stubble-plains with rosy hue;
Then in a wailful choir the small gnats mourn
    Among the river sallows, borne aloft
        Or sinking as the light wind lives or dies;
And full-grown lambs loud bleat from hilly bourn;
    Hedge-crickets sing; and now with treble soft
    The redbreast whistles from a garden-croft;
        And gathering swallows twitter in the skies.
                        —JOHN KEATS

A Vagabond Song

There is something in the autumn that is native to my blood—
Touch of manner, hint of mood;
And my heart is like a rhyme,
With the yellow and the purple and the crimson keeping time.

The scarlet of the maples can shake me like a cry
Of bugles going by.
And my lonely spirit thrills
To see the frosty asters like a smoke upon the hills.

There is something in October sets the gipsy blood astir;
We must rise and follow her,
When from every hill of flame
She calls and calls each vagabond by name.

—BLISS CARMAN

We might note how the varying moods of poets have toned various poems on any subject.

Feel the wind sweeping through these lines:

The Wind Is My Neighbor

Breaking through the brambles where once a road had been,
I came upon the house that the wind lives in.

(Oh how can we work now, at peace with our labor,
Knowing we have only the wind for a neighbor?)

The wind is the farmer who sows the forest seed,
Her home rises stark in an acre of weed.

Through the doors and windows, like wild invisible waters,
Catch-who-can and tumble, race the wind's daughters!

O wind, you have hardly a shutter unbroken,
So rough and so reckless are your wild children.

Somewhere walks a woman who was never meant for child,
She plants all the mountains while her daughters run wild.

(Oh how can we rest here, at peace with our labor,
Knowing we have only the wind for a neighbor?)

—MARGERY MANSFIELD

Notice how the pair, "broken"—"children," contributes to the feeling of broken shutters and reckless children.

Unless a poet tells us how he actually began a poem we cannot know for certain. But it is reasonable to suppose that the mother singing a lullaby feels the quiet that she seeks to create for her child's sleep. Out of her mood grows the cradle song with its restful effect. Note the hush of "Sweet and low."

Sweet and low, sweet and low,
    Wind of the western sea,
Low, low, breathe and blow,
    Wind of the western sea!
Over the rolling waters go,
Come from the dying moon, and blow,
    Blow him again to me;
While my little one, while my pretty one, sleeps.

Sleep and rest, sleep and rest,
    Father will come to thee soon;
Rest, rest, on mother's breast,
    Father will come to thee soon;
Father will come to his babe in the nest,
Silver sails all out of the west
    Under the silver moon:
Sleep, my little one, sleep, my pretty one, sleep.
          —ALFRED, LORD TENNYSON

Cradle Song

Sleep, sleep, beauty bright,
Dreaming in the joys of night;
Sleep, sleep; in thy sleep
Little sorrows sit and weep.

Sweet babe, in thy face
Soft desires I can trace,
Secret joys and secret smiles,
Little pretty infant wiles.

As thy softest limbs I feel
Smiles as of the morning steal
O'er thy cheek, and o'er thy breast
Where thy little heart doth rest.

O the cunning wiles that creep
In thy little heart asleep!
When thy little heart doth wake,
Then the dreadful night shall break.
          —WILLIAM BLAKE

And what a hush falls with the April dew in this 15th century carol. Could anything be stiller than April dew?

Carol, 15th Century

I sing of a maiden
   That is makeles;   *makeles-*
King of all kings   *matchless*
   To her son she ches.   *ches-chose*

He came al so still
   There his mother was,
As dew in April
   That falleth on the grass.

He came al so still
   To his mother's bour,
As dew in April
   That falleth on the flour.

He came al so still
   There his mother lay,
As dew in April
   That falleth on the spray.

Mother and maiden
   Was never none but she;
Well may such a lady
   Goddes mother be.

As you learned in a previous chapter, the little Japanese tercets are atmosphere poems. In the light of this chapter, read them again if you like.

STUDENT POEMS DEVELOPED THROUGH A MOOD

Mood

No sea is sibilant as silence is,
No mellow murmur calms me more than this,
No darkness is so filled with changing thought,
And in no mystery such horror caught,
No bell can chant a quivering tune so long,
Only silence is everlasting song.

—WILLIAM ROEHRICK

Exhilaration

I could not love my life, or you,
Without a beckoning star or two.
Without the fragrant new-born green
I could not laugh. Fresh youth I've seen
Has poured into my soul a clean
Cool draught of water, from a well
Of beauty. Without the spell
Of throbbing song or full refrain,
That calls from near, I would disdain
My life, my love . . . not worth the pain
Of disappointment. Now I sing;
I'm bubbling over with the Spring.

—JOYCE LANCASTER

Song to Yolanda

(So She Will Sleep Well)

Yolanda, yellow moonlight is drenching our hill,
And I can see a nightbird in a tree;
He will sing only if you lie very still,
And at dawn if you will search the wood with me

You may find small footprints in the grass;
I do not promise after fall of dew
They will be there, but where the fairies pass
Only good can ever come to you.

—ESTELLE ROOKS

Abstract subjects seem to lend themselves to a mood. They must be concretely developed to be effective.

Inspiration

I am a flame
Burning the skies,
Scarring the black
Young night as it lies

Screaming with pain;
Yet I do not cease.
The air grows whiter,
The flames increase,

The skies fall apart
And I go beyond—
Doubt is a lily
In a frozen pond

And Life is a cup,
Empty and clean.
Further, beyond
The skies, the keen

White breath of Time
Quickens my speed,
Quickens my soul;
I do not need

Fire or fuel.
Nothing is here
Above the skies
But Time. The queer

Blue light I cast
Consumes the dark.
(This started from
A tiny spark!)

I thrill with heat
And curl about
Till a flood of reason
Puts me out.
—Georgia H. Cooper

Loneliness

Loneliness is a forlorn bird
Crying softly to be heard . . .
Loneliness is an empty street
That's never felt the tread of feet . .
Loneliness is a cloudless sky; . . .
Truly, loneliness is I.
—Sylvia Adelman

Can you not feel age here?

Ancient Night

This night is old.
The moon swings agedly,
Close to the furrowed earth,
Casting down its mellow, brassy light.

A senile breeze,
Bending wearily with the burden
Of many years it has traveled,
Clings to the young flowers,
And clumsily ruffles the hair
Of a slender tree.
His musty sighs tell tales
Of forgotten tombs
And unfound caverns.

The darkness leans heavily
Upon me. . . .
I, too, feel old.
—Jacqueline Hoyt

Night Comes to an Old Lady

Her gray cat yawned and stretched; one sharp claw crept
Out of its cushioned cell, and so she slept.

Hers was deep, downy sleep that wrapped her in,
Warm like a blanket tucked up to her chin;

She regally wore satin in her dream,
And fed her Persian cat on cod and cream.

He drowsed uncertainly and did not rest;
He mewed; his tail twitched in an eager quest

Until at last he caught a fine, sleek mouse.
Contentment came with night to that small house.

—ESTELLE ROOKS

To Four Friends

I could go back, to stand again
Beneath the sun-bright tree,
To run the shadow-blotted path
Where spectral fiends and misty men
Are waiting, where the wind's high wrath
Heaps the leaves in a surging golden sea;

Go back to watch the sunset clouds
On westerly parade,
To puzzle at the glooming hill,
Copper tipped with sunny shrouds,
To wonder till the sky grew chill. . . .
I could go back, but I would be afraid.

—WILLIAM ROEHRICK

Earthward

Winter skies at evening wear
Red lobelias in their hair.
The Palisades stand back, swathed deep
In dusk, grown richly dark, and half-asleep.
The evening presses closer down
And scatters blue dust through the town,
And on the lamp-posts, small and cold,

Hang the first shy drops of gold.
Long ago, lights coming out
Were something to be glad about,
And I had to be alone
To hold the wonder all my own:
The sudden bright uneasiness
That woke within me. It grows less
As I grow knowing.
Tonight I look at blossoms showing
In the grained fields of the sky
Calmly unimpassioned. I
Am a connoisseur in skies
With something dead behind my eyes
That even the first star won't kindle
When red lobelias pale and dwindle.
I used to drink a still delight
From the mirrored pools of night.
The Shy One came to me, and then
There was not any need for men.
I fashioned out of solitude
The peace of nightfall in a wood.
Beauty has no meaning now.
Stars are thick along the bough
Of the evening. Is the fruit
Barren now because the root
Was crushed by wishes one too many,
Or that I have no taste for any
Lusciousness, save to admire
Without any great desire?

The far stars shine with a colder light . . .
What is it beats in the pulse of night?
—Muriel F. Hochdorf

Desert Night

The desert night is clear and cold;
The mountains, in the daylight bold
Against the faded copper skies,
Diminish weirdly in their size
By night. And through each inky fold
Of blackness penetrates the old
White light of stars that once were gold
And tarnished. Sand-filled winds surprise
The desert night,

And sifting through the greasewood, hold
Each restless lizard there, controlled
And still. From far away arise
A weary coyote's lonely cries.
The very sounds like fingers mold
The desert night.

—HELEN HARTMANN

The Haunted House

From the deep dank darkness through the open door
Crept the secret silence of ten years or more.
An age-old moonbeam staggered into sight,
Shivering in the hollow gaping night.
With a rush of wings and a dusty blast
Like memories of an evil past
A swarm of bats flew out, and we
Watched them welter to infinity;
While down from centuries long ago
Ancient voices whispered low,
Making us feel, our hearts filled with dread,
The deserted house was pregnant with dead.

—HARRIET MEYER

SUGGESTIONS

Give yourself up to a mood and see what happens. You will need uninterrupted quiet for any mood to take possession of you. You may induce a mood by thinking of a strain of music, by repeating some lines of poetry and then letting your thoughts drift, or by humming softly. To lie on your back in the grass or in a hammock, to relax in a big chair in the twilight, to sit on the doorstep when "noon hangs heavy on flower and tree,"—these are a few of many other ways to free a mood. A theme will slip into your mood unawares. Materials in tone will take shape out of amorphous experiences.

1. Which will your poem be?

Gay	Reflective	Reminiscent	Whimsical	Eerie
Sad	Optimistic	Pessimistic	Cynical	Ironical
Resentful	Intense	Rebellious	Light	Serious
Flippant	Vivacious			

Test your success by letting a reader with insight tell you what mood you have conveyed through your poem.

2. Try to catch a mood—some moment mood—in the crystal of your verse.

CHAPTER XXXVI

A THOUGHT TO VIGOR AND VITALITY

To GUARD against mere milk-and-water verse let us give a moment's thought to the quality of vigor. Vigor in poetry is the expression of vigor in life. All is not sweetness, music, delicacy. Life includes strength and power and austerity; struggle and sacrifice; exaltation and tragedy. In these things there is a beauty, which in the hands of the masters becomes sublime.

Frailty, grace, gentleness of nature,—such qualities have inspired the tranquil songs of quiet singers. We need those songs. But the might of the thunder, the turbulence of the sea, wind the destroyer, the hardness of steel and stone, the pitilessness of heat, the mechanistic roar of industrial progress, the intensity of social conflicts stir in the soul depths which are adequately expressed only through rich volume of sound.

The jousting Knight in visored helmet, flashing a white plume or his lady's broidered favor, is not more inspiring than the stoker sweating over the *Leviathan's* engine; the lady with her spinet and her Provençal song is no more romantic than the woman of the laboratory over her cultures and test tubes, adventuring toward a cure for cancer. The ideals of every age have been reflected in its poetry. Ours is an age of vigor. For the poet of today there is new romance. Looking skyward he does not miss it. No one would fail to see poetry in flight, whether it be of goldfinches or of airplanes; but it is for a more subtle insight to get at the heart of steel and stone, of mass production, of economic struggle. "Human blessings and human ills commonly flow from the same source," says Longinus. With the glory of man's intellectual achievements goes human tragedy: heights and depths both to inspire the sublime. The very nature of twentieth century living cries for vigorous expression. There is need for words to connote strength, word combinations to interpret hardness, rhythms suitable to skyscrapers moving vertically and high-powered motors endlessly pounding.

One age of discovery, of continent-hunting, produced Sidney and Raleigh, Spenser and Marlowe and Shakespeare. We are in an age of discovery in other realms: science, air, human conduct. If we will lose ourselves in its wonders and in its tragedies some rare unexpected song may startle our too skeptical ears.

To produce a forceful poem we must be energetic in thought. Force will manifest itself in various ways. Here are some.

1. In the theme. It will be one of man's eternal passions and aspirations. It will grow out of brooding upon human or cosmic experiences.

2. In the movement. The lines will sweep along upon the intensity of passion. There will be sparks of fire from the heels of speed.

3. In diction. Forceful words, stark uncompromising words will fit into the movement. There will be a chance for the explosives to have their day. Phrasing will catch the tone of animated voices.

4. Through imagery. The trivial will have no place. Images will be drawn from vital things. They will tend to grandeur.

5. Through the purpose. The end of the poem will be to produce one of the higher, sterner effects, and so inspire one of the strong emotions. For the moment, we shall have done with sweetness, meekness, gentleness, reverence.

6. In the tone. The whole poem will be painted in rich colors and their deeper shades—none of your tints.

> A cry that shiver'd to the tingling stars,
> And, as it were one voice, an agony
> Of lamentation, like a wind that shrills
> All night in a waste land, where no one comes
> Or hath come, since the making of the world.
>   —ALFRED, LORD TENNYSON: *The Passing of Arthur*

7. Through the viewpoint. The young poet's wholesome inquiring attitude toward experience will search out the freshness and vitality of a world essentially wholesome. *He* must translate what he finds.

The young in spirit want to see; they are not afraid to face truth. It is only the old in spirit who are weary and have no hope.

Vigor is a quality not to be acquired through itself but as a natural consequence of the versifier's sharp chiseling out of vital materials. Vigor does not mean coarseness or vulgarity. The young poet will need to approach his exercise with gloves off and sleeves rolled to his elbows; but however stained with the soil may be that which he touches, it should be free of infection.

Printed below are a number of vigorous poems. Read them. Then read the vigorous expression of the young versifiers who tried to be aware of strength and power in human experience.

Prayers of Steel

Lay me on an anvil, O God.
Beat me and hammer me into a crowbar.
Let me pry loose old walls;
Let me lift and loosen old foundations.

Lay me on an anvil, O God.
Beat me and hammer me into a steel spike.
Drive me into the girders that hold a skyscraper together.
Take red-hot rivets and fasten me into the central girders.
Let me be the great nail holding a skyscraper through blue nights into
     white stars.

—CARL SANDBURG

Aftermath

Have you forgotten yet? . . .
For the world's events have rumbled on since those gagged days,
Like traffic checked awhile at the crossing of city ways:
And the haunted gap in your mind has filled with thoughts that flow
Like clouds in the lit heavens of life; and you're a man reprieved to go,

Taking your peaceful share of Time, with joy to spare.
But the past is just the same,—and War's a bloody game. . . .
Have you forgotten yet? . . .
Look down, and swear by the slain of the War that you'll never forget.

Do you remember the dark months you held the sector at Mametz,—
The nights you watched and wired and dug and piled sandbags on
     parapets?
Do you remember the rats; and the stench
Of corpses rotting in front of the front-line trench,—
And dawn coming, dirty-white, and chill with a hopeless rain?
Do you ever stop and ask, "Is it all going to happen again?"

Do you remember that hour of din before the attack,—
And the anger, the blind compassion that seized and shook you then
As you peered at the doomed and haggard faces of your men?
Do you remember the stretcher-cases lurching back
With dying eyes and lolling heads, those ashen-grey
Masks of the lads who once were keen and kind and gay?

Have you forgotten yet? . . .
Look up, and swear by the green of the Spring that you'll never forget.

—SIEGFRIED SASSOON

Meteor

More beautiful than ships or 'planes
Are lightning-flash and thunderbolt
Of runaway night-frightened trains.

Swift, brutal in a wild assault
Of frantic wings and flying heels,
They leap from out the catapult

Of distance, thunder in their wheels
And lightning in their Cyclops' eye
And serpent tail, with warning squeals

As if the shaken stars and sky
Were falling through the holes they rip
In night and silence. Demon cry

And dragon flight, receding, slip
Into the reticence of space—
More terrible than 'plane or ship
In fiery speed and iron grace.
                —BENJAMIN ALBERT BOTKIN

A River Gorge

A savage, ragged throat of red
And splintered rocks, through which a dim stream flows,
So far beneath, its foam becomes a thread
Of melted silver, poured amid the rose
And orange-tinted lichen-spotted walls.

Across the awful chasm, a jay
Flies dauntlessly, with ringing cry.
The shuddering soul goes with him on his way,
Made sick with horror, while the high
Cliffs echo with his fearless calls.
                —HAMLIN GARLAND

There is a planetary sweep suggested in the next poem. The Danish nobleman, Tycho Brahe (1546-1601), was the first of modern observational astronomers, although he died nine years before the invention of the astronomical telescope. To insure accuracy he worked in underground crypts. On his discoveries Kepler, his pupil, formulated planetary laws.

Tycho Brahe

Masked in bright metal, now he makes his home
  In subterranean caverns, red and stark,
    To forge the magic instruments which mark
Fixed constellations and the fires that roam;
Or from a tower of cloud and curling foam,
  With axis and imaginary arc
    He bounds the wild dominions of the dark,
Shadowed in silver on night's sable dome.

A lunar form with opalescent rays
  Lights this lone tower where spheres of crystal swim
    In circles widening to infinity . . .
These talismans about him, he surveys
  Paths of a thousand stars, till gray and dim
    The moon lies moored upon a morning sea.

—THOMAS S. JONES, JR.

The Challenge of Thor

I am the God Thor,
I am the War God,
I am the Thunderer!
Here in my Northland,
My fastness and fortress,
Reign I forever!

Here amid icebergs
Rule I the nations;
This is my hammer,
Miolner the mighty;
Giants and sorcerers
Cannot withstand it!

These are the gauntlets
Wherewith I wield it,
And hurl it afar off;
This is my girdle;
Whenever I brace it,
Strength is redoubled!

The light thou beholdest
Stream through the heavens,
In flashes of crimson,
Is but my red beard
Blown by the night wind,
Affrighting the nations!

Jove is my brother;
Mine eyes are the lightning;
The wheels of my chariot
Roll in the thunder,
The blows of my hammer
Ring in the earthquake!

Force rules the world still,
Has ruled it, shall rule it;
Meekness is weakness,
Strength is triumphant,
Over the whole earth,
Still is it Thor's-Day!

—HENRY WADSWORTH LONGFELLOW

The Eagle

(Fragment)

He clasps the crag with hooked hands;
Close to the sun in lonely lands,
Ring'd with the azure world, he stands.

The wrinkled sea beneath him crawls;
He watches from his mountain walls;
And like a thunderbolt he falls.

—ALFRED, LORD TENNYSON

Re-read "The Man with the Hoe" and "Steel" in the chapter on themes, pages 415 and 417; and "Sea-Sonnet," page 355.

Young poets have given a thought to vigor and vitality. See how well they have succeeded.

Skyscraper

paper, a pen,
group of men,
lump of dirt.
Machines assert
The song of steel.
grinding wheel
Of fire swings round
Upon the ground
Below. Long bands
Of steel, it stands
Alone. It gropes . . .
A web of hopes
Against the sky.
Men live, men die.
But still this wall
Of steel stands tall.
In vain its height
Reaches at night
To touch the vine
Of stars that twine
Above.

—SYDNEY S. ABRAM

Realization

The asceticism of this rock
On which my body rests
Makes my heart tremble.
Sublimity,
I have longed for you all my life,
But now there is a tremor in the air:
The eagle above and the rock beneath.
Oh, I have found you!

—GEORGE KUZNETS

Cosmos

Through the bright day
With ceaseless din,
The engines sway
And the great wheels spin.

Through the dark space
The great spheres roll
In endless race
To an unknown goal.

—LIONEL DAY

To an Idle God

Vulcan, there is not a single proud steed
Left by the gods, for your skilled hand to shoe;
Sorrow not yet, mighty blacksmith, take heed—
There is all manner of work still to do.
Progress is waiting outside of the door,
Tossing his mane, as he chafes to be gone.
Ring on your anvil one sure stroke, one more;
He must beat out many miles before dawn.
Overground, underground, mad is his race,
Shod in the steel of your powerful hand,
Though boulders crumble that slacken his pace,
And the undaunted speed of his hoofs scorch the land,
Charring the flowers and charring the wood.
Smite the stern anvil till heat becomes white;
Fall in exhaustion—he speeds—it is good;
Nothing may hinder his wind-driven flight.
Even yet, Vulcan, I hear you about
Mightier work that can never be through.
How many shoes has the stallion worn out?
How many more will be hammered by you?
Challenge the scoffer; forge on, though your back
Rival the shape of your handcraft that lies
There on the anvil; though stiff fingers crack,
Wear out the muscles and sinews you prize.
Fling out your blows in an ear-numbing roar;
Grow blind beneath lashes the wild sparks have thinned.
This is the price of the joy—this and more—
Of seeing his young head outflung to the wind.

—RUTH H. HAUSMAN

Creation

The City groans and writhes upon her bed,
Tearing mist-veils, and clenching her cold, white hands.
(Surely this pain comes not to other lands!)
Her shrieks resound. She pounds her feverish head.

So Time and the City love and live and bear
New temples in an endless agony.
And none there are who shall remain to see
How all this life will end, or when, or where . . .

—GEORGIA H. COOPER

Melody in Black

I sat alone in thought, quite drowned
By flooding realization found
    In solitude, I wished to be
    The only one . . . to own the sea
And stars, and know the rhythmic sound
Of time and fear, to hear the pound
Of pain and loveliness; so crowned
    With pensiveness, silently
        I sat alone.
I threw from me the earth. Around
My wrists were fragile dreams, and gowned
    In laughter and infinity,
        I banished death delightedly.
In solitude, where life's profound
        I sat alone.

—JOYCE LANCASTER

City Growth

Here, not so long ago, the grass grew rank,
And flowers flirted with the eager bees;
Here, not so long ago, a happy breeze
Ran riot in the hair of stately trees
And taxed their patience with his latest prank.

And what's here now? A wilderness of stone,
With fire-hydrants blossoming around,
And heavy air, twice-filled with smoke and sound
That drags along the hard, cemented ground . . .
Why can't we let the lovely things alone?

—NAOMI ROGIN

SUGGESTIONS

1. Look at the variety about you. Note the wonders man has wrought: bridges, highways, skyscrapers, cathedrals, ocean liners, huge factories roaring with machinery; water power; a system of electricity, of gas for cooking, heating, refrigeration; automobiles—speed; the conquest of rock in laying foundations, tunneling; conquest of air; harnessing of water-falls. Think about one of these things or something related and use it as the basis for a vigorous poem.

2. Do any of these notes suggest poems?

> Infinity   Eternal things   Space   Height   Aridity
> Awe in scientific discovery   Phenomena of the universe   Human struggle   A large idea: such as

> > Our echoes roll from soul to soul
> > And grow forever and forever.

> Moral significance of any commonplace activity   Mode of travel
>   Harmony of an intricate thing: network of cables on a bridge;
> machinery in a watch; machinery of the human body; effect of a sestina
> perfectly wrought   Passionate plea   Passionate protest
> How far from the primitive are you? Would you go back? Why?
>   Tragedies, joys of childhood   Waste—its significance
> Wreckage—significance   Squalor   Sacrifice—triumph of (exalted) ; futility of (tragedy)   Explorations in Arctic regions
> Excavations in Egypt; Pompeii; anywhere else   Futility of explanation   Bitterness   In the wake of drunkenness   Wonder
> at strength: sinews of tiger, panther; skyscraper; a mechanistic thing.

3. Can you move a reader to feel sordidness in a fair-faced thing, to feel the cruelty of hate, the terror of unprovided old age, the agony of being a misfit, the monotony of labor deprived of play time, the hopelessness of life devoid of faith or affection? There must be no moralizing. The images in your poem must create the effect. Do not comment on the effect. To say that a thing is strong does not make it so. Show it in action. Let the action speak strength.

CHAPTER XXXVII

SOME DEVICES FOR CREATING EMOTIONAL EFFECTS

ALL through our study of verse technique we have kept in mind the power of the imaginative element. The imagination of the poet brings together experiences that are worlds apart, and at the impact a magical thing happens; the imagination of the poet visualizes an unseen audience and so makes it possible for his heart to communicate some part, if not all, of what he wants to say; his imaginative ear hears the singing of his song. He may not read his own verse aloud very well; but he reads well to his imaginative ear. As he has thus exercised his imagination he has caught the imagination of his reader and through it has touched his emotions.

The Road Not Taken

Two roads diverged in a yellow wood,
And sorry I could not travel both
And be one traveler, long I stood
And looked down one as far as I could
To where it bent in the undergrowth;

Then took the other, as just as fair,
And having perhaps the better claim,
Because it was grassy and wanted wear;
Though as for that the passing there
Had worn them really about the same,

And both that morning equally lay
In leaves no step had trodden black.
Oh, I kept the first for another day!
Yet knowing how way leads on to way,
I doubted if I should ever come back.

I shall be telling this with a sigh
Somewhere ages and ages hence:
Two roads diverged in a wood, and I—
I took the one less traveled by,
And that has made all the difference.

—ROBERT FROST

This brief poem is a compressed biography. For years the inimitable Robert Frost fashioned his poems without applause because he had chosen to do something original for poetry. He has caught the tones of the American idiom, the elusive inflections of our common speech, in his verse. Had he followed the first road, what?

Perhaps there is no more potent way of touching the reader than through what is suggested or implied. What the poet does not say is more powerful than what he says. Indeed oftentimes what he says has power to move only through what he has not said. Every poem worth anything suggests; but for the moment we shall think only of simple poems whose chief charm lies in what they imply. Through suggestiveness the poet pays a double tribute to his reader: he expects his sympathy and understanding; he takes for granted the insight of his mind and his spirit. See how sharply what is not said speaks to the heart in the following lines:

A Memory

Four ducks on a pond,
A grass-bank beyond,
A blue sky of spring,
White clouds on the wing:
What a little thing
To remember for years—
To remember with tears.

—WILLIAM ALLINGHAM

"Love Came Back at Fall of Dew"

Love came back at fall of dew,
    Playing his old part;
But I had a word or two,
    That would break his heart.

"He who comes at candlelight,
    That should come before,
Must betake him to the night
    From a barrèd door."

This the word that made us part
    In the fall of dew;
This the word that brake his heart—
    Yet it brake mine, too!

—LIZETTE WOODWORTH REESE

Here are student attempts to speak through silence.

Flight

Sudden and silver
Shy as dawn,
So he was here—
In a breath he was gone!

Soft as a bird's wing
Swift in flight,
Lightly withdrawn
As the fingers of night.

Time groans and shakes himself
At our door,—
Loud and garrulous,
He is with us once more.

The days march upon us
As they may,
Now there is nothing
To keep them at bay. . . .

It was an evening
Dark with birds;
He was weary, weary
Of too many words.
—MURIEL F. HOCHDORF

Fact

Wilted roses, pretty tears,
Lyric heart-throbs, charming fears—

Lovely, graceful are such pains . . .
Only these the bard retains.

Ecstasy of love reveals
Dainty scratches music heals.

Once I thought it sweet to go
Sleepless . . . Now I know.
—MILDRED SOLWAN

Another artistic method of creating a powerful emotional effect is through contrast. In Act I, Scene VI of Shakespeare's *Macbeth*, there is an idyllic scene before the castle of Macbeth at Inverness:

> This castle hath a pleasant seat; the air
> Nimbly and sweetly recommends itself
> Unto our gentle senses

says the king; and Banquo, Macbeth's soldier-companion of the recent war, shows a poet's heart in his gentle reply:

> This guest of summer,
> The temple-haunting martlet, does approve
> By his lov'd mansionry that the heaven's breath
> Smells wooingly here: no jutty, frieze,
> Buttress, nor coigne of vantage, but this bird
> Hath made his pendent bed and procreant cradle:
> Where they most breed and haunt I have observ'd,
> The air is delicate.

The atmosphere is one of innocence, beauty and peace. Within, the air is foul with the thought of murder. A heinous crime is committed before the next morning. The tranquillity of that scene outside lingers in the reader's mind to intensify the horror of the later scene.

Sometimes a whole poem is built on contrast. Some of the ballades à double refrain, you remember, are so constructed. Thomas Hardy is very fond of this device. In his handling it frequently becomes irony.

Life and death are nicely balanced below:

Calf in the Goldenrod

> I found a calf in the goldenrod
> Beside the sandy river;
> I saw it lift its little head,
> I saw its nostrils quiver.
>
> The sky above was softly blue,
> And the wild ducks were flying;
> A lovely place to be born, I thought,
> But a sorry place for dying.
>
> For the old cow lay in the goldenrod,
> And she would never rise;
> She watched her little, new-born calf
> With big, bewildered eyes.

And the wind blew through the goldenrod,
And bent and swayed its head;
And the calf called to its mother
—Nor knew that she was dead.

The sky above was softly blue,
And the wild ducks were flying;
A lovely place to be born, I thought,
But a sorry place for dying.

—JULIA VAN DER VEER

These verses by younger poets are based on contrast.

Prisoned

Outdoors there are cherry trees,
In me naught but pain.
Dear God, send a tinted breeze
On the heels of rain.

Outdoors carefree song of birds,—
In me all is numb.
Where are all my pretty words?
What has struck them dumb?

Outdoors, over the hills, they say
Love holds feast with Life.
This can never make me gay,
Who am Sorrow's wife.

—SYLVIA LAPIDUS

Question

Shall life be for Alice
A series of pleasures,
A bright line of flowers,
A ring of gay measures?

Shall life be for Hilda
One without beauty,
One timed to the noon-bell
And driven by duty?

If our God is truly
All goodness and kindness,
It's strange He should show us
Such all-human blindness.

—JEAN ZALESCHITZ

In a light vein:

Rival

I hope that she who stole my place
Is keen of wit and fair of face,
But you'll forgive me if I guess
That she is dumb and looks a mess.

—RUBYE MAE FISHER

Other devices for heightening effects are various figures of speech.

In the union of words there seems to be a spiritual strength that passeth understanding: potential force and vividness to touch the heart. The awakened imagination seeks colorful expression. Through the metaphor things are brought together out of time, across space— and snap! a wondrous thing happens. It is in the nature of the human heart to compare.

Besides the great basic figures, metaphor and simile, there are some other devices of figurative expression which we may wish to know for the greater enjoyment of our reading and for the heightening of effects in our own writing. They are, however, diminutive in size compared to the metaphor!

Allegory is akin to the metaphor, simile, and personification. Like them it is based on resemblance. But the allegory is a connected narrative showing one of the two things compared in action. The reader must supply the reality. The purpose of an allegory is to explain or illustrate an important reality. Something else is intended than is contained in the literal words. Spenser's *The Faerie Queene* and Dante's *The Divine Comedy* are famous allegories in verse. In each case the whole poem is an allegory. Bunyan's *Pilgrim's Progress* and Jonathan Swift's *Gulliver's Travels* are great prose allegories.

The fable and the parable of the Gospels are briefer forms of allegory. Christ in His teachings often explained His allegories so that there would be no doubt of the interpretation He intended: here is a short one to illustrate what an allegory is.

And he spake this parable unto them, saying,
What man of you, having a hundred sheep, if he lose one of them, doth not leave the ninety and nine in the wilderness, and go after that which is lost, until he find it?
And when he hath found *it*, he layeth *it* on his shoulders, rejoicing.
And when he cometh home, he calleth together *his* friends and neighbours, saying unto them, Rejoice with me; for I have found my sheep which was lost.
I say unto you, that likewise joy shall be in heaven over one sinner that repenteth, more than over ninety and nine just persons, which need no repentance.

—LUKE 15:3-7

As it is in the nature of the human heart to compare; it is in the nature of the human heart to make associations.

I must keep a roof over my head! Will you break bread with me? They employed seven hands on the dock. Such expressions are common enough in our speech. Then we have the familiar

I am not fit to touch the hem of his garment.

Oh Lord I am not worthy that Thou shouldst enter under my roof.

A sail, a sail! I see a sail!

The hem signifies the whole garment; the roof is a part of the house; the sail means the boat. The part which I can touch or see suggests the whole but the part is much more vivid than the whole. In one gesture I could not touch the whole garment. Out on the horizon I do not see the hull; I do see the sail. This figure is *synecdoche*: a part for the whole thing. Here are some examples from verse:

> Where's the thane of Cawdor?
> We cours'd him *at the heels*, . . .
> —WILLIAM SHAKESPEARE, *Macbeth*

Macbeth reasons

> He's here in double trust:
> First, as I am his kinsman and his subject,
> Strong both against the deed; then, as his host,
> Who should against his murderer *shut the door*,
> Not bear the knife myself . . .

In the same way but not so frequently we say the whole to suggest the part of a thing or circumstance; that is, we select the genus for the species.

> The *world* is too much with us; late and soon,
> Getting and spending, we lay waste our powers.
> —WILLIAM WORDSWORTH

The world is all-inclusive of the material things of the world.

> Some time let Gorgeous Tragedy
> In Scepter'd Pall come sweeping by.
> —JOHN MILTON

Milton means some special play such as *Othello, Medea, Macbeth,* or *Edward Second.* The class is more vivid in his passage. You see it is closely bound with personification.

There is another kind of association. We associate a crown with a king; the brain with the head; human sympathies with the heart; the works of literature with their author. We say: "He pays tribute to the *crown*," meaning the king or the treasury. "He has a fine head" meaning "the brain in his head is fine," and the brain really means the mind. "She has a warm heart" meaning "she is affectionate." "We are studying Vergil" meaning a "writing of Vergil." "The pen is mightier than the sword." "The kettle (the water) is boiling." "Let us smoke a pipe (tobacco)." In each case we have mentioned something which is very closely associated with another thing. This figure is called *metonymy* from Greek words indicating *change* and *name.* Instead of the parts suggesting the whole, one thing suggests another.

Roughly speaking, the cause suggests the effect and the effect the cause; the sign suggests the thing signified; the container suggests the thing contained.

Here are some examples from poetry. You may find others:

> And noon lay heavy on flower and tree.
>
> —Percy Bysshe Shelley

The effect of the sun at twelve o'clock—*heavy noon.*

> Then to the well-trod stage anon,
> If Jonson's learned *sock* be on.
>
> —John Milton

The sock was the symbol of comedy. Ben Jonson, most learned of the Elizabethan playwrights, wrote many comedies.

> Or what (though rare) of later age
> Ennoblèd hath the *buskined* stage.
>
> —John Milton

Buskins were worn by actors in the Greek tragedies. The buskin is a symbol of tragedy.

> . . . how ennobling thoughts depart
> When men change swords for ledgers, and desert
> The student's bower for gold, . . .
>
> —William Wordsworth

> Is this the *face* that launched a thousand ships
> And burnt the topless towers of Illium?
>
> —Christopher Marlowe

Helen's face stands for her whole beauty.

Another way to secure vivid effect is through reference to some well-known event or fact or expression. Allusion, a metaphor in disguise, is a device of the well-informed. It is taken for granted that most people of average experience and normal life have acquired a background of information from certain great sources: the Bible, mythology, history and so on. Reference to Mary's lamb or Washington's hatchet or Aladdin's lamp, or the doubting Thomas is generally understood through association. An apt allusion will often make a point more quickly than an original figure of speech. Advertisers today recognize the value of allusion, as in Ajax tires.

> . . . Sunny locks
> Hang on her temples like a golden fleece:
> Which makes her seat of Belmont Colchos' strand,
> And many Jasons come in search of her.
>
> —William Shakespeare

> Or hear old Triton blow his wreathèd horn.
>
> —William Wordsworth

Byron laments the ruin of Rome:

> The Niobe of Nations! there she stands,
> Childless and crownless, in her voiceless woe;

Those who know the Greek myths are moved to delight through the significance of the golden fleece and Jason's search; Triton's horn; Niobe weeping over her children, in the passages above. Here are allusions from other sources:

> The glory that was Greece
> And the grandeur that was Rome.
> —EDGAR ALLAN POE

> Some mute inglorious Milton here may rest,
> Some Cromwell, guiltless of his country's blood.
> —THOMAS GRAY

> A Daniel come to judgment!
> —WILLIAM SHAKESPEARE

When poets wrote chiefly for the highly cultured who were classically educated, they used classical allusions so numerous that the school boy today has difficulty in reading their works. Half the pleasure of poetry is lost if one may read it only with a classical dictionary at his elbow. However, wisely chosen allusions may be economical and vivid.

Directly opposite to the figures of comparison and figures of association is one based on an apparent contradiction of terms: *bittersweet; Friendly Enemies; Hell Bent fer Heaven. Oxymoron* it is called—really a literary paradox. To know the paradox read Gilbert K. Chesterton, our living prince of the paradox.

Launcelot, the most trusted of King Arthur's knights, has given his love to the king's wife. Because of his attachment he cannot love Elaine, the lily-maid of Astolat, who idolizes him. Tennyson explains the situation:

> His honor rooted in dishonor stood
> And faith unfaithful kept him falsely true.

You see how the surface contradictions yield rich significance below the surface. There are three in the passage: *honor rooted in dishonor; faith unfaithful; falsely true.*

In "The Hound of Heaven" by Francis Thompson, the soul fleeing from God (the Hound) turns to nature for sympathy:

> I tempted all His servitors, but to find
> My own betrayal in their constancy,
> In faith to Him their fickleness to me.

But when he finds that Nature does not share true fellowship with him, he says:

> . . . in sound I speak—
> *Their* sound is but their stir, they *speak* in *silences*.

We have oxymoron in Milton's

> With wanton heed and giddy cunning.

and in Wordsworth's

> In truth the prison unto which we doom
> Ourselves no prison is: . . .

You will find many other examples as you read. The bringing together of opposite terms this way is a condensation device that holds the shock of pleasure in its united differences. You may want to use it to enhance your writing. The name is of little importance.

As a contradiction in terms may heighten effect, so a contradiction of the inner thought by the words which express it may be intensely effective.

> Here, under leave of Brutus and the rest,
> *(For Brutus is an honorable man,*
> *So are they all, all honorable men)*,
> Come I to speak in Caesar's funeral.
> He was my friend, faithful and just to me;
> *But Brutus says he was ambitious;*
> *And Brutus is an honorable man.*
>
> —WILLIAM SHAKESPEARE

What does Mark Antony mean by the italicized words? Exactly the opposite of what he says. This method of expression is irony. It is a deadly weapon. Spoken, the tone of the voice conveys the true meaning. If you ever use this device in your writing, you must take care to show in some way, by the construction of the sentence, by the circumstances or the like, that your words are to be taken ironically, and not literally. Words thus written in jest have caused many a misunderstanding among friends. Irony may be a powerful weapon, used to great ends. Used by the strong against the weak it is the weapon of a coward.

In his plays Shakespeare makes effective use of what is called dramatic irony. A passage from *Macbeth* will illustrate the device. Banquo, as messenger of guileless King Duncan, says this to Macbeth:

> This diamond he greets your wife withal
> By the name of most kind hostess,

the audience knowing that Macbeth and the "most kind hostess" have planned to murder Duncan while he sleeps.

Enthusiasm for the significant in a circumstance often prompts over-statement. To express how many people responded to the balmy spring weather last Sunday afternoon we may say

> All New York was out walking on the Park mall.

or

> Every car in the City was on the road.

To impress beauty we exclaim,

> The lake is a miracle!
> She is the most beautiful girl I ever met.

These superlatives are exaggerations of the truth, but they differ from mis-statement in that their author expects his hearer to understand the exaggeration. Mis-statement is designed to deceive, or its author is unaware that the statement is false.

An intended exaggeration of fact, which has imaginative quality, is highly effective in impressing the feeling of the literal truth. It is called *hyperbole*. Because of the imaginative element involved in hyperbole, it is always linked with some other figure of speech: metaphor, simile, synecdoche, or the like. This imaginative quality lifts it above mere exaggeration, which is not a figure of speech. Wordsworth gives this lovely picture in "The Daffodils":

> Ten thousand saw I at a glance
> Tossing their heads in sprightly dance.
> The waves beside them danced but they
> Out-did the sparkling waves in glee.

After Macbeth has murdered his king he cries in anguish

> Will all great Neptune's ocean wash this blood
> Clean from my hand? No; this my hand will rather
> The multitudinous seas incarnadine,
> Making the green one red.

and his wife in a feminine way gives expression to the same thought in sleep:

> All the perfumes of Arabia will not sweeten
> This little hand.

The blood on one hand will dye all the oceans of the globe! All Arabia's perfumes will not remove the odor of blood!

And here are others:

> Yea, one to look thereon had thought
> That here the earth, with envy wrought,
> Made strife to be more gay than heaven—
> More flowers to have, like the seven
> Stars that in the welkin be.
>
> —GEOFFREY CHAUCER

and

> So frowned the mighty combatants that Hell
> Grew darker at their frown.
>
> —JOHN MILTON

Hyperbole exaggerates in less as well as in greater degree, understates the fact as well as overstates.

"Not a cough in a carload" is a most familiar example.

Mother Goose says:

> Jack Sprat could eat no fat
> His wife could eat no lean
> And so betwixt them both
> They *licked the platter clean.*

And see how scant the costume:

> Not enough cloth to make a pair of breeches for a humming bird.

Under intense emotional stress a speaker may break off from the regular course of thought to address an object: the absent as though present; the dead as though living; the inanimate as though animate. Such an address is called apostrophe. It is always expressed in the second person.

Before Macbeth murders the king he has a mental struggle. After soliloquizing about the dagger which he imagines he sees, he comments on the atmosphere of the hour. Then breaking off suddenly he turns to the earth as though it were human:

> . . . Thou sure and firm-set earth
> Hear not my steps, which way they walk, for fear
> Thy very stones prate of my whereabout,
> And take the present horror from the time,
> Which now suits with it.

A little later a bell rings which is Lady Macbeth's signal to her husband.

> I go, and it is done: the bell invites me

Then he apostrophizes Duncan as though he were present:

> Hear it not, Duncan; for it is a knell
> That summons thee to heaven or to hell.

In "Childe Harold" Byron is commenting on his love of nature:

> I love not man the less, but nature more,
> From these our interviews, in which I steal
> From all I may be, or have been before,
> To mingle with the universe, and feel
> What I can ne'er express, yet cannot all conceal.

He turns from his contemplation and, lifted on the wings of imagination, is borne to the presence of the sea. His spirit finds expression in this apostrophe:

> Roll on, thou deep and dark blue Ocean,—roll!
> Ten thousand fleets sweep over thee in vain;
> Man marks the earth with ruin,—his control
> Stops with the shore; . . .

Apostrophe is not used so much today as it was formerly.

SUGGESTIONS

1. Plan a poem in which the point of what you have to say is revealed through what you do not say. In the upper corner of the paper write "Suggestive Verse."

2. Plan a poem in which you touch the heart of the reader through a contrast that you work out.

3. See if you can invent each figure of speech considered in this chapter.

4. Look over your poems and see whether or not you have used any figures of speech. You probably have without knowing them by name.

5. In the light of this chapter can you improve what you have written?

CHAPTER XXXVIII

PATTERNS TO TRY

STANZA patterns may be invented by combining lines of any length and of various lengths with an infinite variety of rhyme arrangements. There seems to be no limit to the number of lines that may be bound together as a unit in stanza form. The first metrical ventures in this book were with two. Spenser's "Epithalamion," the greatest marriage hymn in the English language, has stanzas of nineteen lines. Many odes have long and intricate stanza patterns.

The young versifier should delight in making combinations of his own, remembering that stanza forms must suit the thought and the music intended to be sung.

The few stanza patterns given below are to stimulate further invention and to familiarize the curious with some forms which are historically significant.

The five-line stanza or quintet—a very musical form:

a a b b a

Let not the dark thee cumber;	a
What though the moon does slumber?	a
The stars of the night	b
Will lend thee their light,	b
Like tapers clear without number.	a

—ROBERT HERRICK: *The Night-piece, to Julia*

a b a b a

When God at first made man,	a	3 feet
Having a glass of blessings standing by;	b	5
"Let us," said he, "pour on him all we can:	a	5
Let the world's riches, which dispersèd lie,	b	5
Contract into a span."	a	3

—GEORGE HERBERT: *The Pulley*

a b a b b

Go, lovely rose,	a	2 feet
Tell her that wastes her time and me,	b	4
That now she knows,	a	2
When I resemble her to thee,	b	4
How sweet and fair she seems to be.	b	4

—EDMUND WALLER: *Go, Lovely Rose*

Quite a different effect is created by introducing feminine rhymes and changing the line lengths even though the rhyme scheme is the same as that above.

Teach me half the gladness	a	*3 feet*
That thy brain must know,	b	*3*
Such harmonious madness	a	*3*
From my lips would flow	b	*3*
The world should listen then—as I am listening now.	b	*6*

     —PERCY BYSSHE SHELLEY: *To a Skylark*

a b c b b

Here of a Sunday morning	a	*3 feet*
My love and I would lie,	b	*each*
And see the coloured counties,	c	
And hear the larks so high	b	
About us in the sky.	b	

    —A. E. HOUSMAN: *Bredon Hill*

a a b a b

O World! O Life! O Time	a	*3 feet*
On whose last steps I climb,	a	*3*
Trembling at that where I had stood before;	b	*5*
When will return the glory of your prime?	a	*5*
No more—O never more!	b	*3*

    —PERCY BYSSHE SHELLEY: *A Lament*

The six-line stanza:

a b a b a b

She walks in beauty, like the night	a	*4 feet*
Of cloudless climes and starry skies;	b	*each*
And all that's best of dark and bright	a	
Meet in her aspect and her eyes:	b	
Thus mellowed to that tender light	a	
Which heaven to gaudy day denies.	b	

    —LORD BYRON: *She Walks in Beauty*

a b c b d d

Now let my bed be hard,	a	*3 feet*
No care take I;	b	*2*
I'll make my joy like this	c	*3*
Small Butterfly,	b	*2*
Whose happy heart has power	d	*3*
To make a stone a flower.	d	*3*

    —WILLIAM H. DAVIES: *The Example*

a b c b d b

The blessed damozel leaned out	a	*4 feet*
From the golden bar of Heaven;	b	*3*
Her eyes were deeper than the depth	c	*4*
Of waters stilled at even;	b	*3 (off)*
She had three lilies in her hand,	d	*4*
And the stars in her hair were seven.	b	*3*

—DANTE GABRIEL ROSSETTI: *The Blessed Damozel*

a b c b d c

Nor skin nor hide nor fleece	a
Shall cover you,	b
Nor curtain of crimson nor fine	c
Shelter of cedar-wood be over you,	b *(identical)*
Nor the fir-tree	d
Nor the pine.	c

—H. D.: *Lethe*

a a b c c b

Grow old along with me!	a	*3 feet*
The best is yet to be,	a	*3*
The last of life, for which the first was made:	b	*5*
Our times are in His hand	c	*3*
Who saith "A whole I planned,	c	*3*
Youth shows but half; trust God: see all, nor be afraid!"	b	*6*

—ROBERT BROWNING: *Rabbi Ben Ezra*

The seven-line stanza or septet:

a a b b c c b

At her fair hands how have I grace entreated	a	*5 feet*
With prayers oft repeated!	a	*3*
Yet still my love is thwarted.	b	*3*
Heart, let her go, for she'll not be converted.	b	*5*
Say, shall she go?	c	*2*
Oh no, no, no, no, no!	c	*3*
She is most fair, though she be marble-hearted.	b	*5*

—WALTER DAVISON: *At Her Fair Hands*

a b a b c c b

Swiftly walk o'er the western wave,	a	*4 feet*
Spirit of Night!	b	*2*
Out of the misty eastern cave,	a	*4*
Where all the long and lone daylight,	b	*4*
Thou wovest dreams of joy and fear,	c	*4*
Which make thee terrible and dear,—	c	*4*
Swift be thy flight!	b	*2*

—PERCY BYSSHE SHELLEY: *To Night*

Rime royal is a seven-line stanza with the rhyme scheme *a b a b b c c*.
It gets its name from its supposed origin with King James I of Scotland,
but Chaucer had used it in the *Canterbury Tales.*

Flee from the press, and dwell with soothfastness;	a *5 feet each*
Suffice thin owen thing, though it be small;	b
For hoard hath hate, and climbing tickleness,	a
Press hath envy, and weal blent overall;	b
Savour no more than thee behovè shall;	b
Rule well thyself, that other folk canst rede;	c
And truthè shall deliver, it is no drede.	c

—GEOFFREY CHAUCER: *Ballade of Good Counsel*

Soothfastness = truth; tickleness = unsteadiness; blent = blinds; overall = everywhere;
rede = advise; drede = doubt.

Ottava-rima is a stanza of eight iambic pentameter lines rhymed
a b a b a b c c. It is of Italian origin.

Saint Peter sat by the celestial gate,	a *5 feet*
And nodded o'er his keys; when, lo! there came	b
A wondrous noise he had not heard of late—	a
A rushing sound of wind, and stream, and flame;	b
In short, a roar of things extremely great,	a
Which would have made aught save a Saint exclaim;	b
But he, with first a start and then a wink,	c
Said, 'There's another star gone out, I think!'	c

—GEORGE GORDON, LORD BYRON: *The Vision of Judgment*

Still older is the famous eight-line stanza that Chaucer employed
in "The Monk's Tale." It comprises lines of five iambics rhymed
a b a b b c b c.

Although that Nero were as vicious	a *5 feet*
As any feend that lyth in helle adoun,	b
Yet he, as telleth us Swetonius,	a
This wydë world hadde in subjeccioun,	b
Both Est and West, South and Septemtrioun;	b
Of rubies, saphires, and of perlës whytë	c
Were all his clothës brouded up and doun;	b
For he in gemmës gretly gan delytë.	c

The ë is pronounced as a syllable, as is *ci* of "vicious" and "subjec-
cioun."

The Spenserian stanza, so called because Edmund Spenser used it in
The Faerie Queene, is a stanza of nine iambic lines. The first eight are
of five feet; the last of six. This last line is called an Alexandrine. The
extra foot gives a peculiar stateliness to the movement. In the Alexandrine the place of the cæsura is after the third foot.

A gentle Knight was pricking on the plaine,	a *5 feet*
Ycladd in mightie armes and silver shielde,	b
Wherein old dints of deep wounds did remaine,	a
The cruell marks of many a bloudy fielde;	b
Yet armes till that time did he never wield:	b
His angry steede did chide his foming bitt,	c
As much disdayning to the curbe to yield:	b
Full jolly knight he seemd, and faire did sitt,	c
As one for knightly giusts and fierce encounters fitt.	c *6 feet*

—EDMUND SPENSER: *The Faerie Queene*

He is a portion of the loveliness	a
Which once he made more lovely: he doth bear	b
His part, while the one Spirit's plastic stress	a
Sweeps through the dull dense world, compelling there	b
All new successions to the forms they wear;	b
Torturing th' unwilling dross that checks its flight	c
To its own likeness, as each mass may bear;	b
And bursting in its beauty and its might	c
From trees and beasts and men, into the heaven's light.	c

—PERCY BYSSHE SHELLEY: *Adonais*

Of the many poems in the Spenserian stanza here are some: Thomson's "Castle of Indolence"; Scott's "Don Roderick"; Burns's "Cotter's Saturday Night"; Byron's "Childe Harold"; Shelley's "The Revolt of Islam" and "Adonais"; Tennyson's "The Lotos Eaters"; Keats's "The Eve of St. Agnes." You may find most of them in *The Oxford Book of English Verse*, Palgrave's *Golden Treasury, The Winged Horse Anthology* by Auslander and Hill, or in the works of the authors themselves.

Twelve lines have been used effectively by Browning, every other line an echo of the music in the long preceding line. Note the pattern: a a b b c c d d e e f f

Where the quiet-colored end of evening smiles
 Miles and miles
On the solitary pastures where our sheep
 Half-asleep
Tinkle homeward through the twilight, stray or stop
 As they crop—
Was the site once of a city great and gay
 (So they say) ,
Of our country's very capital, its prince
 Ages since
Held his court in, gathered councils, wielding far
 Peace or war.

—ROBERT BROWNING: *Love Among The Ruins*

Terza rima is a kind of chain verse arranged in tercet stanzas of iambic pentameter lines, usually ending in a couplet made by repeating the rhyme of the last tercet stanza: *a b a; b c b; c d c; d d. The Divine Comedy* is written in this form. In Italian the iambic pentameter line always ended in an eleventh unaccented syllable.

The form is excellent for continuous flow but it is difficult to revise because of the interlacing of rhymes. If a mistake is made the writer may have to rip out many lines before he can secure a spontaneous effect.

O wild West Wind, thou breath of Autumn's being,	a
Thou, from whose unseen presence the leaves dead	b
Are driven, like ghosts from an enchanter fleeing,	a
Yellow, and black, and pale, and hectic red,	b
Pestilence-stricken multitudes: O thou,	c
Who chariotest to their dark wintry bed	b
The wingèd seeds, where they lie cold and low.	c
Each like a corpse within its grave, until	d
Thine azure sister of the Spring shall blow	c
Her clarion o'er the dreaming earth, and fill	d
(Driving sweet buds like flocks to feed in air)	e
With living hues and odours plain and hill:	d
Wild Spirit, which art moving everywhere;	e
Destroyer and preserver; hear, oh, hear!	e

—PERCY BYSSHE SHELLEY: *Ode to the West Wind*
(For entire poem see page 433)

Other poems in terza rima are: Shelley's "The Triumph of Life," "Prince Athanase," "The Woodman and the Nightingale"; Byron's "Prophesy of Dante"; Robert Frost's "Acquainted with the Night."

The Limerick consists of five anapestic lines. Lines 1, 2, and 5 are of three feet; lines 3 and 4 a foot shorter. They are rhymed thus: *a a b b a.* Some sort of final twist marks the last line of every interesting limerick. Here is a famous one frequently quoted by the late Woodrow Wilson:

As a beauty I am not a star,	../ ../ ../
There are others more handsome, by far.	../ ../ ../
But my face—I don't mind it	../ ../.
For I am behind it.	./ ../.
It's the people in front that I jar.	../ ../ ../

Here is another:

> There was a young lady from Niger, ./ ../ ../.
> Who smiled as she rode on a tiger. ./ ../ ../.
>   They came back from the ride ../ ../
>   With the lady inside, ../ ../
> And the smile on the face of the tiger. ../ ../ ../.

It is usually better, however, to rhyme the last word of the limerick with the last word in line 2. If the word is repeated only, the effect of surprise is lost.

The ode today is known only by its intensity of utterance. It is usually profound. An ode may be written in any lyric pattern that the author chooses to use. Turn back these pages and note the regular stanza patterns of Shelley's "To A Skylark," Keats's "Ode on a Grecian Urn," his "Ode to a Nightingale," and his "To Autumn." They are all different in form. Odes in regular stanzas are sometimes called Horatian, because Horace wrote in stanza patterns. His odes were written to be read, not sung as were the Greek odes.

Through a misconception of the form of the odes of Pindar, the great Greek lyric poet, Abraham Cowley popularized a ragged form of ode which he called the Pindaric ode, now known as the irregular or false Pindaric ode. This was imitated by many poets. Examples are Dryden's "Alexander's Feast" and "A Song for St. Cecilia's Day," reprinted in this book. Perhaps the greatest ode in this tradition is the following:

Ode on Intimations of Immortality from Recollections of Early Childhood

> There was a time when meadow, grove, and stream,
> The earth, and every common sight
>   To me did seem
>   Apparell'd in celestial light,
> The glory and the freshness of a dream.
> It is not now as it hath been of yore;—
>   Turn wheresoe'er I may,
>   By night or day,
> The things which I have seen I now can see no more.
>
>   The rainbow comes and goes,
>   And lovely is the rose;
>   The moon doth with delight
> Look round her when the heavens are bare;
>   Waters on a starry night
>   Are beautiful and fair;

The sunshine is a glorious birth;
But yet I know, where'er I go,
That there hath past away a glory from the earth.

Now, while the birds thus sing a joyous song,
And while the young lambs bound
As to the tabor's sound,
To me alone there came a thought of grief:
A timely utterance gave that thought relief,
And I again am strong.
The cataracts blow their trumpets from the steep;
No more shall grief of mine the season wrong:
I hear the echoes through the mountain throng,
The winds come to me from the fields of sleep,
And all the earth is gay;
Land and sea
Give themselves up to jollity,
And with the heart of May
Doth every beast keep holiday;—
Thou child of joy
Shout round me, let me hear thy shouts, thou happy
Shepherd-boy!

Ye blessèd Creatures, I have heard the call
Ye to each other make; I see
The heavens laugh with you in your jubilee;
My heart is at your festival,
My head hath its coronal,
The fulness of your bliss, I feel—I feel it all.
Oh evil day! if I were sullen
While Earth herself is adorning
This sweet May-morning;
And the children are culling
On every side
In a thousand valleys far and wide,
Fresh flowers; while the sun shines warm
And the babe leaps up on his mother's arm:—
I hear, I hear, with joy I hear!
—But there's a tree, of many, one,
A single field which I have look'd upon,
Both of them speak of something that is gone:
The pansy at my feet
Doth the same tale repeat:
Whither is fled the visionary gleam?
Where is it now, the glory and the dream?

Our birth is but a sleep and a forgetting;
The Soul that rises with us, our life's Star,
 Hath had elsewhere its setting
 And cometh from afar;
 Not in entire forgetfulness,
 And not in utter nakedness,
But trailing clouds of glory do we come
 From God, who is our home:
Heaven lies about us in our infancy!
Shades of the prison-house begin to close
 Upon the growing Boy,
But he beholds the light, and whence it flows,
 He sees it in his joy;
The Youth, who daily farther from the east
 Must travel, still is Nature's priest,
 And by the vision splendid
 Is on his way attended;
At length the Man perceives it die away,
And fade into the light of common day.

Earth fills her lap with pleasures of her own;
Yearnings she hath in her own natural kind,
And, even with something of a mother's mind
 And no unworthy aim,
 The homely nurse doth all she can
To make her foster-child, her inmate, Man,
 Forget the glories he hath known,
And that imperial palace whence he came.

Behold the Child among his new-born blisses,
A six years' darling of a pigmy size!
See, where 'mid work of his own hand he lies,
Fretted by sallies of his mother's kisses,
With light upon him from his father's eyes!
See, at his feet, some little plan or chart,
Some fragment from his dream of human life,
Shaped by himself with newly-learnèd art;
 A wedding or a festival,
 A mourning or a funeral;
 And this hath now his heart,
 And unto this he frames his song:
 Then will he fit his tongue
To dialogues of business, love, or strife;
 But it will not be long
 Ere this be thrown aside,
 And with new joy and pride
The little actor cons another part;
Filling from time to time his "humorous stage"

With all the Persons, down to palsied Age,
That Life brings with her in her equipage;
      As if his whole vocation
      Were endless imitation.

Thou, whose exterior semblance doth belie
      Thy soul's immensity;
Thou best philosopher, who yet dost keep
Thy heritage, thou eye among the blind,
That, deaf and silent, read'st the eternal deep,
Haunted for ever by the eternal Mind,—
      Mighty Prophet! Seer blest!
      On whom those truths do rest
Which we are toiling all our lives to find,
In darkness lost, the darkness of the grave;
Thou, over whom thy Immortality
Broods like the day, a master o'er a slave,
A Presence which is not to be put by;
Thou little child, yet glorious in the might
Of heaven-born freedom on thy being's height,
Why with such earnest pains dost thou provoke
The years to bring the inevitable yoke,
Thus blindly with thy blessedness at strife?
Full soon thy soul shall have her earthly freight,
And custom lie upon thee with a weight
Heavy as frost, and deep almost as life!

      O joy! that in our embers
      Is something that doth live,
      That Nature yet remembers
      What was so fugitive!
The thought of our past years in me doth breed
Perpetual benediction: not indeed
For that which is most worthy to be blest,
Delight and liberty, the simple creed
Of Childhood, whether busy or at rest,
With new-fledged hope still fluttering in his breast:
      —Not for these I raise
      The song of thanks and praise;
    But for those obstinate questionings
    Of sense and outward things,
    Fallings from us, vanishings;
    Blank misgivings of a creature
Moving about in worlds not realized,
High instincts, before which our mortal nature
Did tremble like a guilty thing surprised:
    But for those first affections,
    Those shadowy recollections,
      Which, be they what they may,

Are yet the fountain-light of all our day,
Are yet a master-light of all our seeing;
    Uphold us, cherish, and have power to make
Our noisy years seem moments in the being
Of the eternal Silence: truths that wake,
        To perish never;
Which neither listlessness, nor mad endeavour,
        Nor man nor boy
Nor all that is at enmity with joy,
Can utterly abolish or destroy!
    Hence, in a season of calm weather
        Though inland far we be,
Our souls have sight of that immortal sea
        Which brought us hither;
        Can in a moment travel thither—
And see the children sport upon the shore,
And hear the mighty waters rolling evermore.

Then sing, ye birds, sing, sing a joyous song!
        And let the young lambs bound
        As to the tabor's sound!
    We, in thought, will join your throng
        Ye that pipe and ye that play,
        Ye that through your hearts to-day
        Feel the gladness of the May!
What though the radiance which was once so bright
Be now for ever taken from my sight,
    Though nothing can bring back the hour
Of splendour in the grass, of glory in the flower;
        We will grieve not, rather find
        Strength in what remains behind;
        In the primal sympathy
        Which having been must ever be;
        In the soothing thoughts that spring
        Out of human suffering;
        In the faith that looks through death,
In years that bring the philosophic mind.

And O, ye Fountains, Meadows, Hills, and Groves,
Forbode not any severing of our loves!
Yet in my heart of hearts I feel your might;
I only have relinquish'd one delight
To live beneath your more habitual sway:
I love the brooks which down their channels fret
Even more than when I tripp'd lightly as they;
The innocent brightness of a new-born day
        Is lovely yet;
The clouds that gather round the setting sun

Do take a sober colouring from an eye
That hath kept watch o'er man's mortality;
Another race hath been, and other palms are won.
Thanks to the human heart by which we live,
Thanks to its tenderness, its joys and fears,
To me the meanest flower that blows can give
Thoughts that do often lie too deep for tears.
                                    —WILLIAM WORDSWORTH

The true Pindaric ode is in strict pattern, made for singing by a chorus. It is divided into three parts which may or may not be repeated in the poem: the strophe (turn), sung as the Greek chorus moved from right to left; the antistrophe (counterturn), exactly the same in form as the strophe, sung as the chorus returned from left to right; and the epode (stand), varying in structure from the other two, sung while the chorus stood. In "The Bard" and "The Progress of Poesy" by Thomas Gray the three parts are twice repeated, making nine divisions in each ode.

The rispetto is an Italian form of varying patterns. The most common form used in English is an eight line poem of two stanzas, rhymed *a b a b; c c d d*. Here is one:

Rispetto

And so I am rejected with a phrase,
Here by the roadside stunned and left alone,
From memory of thee to sing thy praise
With grief instead of joy for overtone.

Wisdom, we know, is but a fool for guide.
Folly will no more travel by my side.
How shall I go without any living laughter,
Through that wide desert that we call hereafter.
                    —O. M. DENNIS in "Left at the Post" from
                              the New York *Evening Post*

The lai is a French form turning on two rhymes in this pattern: *a a b a a b a a b*. The *a* lines have five syllables (not feet); the *b* lines have two syllables. There is no fixed number of lines for a stanza. In a poem of more than one stanza, each stanza has its own set of rhyme sounds. A second stanza for the above pattern would be *c c d c c d c c d*. In accordance with ancient tradition no indention of lines appears.

Here is a simple lai:

Lucy

Lucy was a child	**a**
Wilful as the wild	**a**
Water;	**b**
How an angel smiled,	**a**
Angels undefiled	**a**
Taught her.	**b**
She was song—beguiled	**a**
Sunlight that we styled	**a**
Daughter.	**b**

—J. J.

The virelai is a development of the lai. It has a chain rhyme scheme that goes like this: stanza I, *a a b a a b a a b;* stanza II, *b b c b b c b b c;* stanza III, *c c d c c d c c d;* and so on to the last stanza which takes as its short line the *a* rhyme of stanza I. Modern poets do not limit themselves to five and two syllables.

The lai nouveau is more complicated than either the lai or the virelai ancien. It turns on two rhymes throughout. The opening *a* lines form a refrain for later stanzas alternately as in the villanelle. A^1 closes stanza II; A^2 closes stanza III, and so on to the last stanza when they are united in reverse order to close the poem A^2, A^1.

Analyzed rhyme presents a new approach to rhyme and widens its reaches beyond near rhyme and assonance. It is the invention of Frank Kendon, an English poet living today. In simple rhyme the vowel sound and succeeding consonant sounds are identical: *house, mouse; wide, pride*. In analyzed rhyme the words are ranked in sets of four.

In *Some Modern Poets* Edward Davison, himself a poet, explains Mr. Kendon's method thus:

"Mr. Kendon takes two such words as *soon* and *hide* but separates the vowel from the consonantal sounds before looking for his rhymes. The *oo* of *soon* is united with the *d* of *hide*; and the *i* of *hide* with the *n* of *soon*. This simple analysis produces the rhyming sounds

oon	ine
ide	ood

as a basis for new sets of words. Thus, by means of analyzed rhyme an absolute sound relationship can be established between words that have hitherto seemed alien to each other."

In a poem of Kendon's quoted by Davison appear these sets

down	scene
trees	drowse
city	beauty
(at) tune	(where) in
so	home
fame	(a) way

Hear what lovely music the inventor makes with these:

> From this fair night to draw sweet music down
> A long-benighted wind makes harps of trees,
> And, not to lose the sight while men's eyes drowse,
> The moon gives light and stares upon the scene.
>
> Dew upon dew condenses; from the city
> Chimes of far-away bells the hours attune,
> The silver landscape, no man walks wherein,
> Unto itself is sweet, a secret beauty.
>
> Oh that content, content might softly so
> Steal over me and cheat this longing for fame,
> That I might love the trees about my home,
> Or well enough sing to throw the songs away.

There is a subtlety of effect most pleasing to the trained ear.

Here are short poems with an interesting arrangement of line length and rhyme:

The Wind

> When the wind spoke to me
>   He spoke of the sea
> And of deserts and plains
> And of Devonshire lanes
>   And of harebells of blue
>   That he slips his hands through—
> *Now is that what the wind has spoken to you?*
>
> —C. Lovat Fraser

Summer

'I wonder why a rose is red?'
  The lacewing said;
'I wonder why?'
  Answered I;

'Lacewing, nor you nor I—
Put we all else and other by,
And thought it out and all rules try—
Neither of us could reason why
A rose is red—
Content am I
That it is red
So wondrously.'

  'And so am I,'
    The lacewing said.

—C. LOVAT FRASER

In a lighter vein:

Two Poems on Love

I

I was peeling new potatoes
Near the kitchen door.
Love came down the pathway singing—
Love comes down no more.

Love went scuffing through the peelings
By the kitchen door,
Love fell down and hurt his feelings—
Love will come no more.

II

Love came swimming through the water,
Bubbles in his hair,
Love sank down beneath the water
All for lack of air.
Love went down beneath the water
But I know not where.

—WILLIAM ROEHRICK

You may find it stimulating to work out these patterns:

I.			VI.	
/../	a		/./././.	a
../../	a		/././.	a
../../../.	b		/././.	a
../../	c		/././.	a
../../	c		/././/	b
../../../.	b		/./././.	c
			/./././.	c
II.			/./././.	c
/././/	a		/./././.	c
/./.	b		./././	b
.///./	a			
/./.	b		**VII.**	
			/././.	a
III.			/././.	b
./../	a		/././.	a
./../	a		/././/	b
../.	b			
./../	b		**VIII.**	
../.	b		/././/.	a
../../	c		./../../.	c
../../	c		/../../../..	c
			/./../.	b
IV.				
/././././././	a		**IX.**	
/././././././	a		/././.	a
			/././.	b
V.			/././.	b
/./	a		/././.	a
/./	b			
/../	c		**X.**	
/../	b		./././/	a
/../	a		./././/	b
.././	d		./././/	c
../	c		./././/	a
.././	d		./././/	b
			./././/	c

These poems were derived from patterns:

Hotel

(Pattern in Class)

There were, at least, (despite massages)	./././.
Two chins above each throat,	./././
That quivered as the music shattered	./././.
Brass note on brazen note.	./././
"He's worth six million dollars—"	./././.
She said it with a gloat.	./././
Outside the forest voices rumbled:	./././.
The sharp, dry tongues of oak,—	./././
The pines surged madly up the mountain,	./././.
And rolled, and crashed, and broke.	./././
"You're dummy, Mrs. Sobel."	./././.
The Diamond Collar spoke.	./././

—MURIEL F. HOCHDORF

In truth, the author substituted ../ for the second foot of the last line.
Diamond is a word of three syllables.

Melodies Unsung

Silver-winged birds dart through my brain
  Echoing the Poet's timeless song,
Crooning dark, low melodies of pain,
  Torturing me as they whir along,
  Steadily, a ghostly, rhythmic throng.
Oh, let me be! I am no poet, birds,
Knowing not the craft of weaving words!

—ETHEL GREENFIELD

Here are some poems made in original patterns; that is, the student developed his own without model of any kind.

Snow at Evening

Diana from her frozen height
Lays the coverlet of night
Shaking clouds of dusky white
Out across the blue.

Where the listless birds had flown
Wavering above the town,
Moonlit motes come slowly down
And hide the night from view.

Heaped and blown along the way
Like the leaves of yesterday
You can hide the trodden clay.
Come and hide me too.
—WILLIAM ROEHRICK

Vagabondia

Roads that are straight
And that end at a gate
Are not half so enticing to follow
As are long roads that twist
And are lost in the mist
Like the path of the South-flying swallow.
—GERTRUDE JOAN BUCKMAN

Realization

I saw the flaring plummet drop
Behind the mountain's silvan top
Splashing its brilliance on the western sky.
I watched the colors blend and change until
I could not look away from them, lest I
Should miss some slight nuance. Then still
Bewildered by the splendid quivering sight,
I found its colors were no longer bright.
—WILLIAM ROEHRICK

Song

From the north I blow,
To the south I go,
Rollicking, rollicking, rollicking,
Under and over, high and low
Bringing the snow.

White flakes that flee,
Come! dance with me,
Frolicking, frolicking, frolicking;
Play with a rover. Soon we'll be
Winging to sea.
—JAMES GORHAM

CHAPTER XXXIX

MISCELLANEOUS

IN THE light of accumulating skill and a habit of observation students of poetry find many subjects for expression. Here are a few that their makers labeled "optional." They may suggest other optional poems to their readers.

Sea Weed

I chose to anchor on a shifting stone
That tumbles with the breakers' broken wash
Instead of hitching to a stable cliff.
Often at ebb tide when I am alone,
High on the rippled sand the sea has left
Silent, damp and cold, I think that if
I lived in some huge, rocky home,
How safe, how sheltered I would always be.
Great cliffs—oh, what security they give!
But when I'm tousled by the swishing foam,
And when the ocean drops upon my head,
I'm glad that this is how I chose to live.

—WILLIAM ROEHRICK

Sand Castles

Silent I sat upon the shore,
Between the sea grass swish
And ocean roar,
Building my castle of the damp, salt sand,
Shaping its towers with a thoughtful hand.

But when I had my castle made,
Had planned the place
Where fights were laid,
Upon the sandy field, grown smooth and gray,
The ocean came, and carried it away.

—WILLIAM ROEHRICK

Enchanted Forest

You have the deep-throated midnight,
 (Winds know you),
The far, thin unfurling of stars
In a pennant below you.

You have the stillness of daybreak
Unbroken,
Except for the voices of birds,
As if water had spoken.

Birches are stretching on tip-toe
Around you,
Heavy with sun and with spring;
Far-off hill shadows bound you.

Three times dusk came to the mountain—
 (Oh, holy!)
The woodland was rocked by the night
In its dark cradle slowly.

You have gone proud in the fabric
Spring's made of,
And now the long year holds no grief
That you need be afraid of.

—MURIEL F. HOCHDORF

Spring Song

Let poets and bards the loveliness of spring acclaim—
To me the squalid city is the same;
The streams are freed from winter's icy chain,
And fields grow green beneath the sun again.
The barren rooftops hold no charm for me.
Nor does a granite giant's austerity
Remind me of the fields of Arcady.

—RUBYE MAE FISHER

City Autumn

Here is no wealth of laden apple trees
  Dropping red treasure on a russet world,
Only the challenge of an autumn breeze
  Leaving my mind's bright battle-flag unfurled.
No field of garnered wheat lies with its cheek
  Pressed to the sun releasing slow its hold;
Only the skyscraper in sharp oblique
  Profile upon a sky, steel-blue, steel-cold.
One crackling leaf with too few mates to play
  At somersaults with it,—this is the theme
Which on a diamond-clear October day
  Brings me unbound by steel and smoke, a dream.
                                    —RUTH H. HAUSMAN

Rejuvenation

Heaven sang through me today
And left me full of melody.
I gasped in wonder at the beauty of the voice;
The song lifted me above the earth.
I felt all clean—as though a wind
Had swept my soul.
I felt all young—as though the wind
Had taken years.
I felt all gay—as though the wind
Had taken tears.
                              —GERTRUDE JOAN BUCKMAN

At the Edge of the Garden

The spidery bridge was arched across the stream
And beckoned us to come and share its black
And silhouetted privacy. I thought
Perhaps it found itself a bit
Fatigued with trailing viny fingers through
The ruffled hair of sleepy water
And wanted company. . . . And then
When June was gone, I came alone
To weave my bitterness among the ripples.
                                    —JOYCE LANCASTER

Saturday's Child

I think of blue confetti, amusement parks
And lighted Christmas trees, while carnivals
Parade like Roman candles in my mind . . .
How should I dumb this rage? What should I say?

Within the pagan tent of holiday
Grow memories to brood upon and cherish
—And fling on Monday from the gargoyled church
Of consciousness into a weary heart

Whose large remorse requires expectation
Of every joy that Saturday donates
To taunt that synthesis of monotone
And toil and firecrackers which is life.

—DELMORE SCHWARTZ

For Apathy

Sleep, I have courted you for many a night,
But I will take your sister, second best;
Her face is not so fair nor touch so light;
Bring her to me who cannot hope for rest.
Her opiate is dark and dull of taste,
Not cool and clear, refreshing to the mind,
But it will drug my sense, and work in haste
To deaden thoughts that leave a forehead lined.

She has a sullen visage, but her hand
Has somewhere learned the trick of easing pain,
And though she has no lullaby nor sand
To fling in troubled eyes that wake again
To other troubles, she compensates with peace—
I need not search the earth to find her flown.
Her constancy is great as your caprice.

I hear her footsteps now, as steadily
Her slow processional draws near my side;
And I have gone to meet her, readily,
As though I never sought you for my bride.

—RUTH H. HAUSMAN

Awakening

Were I to look a bit behind,
　　And set my inner mind to trace
The world I knew before that day
　　I woke, I'd find but empty space.

For then I lived, without a life
　　Contained inside my entity;
Without a dream, without a will;
　　My heart had no identity.

Till, lo! one day a breath of wind
　　Called, "Wonder, wonder, child, then learn
How sweet is life, how gold and full;
　　Then wonder more, and more discern!"

Now on my stem of wonder grows
　　A flower sown by ecstasy
With thoughts for petals, fugues for leaves,
　　And for its heart a piece of me.

　　　　　　　　—MILDRED SOLWAN

Marching Song for the Coming Year

I will go back again to where
The old pines face the sunset, bare

And bowed, and without song,
But with a beauty gaunt and strong;

Where evening enters with the sound
That small leaves make on frosty
　　ground;

And night, with slow, cold stars for tears
Will weep for all my hungry years;—

But grief will be a shallow cup,
And bitterness shall drink it up.

Though Beauty be august, austere,
It will not make me weep this year.
　　　　　　—MURIEL F. HOCHDORF

Dirge

The river lies in a chiffon gown,
　　Watching a crooked moon;
I lie among my sickly dreams
　　And pray that Death come soon.

That sound of a fog-horn steals toward
　　me,
(Softly it closes my eyes) . . .
The song of a bird without its mate
(Oh, would that Youth were wise!)

Morpheus, in a long black shroud,
　　Stands weeping at my side;
I turn around too quietly,
　　And see my dreams have died.
　　　　　　—GEORGIA H. COOPER

Secret

The stars are silent-lipped to-night,
　The trees are dumb,
Yet I caught fragments of their talk
　Before they heard me come.

And in the muted leaves that lie
　Like drifted sand,
There is a shy and hidden speech
　I cannot understand.

I came into the woods to-night
　Without belief,
But faith goes up like incense from
　The flame of every leaf.

There is a loneliness, a peace
　That knows no words,
And joys come nestling in my hand
　Like small and eager birds.

If I could live where mountains are,
　Or by the sea,
I might learn how to lift my head
　Upward prayerfully.
　　　　—MURIEL F. HOCHDORF

Schmerzen

"Never" is the end of things,
Closed and finished—all.
Strange that I can be so calm,
Watching darkness fall.

"Never"—such a little word!
Strange I do not cry. . . .
Still, there will be time for that
By and by.

I will gather from my heart
All that once was you,
And sow above the empty ache
Rosemary and rue.

There will be new river roads,
Other summer nights;
Lonesome waters still will hold
Shivering gold lights.

I will listen to the wind
Make the hemlocks moan—
It cannot be so terrible
To be alone!
　　　　—MURIEL F. HOCHDORF

Dirge

I dared not mourn
Beside her long.
Her dead lips were shaping
A frozen song.

I stopped her mouth
With hawthorn bud
And half-opened roses,
The color of blood.

With two gold pennies
I sealed her eyes—
They used to be moon-drunk
Before she grew wise.

I crushed three poppies
For dead desire,
Then I sprinkled incense
And fed the fire.

The flames grew tall
And scorched the moon.
Were the ashes mine?—
It was over soon.

I flung her dust
Away, dry-eyed.
What more can one do
When a dream has died?
　　　　—MURIEL F. HOCHDORF

The Elizabethan age suggested the next two poems. The authors tried to capture the spirit of the Elizabethan lyric.

Sonnet

Fair maid, through hours of endless constancy
I've sung my songs beneath thy window sill;
And thou, thou dost disdain in mockery
The odes I've blown to thee on winds now still,
Hoping that in the garden of thy heart,
Their eager roots might find a fertile soil
For nourishment, and soon become a part
Of thee. But thou hast proven seeds do spoil,
Grow weak and die upon that barren waste
Which nature made the center of thy being.
My very soul has fled on wings of haste
As if alarmed at all too clearly seeing
That though thou, Sweet, be fairer far than fair,
Thou walkest stiffly frozen in warm air.

—HARRIET MEYER

From an Elizabethan Lover to His Lady

O lady mine, since first
I looked upon your face,
A full blown rose athirst
Has sprung within the case,

My heart; ah, be so sweet
To let drop but a tear
And make the sweet more sweet,
Quick—lest the blossom sere.

You feed me pallid dreams,
When I a mortal be,
And mortal wishing seems
To crave less fantasy

And more the living bliss—
Ah, lady, but a kiss!

—MILDRED SOLWAN

Child Secret

I know a secret fairyland,
And there a silken river flows,
Where elves and nymphs play hand in hand.

They sup upon a tiny strand
Where every fragrant flower grows . . .
(I know a secret fairyland.)

They sleep upon blue grains of sand
And wear a spider's web for clothes.
Where elves and nymphs play hand in hand,

On rainy days they form a band
Of robbers round a dripping rose . . .
I know a secret fairyland.

It is so small that when I stand
It seems to slip between my toes.
Where elves and nymphs play hand in hand,

I'm going soon: my trip's all planned,
And I'm the only one who knows.
I know a secret fairyland,
Where elves and nymphs play hand in hand.
—SYLVIA LAPIDUS

Poem

Yesterday was a draftsman's day;
Easy to tell where each house lay,
And the line that parted the heaven and land
Was one clean sweep of a steady hand.

But today, where there *was* a horizon, blues
And vague soft greys and dull greens diffuse.
This subtle art is annoying. I
Like my line straight between earth and sky.
—RUTH H. HAUSMAN

Retreat

I found a flat rock by a brook,
I found a sheltering willow tree,
I found a sun-splashed peaceful nook
Where I could let my thoughts drift free.

I found a spot where just the sighs
And laughter of the water told
The secrets that the fireflies,
The buttercups, and raindrops hold.

Would you have left your mind's retreat
To follow after two bare feet?
—Joyce Lancaster

PARTING SUGGESTIONS

These fragments are intended to send you into bypaths that will take you to a poem. Do with them what you will.

What do I hear? What do I hear? . . . The lines below came out of this suggestion:

Spring

What do I hear? What do I hear
Whispering down the lane?
Sweeter than bird song, blither than
Tunes of the sea and the rain?

What do I hear? A violet's stir.
Why do I thrill? Why do I care?
The simple sound steals into my heart
And finds an answer there.

—Ara Timourian

Rain on the roof   Here troubles shall fall   The word not spoken   Rain on the surf   I shall return to the sea, my mother   Words in moonlight   Wind—"destroyer and preserver"   The soul of an empty house   The soul of a house that knows happy family life   Ice floes in the river   Barge of bricks going down the river   Timber piled on the dock   Passing of things we sometimes see: cart with bells, horse-drawn cabs, old clothes men, umbrella menders   Innovations: radio, airplane travel, mail through the sky, ice cubes, chain store on the site of an exclusive old mansion   Furniture vans in autumn   Arc lights reflected in wet streets   Traveling market   Push carts rolling through congested district   Traffic lights: long line of cars an inch apart waiting; a flash of green and movement!   The feel of the ax in the wood   Toasting marshmallows   Resistance of wood, rock   Resilience of willow   Human bondage   Human freedom   Power of the machine   Limitations of the machine   Gifts of the machine   With slide and lens   Discovery— above, below, on the earth

KEEP OFF—NEWLY SEEDED

As you think of others jot them in your notebook with attendant details for the leisure moment when you will pick up your hollow reed.

> *Piping down the valleys wild,*
> *Piping songs of pleasant glee,*
> *On a cloud I saw a child,*
> *And he laughing said to me:*
>
> *'Pipe a song about a Lamb!'*
> *So I piped with merry cheer.*
> *'Piper, pipe that song again;'*
> *So I piped: he wept to hear.*
>
> *'Drop thy pipe, thy happy pipe;*
> *Sing thy songs of happy cheer!'*
> *So I sung the same again,*
> *While he wept with joy to hear. . . .*
>   —WILLIAM BLAKE

INDEX

* before author's name indicates apprentice poet.